RECENT PROGRESS IN PERCEPTION

Readings from

**SCIENTIFIC
AMERICAN**

RECENT PROGRESS
IN PERCEPTION

with introductions by
Richard Held and Whitman Richards
Massachusetts Institute of Technology

W. H. Freeman and Company
San Francisco

Most of the SCIENTIFIC AMERICAN articles in
Recent Progress in Perception are available as separate
Offprints. For a complete list of more than 950 articles
now available as Offprints, write to W. H. Freeman
and Company, 660 Market Street, San Francisco,
California 94104.

Library of Congress Cataloging in Publication Data

Main entry under title:

Recent progress in perception.

   Bibliography: p.
   Includes index.
   1. Perception—Addresses, essays, lectures.
2. Senses and sensation—Addresses, essays, lectures.
I. Held, Richard.   II. Richards, Whitman.
III. Scientific American.
QP441.R4   612'.8'08   75–43684
ISBN 0–7167–0534–6
ISBN 0–7167–0533–8 pbk.

Printed in the United States of America

9 8 7 6 5 4 3 2 1

Index

CONTENTS

PREFACE

During the past few years research in the area of perception has proliferated, and a sufficient number of relevant new articles have appeared in *Scientific American* to warrant a second set of readings. In our first collection, *Perception: Mechanisms and Models* (PMM), emphasis was placed upon the kinds of experimental results and observations that lend themselves to theorizing in terms of models and mechanisms. In the present collection, we have continued that theme in the first of the two main sections, Peripheral Mechanisms of Perception and Control. But in response to progress as well as popular demand, we have strived for a somewhat broader focus in the second section, Central Determinants of Perception. Both of these main sections contain three subsets of material.

The first subset in Section I presents new results on the basic processing of stimulus input in terms of contrast and sensitivity at retinal and higher levels of the nervous system. The second deals with further developments in our knowledge of the extraction of features from stimulus input and also discusses the elementary processing of such input signals. The third includes new information on the processing of input signals used in controlling the movement of parts of the body, such as the head, eyes, and limbs. There is good reason to believe that the stimuli that control movement are processed separately from those entailed in what we regard as the elaboration of percepts. Both behavioral and neural findings are beginning to delineate these separate control systems.

The first subset of Section II deals with the resolution of ambiguity in stimulation. Stimuli, like reversible figures that may be perceived in two or more different ways, constitute the clearest evidence for central determination of perception. The examples given in these articles show the pervasiveness of ambiguity in the perceptual interpretation of complex scenes and the ways in which the perceptual system resolves that ambiguity. The material of the second continues the thrust of the first by showing how the expectation to perceive in a certain way will influence the perceiver's view of the world and, in particular, of the actions, speech, and writing of his fellow man. The third subset presents the rather limited knowledge we have acquired of the cerebral mechanisms underlying these complex perceptual capabilities.

In writing the introductions to these sections, we have tended to avoid the basic levels of description and analysis. Such material is contained in our first set of readings (PMM), particularly in the fairly extensive introductions to the six sections in that collection. Instead, as the title of this new collection implies, we are concerned here with highlighting the avenues along which progress has been achieved during the past few years, and with presenting current prospects for the future in this science of the brain.

September 1975

Richard Held
Whitman Richards

RECENT PROGRESS IN PERCEPTION

PERIPHERAL MECHANISMS OF PERCEPTION AND CONTROL

I PERIPHERAL MECHANISMS OF PERCEPTION AND CONTROL

INTRODUCTION

If any one neural mechanism holds the key to understanding sensory and perceptual processes, that mechanism must be lateral inhibition. For even at the earliest levels of processing, this mechanism acts to control the sensitivity of the eye. At the same time, it underlies contrast perception by causing neighboring neural elements to respond differentially to one another. Because of this ubiquitous mechanism, sensory systems respond best to changes of input and to new events. Absolute levels of sensory input (such as the actual intensity of light or sound) are ignored; instead, only the light or sound increments are transmitted further on to higher levels of processing. For example, although the absolute level of light intensity may be more than an order of magnitude different in a room illuminated by the afternoon sun as compared with one lit by lamps at night, our perceptions of the color and brightness of objects in the room remain much the same. Lateral inhibition in the visual system is largely responsible for this illusion of brightness and color constancy, whereby the relative differences in the reflectances of the various surfaces are abstracted from the scene and the absolute light levels are ignored.

Contrast and Sensitivity

Lateral inhibition thus serves to maintain constancies as well as to highlight the important, novel features of a scene (or sound pattern). Floyd Ratliff's article "Contour and Contrast," emphasizes the latter function of lateral inhibition in neural networks, using examples drawn from modern neurophysiology and psychophysics, as well as from ancient Oriental art. In the next article, Frank S. Werblin's "The Control of Sensitivity in the Retina," the actual wiring of a network is illustrated in a simple vertebrate retina. Werblin shows that lateral inhibition operates on at least two levels in the retina, one via horizontal cell processes and the second via amacrine cells. These lateral neural elements provide a clear basis for a spatial organization in neural encoding, whereby each fiber in the optic nerve would connect to a region on the retina that would excite the fiber while surrounding retinal regions turn it off (or vice versa). This center-surround property of optic nerve fibers and ganglion cells is one of the first feature detectors, which we identify as a "Kuffler" unit (see Charles R. Michael, "Retinal Processing of Visual Images," in PMM).

Werblin's article goes considerably deeper than a mere description of the contrast-related effects of lateral inhibition. He shows also how the retina is designed to keep the response range of the visual system in register with ambient illumination, thus enabling the retina to form a high-contrast neural image over a broad range of light conditions. We can probably assume with some confidence that similar mechanisms are at work in the auditory and cutaneous sensory pathways. Such mechanisms for the control of sensitivity over a wide dynamic range undoubtedly play a key role in constancy phenomena. A final and further important insight provided by Werblin is the advantage of encoding two types of neural signals: a change-sensitive, transient signal as well as a level-sensitive (sustained) signal. In simple animals, these two types of neural signals appear to go to different visual structures. The sustained class, which is more concerned with visual discrimination of form and pattern, appears to go to the cortex via an intermediate way station (the lateral geniculate), whereas the change or motion-detecting system sends its signal primarily to the midbrain (superior colliculus). (The article by Michael in PMM treats this distinction in more detail.) At higher levels of processing, the motion-or change-detecting system appears most intimately tied to orienting mechanisms, and provides the major sensory input to the control mechanisms considered later.

Although this collection emphasizes visual perception and control, the dichotomy between sustained and transient information processing appears also in other sense modalities, such as somatosensory perception and, in particular, auditory perception. In auditory perception, a useful functional division in the type of signal processing may be made at the first way-station of the cochlear nucleus (Evans and Nelson, 1973). Here, fast-acting transient signals provide the best inputs for auditory localization, whereas the more slowly modulated and sustained inputs better characterize auditory pattern recognition. On the other hand, in somatosensory perception, the analysis of surface texture requires quite a prolonged and sustained input as one's fingers explore a surface, whereas the prick of a pin leads to a rapid withdrawal of the hand.

In the final article of the section, "Contrast and Spatial Frequency," Fergus W. Campbell and Lamberto Maffei tackle the problem of the detection of contrast in mammalian visual systems, principally cat and man. Similar mechanisms and similar behavior have been found, by means of quite different techniques, in each animal. This behavior—in particular, the sine-wave response function (contrast sensitivity) for human and cat—is directly related to the mechanisms described by Ratliff and Werblin for simpler forms. For example, the envelope of the contrast sensitivity curve may be considered to be merely a Fourier representation of the average "Kuffler unit" or of the photocopier's sensitivity to contrast, as illustrated by Ratliff. There is a distinct advantage in describing the sensitivity of such neural units in terms of their sensitivity to sinusoidal gratings, however, for this type of plot emphasizes that the grain, or coarseness, of a pattern will be an important variable in detecting contrast. But the single envelope of contrast sensitivity hides the mechanisms that are actually involved in the analysis of the grain or texture of a pattern. What are these hidden mechanisms? The first article in the next subset, "Experiments in the Visual Perception of Texture," by Bela Julesz, begins to answer this question by describing some properties of higher-level feature analysers.

Feature Extraction

Probably the simplest neural feature analyzer is the Kuffler unit, a neural unit with an antagonistic center-surround organization (see Section III, Physiological Analyzers, in PMM). It is from these simple concentric feature detectors that higher-level analyzers are built, such as the line, edge, and corner detectors of Hubel and Wiesel (see David H. Hubel, "The Visual Cortex of the Brain," in PMM). In mammalian retinae, however, not all Kuffler units are the same size. Even in the same retinal region, where hundreds of such contrast-sensitive units have overlapping receptive fields, there may be a tenfold range of diameters of these units. Together, their combined responses make up the envelope of contrast sensitivity for the eye. Individually, however, these units allow the observer to tell the difference between a coarse and a fine pattern. This is texture discrimination in the simplest sense.

Texture perception also includes higher-level processes. Although the surface of a field of grass or a piece of sandpaper may have the same texture throughout, many texture patterns, such as those of wood, drapes, or rugs, have different textures in each of two dimensions. For example, a rug may be made up of gratings, such as those described in Campbell and Maffei's "Contrast and Spatial Frequency," and also have a graininess typical of grass. Such texture patterns with linear elements must clearly also be analyzed in terms of the line detectors of Hubel and Wiesel (see Hubel's article in PMM) as well as the simpler Kuffler units.

In his article "Experiments in the Visual Perception of Texture," Julesz considers these kinds of linear texture patterns in addition to textures that are uniform in two dimensions. (A random-dot pattern is his simplest illustration of the latter category.) Clearly, when a uniform texture is elongated in one direction to give streaking, the difference will be obvious (see the illustration at the bottom of page 40). This difference may be described in several ways. such as in terms of the coarseness of the pattern (spatial frequency) or in terms of a statistical process. Julesz prefers the statistical descriptor, because this measure yields a remarkable limitation to texture perception: we are not capable of distinguishing textures that differ only in their third-order Markov processes. Julesz demonstrates his conjecture with several very impressive examples, ranging from random-dot matrices to complex arrays of letters and dots. Without an illustration to prove otherwise, how many readers would believe that it is not possible to identify, within an array of R's, a region in which the letters are printed backwards?

In the article following the one by Julesz, Fabio Metelli ("The Perception of Transparency") describes some further properties of the perception of surfaces. A surface may be defined not only by its edges, but perhaps more importantly by its lightness, color, or texture. For each of these attributes, neurophysiologists have found neural feature analyzers (see Section III, PMM). Yet how are these more elemental analyzers put together to yield a percept of an extended area? Ratliff's article "Contour and Contrast" deals with edge-related effects that influence the brightness perception of surfaces, but Metelli extends the problem to the more general case of overlap. When one surface is seen behind a transparent surface, what are the rules governing the brightness in the region of overlap? These rules are not physically determined, but depend instead upon the manner in which the nervous system handles spatial and intensity relations over a relatively wide field. By studying certain mosaics of opaque color and shapes that give rise to the impression of transparency, Metelli is able to formulate a relatively simple model that predicts the conditions under which stationary patterns will appear transparent, one pattern seeming to lie in front of the other.

Clearly, where a separation between two overlying surfaces is possible, some mechanisms of perception in three-dimensional space must be involved. At present, these mechanisms are not well understood. It is known, however, that in mammals with large binocular fields, the cortex has feature detectors that respond to objects located in the third dimension. John D. Pettigrew ("The Neurophysiology of Binocular Vision") describes the properties of these analyzers and their construction. Because they are activated best by edges of a given orientation, one might not be surprised to learn eventually that boundaries or edges that intersect in different depth planes might differentially activate different sets of binocular disparity detectors. Thus, when a vertical edge lies behind a limited horizontal line, the two different sets of disparity detectors (one horizontally oriented and the other vertically oriented) may each define their own regions of brightness, using mechanisms of lateral interaction similar to those described by Ratliff. Is it possible, then, that transparency perception may be based in part upon activities of feature analyzers at this level?

A still higher level of feature analysis is concerned with dynamic stimuli and movements in a three-dimensional world. Gunnar Johansson ("Visual Motion Perception") shows that our visual system does not work like a camera that snaps still shots of the world, but rather as a motion-detecting computer that fits the patterns of flowing images into internal geometrical representations. Although the analysis of these flow patterns may be performed with only one eye, the fact that three-dimensional perceptions are elicited suggests that the internal computation is performed at least in part by analyzers concerned with binocular vision and steropsis, or disparity detection. Johansson's article suggests specific mathematical rules used by the visual system to encode optical flow. Once again, the key is to look at the relations among the parts of the total image—in particular, the relations that remain invariant under perspective transformations. How do our feature-analyzing mechanisms encode these rules of invariance? One answer may be the limitations in the manner by which relatively simple higher-order feature analyzers may interact with one another. Under such a scheme, the computational rules for Johansson's projective geometry would not be found in yet another, higher-order analyzer, but rather in the correlations possible among the activities of lower-order feature analyzers.

In the final article of this subset ("Auditory Beats in the Brain"), Gerald Oster discusses three auditory phenomena that relate to earlier papers on vision: motion perception, binaural localization, and auditory pattern recognition in textured noise. Each of these phenomena demonstrate that sensory processing in different modalities still follows quite similar mechanisms. Clearly, acoustic localization and binaural beats have parallels with stereopsis and binocular vision, as Pettigrew points out in "The Neurophysiology of Binocular Vision." The correlations demanded by the auditory system, however, appear much simpler, requiring less preprocessing than in the visual system. Moreover, some mention is made of two auditory mechanisms for the localization of sounds, one depending on phase differences and a second depending on intensity differences reaching the two ears. Each of these mechanisms has further perceptual correlates. There are even analogies to the model proposed by Johansson in "Visual Motion Perception." For example, motion of a sound image within the head may be generated by appropriate stereophonic input. The motion of the sound image follows its own rules, which appear to be determined in part by the relations between the binaural beats and the two mechanisms by which the brain senses the direction of sounds. The path of apparent motion taken by the illusory sound source depends upon computational rules of invariance not unlike those described for illusory optical flow.

Control Mechanisms in Localization

Before the full power of pattern-analyzing mechanisms may be utilized, it is necessary that objects of interest be presented to the region of central vision and that they be brought directly in front of the head, where both binaural and binocular vision are most sensitive. To bring objects into this central region, an animal makes extremely rapid and coordinated movements of the head, eyes, and often even the limbs. What chain of events leads to such coordinated responses? Is there one center that integrates and coordinates information from the various modalities?

Actually, there are at least two coordinating centers, one handling principally sensory input (the colliculus) and the second concerned mainly with motor coordination (the cerebellum). Articles in this subset describe each of these two structures and also examine the types of behavior they mediate. Details of the superior colliculus in mammals are described by Barbara Gordon in "The Superior Colliculus of the Brain." Although the principal sensory input to this little midbrain structure is visual motion information transmitted directly from the eye itself, the colliculus also receives auditory and somatosensory information. Gordon presents evidence suggesting that these two nonvisual inputs appear as superimposed topographic maps of the animal's auditory and somatic fields. Clearly, an object can be in register on such superimposed maps only when the eyes, head, and body are in a unique position, presumably all oriented "straight ahead." Although not explicitly stated by Gordon, the colliculus may serve to guide the animal's body parts to this straight-ahead position, thus placing objects of interest in the optimal position for further pattern analysis.

Jörg-Peter Ewert ("The Neural Basis of Visually Guided Behavior") shows how localization at a more primitive level is followed by a triggered motor response in the toad. In this simpler nervous system, stereotyped patterns of behavior can be traced to specific sensorimotor pathways, or systems. Two such systems emerge as dominant: the first is a tectal system for localization, which is analogous to the superior colliculus described by Gordon for the cat, and the second is the thalamic-pretectal pathway. The tectal or collicular system generally triggers prey catching, and is clearly dependent upon proper orienting behavior. Ewert calls the thalamicpretectal pathway a "caution" system, as it triggers avoidance reactions. The latter system is thus more concerned with the significance of the nervous system, whereas the colliculus answers the question, "Where is it?" Most remarkable about Ewert's study are the parallels that can be drawn that pertain to the behavior and anatomy of higher mammals, such as the ground squirrel (see Michael's article in PMM), hamster (Schneider, 1969), and even man himself (Trevarthen, 1968).

In man, however, the complete repertoire of the systems that govern eye, head, and body movements is difficult to study (Held, 1968). Each system controls many component movements, all of which must be integrated in proper sequence and synchrony to yield a coordinated movement. These component movements are illustrated very clearly in the eye-movement system, in which three different types of movements occur: saccades, pursuit, and vergence movements. Derek H. Fender ("Control Mechanisms of the Eye") treats saccadic and pursuit eye movements in detail, showing that each responds selectively to either positional or velocity information. By a straight-forward application of systems analysis to the visual processes involved in the pursuit or tracking of a moving object, the eye can be seen to be a servo-mechanism in which retinal-image motion is used as feedback. In contrast, however, the saccadic mechanism, used for orienting, depends upon an entirely different kind of computational routine based upon ballistic movements. Thus the control of eye position consists of separate, quite differently programmed sequences of movement. With such diversity underlying the eye-movement system alone, how can we hope to understand the coordination of the eyes, head, and limbs together?

Nevertheless, Emilio Bizzi ("The Coordination of Eye-Head Movement), in work done with monkeys, shows that considerable understanding can be gained in limited and controlled situations. Both proprioceptive and vestibular inputs are shown to modulate eye movements. Particularly crucial is a reflexive feedback loop from the sensors of the inner ear to the oculomotor command center that causes the eye to counterotate to compensate for head rotations following a rapid eye movement, or saccade. This simple feedback loop suggests that there is no need in this case to postulate a special center in the brain that is responsible for coordinating the eyes with the head. Perhaps, then, the strategy of the mechanisms of many so-called coordinated movements is to program patterns of motor activity that minimize the need to develop coordinated programs, so that internal feedback or servo control mechanisms are relied upon instead.

That part of the brain which has been most carefully examined for links to control mechanisms is the cerebellum. In an exquisitely detailed and illustrative article, "The Cortex of the Cerebellum," Rodolfo R. Llinás dissects the cerebellum into its major parts and then examines its microstructure. With a sure knowledge of the circuitry of the cerebellum, we can specify its function: the control of programmed, synchronous movements necessary for coordination. Although the cerebellum does not initiate movement, it is necessary for the modulation or reorganization of motor commands, and serves to coordinate these signals to obtain maximum efficiency. This "lesser brain" thus allows localization movements to proceed rapidly and accurately, acting in parallel with the pattern-analyzing operations of the cerebral cortex. In time, the cerebral cortex may be understood to the same degree as the cerebellum, whose structure and function are now so elegantly related.

REFERENCES

Evans, E. F., and P. G. Nelson, 1973. On the functional relationships between dorsal and ventral divisions of the cochlear nucleus of the cat. *Experimental Brain Research* **17**, 428–442.

Held, R. 1968. Dissociation of visual functions by deprivation and rearrangement. *Psychologische Forschung* **31**, 338–348.

Schneider, G. E. 1969. Two visual systems. *Science* **163**, 895–902.

Trevarthen, C. B. 1968. Two mechanisms of vision in primates. *Psychologische Forschung* **31**, 299–337.

Contour and Contrast

by Floyd Ratliff

June 1972

We see contours when adjacent areas contrast sharply. Surprisingly, certain contours, in turn, make large areas appear lighter or darker than they really are. What neural mechanisms underlie these effects?

Contours are so dominant in our visual perception that when we draw an object, it is almost instinctive for us to begin by sketching its outlines. The use of a line to depict a contour may well have been one of the earliest developments in art, as exemplified by the "line drawings" in the pictographs and petroglyphs of prehistoric artists. We see contours when there is a contrast, or difference, in the brightness or color between adjacent areas. How contrast creates contours has been thoroughly studied by both scientists and artists. How the contour itself can affect the contrast of the areas it separates has been known to artists for at least 1,000 years, but it is relatively new as a subject of scientific investigation. Although the psychophysiological basis of how contrast enables the visual system to distinguish contours has been studied for the past century, it is only in the past few years that psychologists and physiologists have started to examine systematically the influence of contour on contrast.

You can readily observe how the visual system tends to abstract and accentuate contours in patterns of varying contrast by paying close attention to the edges of a shadow cast by an object in strong sunlight. Stand with your back to the sun and look closely at the shadow of your head and shoulders on a sidewalk. You will see a narrow half-shadow between the full shadow and the full sunlight. Objectively the illumination in the full shadow is uniformly low, in the half-shadow it is more or less uniformly graded and in the full sunlight it is uniformly high; within each area there are no sharp maxima or minima. Yet you will see a narrow dark band at the dark edge of the half-shadow and a narrow bright band at its bright edge. You can enhance the effect by swaying from side to side to produce a moving shadow.

These dark and bright strips, now known as Mach bands, were first reported in the scientific literature some 100 years ago by the Austrian physicist, philosopher and psychologist Ernst Mach. They depend strictly on the distribution of the illumination. Mach formulated a simple principle for the effect: "Whenever the light-intensity curve of an illuminated surface (whose light intensity varies in only one direction) has a concave or convex flection with respect to the abscissa, that place appears brighter or darker, respectively, than its surroundings" [*see bottom illustration on next page*].

The basic effect can be demonstrated by holding an opaque card under an ordinary fluorescent desk lamp, preferably in a dark room. If the shadow is cast on a piece of paper, part of the paper is illuminated by light from the full length of the lamp. Next to the illuminated area is a half-shadow that gets progressively darker until a full shadow is reached. Ideally the distribution of light should be uniformly high in the bright area, uniformly low in the dark area and smoothly graded between the bright and the dark areas [*see top illustration on next page*]. If you now look closely at the edges of the graded half-shadow, you see a narrow bright band at the bright edge and a narrow dark band at the dark edge. These are the Mach bands. Their appearance is so striking that many people will not believe at first that they are only a subjective phenomenon. Some will mistakenly try to explain the appearance of the bands by saying they are the result of multiple shadows or diffraction.

Exact psychophysical measurements of the subjective appearance of Mach bands have been made by Adriana Fiorentini and her colleagues at the National Institute of Optics in Italy. Their technique consists in having an observer adjust an independently variable spot of light to match the brightness of areas in and around the Mach bands. In general they find that the bright band is distinctly narrower and more pronounced than the dark band. The magnitude of the effect, however, varies considerably from person to person.

Since Mach bands delineate contours we expect to see, only a careful observer, or someone who has reason to objectively measure the light distribution at a shadow's edge, is likely to realize that the bands are a caricature of the actual pattern of illumination. Artists of the 19th-century Neo-Impressionist school were unusually meticulous in their observations, and this was reflected in much of their work. A good example is Paul Signac's "Le petit déjeuner." In this painting there are numerous contrast effects in and around the shadows and half-shadows. Particularly striking is how some of the shadows are darkest near their edges and quite light near

NEO-IMPRESSIONIST PAINTER Paul Signac was a meticulous observer of the contrast effects in shadows and half-shadows. On the opposite page is a portion of his "Le petit déjeuner" (1886–1887). Note how the shadow is darker near the unshaded tablecloth and lighter next to the dark matchbox. Similar effects can be found in other shadows. The effects change when the painting is viewed from various distances. The painting is in the Rijksmuseum Kröller-Müller at Otterlo in the Netherlands and is reproduced with its permission.

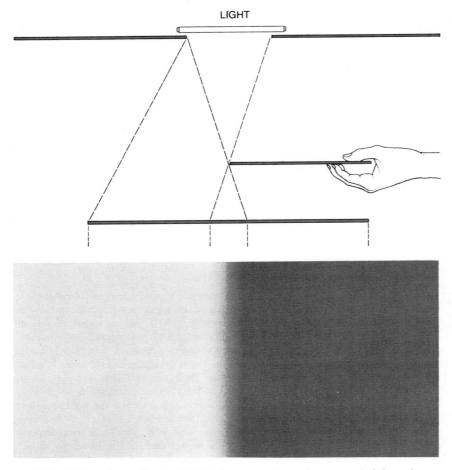

LIGHT

MACH BANDS can be produced with light from an ordinary fluorescent desk lamp (*upper illustration*). Place a sheet of white or gray paper on the desk and the light about a foot or so above it. Covering the ends of the lamp, which usually are not uniformly bright, may enhance the effect. Turn out the other lights in the room and hold an opaque card an inch or less above the paper. Various positions should be tried for optimum results. Note the narrow bright line and the broader dark line at the outer and inner edges of the half-shadow; these are the Mach bands. The lower illustration is a photograph of a half-shadow produced by the method described. The reproduction of the photograph does not retain all the characteristics of the original because of losses inherent in the reproduction process.

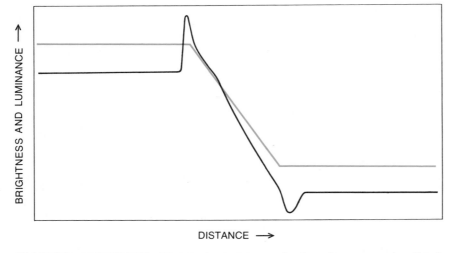

OBSERVED BRIGHTNESS CURVE obtained by psychophysical measurements (*black line*) has two sharp flections, one corresponding to the bright band and the other to the dark band. Measurement of actual luminance (*colored line*) across a half-shadow region reveals that the effect lies in the eye of the beholder and is not an objective phenomenon.

the object casting the shadow. Where Signac saw contrast he painted contrast, whether it was objectively present in the original scene or not. The effects we see in his painting depend of course partly on what Signac painted and partly on how our own eyes respond to contrast. When we view Signac's painting, our own eyes and brain further exaggerate the contrast he painted. As a result the painting appears to have even more contrast than the original scene could have had.

Without precise physical and psychophysical measurements it is difficult to tell how much of the contrast we perceive is objective and how much is subjective. Adding to the confusion is the fact that the subjective Mach bands can seemingly be photographed. All the photograph does, however, is to reproduce with considerable fidelity the original distribution of light in a scene, and it is this distribution of light and dark that gives rise to the subjective Mach bands. Moreover, the photographic process can itself introduce a spurious enhancement of contrast. Edge effects that closely resemble Mach bands can arise as the film is developed. Unlike Mach bands, they are an objective phenomenon consisting of actual variations in the density of the film, and the variations can be objectively measured.

On many occasions scientific investigators have mistaken Mach bands for objective phenomena. For example, shortly after W. K. Röntgen discovered X rays several workers attempted to measure the wavelength of the rays by passing them through ordinary diffraction slits and gratings and recording the resulting pattern on film. Several apparently succeeded in producing diffraction patterns of dark and light bands from which they could determine the wavelength of the X rays. All, however, was in error. As two Dutch physicists, H. Haga and C. H. Wind, showed later, the supposed diffraction patterns were subjective Mach bands.

As early as 1865 Mach proposed an explanation of the subjective band effect and other contrast phenomena in terms of opposed excitatory and inhibitory influences in neural networks in the retina and the brain. The means for direct investigation of such neural mechanisms did not become available, however, until the 1920's, when E. D. Adrian, Y. Zotterman and Detlev W. Bronk, working at the University of Cambridge, developed methods for recording the electrical activity of single nerve cells. The basic excitatory-inhibitory principle

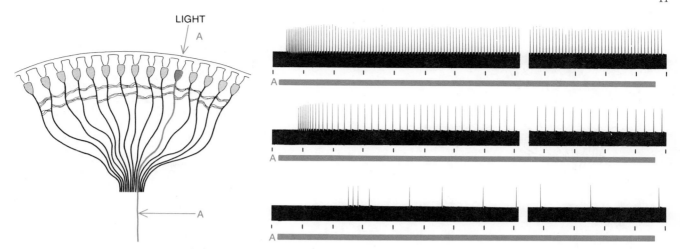

RATE OF DISCHARGE of nerve impulses produced by steady illumination of a single receptor, A, in the eye of the horseshoe crab Limulus is directly related to the intensity of the light. The nerve fibers from the receptor are separated by microdissection and connected to an electrode from an amplifier and a recorder.

The top record shows the response of A to steady, high-intensity light. The middle record shows the response to light of moderate intensity, and the lower record the response to low-intensity illumination. Duration of the light signal is indicated by the colored bar. Each mark above the colored bar indicates one-fifth of a second.

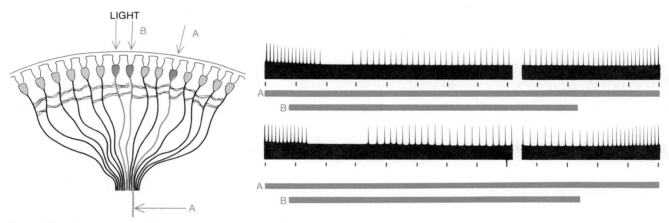

INHIBITION of receptor, A, steadily exposed to moderate illumination is produced when neighboring receptors, B, are also illuminated. The beginning and the end of the records show the initial and final rate of impulses by A. The colored bars indicate duration of light signals. The upper record shows the effects on A of moderate-intensity illumination of B. The lower record shows the effect on A of high-intensity illumination of B. The stronger the illumination on neighboring receptors, the stronger the inhibitory effect.

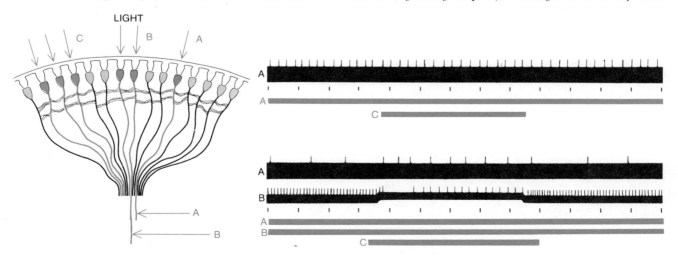

DISINHIBITION of receptor A occurs when the inhibition exerted on it by the B receptors is partially released by illuminating the large area C. The upper record shows that A's activity is not affected when C also is illuminated because of the distance between them. The first part of the lower record shows the inhibitory effect of B on A, then the inhibition of B when C is illuminated and the concomitant disinhibition of A. When the illumination of C stops, B returns to a higher rate of activity and resumes its inhibition of A.

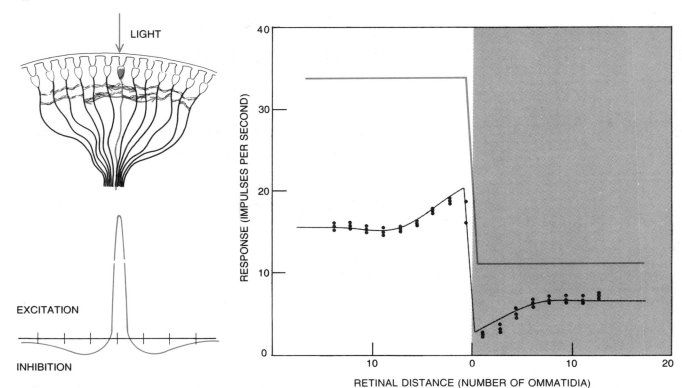

LIGHT

EXCITATION

INHIBITION

LATERAL INHIBITION in the eye of the horseshoe crab is strongest between receptors a short distance apart and grows weaker as the distance between receptors increases. Below the eye section is a graph of the type of excitatory and inhibitory fields that would be produced by the illumination of a single receptor. The colored line in the graph on the right shows what the retinal response would be to a sharp light-to-dark contour if lateral inhibition did not occur. The points on the graph show responses actually elicited by three scans of the pattern across the receptor in an experiment by Robert B. Barlow, Jr., of Syracuse University. The thin line shows the theoretical responses for lateral inhibition as computed by Donald A. Quarles, Jr., of the IBM Watson Research Center.

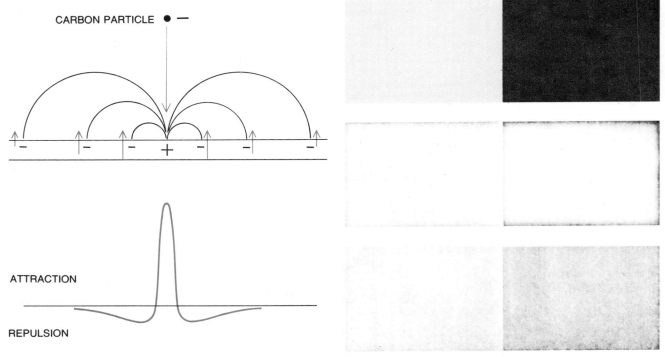

CARBON PARTICLE

ATTRACTION

REPULSION

EDGE EFFECT in xerographic copying is the result of the shape of the electrostatic field (which is quite similar to that of the "neural" field in the top illustration) around a single charged point on the xerographic plate (*upper left*). The first panel on the right shows the original pattern. The middle panel shows a Xerox copy of the original. Note how contrast at the edges is greatly enhanced. The bottom panel shows a Xerox copy made with a halftone screen placed over the original so that the pattern is broken up into many dots.

has been demonstrated to be essentially correct in experiments that H. K. Hartline and I, together with our colleagues, have carried out over the past 20 years.

We measured the responses of single neurons in the compound lateral eye of the horseshoe crab *Limulus*. (The animal also has two simple eyes in the front of its carapace near the midline.) The lateral eye of the horseshoe crab is comparatively large (about a centimeter in length) but otherwise it is much like the eye of a fly or a bee. It consists of about 1,000 ommatidia (literally "little eyes"), each of which appears to function as a single photoreceptor unit. Excitation does not spread from one receptor to another; it is confined to whatever receptor unit is illuminated. Nerve fibers arise from the receptors in small bundles that come together to form the optic nerve. Just behind the photoreceptors the small nerve bundles are interconnected by a network of nerve fibers. This network, or plexus, is a true retina even though its function is almost purely inhibitory.

Both the local excitatory and the extended inhibitory influences can be observed directly. A small bundle of fibers from a single receptor is separated by microdissection from the main trunk of the optic nerve and placed on an electrode. In this way the nerve impulses generated by light striking the receptor can be recorded. Weak stimulation produces a low rate of discharge; strong stimulation produces a high rate. These responses are typical of many simple sense organs.

In addition to the excitatory discharge there is a concomitant inhibitory effect. When a receptor unit fires, it inhibits its neighbors. This is a mutual effect: each unit inhibits others and in turn is inhibited by them. The strength of the inhibition depends on the level of activity of the interacting units and the distance between them. In general near neighbors affect one another more than distant neighbors, and the stronger the illumination, the stronger the inhibitory effect. We discovered that such an organization can produce a second-order effect that we call disinhibition. If two sets of receptors are close enough together to interact, they inhibit each other when both sets are illuminated. Now suppose a third set of receptors, far enough away so that it can interact with only one of the two sets of receptors, is illuminated. The activity of the third set will inhibit one set of the original pair, which in turn reduces the inhibition on

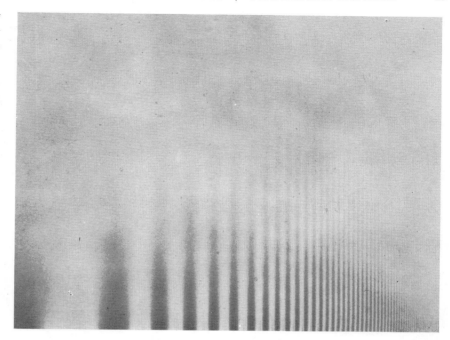

FILTER produced by lateral inhibition at low spatial frequencies and the lack of resolving power of the retina at high spatial frequencies causes intermediate spatial frequencies to be the most distinctly seen. The width of the vertical dark and light bands decreases in a logarithmic sinusoidal manner from the left to the right; the contrast varies logarithmically from less than 1 percent at the top to about 30 percent at the bottom. The objective contrast at any one height in the figure is the same for all spatial frequencies, yet the spatial frequencies in the middle appear more distinct than those at high or low frequencies; that is, the dark lines appear taller at the center of the figure. The effects of changes in viewing distance, luminance, adaptation and sharpness of eye focus can be demonstrated by the viewer.

MACH BAND PHENOMENON created with horizontal lines is shown here. In the illustration at left the black lines are a constant thickness from the left side to the midpoint and then thicken gradually. When the illustration is viewed from a distance, a vertical white "Mach band" appears down the middle. In the illustration at right the horizontal black lines are a constant thickness from the right side to the midpoint and then thin out. When viewed from a distance, the illustration appears to have a vertical black band down the middle.

CRAIK-O'BRIEN EFFECT (this example is known as the Cornsweet illusion) is the result of a specific variation of luminance at the contour, which makes the outer zone appear slightly darker even though it has the same luminance as the inner zone. The effect here is less than in the original because of difficulty in reproducing the actual intensity relations.

RAPID ROTATION of this disk will create the Cornsweet illusion. The white spur creates a local variation near the contour between the two zones that causes the apparent brightness of the inner zone to increase. In the same way the dark spur creates a local variation that causes the outer zone to appear darker. Except in the spur region the objective luminance of the disk when it is rotating is the same in both the inner and the outer region.

the remaining set, thus increasing their rate of discharge [*see bottom illustration on page 11*]. Following the discovery of disinhibition in the eye of the horseshoe crab, Victor J. Wilson and Paul R. Burgess of Rockefeller University found that some increases in neural activity (called recurrent facilitation) that had been observed in spinal motoneurones in the cat were actually disinhibition. Subsequently M. Ito and his colleagues at the University of Tokyo observed a similar type of disinhibition in the action of the cerebellum on Deiter's nucleus in the cat.

The spatial distribution and relative magnitudes of the excitatory and inhibitory influences for any particular receptor unit in the eye of *Limulus* can be represented graphically as a narrow central field of excitatory influence surrounded by a more extensive but weaker field of inhibitory influence [*see top illustration on page 12*].

As Georg von Békésy has shown, the approximate response of an inhibitory network can be calculated graphically by superimposing the graphs for each of the interacting units, each graph scaled according to the intensity of the stimulus where it is centered. The summed effects of overlapping fields of excitation (positive values) and inhibition (negative values) at any particular point would determine the response at that point. In the limit of infinitesimally small separations of overlapping units, this would be mathematically equivalent to using the superposition theorem or the convolution integral to calculate the response. In fact, these inhibitory interactions may be expressed in a wide variety of essentially equivalent mathematical forms. The form Hartline and I used at first is a set of simultaneous equations—one equation for each of the interacting receptor units. Our colleagues Frederick A. Dodge, Jr., Bruce W. Knight, Jr., and Jun-ichi Toyoda have since that time expressed the properties of the inhibitory network in a less cumbersome and more general form: a transfer function relating the Fourier transform of the distribution of the intensity of the stimulus to the Fourier transform of the distribution of the magnitude of the response. This in effect treats the retinal network as a filter of the sinusoidal components in the stimulus, and can be applied equally well to both spatial and temporal variations. The overall filtering effect of the *Limulus* retina is to attenuate both the lowest and the highest spatial and temporal frequencies of the sinusoidal components.

It has long been known that spatial and temporal filtering effects of much the same kind occur in our own visual system. The main characteristics of the spatial "filter" can be seen by viewing the test pattern devised by Fergus W. Campbell and his colleagues at the University of Cambridge [see top illustration on page 13].

Even without considering the filter-like properties of neural networks it is possible to see how the subjective Mach bands can be produced by the interaction of narrow fields of excitation and broad fields of inhibition. Near the boundary between the light and dark fields some of the receptors will be inhibited not only by their dimly lit neighbors but also by some brightly lit receptors. The total inhibition of these boundary receptors will therefore be greater than the inhibition of dimly lit receptors farther from the boundary. Similarly, a brightly lit receptor near the boundary will be in the inhibitory field of some dimly lit receptors and as a result will have less inhibition acting on it than brightly lit receptors farther away from the boundary. Because of these differential effects near the boundary the response of the neural network in the *Limulus* retina will show a substantial maximum and minimum adjacent to the boundary even though the stimulus does not have such variations.

Opposed excitatory and inhibitory influences can mediate some highly specialized functions in higher animals. Depending on how these opposed influences are organized, they can detect motion, the orientation of a line or the difference between colors. No matter how complicated the visual system is, however, the basic contrast effects of the excitatory-inhibitory processes show up. For example, recent experiments by Russell L. De Valois and Paul L. Pease of the University of California at Berkeley show a contour enhancement similar to the bright Mach band in responses of monkey lateral geniculate cells. The simple lateral inhibition that produces contrast effects such as Mach bands may be a basic process in all the more highly evolved visual mechanisms.

Contrast phenomena are by no means found only in the nervous system. Indeed, contrast is found in any system of interacting components where opposed fields of positive (excitatory) and negative (inhibitory) influences exist. Whether the system is neural, electrical, chemical or an abstract mathematical model is irrelevant; all that is needed to produce a contrast effect is a certain distribution of the opposed influences. A familiar example is the contrast effect in xerography. The xerographic process does not reproduce solid black or gray areas very well. Only the edges of extended uniform areas are reproduced unless some special precautions are taken. This failing is inherent in the basic process itself. In the making of a xerographic copy a selenium plate is first electrostatically charged. Where light falls on the plate the electrostatic charge is lost; in dark areas the charge is retained. A black powder spread over the plate clings to the charged areas by electrostatic attraction and is eventually transferred and fused to paper to produce the final copy.

The electrostatic attraction of any point on the plate is determined not by the charge at that point alone but by the integrated effects of the electrostatic fields of all the charges in the neighborhood. Since the shapes of the positive and negative components of the individual fields happen to be very much like the shapes of the excitatory and inhibitory components of neural unit fields in the retina, the consequences are much the same too [see bottom illustration on page 20]. Contours are enhanced; uniform areas are lost. To obtain a xerographic copy of the uniform areas one merely has to put a halftone screen over the original. The screen breaks up the uniform areas into many small discontinuities, in effect many contours.

Similar contrast effects are seen in photography and in television. In photography a chemical by-product of the development process at one point can diffuse to neighboring points and inhibit further development there, causing spurious edge effects; in television the secondary emission of electrons from one point in the image on the signal plate in the camera can fall on neighboring points and "inhibit" them, creating negative "halos," or dark areas, around bright spots. The similarity of the contrast effects in such diverse systems is not a trivial coincidence. It is an indication of a universal principle: The enhancement of contours by contrast depends on particular relations among interacting elements in a system and not on the particular mechanisms that achieve those relations.

How a contour itself can affect the contrast of the areas it separates cannot be explained quite so easily. This effect of contour on contrast was first investigated by Kenneth Craik of the University of Cambridge and was described in

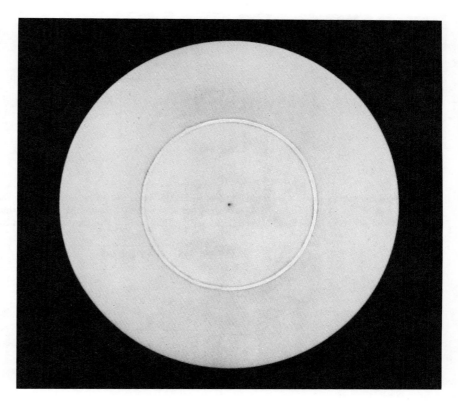

SOURCE OF CRAIK-O'BRIEN EFFECT can be demonstrated by covering the contour with a wire or string. When this is done, the inner and outer regions appear equally bright.

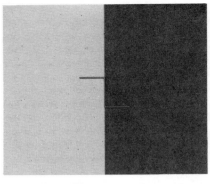 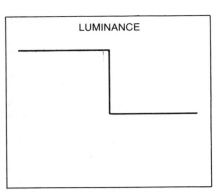 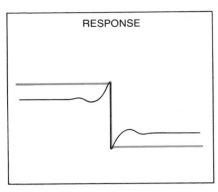

STEP PATTERN of illumination (*left*) also has a step-pattern luminance curve (as measured by a photometer) across the contour. A computer simulation of the response of the *Limulus* eye to the pattern (*black curve at right*) shows a maximum and a minimum that are the result of inhibitory interaction among the receptors. The colored curve at right shows how the pattern looks to a person; the small peak and dip in the curve indicate slight subjective contrast enhancement at the contour known as "border contrast."

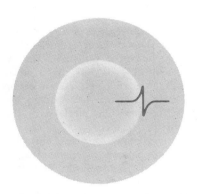 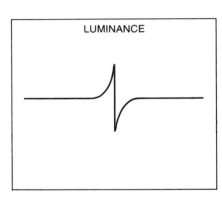 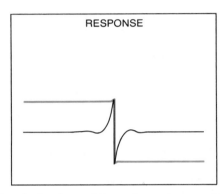

LUMINANCE on both sides of the Craik-O'Brien contour is the same but the inside (here simulated) is brighter. The human visual system may extrapolate (*colored curve*) from the maximum and minimum produced by inhibitory processes (*black curve at right*).

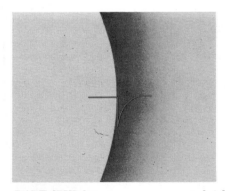 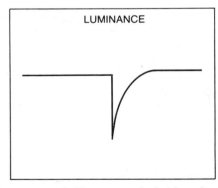 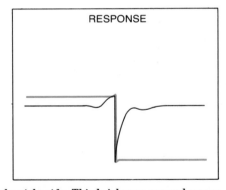

DARK SPUR between areas can create brightness reversal. Objectively the area at left of the contour is darker than the area at far right, but to an observer the left side (here simulated) will appear to be brighter than the right side. This brightness reversal agrees with the extrapolation (*colored curve*) from the maximum and minimum produced by inhibitory processes (*black curve at right*).

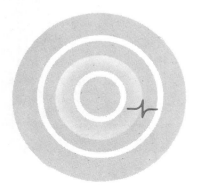 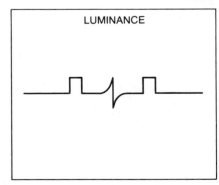 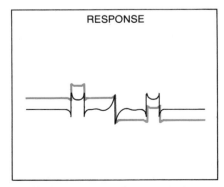

TWO BANDS OF LIGHT of equal intensity are superimposed on backgrounds of equal luminance separated by a Craik-O'Brien contour. The lights add their luminance to the apparent brightness (*colored curve*) and one band appears brighter than the other.

his doctoral dissertation of 1940. Craik's work was not published, however, and the same phenomenon (along with related ones) was rediscovered by Vivian O'Brien of Johns Hopkins University in 1958. The Craik-O'Brien effect, as I shall call it, has been of great interest to neurophysiologists and psychologists in recent years.

A particular example of this effect, sometimes called the Cornsweet illusion, is produced by separating two identical gray areas with a special contour that has a narrow bright spur and a narrow dark spur [see top illustration on page 14]. Although the two uniform areas away from the contour have the same objective luminance, the gray of the area adjacent to the light spur appears to be lighter than the gray of the area adjacent to the dark spur. When the contour is covered with a thick string, the grays of the two areas are seen to be the same. When the masking string is removed, the difference reappears but takes a few moments to develop. These effects can be very pronounced; not only can a contour cause contrast to appear when there actually is no difference in objective luminance but also a suitable contour can cause contrast to appear that is the reverse of the objective luminance.

With the choice of the proper contour a number of objectively different patterns can be made to appear similar in certain important respects [see illustrations on opposite page]. It is reasonable to assume that in all these cases the dominant underlying neural events are also similar. With the mathematical equation for the response of a *Limulus* eye one can calculate the neural responses to be expected from each type of pattern when processed by a simple inhibitory network. When this is done, one finds that the calculated responses are all similar to one another. Each has a maximum on the left and a minimum on the right. Furthermore, there is a certain similarity between the calculated neural response and the subjective experience of a human observer viewing the patterns: where the computed response has a maximum, the pattern appears brighter on that side of the contour; where the computed response has a minimum, the pattern appears darker on that side of the contour. Indeed, merely by extending a line from the maximum out to the edge of that side of the pattern and a line from the minimum out to the edge of that side of the pattern one obtains a fair approximation to the apparent brightness. This correspon-

dence suggests that opposed excitatory and inhibitory influences in neural networks of our visual systems are again partly responsible for creating the effect. Even so, much would remain to be explained. Why should the influence of the contour be extended over the entire adjacent area rather than just locally? And why do three distinctly different stimuli, when used as contours, produce much the same subjective result?

The answer to both of these questions may be one and the same. Communication engineers have experimented with a number of sophisticated means of data

compression to increase the efficiency of transmitting images containing large amounts of redundant information. For example, if a picture is being transmitted, only information about contours need be sent; the uniform areas between contours can be restored later by computer from information in the amplitudes of the maxima and minima at the contours. By the same token signals from the retina may be "compressed" and the redundant information extrapolated from the maximum and the minimum in the neural response. Such a process, which was postulated by Glenn A. Fry

KOREAN VASE from the 18th century provides an excellent example of the effect of a dark spur between areas. The moon appears to be brighter than the sky directly below it, but the actual luminance is just the reverse. If only a portion of the moon and an equal portion of the sky about one moon diameter below it are viewed through two identical small holes in a paper so that the dark contour is masked, the moon appears darker than the sky.

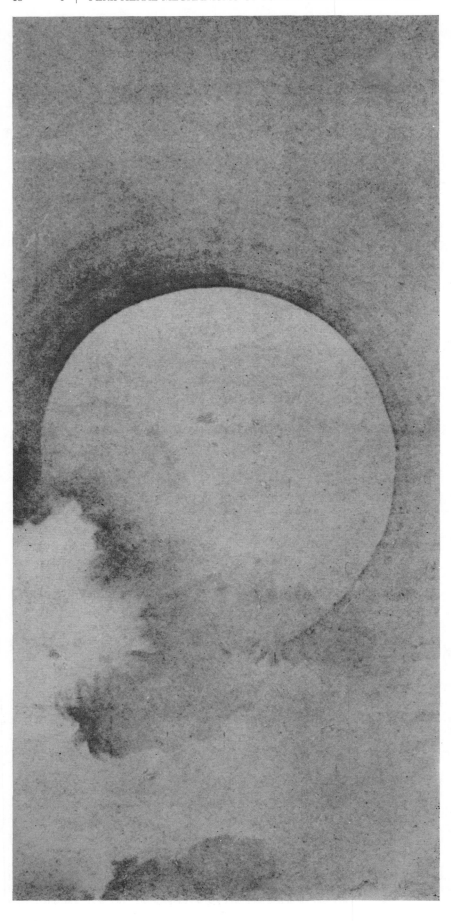

of Ohio State University many years ago, could explain the Craik-O'Brien effect.

What the actual mechanisms might be in our visual system that could "decode" the signals resulting from data compression by the retina and "restore" redundant information removed in the compression are empirical problems that have not yet been directly investigated by neurophysiologists. The problem as I have stated it may even be a will-o'-the-wisp; it is possible that there is no need to actually restore redundant information. The maximum and minimum in the retinal response may "set" brightness discriminators in the brain, and provided that there are no intervening maxima and minima (that is, visible contours) the apparent brightness of adjacent areas would not deviate from that set by the maximum or the minimum.

Some evidence that apparent brightness is actually set by the maximum and minimum at a contour or discontinuity and is then extrapolated to adjacent areas can be found in experiments conducted by L. E. Arend, J. N. Buehler and Gregory R. Lockhead at Duke University. They worked with patterns similar to those that create the Craik-O'Brien effect. On each side of the contour they produced an additional band of light. They found that the difference in apparent brightness between each band of light and its background depended only on the actual increment in luminance provided by the band, but that the apparent brightness of the two bands in relation to each other was determined by the apparent brightness of the background. For example, if two bands of equal luminance are superimposed on two backgrounds of equal luminance that are separated by a Craik-O'Brien contour, one of the bands of light will appear brighter than the other [see bottom illustration on page 16]. A number of related phenomena, in which contrast effects are propagated across several adjacent areas, are under investigation by Edwin H. Land and John H. McCann at the Polaroid Corporation. These experi-

JAPANESE INK PAINTING, "Autumn Moon" by Keinen, has a moon that objectively is only very slightly lighter than the sky. Much of the difference in apparent brightness is created by the moon's contour. The extent of the effect can be seen by covering the moon's edge with string. The painting, made about 1900, is in the collection of the late Akira Shimazu of Nara in Japan.

ments lend further support to the general view outlined here.

Of course, the human visual system is far too complex for the simple notion that apparent brightness is determined by difference at contours to be the whole story. Nonetheless, the general idea contains at least the rudiments of an explanation that is consistent with known physiological mechanisms and with the observed phenomena. Several entirely different distributions of illumination may look much the same to the human eye simply because the eye happens to abstract and send to the brain only those features that the objectively different patterns have in common. This type of data compression may be a basic principle common to many different kinds of neural systems.

Even if the cause of the Craik-O'Brien effect is in doubt, the effect itself is incontrovertible. Although the effects of contour on perceived contrast are relatively new to the scientific community, the same effects have long been known to artists and artisans. One can only speculate on how the effects were discovered. Very likely they emerged in some new artistic technique that was developed for another purpose. Once such a technique had been perfected, it doubtless would have persisted and been handed down from generation to generation. Furthermore, following the initial discovery the technique would probably have been applied in other media. In any event such techniques date back as far as the Sung dynasty of China (A.D. 960–1279), and they are still employed in Oriental art. For example, in a Japanese ink painting made about 1900 a single deft stroke of the brush greatly increases the apparent brightness of the moon [*see illustration on opposite page*]. If the contour is covered with a piece of string, the apparent brightness of the moon diminishes and that area is seen to be very little brighter than its surround.

A similar effect is found in a scene on an 18th-century Korean vase [*see illustration on page 17*]. Here the moon is actually darker than the space below it. Measurements of a photograph of the vase with a light meter under ordinary room lights showed that the luminance of the moon was 15 foot-lamberts and the space one moon diameter below was 20 foot-lamberts. The contour effect is so strong that the apparent brightness of the two areas is just the reverse of the objective luminance.

The contour-contrast effect can be produced on a ceramic surface by still another technique. This technique was

CHINESE TING YAO SAUCER is an example of the famous Ting white porcelain produced in the Sung dynasty of about A.D. 1000. Although the entire surface is covered with only a single creamy white glaze, the incised lotus design appears brighter than the background because of the incisions, which have a sharp inner edge and a graded outer edge, producing exactly the kind of contour that creates an apparent difference in brightness.

developed more than 1,000 years ago in the Ting white porcelain of the Sung dynasty and in the northern celadon ceramics of the same period. In the creation of the effect a design was first incised in the wet clay with a knife. The cut had a sharp inner edge and a sloping outer edge. The clay was then dried and covered with a white glaze. The slightly creamy cast of the glaze inside the cuts produces the necessary gradient to create the Craik-O'Brien effect. The result is that the pattern appears slightly brighter than the surround [*see illustration above*]. Since the effect depends on variations in the depth of the translucent monochrome glaze, it is much more subtle than it is in the Japanese painting and in the Korean vase. But then subtlety and restraint were characteristic of the Sung ceramists.

These examples of the effects of contrast and contour from the visual sciences and the visual arts illustrate the need for a better understanding of how elementary processes are organized into complex systems. In recent years the discipline of biology has become increasingly analytical. Much of the study of life has become the study of the behavior of single cells and the molecular events within them. Although the analytic approach has been remarkably productive, it does not come to grips with one of the fundamental problems facing modern biological science: how unitary structures and elementary processes are organized into the complex functional systems that make up living organs and organisms. Fortunately, however, we are not faced with an either-or choice. The analytic and the organic approaches are neither incompatible nor mutually exclusive; they are complementary, and advances in one frequently facilitate advances in the other. All that is required to make biology truly a life science, no matter what the level of analysis, is to occasionally adopt a holistic or organic approach. It is probably the elaborate organization of unitary structures and elementary processes that distinguishes living beings from lifeless things.

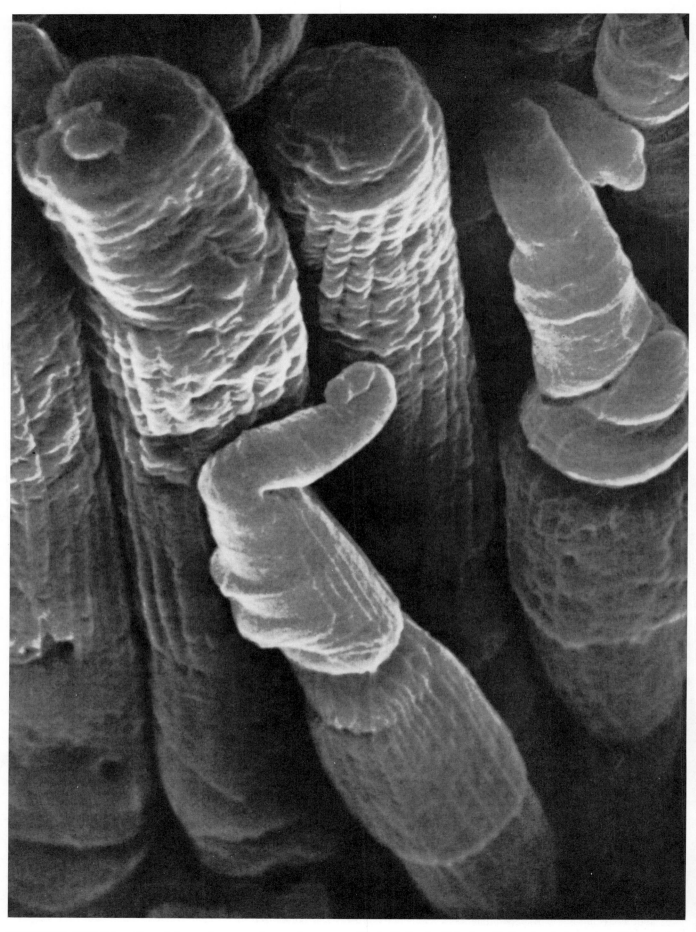

RECEPTOR CELLS in retina of the mudpuppy, a large salamander, are seen end on in a scanning electron micrograph made by Edwin R. Lewis, Yehoshua Y. Zeevi and the author. The cylindrical rods and the pointed cones are enlarged about 5,000 diameters.

The Control of Sensitivity in the Retina

by Frank S. Werblin
January 1973

*Interactions among nerve cells keep the response range
of the system in register with ambient illumination,
enabling the retina to form a high-contrast neural
image over a broad range of light conditions*

A good photographer can make pictures with the same camera and the same roll of film on a sunny beach at noon and then while driving home at dusk, even though the average light intensities may differ by more than a million to one. By adjusting the aperture and the shutter speed to control the amount of light that reaches the film, he keeps the response range of the film in register with the available light. In the eye as in the camera there are "settings" that need to be made in order to adapt the visual system to cope with a wide range of light conditions. The difference is that the aperture of the eye, the pupil, plays only a small part in these operations; most of the adjustments are made within the retina, which, like the film, must encode the differences in light intensity in the scene.

All visual information passes through the retina, which can be thought of as a special subsystem of the brain that has been brought out to the periphery to perform some essential early processing of the visual message. The retina communicates with higher centers of the brain through the optic nerve, which consists of about a million individual nerve fibers, each serving a different area of the visual field. Since the individual fibers of the optic nerve (and fibers in other parts of the nervous system as well) cannot accurately signal levels of activity over a range of more than about 100 to one, the retina must compress the very large range of intensities presented by the outside world into a narrower range that can be adequately handled by the optic-nerve fibers.

One possible method would be for the retina to generate for each point in visual space a signal that is proportional to the logarithm of the incident intensity. That is one of the solutions the camera-film system uses. Such a system, however, if it were used to span the entire range of intensities over which the visual system operates, would provide poor contrast discrimination because very little signaling capability would be available for each small increment in intensity. In order to solve this problem the system might use the full signaling capabilities of each of several different populations of neurons to cover different narrow ranges of intensities, for example one set of neurons for noon on the beach and another for dusk. Such a system would provide better contrast sensitivity, but the visual system would suffer from poor acuity because only a small population of neurons would be operational at any one time.

The retina actually performs operations that incorporate the best features of both of the foregoing solutions. As a result it is capable of signaling with high contrast sensitivity over a broad range of field intensities without sacrificing acuity. It is these operations I shall discuss, first describing the structure of the retina: the types of cell represented and the "wiring diagram," or the routes along which the cells communicate with one another.

In all vertebrates the retina is constructed with the same five basic types of cell [see "Retinal Processing of Visual Images," by Charles R. Michael; SCIENTIFIC AMERICAN, Offprint 1143]. I have worked with the retina of the mudpuppy (*Necturus maculosus*), which is remarkable for the size of its cells and is therefore particularly suitable for electrophysiological experiments at the level of individual cells. Information is carried in two different directions through the retina [*see bottom illustration on next page*]. It is carried in the input-output direction by a sequence of three cell types: receptor cells to bipolar cells to ganglion cells. Only the receptor cells contain photopigments and act as transducers, converting light energy into neural signals that are processed by succeeding retinal cells. The receptor cells drive the bipolar cells, which then pass the signal on to the ganglion cells. The ganglion cells generate the retinal output; their outgoing fibers comprise the optic nerve and carry information to higher centers. Information is also carried laterally, at right angles to the input-output pathway, by the horizontal and amacrine cells, which are strategically positioned to perform important operations that relate activity across different parts of the visual field. The actual connections among the cells can be inferred from information available in electron micrographs. Each neuron communicates with another at a synapse, or junction, probably by releasing a chemical transmitter substance that travels across the small space between the membranes of the two cells. The transmitter is presumably stored in and later released by synaptic vesicles: small packets within the cytoplasm that can be discerned in electron micrographs. One good indicator of the site and direction of synaptic transmission across cell membranes is therefore the presence of vesicles inside the membrane of the transmitting cell.

On this evidence the general scheme of the retinal wiring diagram is quite simple. Each lateral interneuron receives from the cell that precedes it in the input-output pathway, and it is capable of transmitting back to that cell, across to its neighbors or forward to the succeeding input-output cell. This means that horizontal cells can transmit to receptor cells, to other horizontal cells and to bipolar cells; amacrine cells can transmit to bipolar cells, to other ama-

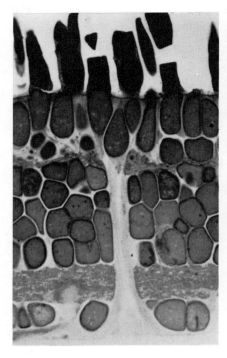
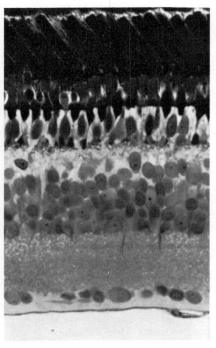

RETINAL CELLS of the mudpuppy, *Necturus maculosus* (*left*), and of the frog (*right*) are enlarged 400 diameters in photomicrographs of sections of retinas made by John E. Dowling, now at Harvard University. The light-sensitive receptor cells are at the top and the ganglion cells, which form the output of the retina and send signals to the brain along the optic nerve, are at the bottom. The remarkably large size of the mudpuppy cells is evident.

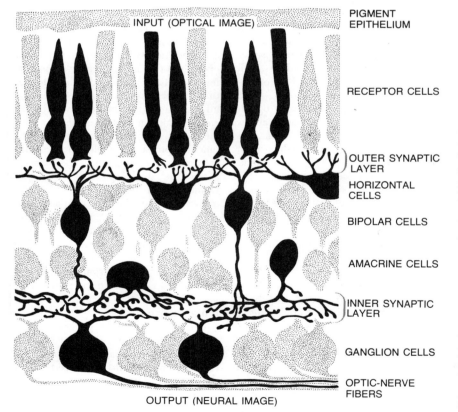

STRUCTURE of the vertebrate retina is emphasized in a drawing based on a micrograph of a retina prepared by the Golgi method, which selectively stains a few cell bodies and their processes. The vertically oriented receptor, bipolar and ganglion cells constitute the input-output pathway. Laterally oriented horizontal and amacrine cells carry information across the retina at two distinct levels to relate activity in different parts of the visual field.

crine cells and to ganglion cells. The functional result of these anatomical relations is that each input-output pathway is strongly influenced by activity in neighboring pathways through the laterally oriented interneurons.

Although intercell communication is mediated by chemical transmitters, information is carried within each cell by means of changes in electrical activity. The following is a typical sequence of events: On receipt of the chemical transmitter the electrical properties of the receiving cell's membrane are altered; that leads eventually to a change in the electric potential across the membrane, which is related to the strength of the incoming chemical signal; the change in electric potential in turn affects the release of chemical transmitter from the neuron to the next cell. It is fortunate that the chemical events by which cells communicate with one another have an intermediate electrical correlate within each cell because changes in the electrical activity of cells are easily measured.

The measurement is made by passing a fine glass tube with a conducting center through the cell membrane and reading the potential across the membrane. The potential measured by this fine micropipette electrode gives an index of cellular activity, and it is usually recorded as a function of time following a flash of light. The electrophysiologist, then, has a fairly thorough description of the wiring diagram for the retina showing clearly all possible synaptic relations between cells, but he cannot study these synapses directly; with his electrodes he has access only to the electrical activity of the cells that results from synaptic interactions. He must infer the nature of synaptic function from his indirect electrical measurements.

In most animals the cells of the retina are too small to be penetrated without damage by existing micropipettes, and so Alexander Bortoff of the State University of New York Upstate Medical Center at Syracuse began in 1964 to take advantage of the large cells of the mudpuppy retina. He also showed that the cells could be filled with a stain passed through the recording electrode, so that they could be identified later. Working first with John E. Dowling at Johns Hopkins University and later in my laboratory at the University of California at Berkeley, I have followed up Bortoff's initial efforts.

As a first step toward understanding the functional significance of synaptic interactions in the retina, I recorded from each cell type with a micropipette while flashing spots of light of various configurations on the retina. The pipettes were filled with a stain that I could drive out of the tip into the cell after recording its electrical activity. By identifying the stained cell later I could relate the recorded electrical activity to a specific anatomical category. The most satisfying result of the initial study was that five basic types of electrical response were recorded from cells in the retina, and each response matched up with a particular cell type as determined by the stain-identification technique. From then on the type of cell could be determined simply on the basis of the characteristic form of the response without resorting to the tedious staining procedure.

The flashing-light studies can be made to yield more detailed information about the retina if one activates separately the two distinct pathways that enter each synaptic complex. A bipolar cell can be driven either by the receptor cell immediately preceding it or by horizontal cells, depending on the form of the stimulus. A small spot of light illuminating only the receptors above the bipolar cell will selectively activate the receptor-to-bipolar synapse. Illumination by a surrounding ring of light will excite only more distant receptors, which communicate with the central bipolar cell only through horizontal cells, and so the ring preferentially activates the horizontal-to-bipolar (or horizontal-to-receptor) synapse. A similar set of stimulus conditions can be generated in order to activate the various synapses at the base of the bipolar cell.

Let us first consider the general forms of the response to light and the ways in which these forms change for the different cell types as information proceeds from the retinal input to its output [see illustration on next page]. The receptor cells, the horizontal cells and (in some cases) the bipolar cells polarize in the negative-going direction, or hyperpolarize, with illumination. This form of behavior is most unusual for a neuron: most nerve cells polarize in the positive-going direction, or depolarize, when they are excited. Furthermore, nerve cells usually propagate nerve impulses along their length when they are excited, but there is no indication of such impulse activity in the three cells at the input end of the retina. The form of the retinal message changes dramatically after leaving the bipolar cell. The amacrine and ganglion cells behave more like classical neurons in that they depolarize and also seem to generate more typical

nerve impulses when they are excited. The nerve impulse is an essential feature in neurons that need to communicate over great distances, for instance from the retina to the brain along the optic nerve, but it may not be required within the retina itself, where communication takes place over short distances.

The effect of interaction of the two pathways through the retina is most apparent in the recordings from the bipolar cell. It is responsive over a

broad area of the retina—its receptive field—but illumination in different regions of the field has different effects. When the flashed spot of illumination falls only on receptor cells that are in direct contact with the bipolar cell, the cell hyperpolarizes; when neighboring receptor cells that have no direct connection with it are illuminated, the cell depolarizes. These neighboring receptor cells communicate with the bipolar cell only by means of horizontal cells carrying information laterally across the ret-

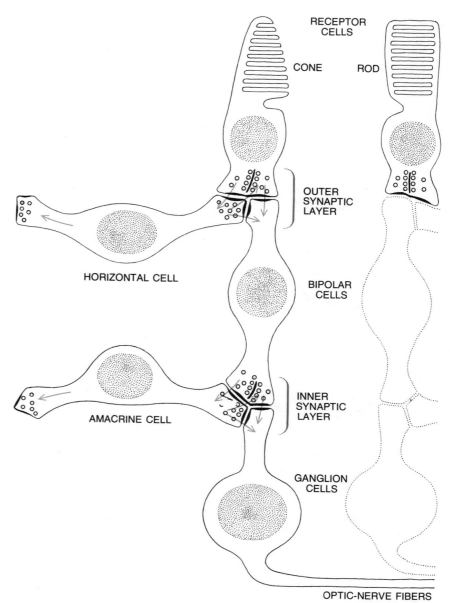

CONNECTIONS among cells were deduced by examining electron micrographs made by Dowling. Cells communicate by releasing a chemical transmitter substance at synapses, or junctions, with other cells; the substance is contained in synaptic vesicles (small circles). Messages can therefore be sent from cell terminals that have vesicles. All possible sites and directions of transmission of such messages are shown (arrows), as inferred from electron micrographs. Bipolar and ganglion cells simply "read out" and pass along signals formed by interactions of vertical and lateral neurons; lateral interneurons transmit back to cells that drive them, across to one another and on to succeeding input-output cells.

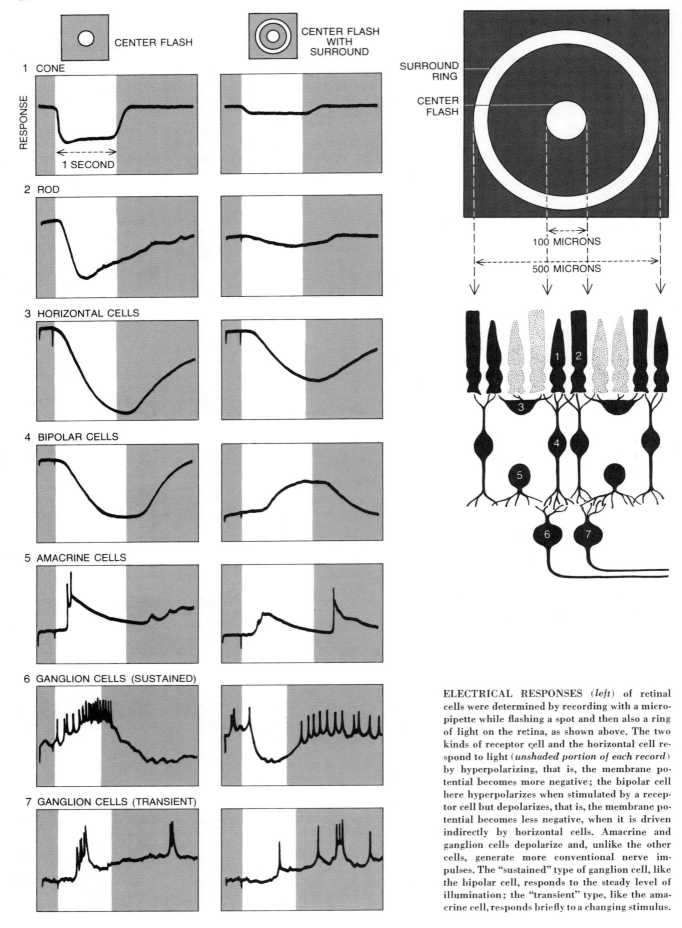

ELECTRICAL RESPONSES (*left*) of retinal cells were determined by recording with a micropipette while flashing a spot and then also a ring of light on the retina, as shown above. The two kinds of receptor cell and the horizontal cell respond to light (*unshaded portion of each record*) by hyperpolarizing, that is, the membrane potential becomes more negative; the bipolar cell here hyperpolarizes when stimulated by a receptor cell but depolarizes, that is, the membrane potential becomes less negative, when it is driven indirectly by horizontal cells. Amacrine and ganglion cells depolarize and, unlike the other cells, generate more conventional nerve impulses. The "sustained" type of ganglion cell, like the bipolar cell, responds to the steady level of illumination; the "transient" type, like the amacrine cell, responds briefly to a changing stimulus.

ina. The response of the bipolar cell is inverted when the surround is illuminated because an input from the horizontal cell and an input from the receptor cell through the synaptic structure at the base of the receptor cell affect bipolar cells in opposite ways. The receptive field for the bipolar cell is therefore said to be concentrically organized, with antagonistic center-surround components. (This form of lateral antagonism is a characteristic of most sensory systems, including the auditory and somatic systems and the visual system of invertebrate animals. The retina of vertebrates is unique in that the cells associated with lateral antagonism generate only slow potentials and show no sign of nerve-impulse activity.)

In our experiments the receptor cells themselves behaved quite differently. They were driven strongly by the spot of light that illuminated them directly, but their response was feeble when neighboring receptor cells were illuminated with the stimulating ring. Alan Baylor and his co-workers at the National Institutes of Health have shown that in the retina of the turtle under certain conditions the receptor cells can be driven in the opposite direction by horizontal cells, which is good evidence that the horizontal cells are feeding back to the receptor cells. In this sense receptor cells also have a broad receptive field with an antagonistic surround.

The horizontal cells extend across the retina, communicating with many receptor cells, and so it is not surprising that they are well driven by either the spot stimulus or the ring; even the ring falls on receptor cells to which the far reaches of the horizontal cells extend. Each form of receptive field is thus the direct manifestation of the structural organization of cells and synapses.

The retinal wiring diagram shows that bipolar cells drive both amacrine and ganglion cells, so that the antagonistic form of the bipolar-cell receptive field should also be represented in these subsequent cells. One type of ganglion cell, the sustained-response type, appears to be driven directly by the bipolar cells. Its activity (now in the form of nerve impulses) is elicited by the central spot but inhibited by the ring stimulus, following closely the general form of antagonistic activity in the bipolar cell. This sustained, concentric, antagonistic function measured at the ganglion cells seems to be one of the important components of the retinal output that is sent to the brain.

There is another form of retinal output, represented by another set of gan-

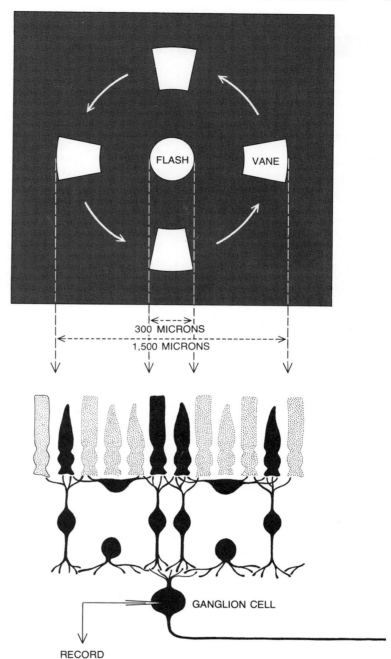

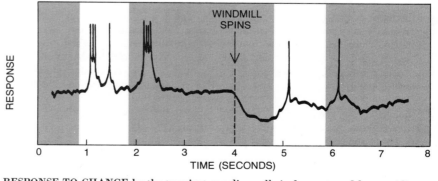

RESPONSE TO CHANGE by the transient ganglion cells is demonstrated by providing a "windmill" light, spinning in the ganglion cell's surround and continuously stimulating amacrine cells below the vanes. The amacrine activity propagates across the retina and impinges on the ganglion cell at the center. As a result the change-detecting response of the ganglion cell at the center of its field is reduced by change in surrounding region (*bottom*).

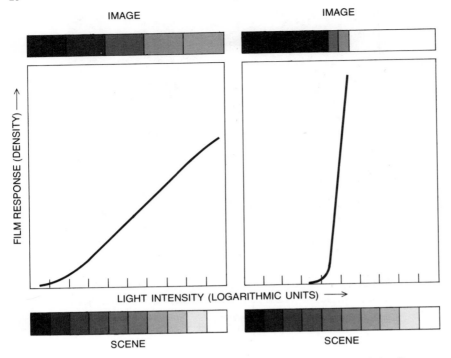

IMAGE   IMAGE

FILM RESPONSE (DENSITY) →

LIGHT INTENSITY (LOGARITHMIC UNITS) →

SCENE   SCENE

PHOTOGRAPHIC FILM can have low-contrast or high-contrast characteristics. Low-contrast film has a shallow operating curve spanning the full intensity range (left). High-contrast film has a steep curve spanning a narrow range (right). The bars represent the light intensities in a scene (bottom) and film response (top) as displayed in a positive print.

glion cells. These cells depolarize and fire nerve impulses only when the intensity or the configuration of illumination presented to the retina is changing, that is, when the bipolar cells that make synaptic contact with them are "turning on" or "turning off." Their response is affected by a lateral interneuron, the amacrine cell, that seems to have quite similar change-detecting response properties. In responding to change the amacrine cells appear to have an antagonistic effect on the change-sensitive ganglion cells, in a manner analogous to the effect of horizontal cells on bipolar cells. This was demonstrated by spinning a "windmill" light to introduce a constant rate of change in the surround of the input-output pathway to the ganglion cell. The spinning of the windmill decreased the response of the change-detecting ganglion cell at the center of the configuration [see illustration on preceding page].

The retina, then, appears to have two structurally similar systems of lateral interactions, one at the base of the receptor cells and the other at the base of the bipolar cells. At each site the lateral interneuron has the synaptic machinery necessary to modulate the signal that is being transmitted along the input-output pathway. Horizontal cells responding to sustained levels of illumi-

nation affect the magnitude of the sustained bipolar-cell signal; amacrine cells, responding to change, affect the responsiveness of the change-detecting ganglion cells. As a general principle of organization, the lateral interneurons receive input over a broad retinal area (the receptive-field surround) and form an averaged signal by which they modulate the local input-output pathways (receptive-field centers) of the bipolar and ganglion cells. Both the sustained-signal detectors and the change detectors have representatives among the ganglion cells that form the retinal output, so that messages about both the presence and the change of illumination are transmitted to the brain.

The two systems of modulation by lateral interneurons are two elements of the total process by which the retina adjusts its operating characteristics to prevailing light conditions. One aim of these adjustments is to generate a high-contrast visual signal, and so it will be useful to review the analogous procedures in photography before examining the retinal mechanisms. There is low-contrast film and there is high-contrast film. Each is defined by a characteristic operating curve that relates the intensity of the light striking it (in logarithmic units) to the response of the film: the density of the developed silver-salt grains in the emulsion. The operating

curve of a low-contrast film spans about 10 logarithmic units (or 10^{10} units) of intensity, the same range that human vision spans. Its slope is correspondingly gradual: there is not much difference in response (film density) for a small difference in intensity. Low-contrast film is easy to use since all possible image intensities fall somewhere on the curve and therefore produce a response density on the film. The film's ability to separate different intensities—its contrast sensitivity—is minimal, however; the picture may be too "soft," or washed out. The operating curve of a high-contrast film, on the other hand, spans only about one logarithmic unit. It is correspondingly steep, and so the film gives good separation of different intensities and a sharply contrasting image. High-contrast film is harder to use. The photographer must move the significant intensities in the scene into accurate register with the film's response range. He does this by adjusting the camera's aperture and shutter speed. His adjustments take a few seconds to complete; then he exposes the film for a fraction of a second to make the picture.

With the flashing-light experimental setup we set out to establish the characteristics of each cell type's graded response. We determined the operating curve of a cell by flashing light at various intensities and measuring the graded amplitude of the response, from threshold to saturation. The resulting operating curve, as in a photographic film, represents the peak response of the cell, which is reached within a fraction of a second. We then changed the ambient conditions by increasing the background luminance in order to see how the operating curves were adjusted. By flashing the surround ring or spinning the windmill we activated the lateral pathways that modulate the visual message as it passes through the retina. What then happens to the operating curve represents the "setting" of the cell's response as a function of conditions in the visual field.

There are two kinds of receptor cell, the well-known rods and cones, and Richard Normann of our laboratory showed that they have different operating characteristics relating neural activity (rather than density) to the incoming light intensities. The rods are somewhat more sensitive, coming into operation at intensities about one logarithmic unit lower than the cones. At any one background level each receptor operates over a curve that spans about three logarithmic units and is therefore intermediate in slope between the

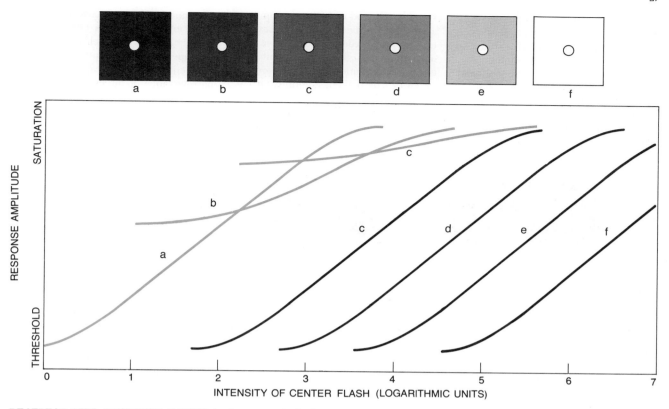

RECEPTOR-CELL RESPONSE RANGE is shown at six background-illumination levels. The rods (*colored curves*) are more sensitive than the cones in that they begin to respond at lower intensity levels, but they saturate quickly with increasing background illumination. Cones, however, appear not to saturate; their operating curves (*black*) shift along the intensity axis with increasing background illumination, so that they are optimally responsive over a narrow intensity range near each background level.

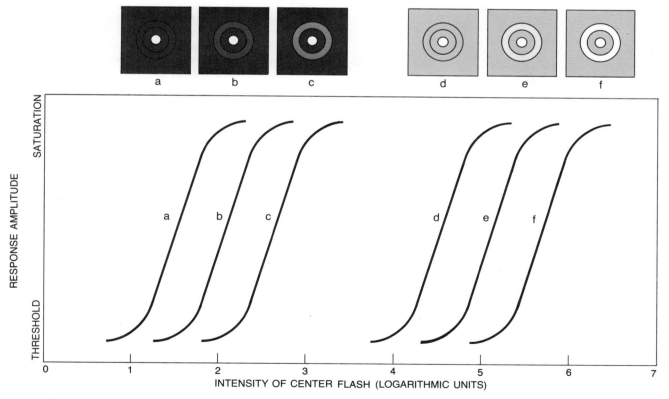

FIRST TRANSFORMATION of operating curves comes between receptor cells and bipolar cells. The response range of the bipolar cells follows that of the receptor cells with increasing background illumination but the narrower bipolar-cell curve is further fine-tuned within the receptor-cell range by input from the surround: an increase in the ring brightness shifts the curve to the right.

curves of low-contrast and high-contrast film. When the background level is raised, photochemical mechanisms that are still not fully understood come into play and somehow reduce the sensitivity of the receptor cells. These mechanisms move the cone operating curve along the intensity axis to keep it in register with ambient conditions; the shift takes place slowly, within about five seconds. The rod curves are compressed as the background level increases, saturating and becoming inoperative after only about four logarithmic units; the cone curves continue to shift along the intensity axis without compressing [*see top illustration on preceding page*].

This receptor-cell function is the first in a series of events that lead finally to a high-contrast output from the retina. Since each curve covers only about three logarithmic units of the 10 logarithmic units over which the visual system operates, the receptor cells can use their entire signaling capacity over this narrow range of intensity, thus making more millivolts of signal available per unit of intensity than if they had a shallow curve extending across the entire operating range.

In the camera, then, the light intensity is adjusted to fit the response range of the film. In the retina the response range of the cells is adjusted to fit the light intensity. The major "exposure setting" function is carried out by the receptor cells; fine-tuning and accentuation and modification of contrast are carried out at subsequent levels.

The receptor cells constitute the window through which all subsequent visual cells must view the world, so that the response range for all other retinal neurons always falls within the three logarithmic units spanned by the receptor cells. Horizontal cells, for example, have an operating curve that is similar to that of the receptor cells and shifts with it.

The bipolar cell's response curve is steeper than that of the receptor cells or horizontal cells. Its graded response goes from threshold to saturation within a little more than one logarithmic unit, much as the curve for a high-contrast film does. Since the bipolar-cell curve is responsive over such a narrow range of intensities it must be positioned even more accurately than the receptor-cell curve; so positioned it can signal, with a higher contrast function, the presence of important boundaries in the visual field. It is at this point that the antagonistic effect of the horizontal-cell input comes into operation. Remember that when the ring stimulus was flashed, the processes of the horizontal cells carried across the retina a signal related to the average light intensity in the immediate surround. The effect of the signal was to reduce the magnitude of the bipolar cell's response. The reduction is actually manifested as a shift of the bipolar-cell operating curve to the right—to a higher range of intensities—with increasing surround luminance. The shift is accomplished very quickly, within the fraction of a second that it takes for the horizontal cells to respond.

By this mechanism the high-contrast operating curve of various groups of bipolar cells can be moved to different regions of the intensity axis in different parts of the visual field. Such a system outdoes any exposure-setting device on a camera. Imagine being able first to

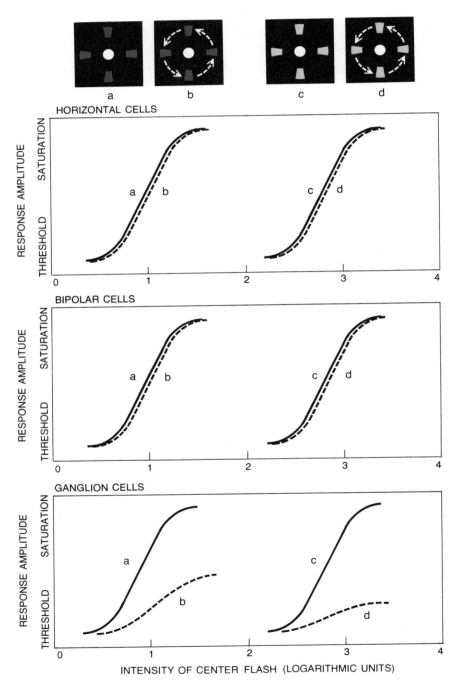

SECOND TRANSFORMATION comes between bipolar and ganglion cells. Bipolar-cell curves are shifted by increasing surround illumination (brighter windmill vanes). The curves for both sustained and transient ganglion cells driven by bipolar cells follow these shifts. When the windmill is spun (*broken curves*), the amacrine system suppresses the activity of the change-detecting transient ganglion cells: their operating curves are compressed.

control for general illumination in the visual field (through the exposure-setting function of the receptor cells) and then to fine-tune the exposure in local regions of the field as a specific function of the local intensity level! The system does have one disadvantage: since intensity discrimination in any part of the retina is controlled by the activity in the area immediately surrounding it, two separated points in the scene that actually reflect the same amount of light can appear to have different intensities if they are surrounded by "control regions" of different intensities.

The full mosaic of bipolar cells brings its high-contrast neural image to the inner retina. Here in the inner synaptic layer bipolar cells are connected to the amacrine and ganglion cells much as receptor cells are connected to bipolar cells and horizontal cells in the outer synaptic layer. Some ganglion cells simply pass along to the brain the sustained signals they receive from the bipolar cells; they are unaffected by the amacrine cells. Other ganglion cells, however, respond to change in the signal from the bipolar cells, which corresponds to the presence of movement or fluctuating intensities in the visual field. These change-detecting ganglion cells are embedded in a system of amacrine cells that also respond to change but that exert an antagonistic effect on the ganglion cells. When the amacrine system is activated, as by the moving windmill or other spatiotemporal change, it serves to reduce the effectiveness of the bipolar-to-ganglion signal and reduces the slope of the ganglion-cell operating curve. In other words, the change-detecting ganglion cells are activated by change at the center of their receptive field, but change in the surround activates the amacrine-cell system that acts to reduce ganglion-cell activity. This is another example of a concentric, antagonistic receptive field, but here both antagonistic components are driven by change. As a result change over broad regions acts to reduce the response to change occurring locally. Such a system has no analogy I know of with the technology of photography, although a similar technique is used in television. It is as if a camera system could switch automatically from a high-contrast film to a low-contrast film when it encountered a rapidly changing or very contrasty scene.

How can this system, which responds to local change but is antagonized by steady broad-field change, be an asset to the organism? The answer is that it provides for detection of the movement

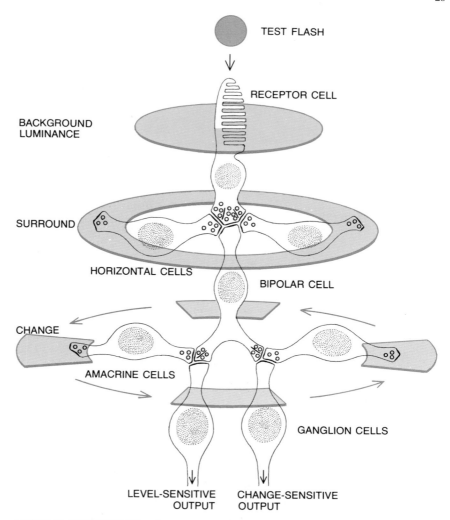

RETINAL SENSITIVITY is determined by three distinct properties of the visual scene, each activating a specific mechanism. Average background luminance affects photochemical processes in receptor cells. Luminance in surrounding regions affects interactions mediated by horizontal cells at the receptor-cell terminals. Spatiotemporal change in surrounding regions affects interactions mediated by amacrine cells at the bipolar-cell terminals. At any background ganglion cells carry signals that are related to luminance or change at local regions but are modified by corresponding activity in surrounding regions.

of small objects within the visual field but is not overwhelmed by the vast changes in contrast, covering broad retinal regions, that result, for example, from blinking or eye movements.

In summary, both ends of each neuron in the input-output pathway of the visual system are subject to some form of signal control. The first effect is at the outer end of the receptor cells, where photochemical processes somehow adjust the efficiency of the transducer so that the receptor cells operate best over different ranges of intensity depending on the average ambient intensity level. In the mudpuppy this operation takes many seconds to complete. Next, the narrow operating range of the high-contrast bipolar cell can be shifted, within the broader operating range of the re-

ceptor cells, according to the luminance level in the local surround of each bipolar cell. This shifting, mediated by horizontal cells carrying information across the retina, is accomplished within a fraction of a second and serves to "fine-tune" each bipolar-cell operating curve to the appropriate intensity range. Finally, the contrast sensitivity of the change-detecting output of the retina can be modulated by the presence of change in local surrounding regions; this is done through the lateral system of amacrine cells. With these mechanisms the retina can transmit a high-contrast, high-acuity message to the brain carrying information about the presence and movement of boundaries within the visual field, information that is essential to the brain's function of reconstructing the visual world.

3

Contrast and Spatial Frequency

by Fergus W. Campbell and Lamberto Maffei
November 1974

The visible details of an object often consist of contrasting areas with a regular spacing, or spatial frequency. The visual system is more sensitive to certain of these frequencies than it is to others

The ability of men and other animals to perceive the details of objects and scenes is determined to a large extent by how well their visual system can discern contrasts: the differences in brightness of adjacent areas. The size of the visual image on the retina also plays an important role in the perception of detail. We all know from experience that as an object recedes from us and becomes smaller, details with low contrast become difficult to perceive. The reason for this loss in contrast perception is not that the relative brightness of adjacent areas changes but rather that the visual system is less sensitive to contrast when the spacing of the contrasting areas decreases. If the spacing of the contrasting areas is regular, it can be called a spatial frequency. It is a remarkable fact that the visual system is much more sensitive to contrast at certain spatial frequencies than it is to contrast at other spatial frequencies, just as the ear is more sensitive to certain frequencies of sound than it is to others.

The simplest sound signal is a pure sine wave. In vision the equivalent is a grating pattern whose brightness varies in a simple sinusoidal manner [*see "a" in illustration on opposite page*]. The contrast of the grating is defined as the modulation of its brightness around a mean level. Spatial frequency can be described as the number of whole cycles of contrasting areas over some unit of distance. In dealing with the visual system it is convenient to define spatial frequency as the number of cycles of the grating that subtend one degree at the eye of the observer [*see top illustration on page 32*].

One can build up a complex spatial waveform by adding together a number of sinusoidal waveforms. For example, if one begins with a simple sine-wave grat-

ing and adds a third harmonic with a third the amplitude and three times the frequency of the initial sine wave, the resulting grating appears to have additional light and dark bands [*see "b" in illustration on opposite page*]. The addition of a fifth harmonic, a seventh and so on will eventually give rise to a square-wave grating with abrupt changes in contrast between the dark and the light areas. If we begin with the assumption that the visual system analyzes a spatial frequency in terms of the simple sum of the harmonics in it, the first step is to study the responses of the system to simple sine-wave gratings. Understanding may then come of how the visual system deals with more complex waveforms.

In order to obtain accurate information on the relation between the size of the bars of a grating and the contrast at which they can just be detected, it is convenient to display a grating on a cathode ray tube and have the subject adjust the contrast until the bars of the grating can no longer be seen. In this way the threshold of contrast perception can be determined for a series of different gratings ranging from very high spatial frequencies to very low ones.

John G. Robson, who was working with one of us (Campbell) at the Physiological Laboratory of the University of Cambridge, found that the best sensitivity to low contrast in the human visual system occurs with simple sine-wave gratings that have a spatial frequency of about three cycles per degree. If maximum contrast is 1, at this frequency the contrast can be as low as .003 [*see top illustration on page 35*]. As the frequency of the grating is increased, contrast sensivity drops. The highest spatial frequency the human eye can per-

ceive is about 50 cycles per degree. For this frequency to be perceived very high contrast is required. Contrast sensitivity also decreases as the spatial frequency is decreased below the optimum of three cycles per degree.

It may be surprising at first that the bigger the bars of the grating become, the less sensitive the eye is in detecting them. This can be demonstrated by viewing the grating on page 32 from a distance of about three feet. At that distance the grating has a spatial frequency of about three cycles per degree, and the reader should be able to detect the grating pattern at very low contrast; indeed, the grating is visible right up to the top. Now move closer, say to a distance of 12 inches, and the grating in the low-contrast region will disappear. At that distance the grating has a frequency of less than three cycles per degree. This method of measuring contrast sensitivity is rather crude, however, because the photographic process required to reproduce the grating introduces a loss of contrast, particularly at the higher spatial frequencies.

When an optometrist tests our visual acuity by having us look at black letters on a white background, he is measuring our acuity only for very high contrast. Most of what we view in daily life has a much lower contrast; in fact, the contrast level can go down to the point where we cannot detect the pattern or object at all. Alice, in *Through the Looking Glass*, remarked, "I see nobody on the road," and the White King replied, "I only wish I had such eyes to be able to see nobody and at that distance too." This effect can be demonstrated by viewing the bottom illustration on page 32 from a distance of 30 feet. From that distance no portion of the grating is visible. As one approaches

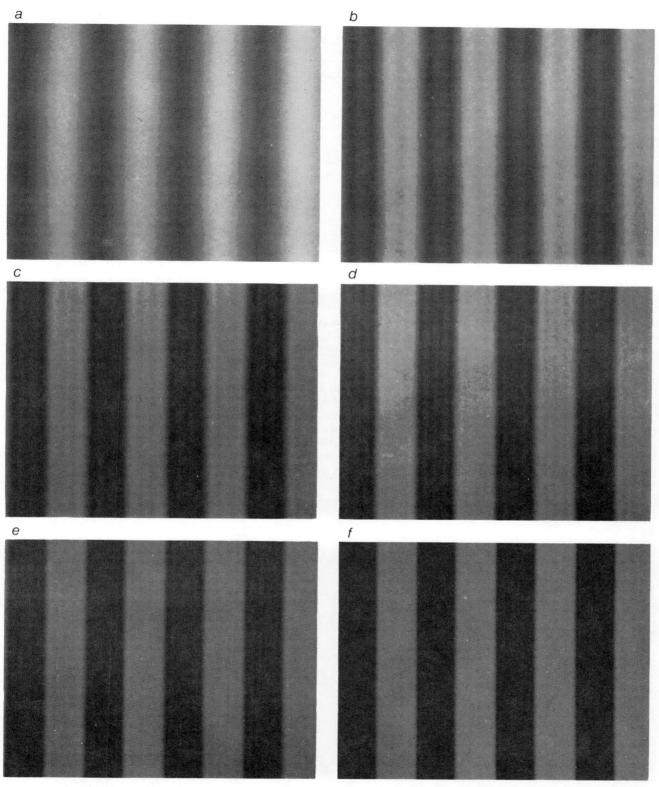

GRATING PATTERNS shown here are photographs of patterns produced on the screen of a cathode ray tube by a voltage-modulating generator. A simple grating (*a*) is produced by a single sine-wave signal from the voltage generator. The brightness of each vertical bar in this simple grating varies in a sinusoidal manner in the horizontal direction across the pattern. A more complex grating (*b*) is formed by the addition of the third harmonic of the fundamental sine wave. The third harmonic has three times the frequency and a third of the amplitude of the fundamental wave. As the frequency of the light and dark bands increases with the addition of the fifth harmonic (*c*), the seventh (*d*) and the ninth (*e*), the individual bands formed by the harmonics become progressively more difficult to see. With the addition of the 15th harmonic only a square-wave pattern is perceived (*f*). Studies of contrast perception with simple and complex grating patterns such as these indicate that the visual system possesses a number of separate "channels," each channel tuned to detect a relatively narrow range of spatial frequencies and each with its own range of sensitivity to contrast.

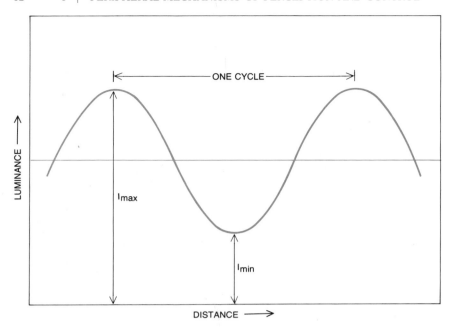

SINE WAVE depicts the sinusoidal variation in the brightness of a simple sine-wave spatial grating. Contrast of the grating is defined as $(I_{max} - I_{min}) \,/\, (I_{max} + I_{min})$. The spatial frequency is the number of cycles of the grating that subtend one degree at eye of the observer.

the grating it is the high-contrast part at the bottom that becomes visible first.

Sensitivity to contrast is thus a function of spatial frequency. The advantage of the contrast-sensitivity thresholds determined by the sine-wave-gratings technique is that they describe how the eye performs at all contrast levels and not just at very high contrast. The threshold curve also delineates the boundary of a low-contrast world we never perceive. Is there some way of measuring thresholds other than asking someone if he sees a pattern? Such a

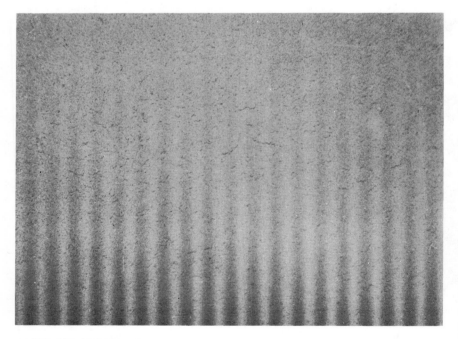

CONTRAST OF SINE-WAVE GRATING decreases logarithmically from the bottom to the top. When the grating is viewed from a distance of three feet, it has a spatial frequency of about three cycles per degree, and the grating is visible to very low contrasts. When the grating is viewed from a much closer range, say one foot or less, the spatial frequency is much lower and the grating in the low-contrast region near the top is no longer visible.

method does exist; it involves recording small electrical signals, called evoked potentials, that arise from the visual cortex of the brain at the back of the head.

The subject looks at an oscilloscope screen on which a grating flashes on and off at the rate of eight times per second. The overall luminance of the screen is the same whether the grating is present or absent. Each time the grating appears a small evoked potential is generated. Because individual evoked potentials are masked by signals from other parts of the brain, the signals are fed into a computer where the evoked potential can be retrieved by an averaging technique [*see top illustration on opposite page*]. We recorded the evoked potentials generated by gratings with low, moderate and high spatial frequencies. The contrast of each grating was varied from high to low. We found that the higher the contrast, the greater the amplitude of the evoked potential. More important was the finding that when the evoked potentials for a specific spatial frequency were plotted against the contrast level (with the contrast level on a logarithmic scale), they fell on a straight line. By extrapolation to zero voltage the theoretical threshold could be obtained. These extrapolated thresholds correspond quite well with the thresholds obtained by asking the subject to indicate when the grating is no longer perceptible. Thus it is possible to find the subject's threshold objectively without asking him any questions. In this case we have been able to take the "psycho" out of psychophysics.

This may seem to be a roundabout and complicated way of obtaining a threshold, but we are interested not only in how human beings see contrast but also in how animals do so. Alice said of her cat, "If they would only purr for 'yes' and mew for 'no,' or any rule of that sort, so that one could keep up a conversation! But how can you talk with a person if they always say the same thing?"

We applied the evoked-potential technique to a cat and came up with some interesting results. The amplitude of the potential we obtained was plotted against the logarithm of the contrast of the grating involved. We extrapolated the curves to zero voltage and assumed that this contrast level is the threshold for the cat, as it is for human beings [*see bottom illustration on page 34*]. When the contrast thresholds for cats are plotted together, the curve is very similar to the threshold curve for humans, except that it is displaced toward the lower

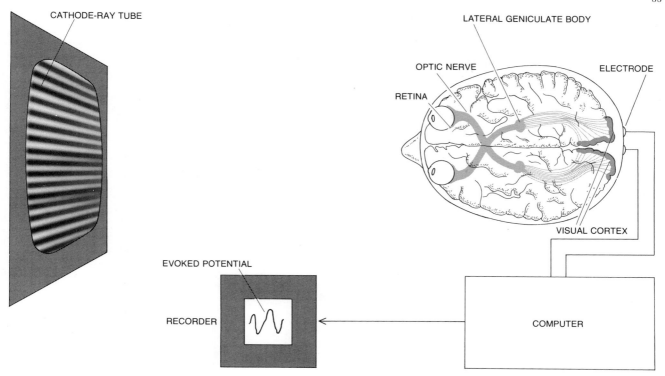

EXPERIMENTAL ARRANGEMENT for recording electrical potentials evoked in the brain by a grating is depicted. When a grating on the screen is flashed on and off at the rate of eight times per second, a characteristic evoked potential is generated in the visual cortex. These potentials are small and are masked by electrical signals arriving from other parts of the brain. Electrodes at the back of the head pick up the signals and transmit them to a computer, which extracts the evoked potential from background noise by an averaging technique. For a given spatial frequency the amplitude of the evoked potential is proportional to contrast of the grating.

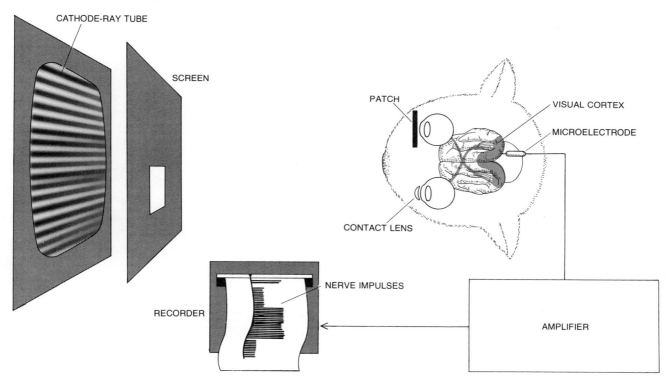

ARRANGEMENT FOR MEASURING the response of cells in the visual cortex of the cat during stimulation by grating patterns is shown in simplified form. The microelectrode is surgically implanted while the cat is anesthetized. As the cat views a grating pattern on a cathode ray tube the elecrical discharges of individual cells are picked up by the microelectrode, amplified and recorded. The results of several studies show that there are single cells in the visual cortex that respond to a small range of spatial frequencies.

spatial frequencies [*see bottom illustration on opposite page*]. Where the human sensitivity to contrast peaks at three cycles per degree, the cat's best sensitivity is about .3 cycle per degree. At frequencies above .5 cycle per degree the contrast sensitivity of cats is less than that of human beings. This means that at the higher spatial frequencies the cat can see only high-contrast details. On the other hand, at the lower spatial frequencies the cat can see detail at lower contrast than human beings can. One could summarize these results by saying that the cat is attuned to seeing spatial frequencies some 10 times lower than those human beings can see, and that at the lower frequencies a cat sees low-contrast details that a human being cannot perceive at all.

David H. Hubel and Torsten N. Wie-

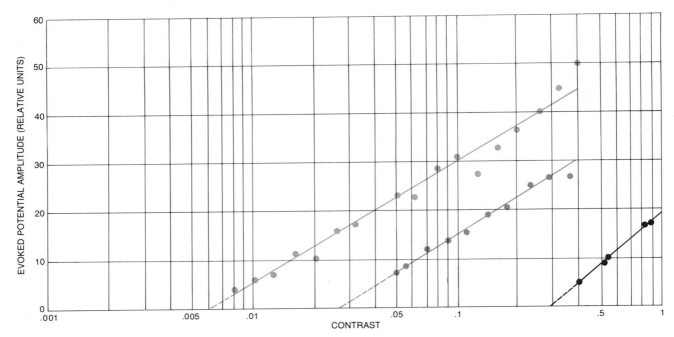

HUMAN EVOKED POTENTIALS for three different spatial frequencies show a regular decrease in their amplitude as the contrast decreases. The evoked potentials were obtained while subjects viewed gratings with spatial frequencies of 3.5 cycles per degree (*color*), nine cycles per degree (*gray*) and 18 cycles per degree (*black*). Extrapolation to zero amplitude (*broken lines*) yields the theoretical contrast threshold for each spatial frequency. These extrapolated thresholds correspond well with the subjective thresholds obtained by asking subject to indicate the lowest contrast at which a grating of a particular spatial frequency is just perceptible.

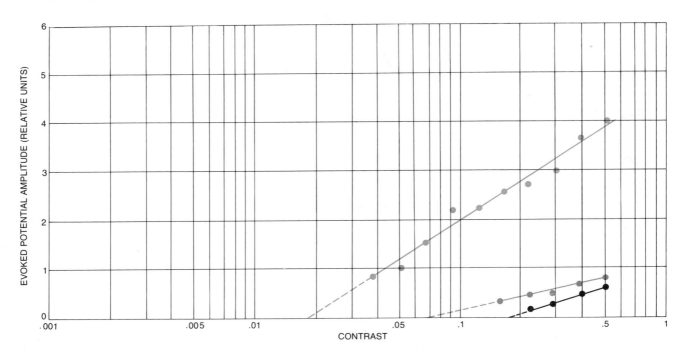

EVOKED POTENTIALS FROM CATS are plotted against the logarithm of the contrast of the gratings and extrapolated to zero amplitude in order to determine the threshold contrast sensitivity of the cat for each spatial frequency. These evoked potentials were obtained from cats viewing gratings of .6 cycle per degree (*color*), three cycles per degree (*gray*) and 5.5 cycles per degree (*black*).

sel of the Harvard Medical School, working with microelectrodes implanted in the brain, discovered that in the visual cortex of the cat and the monkey there are cells that respond to edges or bars of a particular orientation or a particular direction of motion [see "The Visual Cortex of the Brain," by David H. Hubel; SCIENTIFIC AMERICAN, Offprint 168]. Robson, Grahame F. Cooper and one of us (Campbell), working in Christina Enroth-Cugell's laboratory at Northwestern University, applied the microelectrode techniques to determine the response of individual cells in the cortex (and other parts of the visual system) of the cat to gratings of various spatial frequencies. The results revealed that there are individual cells in the visual cortex of the cat that respond to a fairly narrow range of spatial frequencies. Each cell that was tested was tuned to a particular part of the spatial-frequency spectrum. The response of each cell peaked at one frequency and fell off rapidly when the frequency was higher or lower. We also found individual cells in other parts of the visual system (the lateral geniculate body and the retina) that respond to specific spatial frequencies.

Even though it is not possible to ask a cat if it sees something when a particular cortical cell fires or when an evoked response is generated, it is possible to train a cat to give a sign when it sees a grating on the oscilloscope screen. This is accomplished by giving the cat a food reward when it responds correctly. If the animal responds when the grating is not present, no reward is given. Once the cat is trained, it is possible to find the threshold of contrast sensitivity for a grating by progressively reducing the contrast of the grating. Sylvia Bisti, working with one of us (Maffei) at the University of Pisa, has directly measured the contrast threshold for two cats. The training takes many months and requires great patience and persistence. There is good agreement between the results obtained in a few hours with the evoked-potential technique and those obtained with the lengthy behavioral method.

How, then, does the visual world of the cat compare with ours? Since the contrast sensitivity of the cat compared with that of human beings is displaced to lower spatial frequencies by a factor of 10, it could be argued that to detect a small object the cat would have to be 10 times closer to it than a man would need to be. One might suspect that the smaller size of the cat's eye accounts for the

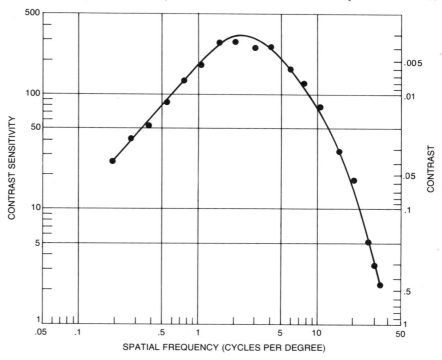

CONTRAST SENSITIVITY OF A HUMAN SUBJECT is plotted as function of spatial frequency. The scales are logarithmic. Very high contrast is given a value of 1, and contrast sensitivity is the reciprocal of contrast. The human visual system is more sensitive to contrast with sine-wave gratings that have spatial frequencies of about two or three cycles per degree. Contrast sensitivity drops off at higher and at lower spatial frequencies. Data were obtained by asking the subject to indicate when a particular grating could just be seen.

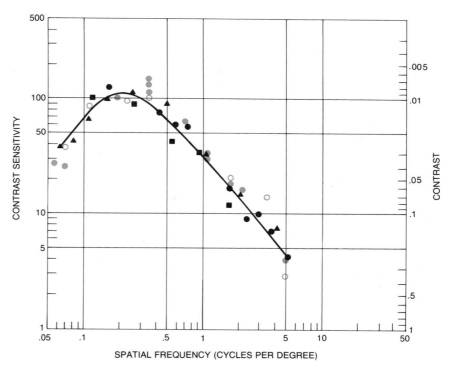

CONTRAST-THRESHOLD CURVE FOR THE CAT is similar to the curve for man (*see illustration at top of page*), but it is displaced toward the lower spatial frequencies. Below .5 cycle per degree the cat sees low-contrast detail that man does not perceive. Above .5 cycle per degree man sees low-contrast detail that is not visible to the cat. Cat data were obtained from evoked-potential responses of three cats to grating patterns (*black symbols and curve*) and from conditioned behavioral responses of two other cats (*colored symbols*).

difference, but for a given object at a given distance the size of the image on the cat's retina is only 1.3 times smaller than the image on a man's retina. Hence the size of the eye cannot account for the difference in the perception of spatial frequencies.

In order to understand the cat's visual world let us start with the familiar situation in which we are viewing an eye-test chart from a distance of 20 feet. If we can read what is called the 20-foot line, we have normal visual acuity (20/20 vision). Since the cat's resolving power is lower by a factor of 10, it should be able to "read" only the large letter on the 200-foot line (20/200 vision). We can try to simulate the cat's vision by placing in front of our eyes lenses that will render them myopic to the point where we can discern the 200-foot line at 20 feet only. If we then look at a distant scene with such a degree of myopia,

everything will be quite blurred, even objects we can discriminate. The myopic lenses act as a spatial filter that attenuates the higher spatial frequencies more than it does the lower frequencies. The sensation of blurring is the result of the relative inactivity of the visual nerve cells that are stimulated by the higher frequencies. The cat, however, does not possess nerve cells attuned to these higher spatial frequencies, and so its distant view cannot be blurred and cannot be simulated by artificial myopia.

Let us seek a more realistic and fruitful simulation. Instead of blurring our vision, let us look at the test chart through a pair of binoculars with a magnifying power of 10. If we reverse the binoculars and look at the chart from 20 feet away, we will be able to read only the 200-foot line but there will be no blurring of the remainder of the chart. In order to read the 20-foot line we

would have to go 10 times closer, to a distance of two feet, and refocus the binoculars. Although the binocular analogy of cat vision is better than the blurring one, it is not entirely satisfactory because it introduces a change in perspective. The reversed binoculars make everything 10 times smaller. We do not know if the cat sees everything 10 times smaller. Its peripheral vision could be wired up so that its perspective is the same as ours.

It could be assumed that cat vision is quite sharp and clear, just as our vision is, but that it is different from ours in being attuned to seeing well at much closer range, if seeing well means a mechanism for detecting low-contrast details at low spatial frequencies. An informal experiment can demonstrate the visual performance of a cat. Swing in front of a playful cat a small white ball on the end of a black thread. If the ball is about a centimeter in diameter, the cat will approach it from a distance of several meters and play at catching it. If we swing the ball away, the cat will chase after it even when we move it a considerable distance. If the ball is replaced with one that is four millimeters in diameter, however, the cat will not approach it until the swinging ball is less than a meter away. Even more convincing is to let the cat play for a while with the smaller ball and then swing the ball away suddenly to a distance of about a meter. The cat will stop playing and will look around for the ball without success. A person with normal vision, on the other hand, would have to move back to a distance of about eight meters before a moving four-millimeter ball would become invisible.

Let us assume that the cat sees slightly better in daylight because of the increased illumination and that it can detect a high-contrast object that subtends a visual angle of 10 minutes. Under such circumstances the cat should be able to detect a flying bird with a wingspan of 20 centimeters from a distance of 60 meters, although the details of the bird would not be visible. At dusk the cat should see the moon quite distinctly as a disk, since it subtends an angle of 30 minutes. It would not see any surface details on the moon.

We now have an inkling of what the visual world of the cat may be like. It may prove fruitful to use the evoked potential technique to study the contrast sensitivity of a number of animals, particularly those that are assumed to have a higher acuity than man, such as the eagle.

SINUSOIDAL GRATING with a logarithmic variation in spatial frequency and in contrast demonstrates the loss of contrast sensitivity at low and high spatial frequencies. The contrast decreases from the bottom to the top, but at any one height it is the same for all spatial frequencies. When the grating is viewed, it is apparent that the intermediate spatial frequencies are visible to much lower contrast than either the low or the high spatial frequencies.

Experiments in the Visual Perception of Texture

by Bela Julesz
April 1975

*The discovery of textures that are indistinguishable
even though their constituent elements are different
suggests how the visual system organizes patterns
into the percepts "figure" and "ground"*

When we are confronted with a device or a system whose workings we do not understand, the first question we usually ask is: What can it do? One often finds that having detailed information about the internal structure of the device or system does not help much in establishing its capabilities. When we are confronted with an ultracomplex system, such as the human brain or a large computer, it is sometimes more pertinent to ask: What can it not do? Indeed, one of the profound mathematical insights of this century is the discovery by Alonzo Church and others that there are important mathematical problems that cannot be solved by a class of computers that had been thought to be very powerful, the class of hypothetical mechanisms known as Turing machines.

I shall not dwell here on the controversial question of whether the human brain is more powerful than a Turing machine. What I shall take up is certain limitations that seem to be inherent in the human visual system, a part of the most complex system yet known in the universe. My colleagues and I at the Bell Laboratories have spent much time trying to find perceptual tasks that are beyond the visual system's processing capabilities. In order to clarify the role the visual system plays in perception we have tried to confine our studies to tasks involving pure perception, that is, tasks that can be performed spontaneously and do not require help from cognitive processing stages of the brain that involve scrutiny. My distinction between pure perception and cognition is best illustrated by a few examples.

The first example was devised a few years ago by Marvin L. Minsky and Seymour A. Papert of the Massachusetts Institute of Technology. It consists of two spiral patterns that appear to be similar to each other [*see illustration at left at top of following page*]. Actually one of the patterns is drawn with a continuous line and the other is not. This fact cannot be perceived spontaneously. You have to trace the lines point by point with your finger (or perhaps by slow scanning eye movements) to convince yourself that one pattern is formed by an unbroken line and the other is not. Any visual task that cannot be performed spontaneously, without effort or deliberation, can be regarded as a cognitive task rather than a perceptual one. It is evident that one could simplify the Minsky-Papert spiral patterns to the point where their connectedness or lack of it would be instantly apparent [*see illustration at right at top of following page*].

The second example demonstrates even better what we mean by pure perception. The illustration at the bottom of the opposite page shows three squares containing patterns of black and white cells. In the square at the left the cells are completely random. The square in the middle also seems to contain a random array. On closer scrutiny, however, one can see that it consists of four quadrants, all identical. If we now take the same four quadrants and mirror them across the horizontal and vertical axis, we obtain the pattern at the right, in which the twofold symmetry can be perceived without effort. In this example the redundancy of the four repeated quadrants and of the mirrored quadrants is the same, yet symmetry is perceived and repetition is not. The scrutiny needed for the latter again requires some cognitive processes, which we want to exclude.

These examples were not meant to show the limitations of visual perception but rather to illustrate the difference between effortless perception and some other processes that require scrutiny. To clarify further, one should not conclude that the mere presence of randomness in an array presents a barrier to the perception of periodicity. Thus if the periodic distance is sufficiently reduced, the periodicity of random arrays can be perceived immediately [*see top illustration on page 39*]. This even suggests that perception of symmetry does not depend on the entire pattern, only on the presence or absence of symmetrical pairs of cells near the symmetry axis. Indeed, if one takes an array of black and white cells with twofold symmetry and inserts a stripe of random black cells eight cells wide across the horizontal and vertical axes of symmetry, the overall symmetry of the array is largely if not totally destroyed [*see top square in bottom illustration on page 39*]. Conversely, if one inserts two symmetrical stripes eight cells wide in the same position in an otherwise random array, the overall array appears to be surprisingly symmetrical [*see bottom square in bottom illustration on page 39*].

These demonstrations clearly illustrate a basic limitation of the human perceptual system. It can perform certain kinds of perceptual task well until the system is overloaded in some way. There are, of course, many limitations of no particular interest. One can imagine many properties of images that were irrelevant to survival during animal evo-

LIMITATIONS OF PURE PERCEPTION are demonstrated in these two figures devised by Marvin L. Minsky and Seymour A. Papert of the Massachusetts Institute of Technology. It is not spontaneously apparent that the figure at left consists of one continuous line and that figure at right has two discontinuous elements.

EXAMPLE OF PURE PERCEPTION, requiring no assistance from cognitive processes, is demonstrated by these figures in which the connectedness or lack of it is instantly apparent. Limitations of pure perception in perceiving connectedness of more complex patterns result from gradual overloading of perceptual system.

lution; accordingly the perceptual machinery provides no means for their extraction. Hence when a certain image property cannot be perceived, it implies either that perception of the property was not crucial for the survival of our remote ancestors or that the extraction of the property exceeds the processing power of the perceptual system.

Let us therefore examine more closely the phenomenon of visual texture discrimination, a task with obvious survival value, and see what we can learn by manipulating the complexity of the textures. We shall see that texture discrimination ceases rather abruptly when the order of complexity exceeds a surprisingly low value. Whereas textures that differ in their first- and second-order statistics can be discriminated from each other, those that differ in their third- or higher-order statistics usually cannot. In due course I shall explain more precisely what is meant by order of statistics; for the moment, speaking roughly, it is like describing a structure or a phenomenon

by increasing the number of variables (degrees of freedom or number of dimensions).

Each new variable gives a more detailed description of the structure, but the number of parameters increases exponentially with the number of variables. As a result the jump from a second-order statistical description to a third-order one brings with it a vast increase in computational requirements that seems to surpass the capabilities of the perceptual system. Thus we encounter a case where the visual system is genetically programmed for texture discrimination (think of the importance of penetrating animal camouflage) but cannot cope with structures beyond a certain complexity.

One might regard this overloading of the visual system as being analogous to what happens when the system is unable to perceive periodicity or connectedness, as in the examples given above. In the perception of periodicity or connectedness, however, the overloading of the system occurs gradually as the periodic-

ity distance or complexity is increased. Any number of models can be proposed to explain such a gradual decrease in performance. The abrupt decrease in performance that occurs in texture discrimination is quite another matter, suggesting a clear structural constraint on the interconnecting neural network of the perceptual machinery.

My interest in texture discrimination dates back to 1962, when I first used a computer to generate pairs of textures, presented side by side, and studied the conditions under which they could or could not be discriminated. I found that for a limited class of textures generated by Markov processes the texture pairs could not be discriminated if they agreed in their second-order statistics. In a Markov process the content of each unit cell in a linear sequence—that is, whether a cell is to be black, white or some intermediate shade of gray—is determined by the content of some number of preceding cells according to a prescribed mathematical formula. I should

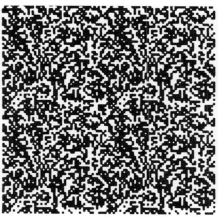

PERIODIC AND SYMMETRICAL ARRAYS provide further examples of the difference between pure perception and processes requiring cognitive effort. The computer-generated array at the left is random. The array in the middle may appear equally random, but on closer inspection one can see that it consists of four identical quadrants. If one of the quadrants is now mirrored across the vertical midline, and result is mirrored again across horizontal midline (right), the twofold symmetry of final array is apparent.

also explain that if two textures are the same in their second-, third- or nth-order statistics, they are necessarily the same in all statistics of lower order, that is, in their first-, second- and $(n-1)$th-order statistics, since from statistics of a given order statistics of any lower order can be uniquely determined.

Because of certain limitations in these first experiments with computer-generated textures it was highly questionable whether one could make a "mathematical," or quantitative, conjecture about the limits of human texture perception, for example by stating in general that "no texture pairs can be discriminated if they agree in their second-order statistics." Indeed, 10 years ago, when I reviewed some of my earlier findings in these pages, I was skeptical of statistical considerations in texture discrimination because I did not see how clusters of similar adjacent dots, which are basic for texture perception, could be controlled and analyzed by known statistical methods [see "Texture and Visual Perception," by Bela Julesz; SCIENTIFIC AMERICAN Offprint 318].

In the intervening decade much work went into finding statistical methods that would influence cluster formation in desirable ways. The investigation led to some mathematical insights and to the generation of some interesting textures. What is more, the conjecture that "no texture pairs can be discriminated if they agree in their second-order statistics" seems to hold for a surprisingly large class of textures. Although a few rather weak counterexamples have been found, the conjecture can still be maintained with only minor modifications. Only time will tell if stronger counterexamples exist. In any event the new textures that have come out of the work of the past decade are so striking and so contrary to expectation that I think the texture-discrimination problem is worth revisiting.

Let me begin by defining what I mean by texture discrimination. If you look at the top illustration on the opposite page, you will see two square arrays of black dots, with each dot containing a white U. Moreover, each array contains a region of one texture embedded in a region of a different texture. In the array at the left the regions containing the two dissimilar textures can be perceived at a glance. In the array at the right, however, the areas defined by the two textures are not immediately evident. Only after close scrutiny is one able to detect that the U's are upside down in one quadrant of the entire

array. Such an array will be regarded as a nondiscriminable texture pair.

Although the distinction between discrimination and nondiscrimination is self-evident, it can be precisely quantified. One can present patterns such as those just described in a brief flash and ask a subject whether or not he saw a square area different from the rest and which quadrant it was in. The strength of discrimination can be measured by the duration of the presentation and the number of errors in identification of the quadrants.

The next question is how to specify textures. In the case of the random textures that we usually employ we can describe the textures by their statistics of different order. The first-order statistics have to do with brightness, or, to be precise, luminance: the frequency that any given point of the texture will have a certain luminance. For example, one texture might have first-order statistics indicating that it is composed of dots of only three luminances: black, white and gray, each occurring with a probability of one-third. Another texture might be made up of dots of the same three luminances, but the black dots might occur with a probability of .5 whereas the gray and white dots each occur with a probability of .25. The second texture can easily be discriminated from the first texture because the second will appear much darker.

Let us now consider textures that share the same first-order statistics but differ in the second order. Such a texture pair is shown in the middle illustration on the opposite page. Both the left field and the right field contain an equal number of black dots placed at random, hence the overall luminance of the two fields is the same. In the right field, however, no two dots were allowed to fall within 10 dot diameters of any other dot, whereas in the left field there is no such restriction. Clearly the first-order statistics, that is, the f_0 ratio of black to white dots, are the same for both textures, but their second-order statistics differ. The difference can be demonstrated and quantified by dropping a dipole r (such as a needle) on the two textures and observing the frequency with which both ends of the dipole land on black dots. The probability, $f(r)$, of this happening on the two different textures would be quite different and would provide a measure of the difference in the second-order statistics of the two textures. When one looks at the two textures, one sees instantly that they have a different granularity.

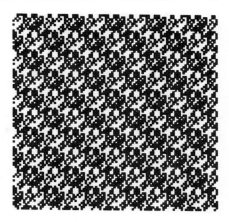

PERIODICITY of random-array figures can be perceived without special effort if the distance of the periodicity is not too large.

PERCEPTION OF SYMMETRY seems to require the presence of symmetrical pairs of cells near the symmetrical axis only. Thus the twofold symmetry in the image at the top is largely destroyed by the insertion of random black cells in two stripes eight cells wide (*marked by faint color*) across horizontal and vertical axes of symmetry. On the other hand, insertion of symmetrical stripes eight cells wide in same location in an otherwise random array (*bottom*) creates impression the entire image has twofold symmetry.

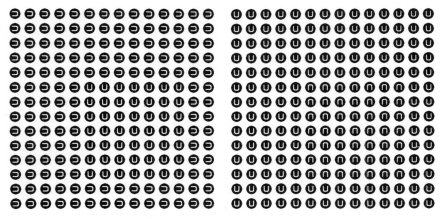

VISUAL TEXTURE DISCRIMINATION is studied by the author by flashing on a screen images with controlled statistical properties such as these and asking the subject if he can see an area of one texture embedded in an area of similar but different texture. In the image at the left the two textures have identical first-order statistics but different second-order statistics; the difference in textures can be perceived without effort. In the image at the right the two textures have identical second-order statistics in addition to identical first-order statistics. Here discriminating between the two textures requires deliberate effort.

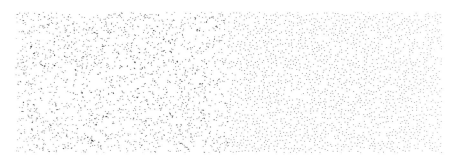

DIFFERENCE IN SECOND-ORDER STATISTICS, which is readily visible here, is exemplified by these two textures, which have identical first-order statistics. The first-order statistics of the textures are identical because each texture consists of the same number of black dots; hence there is the same probability in both textures that a given point will have same luminance. In the left field the dots fall at random. In the right field, however, there are at least 10 dot diameters between dots. Thus if a dipole such as a needle were dropped on the two fields, the probability of both ends' touching a dot would be different in the two cases. Difference in probabilities signifies a difference in second-order (dipole) statistics.

DIFFERENCE IN THIRD-ORDER STATISTICS, which eludes spontaneous detection, is demonstrated in the image at the left. The left and right half-fields in that image have textures that are generated by a Markov process so as to have identical first-order and second-order statistics but to have different third-order statistics based on the sequential arrangement of cells of four different luminance levels: black, dark gray, light gray and white. Only by careful inspection can one see that the left half-field contains a few horizontal stripes of uniform luminance that are formed by three adjacent cells whereas the right half-field contains practically no stripes. In comparison the two textures in the image at the right can instantly be discriminated because they have different second-order statistics, which appear as a difference in granularity. In both textures cells of three luminance levels (black, gray and white) occur with equal probability; hence first-order statistics are the same. In the texture that largely fills the left side adjacent cells are statistically independent of one another in luminance whereas in the surrounding texture adjacent cells are related mathematically by a Markov process. This gives rise to different second-order statistics.

In 1962 I asked what would happen if textures had identical first- and second-order statistics but different third- or higher-order statistics. Could the textures be discriminated or not? One way to describe third-order statistics is to throw a triangle on a texture and note the probabilities with which its three vertexes land on dots of certain luminances.

In 1962, after I drew attention to this problem, two mathematicians, Murray Rosenblatt of the University of California at San Diego and David Slepian of the Bell Laboratories, invented a class of Markov processes that have identical first-, second- and nth-order statistics but that differ in their $(n + 1)$th-order. When I used these Markov processes to generate pairs of textures with identical first- and second-order statistics but different third-order statistics, I found they could not be discriminated from each other [see left half of bottom illustration on this page]. When a difference occurs in the second-order statistics, however, the difference is immediately seen as a difference in granularity [see right half of illustration].

Since Markov processes are inherently one-dimensional, they can be generated by scanning an image from left to right row by row, in the same way that a television image is scanned. Each texture point depends on the luminance of the preceding two points on the left; the resulting trigrams have different probabilities in the two textures, yet the textures cannot be discriminated from each other. The finding that the visual system cannot keep track of the presence or absence of the luminance combinations of three adjacent dots was rather unexpected. It is true that these Markov processes must have at least three luminance values (black, white and gray); thus the number of possible trigrams is 27. With four luminance values (black, two shades of gray and white) the number of trigrams jumps to 64. These are nevertheless low numbers. Furthermore, to simplify the discrimination task we selected texture pairs from the 64 trigrams such that, for example, one texture contained 32 trigrams and the other contained the remaining 32. (In other words, the two textures did not contain any trigrams in common.) With Newman Guttman, I tried the same Markov processes with musical "textures" and found that random melodies could be perceived as being different only if they possessed different second-order statistics; if the first- and second-order statis-

NONDISCRIMINABLE TEXTURE PAIRS are produced when the textures have identical second-order statistics, as is demonstrated by these two examples. In each case a square area of one texture is embedded in a large square of different but closely similar texture. In the example at the left texture A in the large square is composed of identical micropatterns consisting of R's in random orientations whereas texture B in the small square consists of mirror-image R's. In the example at the right the two textures are made up of octopus-shaped micropatterns. The arms bend clockwise in texture A and counterclockwise in texture B. In both of the displays the second-order as well as the first-order statistics are the same. How identity of statistics can be simply demonstrated is explained in text of article.

LOCATION OF TEXTURE B in the texture pairs presented in the illustration above this one is indicated by light blocks of color. Color is not used, of course, when the texture pairs are flashed on the screen before an observer in actual studies of perceptual mechanism.

tics were the same, the ear (like the eye) could detect no difference.

Unfortunately Markov processes are inherently one-dimensional, whereas vision is two-dimensional. Therefore I was not convinced of the general validity of the results obtained with the linearly generated Markov textures. A ubiquitous characteristic of naturally occurring textures is the presence of clusters of various sizes and shapes. Most of these two-dimensional clusters cannot be generated by one-dimensional Markov processes, and the few clusters that form by chance depend on the scanning rules in arbitrary ways. Obviously the clusters that do form are very different, depend-

ing, for example, on whether the dots are scanned line by line or generated along a spiral path starting in the center of the display. It is well known from neurophysiological studies that the visual systems of cats and monkeys incorporate cluster detectors in several stages of hierarchically increasing complexity, beginning at the retina of the eye and extending to the highest levels of the cerebral cortex.

Typically these cluster detectors, or feature extractors, are neurons that fire only if in a local retinal domain to which they are connected (their "receptive field") certain features are present. The simplest of these receptive fields are con-

centric, with an excitatory center and an inhibitory surround (or vice versa), and they connect to neurons in the retina and in the lateral geniculate nucleus, a major switching center on the pathway to the visual region of the cortex. The simplest feature extractors in the visual cortex have similar antagonistically organized receptive fields, but their shapes are narrow ellipses. Both types of feature extractor ignore uniform illumination but fire for clusters whose shapes optimally match those of the receptive field. As a result they detect dots and line segments of particular diameters, widths and orientations. Some of the complex and hypercomplex feature extractors in higher cortical areas detect a hierarchy of increasingly complex stimulus features, which together make possible the remarkable feats of form recognition.

In view of these neurophysiological findings it seemed important to find ways to generate textures by some non-Markovian process that would incorporate clusters of desired shapes in a statistically describable manner. Therefore we looked for ways to generate two-dimensional textures of black and white dots (omitting shades of gray) in which the area fractions of black to white f_0 would be identical (thus providing identical first-order statistics) and in which the $f(r)$ dipole (or second-order) statistics would also be identical, but in which the third- or higher-order statistics would be different. Such two-dimensional textures would enable us to study the role of clusters in texture discrimination and to test the conjecture under the most general conditions in which such texture pairs cannot be discriminated.

Only recently, with the help of two other Bell Laboratories mathematicians, Edgar N. Gilbert and Lawrence A. Shepp, and a physical chemist, H. L. Frisch of the State University of New York at Albany, were we able to find ways to generate the desired two-dimensional textures. As a matter of fact, we now have three different methods that generate the pairs of textures desired. Throughout our investigations we tried to generate texture pairs that would disprove the conjecture. To our mounting surprise many trivial counterexamples that we thought would certainly disprove the conjecture failed, and micropatterns that individually appeared very different yielded textures that could not be discriminated. Finally we did find a few subtle cases that could be regarded as counterexamples. As we shall see, however, a slight modification of the conjecture explains even these cases. In the rest of this discussion I want to share with the reader the thrill of this quest and the unexpected demonstrations that resulted from our efforts.

All our methods use texture pairs composed of identical micropatterns, either regularly spaced or thrown at random, with or without rotation, except that the micropattern b in texture B is derived from micropattern a in texture A by

some rule. The procedure involved can be clarified by returning to the top illustration on page 40. On the left are two textures, A and B, derived by repeating the micropatterns a and b with a regular spacing, where b is derived from a by a rotation of 90 degrees. Obviously the second-order statistics for textures A and B must be different, because if one were to scatter needles (as dipoles) over the two textures, one would find needles on texture A whose end points fall on the

U-shaped micropatterns in orientations that cannot be reproduced on the micropatterns of texture B, or if they can be reproduced, they can occur only with a different frequency. Because of this demonstrable difference in second-order statistics the left image is strongly discriminable in texture.

Now consider the image at the right in the same illustration. Here texture B embedded in texture A defies instant discrimination, evidently because micropat-

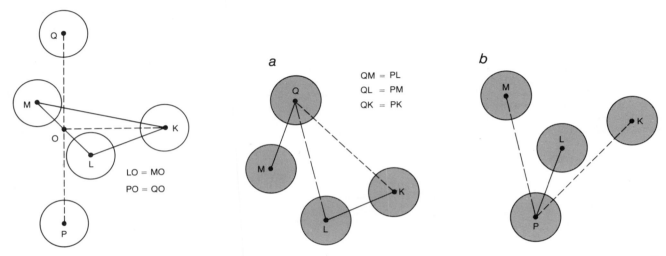

METHOD OF GENERATING MICROPATTERNS that yield texture pairs with identical second-order statistics begins with the construction of a triangle of arbitrary dimensions, KLM. At the midpoint of one side, say LM, a line is drawn perpendicular to OK, and on it points P and Q are placed so that PO equals QO. Five nonoverlapping disks are drawn with centers at K, L, M, P and Q. The three central disks and disk Q form the micropattern a; the same central disks and disk P form the micropattern b. The

micropatterns have identical second-order statistics because any dipole whose ends touch any two disks in micropattern a can be matched by a dipole of equal length touching two disks in micropattern b. If micropatterns are also randomly rotated, a dipole of given orientation will touch pairs of disks with equal frequency in each micropattern. The micropatterns differ in third-order statistics, however, because a triangle, for example KLQ, can be placed on micropattern a in a manner that cannot be duplicated on b.

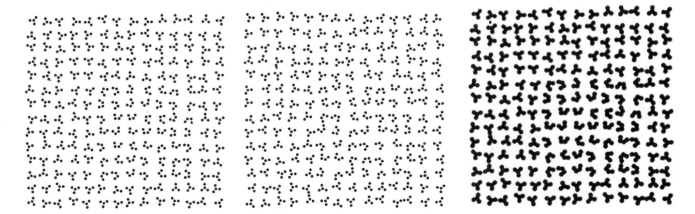

ONLY WEAKLY DISCRIMINABLE TEXTURE PAIRS are generated from the micropatterns a and b that are described in the illustration above this one, even though a and b in isolation appear very different. In each of the three displays a square of texture B, consisting of b micropatterns, is embedded in a large square of texture A, consisting of a micropatterns. In the display at the left the micropatterns are randomly rotated on evenly spaced

centers. In the display in the middle the micropatterns are randomly thrown without overlapping, yielding texture pairs that are even harder to discriminate than the ones in the first example. In the display at the right the micropatterns are arranged exactly as in the first example except that now micropatterns have been fused by throwing them out of focus. Since second-order statistics are made different by this process, texture discrimination is enhanced.

tern b in texture B is derived by rotating micropattern a 180 degrees, with the result that textures A and B have the same second-order statistics in addition to the same first-order statistics. This can easily be verified by scattering dots and needles on texture A alone and placing the result on a table between two subjects who are facing each other. To one subject the U's look right side up; to the other they look upside down. Yet both see the same probing dots and needles (only the end points of the needles interchange) touching the same parts of the same micropatterns. If, however, the demonstration is repeated to test third-order statistics by using triangles instead of needles, the statistics turn out to be different because a triangle of a given orientation (unlike a dipole, whose two ends are considered interchangeable) can be placed on a right-side-up U in a way it cannot be placed on an upside-down U.

A second method of generating texture pairs that contain clusters and identical second-order statistics involves using the mirror image of micropattern a of texture A to produce micropattern b of texture B. Here the micropatterns are allowed to rotate in random orientations. The verification that the two textures, A and B, have identical first- and second-order statistics but different third- and higher-order statistics is similar to the preceding verification except that now one observer views texture A in a normal manner and the second observer views the texture from behind, as if the plane on which the micropatterns a were thrown were transparent. It is clear that the first-order (single point) statistics and the second-order (dipole) statistics (because of random rotation) will be the same for both observers but in general will not be the same when the probing points are the corners of triangles or of polygons with more than three sides. (The special case of symmetrical triangles and symmetrical polygons must be excluded in such analyses.)

The left half of the upper illustration on page 41 is an example of textures composed of micropatterns that are mirror images of each other. The micropattern of texture A is the letter R; the micropattern of texture B is the mirror image of the same R. Both R's are thrown in all possible orientations. It is impossible to discriminate the two textures. As a further experiment we designed an abstract micropattern, an octopuslike structure that is invariant under rotations that are multiples of 45 de-

grees. Micropatterns consisting of this structure and its mirror image provide the two textures shown in the right half of the upper illustration on page 6. Inspection of this image will reveal that in it texture discrimination is exceedingly difficult, if not impossible.

The third method of generating texture pairs that have identical second-order but different third- or higher-order statistics is shown in the upper illustration on the preceding page. One begins by drawing a triangle KLM. In the middle of one of its sides, say LM, a point O is placed. Line OK connects O with the opposite vertex K, and a line perpendicular to OK is drawn through O. Finally, two points, P and Q, are selected on this line such that PO is equal to QO. The micropattern a consists of four non-overlapping disks of equal size with their centers at the points K, L, M and Q. The micropattern b consists of disks of the same size centered on K, L, M and P. The micropatterns a and b are used, with random rotations, to generate textures A and B. From the geometry of construction it is obvious that QM is equal to PL, QL is equal to PM and QK is equal to PK. Thus any distance between a pair of points on the disks of micropattern a has a corresponding equal distance between a pair of points on the disks of micropattern b. The dipoles between these pairs of points have the same length but different orientations for a and b respectively. This difference in orientation does not count, however, because the micropatterns are randomly rotated (pivoted through the point O). As a result the second-order statistics $f(r)$ (and, of course, the first-order statistics f_0) are identical for textures A and B. On the other hand, the reader can easily find three points that fall on micropattern a to form a triangle that has no counterpart on micropattern b. Hence the third-order statistics of textures made from a and b likewise differ.

The important advantage of this method over using mirror-image micropatterns is that one can choose KLM triangles whose resulting micropattern pairs look quite different from each other. Thus the KLM triangle in the upper illustration on the preceding page generates an open C-shaped micropattern and a compact Y-shaped micropattern, which are impossible to confuse when they are viewed side by side. When the two textures are assembled into arrays, however, they are as hard to discriminate as the textures based on the letter R and its mirror image [see array at left in lower illustration on preceding page].

Up to this point I have not presented textures in which the positions of the micropatterns are randomized. The fact that texture discrimination is difficult, if not impossible, even with orderly spacing of the micropatterns tends to strengthen our conjecture about the limitation of the visual system. If we now randomize the position of the C-shaped and Y-shaped micropatterns (avoiding overlapping), discrimination becomes even more difficult, if not impossible [see array in middle in lower illustration on preceding page].

Texture discrimination becomes easier, however, if the images are slightly blurred, or thrown out of focus, because now the second-order statistics between the two textures become different [see array at right in lower illustration on preceding page]. The difference arises because the slightest blur can cause some "rounding off" in the areas where the disks are adjacent, thereby affecting the second-order statistics.

Our results with many observers have shown that some slight texture discrimination is possible when the micropatterns are derived from KLM triangles, whereas discrimination is totally impossible with, say, textures based on R and its mirror image. Thus the KLM textures might be regarded as weak counterexamples to our hypothesis that visual texture discrimination involves processes that cannot "compute" third- or higher-order statistics. Indeed, it would be going too far to believe texture discrimination depends entirely on the statistical properties of the textures alone, and to ignore all additional factors such as the idiosyncrasies of the various feature extractors.

What would happen if we were to experiment with other KLM triangles that yielded simpler feature differences between the micropattern pairs, hoping thereby to see if the differences could be detected by the simplest kinds of line detectors? A micropattern pair with the desired simplicity is produced by the KLM triangle in the top illustration on the opposite page, suggested by my colleague William Tyler. The triangle is a right triangle in which the perpendicular sides are in the ratio 2 : 1. Micropattern a consists of four disks that form an inverted T; micropattern b consists of four disks that define the corners of a rectangle. One can imagine that the three colinear disks in micropattern a might serve to stimulate a thin line detector three times. Similarly, micropattern b might serve to stimulate a thick line detector (of the same length) four times. Therefore if the visual mechanism of texture discrimination were to employ simple line detectors, they should be able to differentiate between textures composed of the "thin" clusters of micropattern *a* and the "thick" clusters of micropattern *b*.

The middle illustration on the opposite page shows three pairs of textures generated by micropatterns *a* and *b*. Contrary to the prediction of the line-detector hypothesis, texture discrimination is not notably stronger in the left and middle texture pairs than it is in the texture pairs composed of the *C*- and *Y*-shaped micropatterns. In the left texture pair the micropatterns are regularly spaced but are rotated in all possible orientations around point *O* in the *KLM* construction diagram. In the middle texture pair the two micropatterns are randomly thrown but are not allowed to overlap. As one would expect, texture discrimination is made still more difficult by the randomization. In forming textures from these particular micropatterns it is important to jitter the patterns randomly, since the disks in micropattern *b* are capable of forming long horizontal and vertical sequences in a manner not possible with micropattern *a*. These sequences are readily visible even though the second-order statistics are still identical for both textures. This is demonstrated in the texture pair at the right in the middle illustration on the preceding page, where the micropatterns *a* and *b* not only are regularly

spaced but also are allowed only two rotations: 0 degrees and 90 degrees. Even so the eye does not spontaneously perceive that texture *B* fills a square in the lower left quadrant of the total array. To sum up, simple dot detectors and line detectors, which are believed to exist in the human visual system, evidently contribute something to texture discrimination, but they contribute surprisingly little.

Perhaps the most interesting outcome of these demonstrations is not that simple feature extractors can sometimes discriminate between textures with higher than second-order statistics owing to some local feature formed by chance, but rather that the many complex and hypercomplex feature extractors present in the visual system do not facilitate pure perception in texture discrimination. Thanks to a hierarchy of increasingly complex feature extractors a pattern can be analyzed in minute detail, but for texture discrimination only the simplest feature extractors come into play; moreover, the outputs of these extractors are evidently compared only in pairs.

These hypotheses about the visual system are depicted schematically in the illustration below. The diagram at the left shows the retina and a hierarchical level of feature extractors of increasing complexity. (Whether the increasingly complex feature extractors actually get their multiple inputs from the preceding stage of feature analyzers or from much earlier stages is not important in this context.) The analyzers at the highest level

constitute the form-recognizer stage that effectuates scrutiny of any local micropattern. The diagram at the right in the same illustration represents a model of the global (as opposed to the local) texture-discrimination network that employs only the earliest stages of feature extractors, that is, the simplest units, and only pairs of these elements are connected to the comparison units whose outputs are combined by the texture-discrimination processor. (If more than two simple units were connected to the next stage, the network could process statistics higher than second-order statistics.)

According to this model, the comparison units and their combinations have a structure that computes second-order statistics. It may be that for texture discrimination complete second-order statistics are not necessary, only some statistical parameters that can be derived from them. Indeed, there are some special cases where texture pairs with different second-order statistics cannot be discriminated. For example, in the illustration on the opposite page micropattern *b* is simply the mirror image of micropattern *a*. Since *a* and *b* are not randomly rotated in all possible orientations, they obviously have different second-order (dipole) statistics, yet the two textures resist discrimination. We conclude, therefore, that the texture-discrimination mechanism can at most compare the output of two simple extractor units. Conceivably the texture-discrimination process takes only the first-order

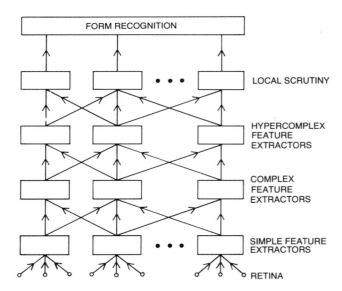

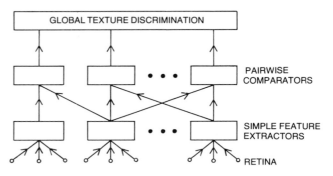

NEUROPHYSIOLOGICAL MODELS incorporate the author's conclusions about the levels of visual information processing required for detailed form recognition, or local scrutiny (*left*), and global texture discrimination (*right*). In detailed form recognition

visual information received at the retina passes through a hierarchy of feature extractors, culminating in recognition. Global discrimination seems to employ only simple feature extractors whose outputs are combined in pairs by a texture-discrimination processor.

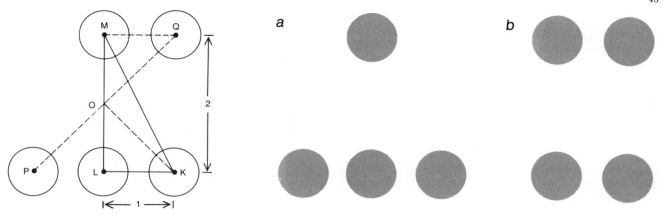

ANOTHER PAIR OF MICROPATTERNS that yield pairs with identical second-order statistics form an inverted *T* and a rectangle.

It was expected that such micropatterns might stimulate "line detectors" of the type known in visual systems of cats and monkeys.

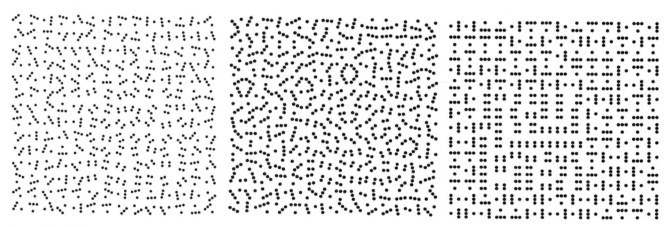

THREE TEXTURE PAIRS are based on the inverted-*T* and rectangle micropatterns depicted in the illustration above this one. In the example at the left the micropatterns are randomly rotated on regularly spaced centers; the discriminability of the texture pairs is very weak. In the middle example the micropatterns are randomly jittered without any overlap, making discrimination still more difficult. With these particular micropatterns random orientations are necessary. Otherwise, as in the example at the right, in which the micropatterns are regularly spaced and are limited to two rotations (0 degrees and 90 degrees), the dots may form long horizontal and vertical sequences that are quite different for the two textures even though their second-order statistics are the same.

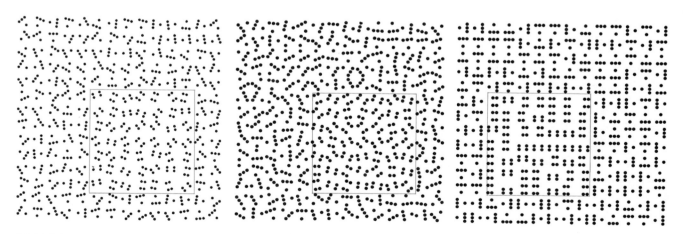

LOCATION OF EMBEDDED TEXTURE in each of the texture pairs in the illustration above this one is indicated by a thin color outline. It is surprising that even with this perceptual assistance the textures themselves are still rather difficult to discriminate.

statistics of various simple feature extractors that can be pooled according to diameter or to width, length and orientation.

Do animals share human perceptual limitations? Obviously I do not mean limitations in retinal resolution (a falcon's visual acuity, for example, is known to exceed our own) but limitations in perceptual processing power. It could be argued, for instance, that the processing power of our visual system should exceed that of other animals because our brain is structurally more complex. On the other hand, one could counter, we can afford to have a less powerful perceptual system because we can always implement its shortcomings with the symbolic processes of language, logic and mathematics. Lacking these processes, animals might have been forced to evolve a more powerful perceptual machinery that enables them to compute statistics higher than second-order statistics.

The question could be decided by conducting texture-discrimination experiments, using patterns of the type discussed here, with animals in the laboratory. Even before attempting such an investigation one can get some preliminary answers by exploiting the fact that nature has been conducting such experiments for aeons. Animal camouflage is based on the perceptual limitations of predators. Some animals, through evolutionary selection, exhibit a replica of the color and texture of their natural environment as it is perceived by their enemies. It is well known that human beings have much difficulty discriminating camouflaged animals from their natural background. For example, the light-colored peppered moth is almost invisible when it is resting on the light-colored bark of an oak tree.

Such difficulties in discrimination suggest that our perceptual system does not surpass the perceptual mechanisms of all the predatory animals whose camouflaged prey is also invisible to us. Whether or not some of these animals actually excel us in perceptual ability remains to be seen. It seems most unlikely, however, that the texture of a camouflaged moth and the texture of bark have identical third-order statistics in addition to identical second-order statistics. Only if we were able to find animals that mimicked their environment to the third order in their appearance could we conclude that their predators possessed a global perception superior to our own.

Let me clarify a few questions that are often asked about the material covered in this article. One frequent question is: Could one perhaps learn to improve one's texture discrimination by noticing statistical properties higher than those of the second order? The reader will remember that some of the textures presented here included such highly familiar micropatterns as the letters U and R, yet when these letters are used to form textures, they do not yield better texture discrimination than unfamiliar patterns do. Thus we can be quite confident that learning has no effect. What happens is that with familiar micropatterns it is more difficult to refrain from local scrutiny. As long as we can adhere to this taboo, however, texture discrimination is not aided by familiarity.

A related question is: Why do I regard scrutiny in texture discrimination as a cognitive process? Even if scrutiny meant only the local form recognition of, say, a letter R or its mirror image, it is a question of taste whether the reading of the alphabet is a perceptual process or a cognitive one. When we try to decide the shape of an area that is composed of certain letters, however, we have to augment local form recognition with a letter-by-letter scan and have to memorize the trace of the boundaries between different letters. This compound task of form recognition, scanning and memorizing is certainly more complex than pure perception.

Another question is: Will the conjecture hold for textures with decreased micropattern densities and increased viewing angles? The reader can easily verify that texture discrimination in the demonstrations is not improved as one varies the viewing distance over a wide range. Of course, if the density of the micropatterns is greatly reduced and the array is viewed from close range, then too few micropatterns are presented in any instant, and instead of seeing the micropatterns as forming a texture one sees them in isolation, which leads to local scrutiny.

This brings us to the main question: Why did two systems evolve in vision, one for the local scrutiny of form and the other for global perception? The answer lies in the fundamental dichotomy of perception that separates things into "figure" and "ground." Any object in our environment can be seen either as figure or as ground, but it can be seen only one way at a time. This point can be illustrated by an example. Imagine that we are told we will witness a crime in a brief motion-picture scene and that we are asked to concentrate on the crim-

SPECIAL CASE shows that a texture pair may resist discrimination even when the second-order statistics of the two textures are different. Here micropattern b, which forms the texture of the small embedded square, is a mirror image of micropattern a, which forms texture of large surrounding square. Since micropatterns are not randomly rotated, dipole statistics are not identical.

inal for later identification. To our surprise the experimenter asks us instead to describe the texture of the background. Although we might be able to describe the criminal in great detail, we are able to report only some vague properties of the background (for example its color or granularity). Indeed, all we are able to report about textures we have not selectively attended to is governed by first- and second-order statistical constraints. Hence "selective attention" separates figure from ground and local form recognition from global texture perception. It is interesting that children suffering from dyslexia, many of whom are highly intelligent but have difficulty reading, also have problems with perceptual attention and often confuse letters with their mirror images. When we agreed in the framework of texture discrimination to refrain from local scrutiny, we too in a sense became dyslexic, and it is no wonder that we could not discriminate between texture pairs made up of letters and their mirror images.

Thus we can regard global texture discrimination as a very general process, encompassing the perception of all things that fall outside the limelight of our attention. Until now it has been said that all unattended objects at a given instant formed a ground; now we can say that they form a texture. Therefore as long as the conjecture holds for texture perception we can endow ground perception with the properties and limitations of texture perception.

5

The Perception
of Transparency

by Fabio Metelli
April 1974

*Certain mosaics of opaque colors and shapes give rise
to the impression of transparency. A simple theoretical
model predicts the conditions under which
perceptual transparency will occur*

What do we mean when we say that something is transparent? Actually the term has two meanings. If we are referring to the fact that light can pass through a thing or a medium, then the meaning of "transparent" we intend to convey is physical; if, on the other hand, we mean to say that we can see through something, then the meaning we intend to convey is perceptual. The distinction would not be very important if physical and perceptual transparency were always found together. Such, however, is not the case. Air is physically transparent, but normally we do not speak of "seeing through" it. Nor do we always perceive plate glass doors, since we occasionally run into them. It seems useful, therefore, to give a more precise definition of the perception of transparency: One perceives transparency when one sees not only surfaces behind a transparent medium but also the transparent medium or object itself. According to this definition, air and plate glass are not perceptually transparent unless there is fog in the air or there are marks or reflections on the glass.

The fact that physical transparency is not always accompanied by perceptual transparency can be demonstrated. Take a square of colored transparent plastic and glue it onto a larger square of black cardboard. Provided that the layer of glue is spread evenly, the plastic no longer is perceived as being transparent; it appears to be opaque. Changing the color of the cardboard, say from black to white, does not alter the effect [*see top illustration on following page*].

There also are instances where physical transparency is absent and perceptual transparency is present. Wolfgang Metzger of Münster has shown that mosaics of opaque cardboard can give rise to a perception of transparency even though there are no elements in the mo-

saic that are physically transparent [*see second illustration from top on facing page*]. These two examples make it clear that physical transparency is neither a necessary nor a sufficient condition for the perception of transparency. Physical transparency cannot explain perceptual transparency.

What causes perceptual transparency? As with other visual phenomena, the causes must be sought in the pattern of stimulation and in the processes of the nervous system resulting from retinal stimulation. Light reaches the retina only after having passed through several transparent mediums (air and the transparent mediums of the eye). The input to the retina, however, does not contain specific information about the characteristics of the transparent layers through which the light has traveled and been filtered. The perception of transparency is thus not the result of filtration; it is a new fact originating in the nervous system as a result of the distribution of the light stimuli acting on the retinal cells.

Perceptual transparency depends on the spatial and intensity relations of light reflected from a relatively wide field and not on light reflected only from a local area. This can be demonstrated by juxtaposing two sets of squares that do not appear to have any transparent areas [*see third illustration from top on following page*]. The juxtaposition produces a change from apparent opacity to transparency even though the light reflected from each region has not changed.

The conditions under which transparency is perceived have been studied by several eminent investigators, beginning in the 19th century with Hermann von Helmholtz and his contemporary Ewald Hering. They were at odds on al-

most all points. In his treatise on physiological optics Helmholtz described the perception of transparency as "seeing through" and studied it with a simple device in which images of two strips of paper of different colors were perceived one behind the other. The colors were superposed by reflection and transparency. Similar dual images can be found on windows under certain conditions, for example in the evening when one looks outside and sees both the reflection of the illuminated room and the external landscape.

Hering denied the possibility of seeing one color behind another. He argued that when light reflected by two different colors reaches the same retinal region, an intermediate or fusion color will be perceived. He supported his argument with new observations. When an observer concentrated only on the region where the two color images were superposed, just one color, the fusion color, was perceived.

In 1923 the German psychologist W. Fuchs was able to solve the Helmholtz-Hering controversy. He showed that both colors are perceived only when the transparent object and the object seen through it are perceived as independent objects. If the region of superposition of the two objects is isolated (even if it is just by the attitude of the observer), then only the fusion color is perceived. In the following years important findings were made by the Gestalt psychologist Kurt Koffka and some of his students at Smith College. B. Tudor-Hart showed that transparency on a totally homogeneous ground is not possible (for example the transparent plastic on a black cardboard). In 1955 Gaetano Kanizsa of the University of Trieste pointed out that whereas investigators had been concentrating only on the region of superposition of two figures, the conditions for perceiving transparency also applied

COLORED SQUARES OF TRANSPARENT PLASTIC glued onto a black cardboard (*left*) or a white one (*right*) no longer appear to be transparent. This demonstrates that perceptual transparency is not possible when the underlying field is homogeneous.

MOSAIC METHOD for constructing a figure with perceptual transparency out of opaque pieces is depicted. There is a strong impression of transparency in the central region where the two rectangles overlap. The method was originally developed by Wolfgang Metzger.

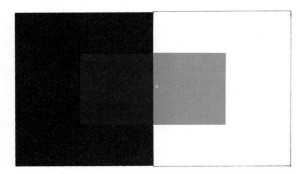

CHANGE FROM OPACITY TO TRANSPARENCY is obtained when the two figures depicted in the illustration at the top of the page are juxtaposed in the manner shown here.

TRANSPARENCY EFFECT is much more evident on an opaque figure than on the background, but conditions required to perceive transparency are the same in both instances.

to the regions in which the background could be seen through the transparent surface. The fact that this point had been neglected indicates that transparency on a figure is much more evident than transparency on the background [*see bottom illustration at left*].

The early investigators worked with filters or transparent objects, but after it became clear that physical transparency is not essential for the perception of transparency the use of physically transparent objects was generally abandoned. A number of investigators worked with the episcotister: a wheel with sectors cut out. The wheel generates a strong impression of transparency when it is rotated at high speed [*see top illustration on opposite page*]. This technique enables the experimenter to independently vary the size of the missing sectors (which affects the degree of transparency) and the color of the remaining sectors (which determines the color of the transparent layer).

In my own work I have used the mosaic method developed by Metzger because it offers a means of independently varying the color, the size and the shape of each region of a configuration. With this method it is easy to demonstrate that transparency depends on form as well as on color [*see middle illustration on opposite page*].

There are three main figural conditions for perceiving transparency in overlapping figures: figural unity of the transparent layer, continuity of the boundary line and adequate stratification. Let us examine each condition in turn.

When the unity of the central region of a transparent shape is broken, the perception of transparency is lost [*see bottom illustration on opposite page*]. On the other hand, modification of the shape that does not break up figural unity will not cause transparency to be lost. Figural unity of the transparent layer alone, however, is not sufficient to give rise to the perception of transparency. The boundary that divides the figure into two regions (one light and one dark) must be perceived as belonging to the opaque regions. A break in the continuity of the boundary line where it intersects the transparent layer can destroy the transparency effect. Abrupt changes in the boundary at points other than this intersection do not hinder the perception of transparency [*see top illustration on page 50*].

We have defined the perception of transparency as seeing surfaces behind a transparent medium or object. This means that the layer having the conditions necessary to become transparent must be located on or above the surface of the opaque object. It is not sufficient, however, for one surface to be perceived as being on top of another in order to obtain the effect of transparency. It is possible to perceive different strata in figures where no transparency is seen [see bottom illustration on following page]. In order to create adequate stratification for transparency the underlying regions must appear to meet under the whole of the transparent layer.

Let us take as a model a figure in which the underlying region is composed of two squares, one black and one white. On these are superposed two smaller squares, one light gray (over the white) and the other dark gray (over the black) [see illustration on page 52]. When all the figural and color conditions for transparency are met, then the gray regions appear to be a single transparent surface. (Unbalanced transparency is possible, but here we shall for the most part discuss cases where the transparent layer appears to be uniform.)

How is it that two shades of gray give rise to the same shade of gray in the transparent layer that is perceived? This phenomenon has been described as a case of perceptual scission, or color-splitting. The original gray is called the stimulus color. With the perception of transparency the stimulus color splits into two different colors, which are called the scission colors. One of the scission colors goes to the transparent layer and the other to the surface of the figure below. In 1933 Grace Moore Heider of Smith College formulated the hypothesis (and gave an experimental demonstration) that there is a simple relation between the stimulus and the scission colors: when a pair of scission colors are mixed, they re-create the stimulus color.

The process of color scission works in a direction opposite to that of color fusion. The law of color fusion, also known as Talbot's law (although it actually goes back to Isaac Newton), enables us to predict what color will be perceived when two colors are mixed. The same law, as Heider demonstrated, can be used to describe the color scission that gives rise to transparency. Since measuring chromatic colors such as yellow, red and blue is relatively complex, we shall limit our discussion to the achromatic colors (white, gray and black), which can be measured in a simple way. The achromatic colors vary only in one dimension: lightness. They can be defined by their albedo, or coefficient of reflectance: the percentage of light they reflect.

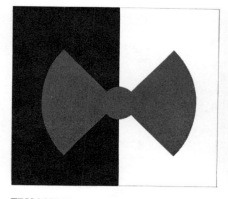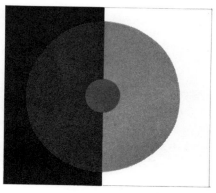

EPISCOTISTER is a wheel with cutout sectors (*left*). When the wheel is rapidly rotated with a suitable background behind it, a strong impression of transparency is created (*right*).

PERCEIVED TRANSPARENCY of the gray circle (*figure at left*) can be abolished either by an abrupt change of form (*middle*) or by an alteration in the color relations (*right*).

FIGURAL UNITY OF THE TRANSPARENT LAYER is a necessary condition for perceiving transparency (*top left*). When the unity of the shape is broken, the transparency effect is lost. Changes in the shape, however, do not destroy transparency (*bottom right*).

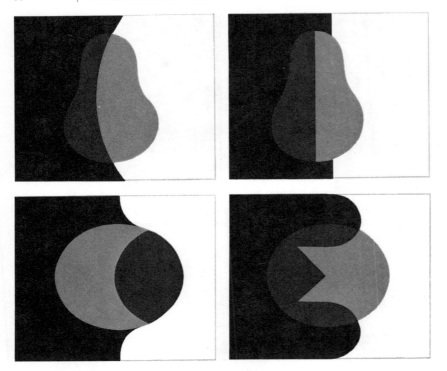

BOUNDARY LINE must appear to belong to the underlying opaque regions and must be visible through the transparent layer for transparency to be perceived (*top left*). Sudden change of the boundary line at the points of intersection causes transparency to be lost (*top right and bottom left*), but in other locations, even in the region that appears to be transparent, it can make abrupt changes without affecting the transparency (*bottom right*).

STRATIFICATION OF SURFACES is another necessary condition for the perception of transparency. If the light gray and the dark gray regions of a figure are perceived as being two different strata, figural unity is lost and transparency is not perceived (*top left*). Another example of inadequate stratification is when the gray regions appear to have an opaque layer above them (*top right*). The underlying opaque regions must meet under the whole of the gray regions in order for transparency effect to occur (*bottom left and right*).

Every surface absorbs and reflects part of the light falling on it. An ideal white that reflects 100 percent of the light falling on it would have a reflectance of 100; an ideal black that absorbs 100 percent of the light falling on it would have a reflectance of zero. These limits are never reached; a piece of white cardboard typically has a reflectance of about 80 and a piece of black cardboard a reflectance of about 4. Grays have a reflectance ranging from 4 to 80.

A device for studying color fusion is the color wheel. Two or more colors are placed on the wheel, which is then rotated rapidly. The fusion color perceived depends on two factors: the component colors and the proportions in which they are mixed [*see illustration on opposite page*]. With achromatic colors the resulting fusion color can readily be predicted, but with color scission there is a great variety of ways in which the stimulus color can split. How can we determine how much of the stimulus color will go to the transparent layer and how much to the opaque layer?

Let us consider first the transparent layer. By way of example imagine what happens when you add a dye to a glass of water. As more dye is added the water becomes less transparent and objects seen through the water become less visible. It is therefore plausible that in the scission process the greater the proportion is of color going to the transparent layer, the less its perceived transparency will be.

Now let us consider the opaque surface. Suppose that as you view it through a glass of water it is painted with a dye. Obviously the visibility of the opaque surface will increase as more dye is put on it.

The limiting case in the scission process is when all the color goes to one layer. If all the color goes to the transparent layer, it becomes opaque. If all the color goes to the underlying surface, then the transparent layer becomes invisible. Transparency is perceived only when there is a distribution of the stimulus color to both the transparent layer and the opaque layer. Moreover, transparency varies directly with the proportion of color going to the opaque layer. As more color goes to the opaque layer, less goes to the transparent one and the more transparent it appears. The proportion of color going to the opaque layer, which is described by an algebraic formula, can therefore be regarded as an index of transparency.

With achromatic colors it is possible to

derive a second algebraic formula that states a relation between the reflectances of the surfaces involved and the color of the transparent layer [*see the illustration on page 52*]. If the reflectances of the four surfaces in the figure are known, then the index of transparency can be calculated and the relative lightness of the transparent layer can be predicted. Such predictions are possible when (in most cases, as it happens) the transparent layer is perceived to be uniform in color as well as in the degree of transparency;

in other words, the transparent layer is a perceptual unit, not divided by the boundary belonging to the opaque layer below.

The validity of the theoretical algebraic formulas can be tested by taking our model figure and altering the color (black, gray and white) of individual regions. When the reflectance values of the gray squares are very different, the calculated coefficient of transparency is large and therefore transparency should be readily perceived. When the gray re-

gions are similar, the coefficient is very small and transparency usually is not perceived. Some necessary color conditions of transparency can be deduced from the theoretical formulas. Transparency is possible only when the darker gray square is on the darker underlying surface and the lighter gray square is on the lighter underlying surface. If these conditions are not met, transparency cannot be perceived. Finally, the difference of reflectance of the colors in the transparent layer must always be less

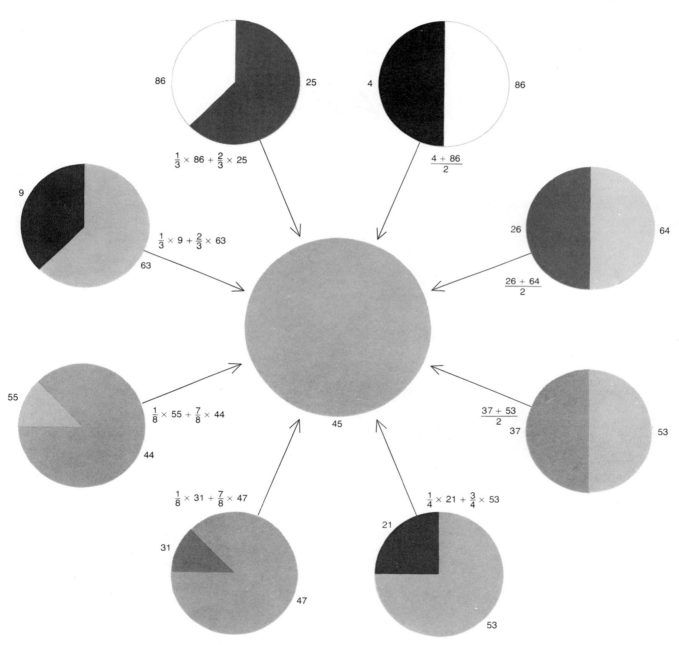

COLOR FUSION is produced when a wheel with sectors of different colors is rapidly rotated. With achromatic colors (black, gray and white) the fusion color can be calculated. For example, if the disk has two sectors of equal size, then the fusion color perceived will be the simple average of the reflectance of each sector. If the sectors are of unequal size, the fusion color is the weighted average. The reflectance figures given here are only representative. The same shade of gray (*center*) can be produced by a variety of color mixtures. Since color scission is the reverse of color fusion, it is apparent that a particular gray can split in a great variety of ways.

1

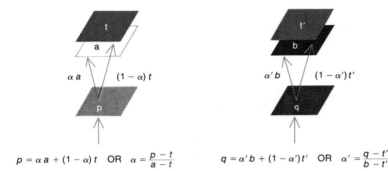

2

$$p = \alpha a + (1 - \alpha) t \quad \text{OR} \quad \alpha = \frac{p - t}{a - t} \qquad\qquad q = \alpha' b + (1 - \alpha') t' \quad \text{OR} \quad \alpha' = \frac{q - t'}{b - t'}$$

3

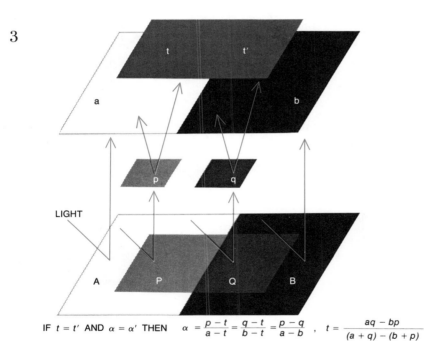

$$\text{IF } t = t' \text{ AND } \alpha = \alpha' \text{ THEN } \quad \alpha = \frac{p - t}{a - t} = \frac{q - t}{b - t} = \frac{p - q}{a - b} \;,\quad t = \frac{aq - bp}{(a + q) - (b + p)}$$

4

LEFT HALF					RIGHT HALF		
$\alpha = \dfrac{p - t}{a - t}$					$\alpha = \dfrac{q - t}{b - t}$		
a > p > t			AND		b > q > t		
a > p > t			AND		t > q > b		
t > p > a			AND		t > q > b		
t > p > a			AND		b > q > t		

than the difference of reflectance of the colors in the underlying layers [*see top illustration on page 54*].

Another powerful factor in perceiving transparency (in addition to the proportion of color going to the opaque and the transparent layer) is the color of the transparent layer itself. All other conditions being equal, the darker the transparent layer, the greater its perceived transparency.

The conditions for the perception of transparency that are deduced from the algebraic formula also enable us to predict the degree of lightness of the transparent layer when the colors of the stimulus regions are varied. With our model figure it is not always easy to judge the color of the transparent layer. With a checkerboard pattern, however, such estimations are easier to make and predictions about the transparent layer are visually confirmed [*see bottom illustration on page 54*].

The color conditions for perceptual transparency discussed here are theoretically derived without any empirical correction or adaptation. They state relations for "pure" achromatic conditions. Figural conditions, as has been noted, play a role and cannot be entirely excluded, but they can be held constant. It must be stressed that the inferences drawn from the theory should be considered as describing some (but not all) necessary conditions for the perception of transparency. In other words, certain instances are described where the perception of transparency is possible and instances where it is impossible. Of

THEORY OF COLOR SCISSION explains transparency as a case of perceptual colorsplitting. The achromatic colors can be defined simply by the percentage of light they reflect (*1*). When transparency is perceived, the areas *P* and *Q* split and appear to consist of two surfaces, equal in form and size but different in color. Assuming that this color scission follows the same law as color fusion, then the proportion of the stimulus color going to each of the perceived surfaces can be described by an algebraic formula (*2*). The symbols α and α' stand for the proportion of color (which can vary from zero to one) going to the opaque layers *a* and *b* respectively. The remainder of the color goes to the transparent layers *t* and *t'*. If $\alpha = \alpha'$ and $t = t'$ (*3*), then the algebraic equations can be solved for α (transparency) and for *t* (color of transparent layer). From the formulas certain predictions about the perceived lightness of the transparent layer can be made from the relations of the colors of the *A*, *P*, *Q* and *B* regions (*4*). The symbol > here means "lighter than."

TRIANGLE IS PERCEIVED as being transparent and on top of the black and white concentric circles even though no elements of the illustration actually are physically transparent. The triangle is a mosaic composed of individual light gray and dark gray sections.

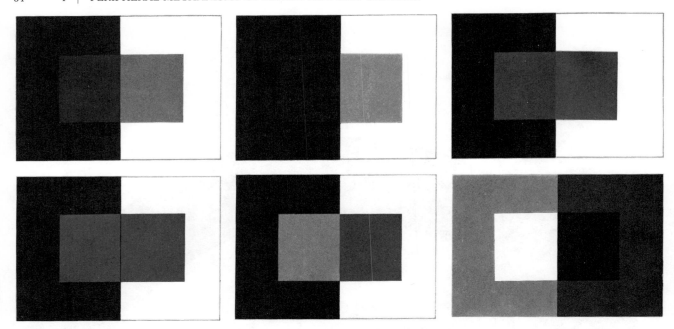

COLOR CONDITIONS necessary for the perception of transparency are demonstrated. In the model figure transparency is readily perceived (*top left*). According to the author's theoretical formula, the degree of perceived transparency increases when the difference between the dark and light gray regions is increased (*top middle*). When the gray regions are similar, perceived transparency is low (*top right*). When the grays are identical, no transparency is perceived (*bottom left*). Transparency is impossible when the darker gray is over the lighter background (*bottom middle*). If the difference between light and dark colors of the background is less than the difference between the colors of the central region, then the central region is not perceived as transparent (*bottom right*).

course, not everyone will perceive transparency when it is theoretically possible. On the other hand, when it is predicted that it is impossible for transparency to exist in a figure, no one should be able to perceive it.

There is an important limitation to the index of transparency that has been discussed: it measures the degree of transparency only if the lightness of the transparent layer is held constant. It is possible to develop a new formula in which the color of the transparent layer is variable, but this can only be done empirically, and it would not give rise to the interesting deductions possible with a theoretical formula. We have dealt here primarily with instances of balanced transparency, that is, instances where the perceived transparent layer is uniform in degree of transparency and color. There are instances of unbalanced transparency, where the perceived transparent layer varies in degree of transparency. A special case is that of partial transparency, where one part of the upper layer is perceived as being transparent and the other as being opaque. Unbalanced transparency and partial transparency, of course, require different formulas for their theoretical description. Other factors such as motion and three-dimensionality are often involved in the phenomenon of transparency. It appears, however, that the main conditions for the perception of transparency are to be found in the figural and chromatic conditions that have been described here.

PERCEIVED LIGHTNESS OF TRANSPARENT LAYER depends on the relation of the colors in the figure and can be deduced from the author's theoretical formulas given in the illustration on page 41. According to his theory, if region A is lighter than P and region Q is lighter than B, then the perceived transparent layer appears to be darker than P and lighter than Q (*left*). If region P is lighter than A and region Q is lighter than B, then the transparent layer appears to be lighter than any of the colors (*middle*). If region A is lighter than P and region B is lighter than Q, then the transparent layer appears to be darker than any of the colors (*right*).

The Neurophysiology of Binocular Vision

by John D. Pettigrew
August 1972

*The ability of certain mammals, including man,
to visually locate objects in the third dimension
is traced to the selective activity of single binocular
nerve cells in the visual cortex of the brain*

Man, along with cats, predatory birds and most other primates, is endowed with binocular vision. That is to say, both of his eyes look in the same direction and their visual fields (each about 170 degrees) overlap to a considerable extent. In contrast, many animals, such as rabbits, pigeons and chameleons, have their eyes placed so as to look in different directions, thereby providing a more panoramic field of view. Two questions come to mind: First, why do we have binocular vision instead of panoramic vision? Second, how is it that our single impression of the outside world results from the two different views we have of it by virtue of the separation of our eyes?

In answer to the first question, it is now known that binocular vision provides a powerful and accurate means of locating objects in space, a visual aptitude called stereopsis, or solid vision. Of course, it is possible to judge distance from the visual image of one eye by using indirect cues such as the angle subtended by an object of known size, the effort used in focusing the lens of the eye or the effect of motion parallax (in which the relative motions of near and far objects differ). These cues cannot be used in all situations, however, and they are not as accurate or as immediate as the powerful sensation of stereopsis, which is perhaps most familiar in the context of stereoscopic slide-viewers, three-dimensional motion pictures and so on. Some 2 percent of the population cannot enjoy stereopsis because of undefined anomalies of binocular vision. It is the aim of this article to give an account of recent work that shows how the brain achieves the very first stages of binocular depth discrimination.

Although it was not until the 19th century that the advantages of binocular vision were clearly demonstrated, man has pondered the arrangement of his eyes from earliest times. Of more concern to early investigators was not the first question, "Why binocular vision?" but rather "How does my single unified impression of the world result from the two views I have of it?" This second question is almost as difficult to answer today as it was when it was first asked by the ancient Greeks. The problem of "fusing" two slightly differing views of the world, however, is closely akin to the problem of using the slight differences between the views to achieve stereopsis. Thus a better understanding of the events in the nervous system underlying stereopsis should also throw some light on the problem of binocular fusion.

Galen taught in the second century that the fluid-filled ventricles of the brain were the seat of union, with a flow of visual spirit outward to both eyes. Galen's teachings were influential until the Renaissance, when scholars realized that the transfer of information is from the world to the eye, rather than in the reverse direction. René Descartes proposed in the 17th century that fibers from each eye might converge on the pineal gland for unification [see illustration on page 57]. His scheme, although incorrect, clearly indicates the now established principle that fibers from roughly corresponding regions of each eye converge on a single site in the brain. It was Isaac Newton who in 1704 first proposed that where the optic nerves cross in the optic chiasm there is an exchange of fibers. An early drawing of this concept, called partial decussation, shows how the fibers come together to carry information from corresponding parts of each eye [see illustration on page 58].

Newton's proposal, unlike that of Galen or Descartes, has been extensively verified. The number of uncrossed fibers in the optic chiasm depends on the amount of overlap of the two visual fields, and this number tended to increase as animals evolved with eyes occupying a more frontal position [see illustration on page 59]. The rabbit, with only a tiny binocular portion in its visual field, has a very small number of ipsilateral, or uncrossed, fibers in the optic chiasm, whereas each of its cerebral hemispheres is heavily dominated by contralateral, or crossed, fibers from the opposite side. As the amount of binocular overlap increases from animal to animal, so does the number of ipsilateral fibers. In man there is almost complete overlap and 50 percent of the fibers of the optic nerve are uncrossed.

Although partial decussation provides the opportunity for the optic nerve fibers to come together in the brain, for a long time there was controversy over whether this coming together does in fact occur. For instance, at the first way station for the optic-nerve fibers in the brain, the lateral geniculate nucleus, the inputs from the two eyes are carefully segregated into layers. The more binocular overlap the animal has, the more obvious the layering is. The segregation is confirmed by physiological recordings that show that a neuron, or nerve cell, in a given layer can be excited by light stimuli falling on one eye only. The segregation is reinforced by inhibitory connections between corresponding neurons in adjacent layers.

At the level of the visual cortex of the brain, however, single neurons do receive excitatory inputs from both eyes. David H. Hubel and Torsten N. Wiesel of the Harvard Medical School demonstrated this effect for the first time in

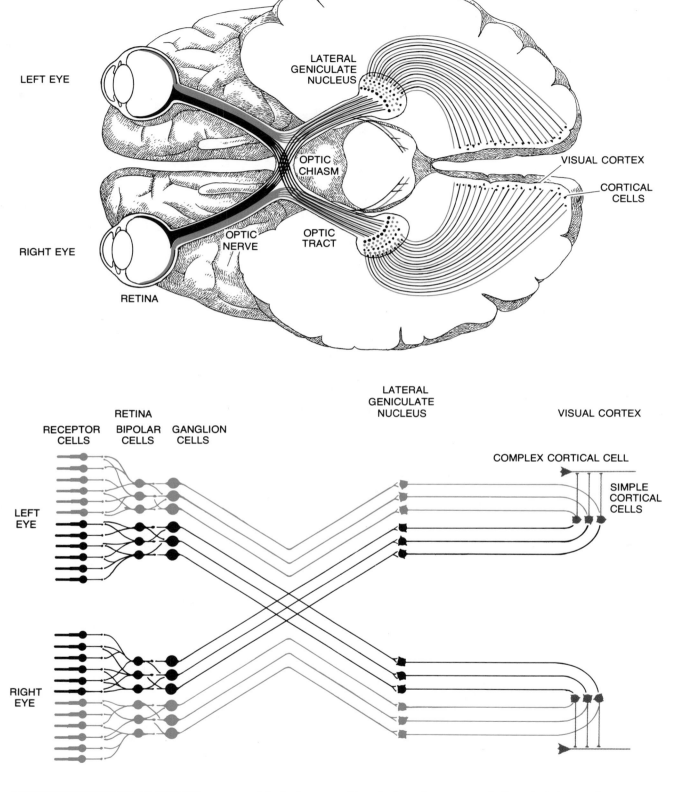

LEFT EYE

RIGHT EYE

RETINA

LATERAL
GENICULATE
NUCLEUS

OPTIC
CHIASM

OPTIC
NERVE

OPTIC
TRACT

VISUAL CORTEX

CORTICAL
CELLS

LATERAL
GENICULATE
NUCLEUS

RETINA

RECEPTOR
CELLS

BIPOLAR
CELLS

GANGLION
CELLS

VISUAL CORTEX

COMPLEX CORTICAL CELL

SIMPLE
CORTICAL
CELLS

LEFT
EYE

RIGHT
EYE

ANATOMY OF BINOCULAR VISION is represented in the drawing at top, which shows the human brain as viewed from below. The visual pathway from retina to cortex consists essentially of six types of neurons, or nerve cells, of which three are in the retina, one is in the lateral geniculate nucleus and two are in the cortex (*see schematic diagram at bottom*). Roughly half of the fibers of the optic nerve from each eye remain uncrossed at the optic chiasm. These ipsilateral, or uncrossed, fibers (*color*) from the outer part of the retina of one eye join with the contralateral, or crossed, fibers (*black*) from the inner part of the retina of the other eye, and the two types of fiber travel together along the optic tract to the lateral geniculate nucleus, where fibers from each eye are segregated into layers. The fibers that emerge from this body carrying an input from both eyes converge on single neurons in the cortex.

1959 by recording from single neurons in the visual cortex of the cat [see "The Visual Cortex of the Brain," by David H. Hubel; SCIENTIFIC AMERICAN Offprint 168]. For almost every nerve cell studied two areas could be defined where light stimuli evoked a response, one associated with each eye. The proportion of binocularly activated neurons found has increased as the technique of presenting stimuli has become more refined. Recent work by P. O. Bishop, Geoffrey H. Henry and John S. Coombs of the Australian National University shows that all the cells in the striate cortex of the cat receive an excitatory input from both eyes. Since each neuron in the striate cortex is simultaneously "looking" in two directions (one direction through each eye), the striate cortex can be regarded as the "cyclopean eye" of the binocular animal. The term cyclopean eye, derived from the mythological Cyclops, who had one eye in the center of his forehead, was first used by Ewald Hering and Hermann von Helmholtz in the 19th century to describe the way the visual cortex resolves the different directions of a given object as seen by each eye. Besides assessing visual direction, the cyclopean eye has an ability not possessed by either eye alone: it can use binocular parallax to ascertain the distance of an object.

Imagine looking down on an upturned bucket [see illustration on page 60]. If one directs each eye's fovea (the central high-resolution area of the retina) toward the cross at the center of the bucket, each eye will receive a slightly different view. The difference between the two views is called binocular parallax. Since each retinal image of the bottom of the bucket (small circles) is equidistant from the fovea, these two images must lie on exactly corresponding retinal points and are said to have zero disparity. Because of the horizontal separation between the eyes, the images of the rim of the bucket (large circles) are displaced horizontally with respect to the small circles and the foveas. These images lie on disparate retinal points. The retinal disparity between two such images is measured as an angle that corresponds to the difference between the angular separations of the two images from some known point such as the fovea (in the case of absolute disparity) or the smaller circle (in the case of relative disparity). If the disparity between the retinal images of the large circle is not too great, one sees not two large circles but a single large circle floating in depth behind the small one.

The basis of this powerful depth sensation of stereopsis was first demonstrated by Sir Charles Wheatstone (of

Wheatstone-bridge fame) in 1838. By providing very precise localization of objects in visual space, stereopsis can be regarded as the *raison d'être* of binocular vision. Whenever in evolution the need for the protection of panoramic vision was lessened (by the animal's taking to the trees as in the case of the primates, or by the animal's becoming predatory as in the case of the cats), then binocular vision developed to make it possible to use a depth cue more direct and accurate than the depth cues available to one eye alone. In addition, stereopsis enables a predator to penetrate the camouflage used by its prey, because monocular form perception is not a necessary prerequisite for stereoscopic vision. For example, an insect disguised as a leaf may be invisible monocularly but stand out in a different depth plane from real leaves when it is viewed stereoscopically. One can readily demonstrate this effect for oneself with the aid of random-dot stereograms devised by Bela Julesz of the Bell Telephone Laboratories [see "Texture and Visual Perception," by Bela Julesz; SCIENTIFIC AMERICAN Offprint 318]. Here a given pattern, such as a square, may be invisible to monocular inspection but stand out vividly when viewed stereoscopically.

The sole basis of stereopsis is the horizontal disparity between the two retinal

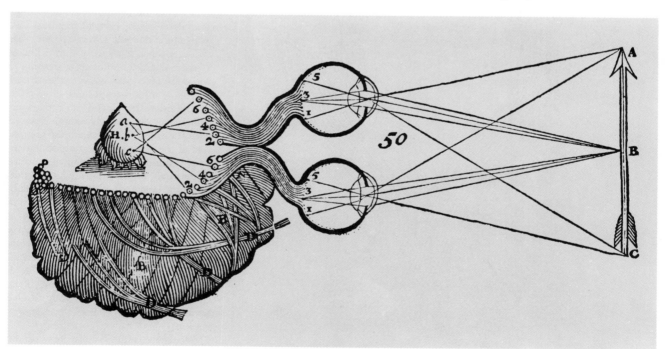

CONVERGENCE of nerve fibers from corresponding regions of each eye on a single site in the brain was proposed more than 300 years ago by René Descartes. In this early drawing of Descartes's scheme, reproduced from his study *Traite de l'Homme*, the optic-nerve fibers from each eye are shown converging on the pineal gland (*H*), where they are rearranged, with those from corresponding retinal regions merging together. It is now known that fibers from both eyes do in fact converge, but not on the pineal.

PARTIAL DECUSSATION, or crossover, of nerve fibers at the optic chiasm was first proposed by Isaac Newton in 1704. This drawing, made by a contemporary of Newton's, shows how fibers carrying information from corresponding parts of the eye come together on the same side of the brain in the interests of binocular vision. Newton's scheme was verified in the 19th century by the first ophthalmologists, Heinrich Müller and Bernhard von Gudden.

images. Of course, the brain must have a means by which it can first select those parts of the two images that belong to each other in the sense that they are images of the same feature in space. The horizontal disparities between the paired parts give the cue to depth. Julesz' experiments show that the binocular assessment of depth does not require the prior recognition of form, suggesting that the disparity information is processed by the brain fairly early in visual perception. Encouraged by this suggestion, neurophysiologists have examined the properties of binocularly activated neurons in the visual cortex, and over the past five years they have learned more about the neural mechanisms of binocular depth discrimination.

The experimental arrangement for studying binocularly activated neurons in the visual cortex is shown in the illustration on page 61. A cat that has been anesthetized and given a muscular paralyzing agent to prevent eye movements faces a screen onto which a variety of visual stimuli can be projected. A microelectrode inserted into the visual cortex samples activity from single nerve cells, and this activity is amplified so that it can be displayed on an oscilloscope, recorded and fed into a loudspeaker, in order that the experimenter can readily follow the response. Unlike neurons in the retina or the lateral geniculate nucleus, cortical neurons need exquisitely defined stimuli if they are to fire. Each cell requires that a line of a particular orientation (for instance a white slit on a dark background, a dark bar on a light background or a dark-light border) be placed on a narrowly defined region of each retina. Neurons with the same requirements for orientation of the stimulus are grouped together in columns that run from the surface of the brain to the brain's white matter. For some neurons within the column absolute position of the line is very important. Plotting with small spots of light suggests that such neurons receive a fairly direct input from the fibers coming into the cortex. These are "simple" neurons. Other neurons, called "complex," probably signal the output of the column; they behave as if they receive an input from a large number of simple neurons.

The speed and the direction of the moving stimulus are also important. Each of these stimulus requirements is more or less critical and each varies from neuron to neuron. As one slowly advances the electrode to pick up neurons, one must be continually moving a complicated pattern in front of the animal's eyes, in order to activate neurons that would otherwise be missed because of their lack of activity in the absence of the specific stimulus. (I sometimes wear a knitted sweater with a regular design as I move about in front of the cat.) Once one has found the specific stimulus for a given neuron, it is possible to define a region in the visual field of each eye where that stimulus will cause excitation of the cell. This region, called the response field, is plotted for each eye on a screen in front of the animal. The eye on the same side of the brain as the neuron in question is called ipsilateral; the eye on the opposite side is called contralateral. The study of a number of neurons in succession gives an array of ipsilateral and contralateral response fields [*see illustration on page 63*]. The arrays for each eye are separated on the screen because of the slightly divergent position the eyes assume in paralysis. Normally the eyes would be lined up so that the arrays could overlap and a single object might stimulate both response fields for a given neuron.

The highly specific stimulus requirements of cortical neurons could provide a means of identifying the parts of the two images corresponding to a single feature in object space. Because the number of identical features in a small part of the image in one eye is likely to be low, similar features lying in roughly corresponding regions in each eye can be assumed to belong to the same object. For example, a black line with a particular orientation and direction of movement in one image would be associated with a similar line at the most nearly corresponding position in the other image, because both are likely to be images of the same object. Since binocular cortical neurons have properties suited to the detection of the pair of retinal images produced by a given object, it was of great interest to see if they could also detect disparity between the pairs of images.

When one takes a close look at the position of each response field compared with the position of its partner in the opposite eye, it is immediately obvious that it is not possible to superimpose every response field on its partner simultaneously because of the greater scatter in the fields of the ipsilateral eye compared with those of the contralateral eye. The response fields therefore do not lie in corresponding regions of each retina and may be said to show disparity. I had

AMOUNT OF BINOCULAR OVERLAP of an animal's two visual fields is proportional to the percentage of uncrossed fibers in the optic chiasm. As animals evolved with eyes occupying a more frontal position this percentage tended to increase. The rabbit, for example, has only a tiny amount of binocular overlap and accordingly has a very small number of uncrossed fibers (*top*). The cat, in contrast, has a much larger binocular overlap and a correspondingly higher percentage of uncrossed fibers (*bottom*). In man there is almost complete binocular overlap and 50 percent of the fibers are uncrossed. The uncrossed nerve fibers carry information from the outer part of retina, the region responsible for binocular vision.

noticed this phenomenon in 1965 while working with Bishop at the University of Sydney and had considered the possibility that the variation in the position of one eye's response field with respect to the position of the corresponding response field of the opposite eye might play a role in the detection of retinal-image disparity and therefore in binocular depth discrimination. At that time, however, there were two major difficul-

ties involved in the interpretation of the phenomenon.

The first difficulty was residual eye movement, which is present in small amounts even after the standard muscular paralyzing agents are applied. Since determination of the two response fields for one neuron can take hours (because one has to find the best stimulus orientation, speed of movement, exact position on the screen and so forth), one has

to be sure that the eyes do not move in that time. Eye movement would produce spurious response-field disparities.

The second problem concerns the specificity of a neuron to binocular stimulation in the situation where a single stimulus is presented simultaneously to both eyes. It could be argued that the response-field disparities observed are not significant functionally since the neuron might tolerate large amounts of

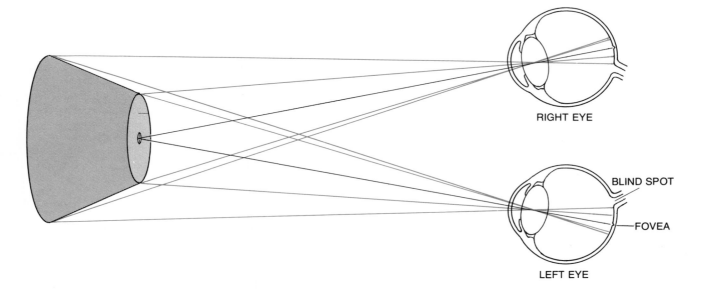

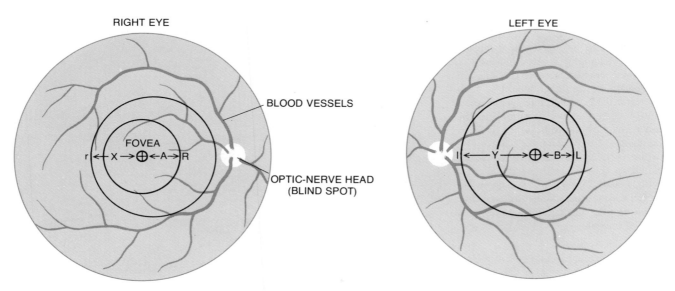

BINOCULAR PARALLAX is the term used to describe the disparity produced between two retinal images when one views a three-dimensional object. In this case a subject has been instructed to direct each eye toward the cross at the center of an upturned bucket (top). The drawings at bottom show how the fundus of each eye would look in an indirect ophthalmoscope. The fovea, the central high-resolution area of each retina, would appear as a shallow depression on which the cross would be imaged. The optic-nerve head, or blind spot, where the fibers of the optic nerve leave the retina and the blood vessels enter, would appear as a white disk.

Since the small circles corresponding to the retinal images of the bottom of the bucket are each equidistant from the fovea (that is, distance A is equal to distance B), these two images must lie on exactly corresponding retinal points (R and L); these images are said to have zero disparity. The large circles corresponding to the images of the rim of the bucket, on the other hand, are displaced horizontally with respect to the small circles and the foveas (that is, distance X is not equal to distance Y); these images are said to lie on disparate retinal points (r and l). The amount of retinal disparity, usually expressed as an angle, is the difference between X and Y.

overlap of its receptive fields without changing its response. If the tolerated overlap were of the same order of magnitude as the variation in response-field disparity from neuron to neuron, then the latter variation would be of no use.

Both of these problems were worked out in the succeeding years by me in collaboration with Bishop and Tosaku Nikara at Sydney, and with Horace

B. Barlow and Colin Blakemore at the University of California at Berkeley. The problem of eye movement was solved by resorting to a number of measures simultaneously. A particularly potent mixture of neuromuscular blocking drugs was developed to reduce eye movement to a minimum without toxicity to the cat's heart and blood vessels. The sympathetic nerves to the orbit of the eye were cut to eliminate movements

due to the involuntary muscles near the eye. Any residual drift was carefully monitored by plotting the projection of some small blood vessel inside the eye onto a screen. Any tiny amount of movement between response-field plots could then be corrected. In the Berkeley experiments we carefully attached the margins of each eye to rigidly held rings, which kept the eyes fixed for the duration of the long measurements.

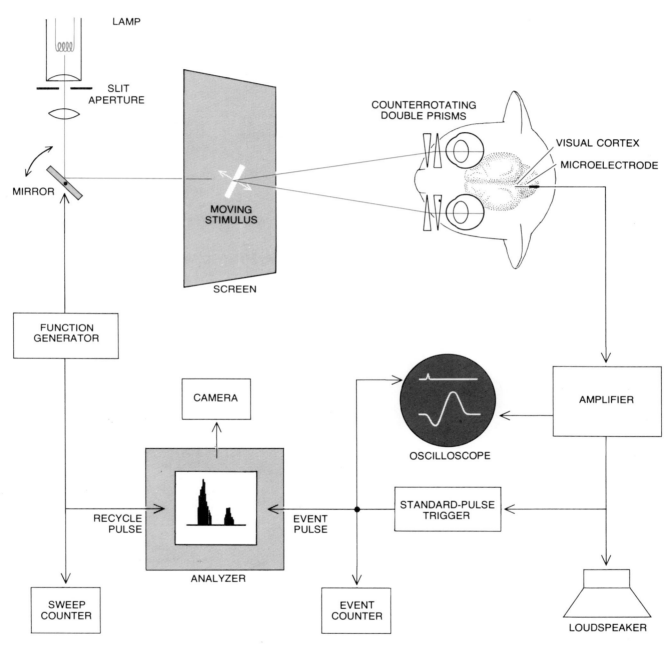

EXPERIMENTAL SETUP used by the author and his colleagues to study binocularly activated neurons in the visual cortex of the cat is depicted here. A cat that has been immobilized by a number of measures faces a screen onto which a moving line stimulus of any orientation, direction and speed can be projected from behind. A microelectrode inserted into the visual cortex samples activity from single neurons, and this activity is amplified so that it can be displayed on an oscilloscope, recorded and fed into a loudspeaker. Once a particular orientation and direction are discovered that will make the neuron fire, the stimulus is moved back and forth repeatedly while the neuron's response pattern is worked out. Counterrotating double prisms of variable power placed before the eyes enable the experimenter to determine the effect of changing retinal disparity as the stimulus moves in a fixed plane in front of the cat.

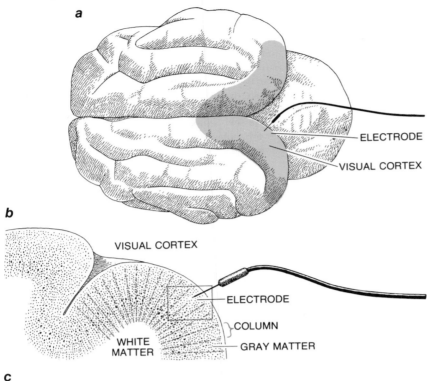

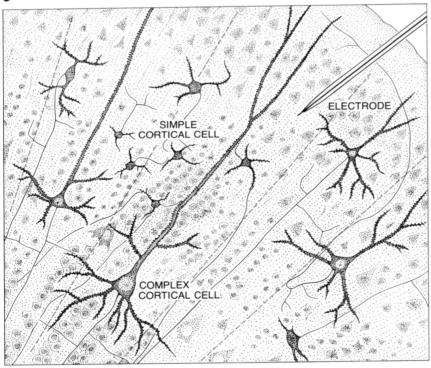

PENETRATION of the microelectrode through the cat's visual cortex is represented in this sequence of successively enlarged views. The top view of the entire brain (*a*) shows that the cortical region associated with vision (*color*) corresponds to a single gyrus, or fold, located toward the rear of each of the brain's two hemispheres. The cross section of this gyrus (*b*) reveals that the visual cortex is functionally divided into an array of tiny columns (*broken colored lines*) that run from the surface of the brain to the interior white matter. The magnified cross section (*c*) shows that each of these columns (which are not visible under the microscope) consists of a group of neurons with the same requirements for orientation of the stimulus. "Simple" neurons are those that appear to receive a fairly direct input from the fibers coming into the cortex. "Complex" neurons, which behave as if they receive an input from a large number of simple neurons, probably signal the output of the column.

The question "How specific is the response of a single neuron for the retinal disparity produced by a stimulus presented to both eyes?" was answered with the help of the following technique. The specific stimulus was swept forward and backward over both of the response fields of a cortical neuron when these had been lined up on the screen by the use of a double prism of variable power. The double prism was used to vary the visual direction of one eye (and therefore any response fields of that eye) in finely graded steps. Since the eyes are fixed, this maneuver changes the disparity between the retinal images of the moving stimulus, and if the change in prism power for one eye is in the horizontal plane, then the effect is identical with the one produced by a change in the distance of the stimulus along a line through the opposite eye and its response field.

We found that the binocular response of a particular cortical neuron in the left visual cortex to a moving slit of light varies considerably as the disparity is changed [*see illustration on page 65*]. The responses were averaged for stimulation of each eye alone and for binocular stimulation when the two response fields have different amounts of overlap on the tangent screen where the light stimulus is moving forward and backward. The cortical neuron responded only to an oblique slit, and there was no response when the orientation was rotated more than 10 degrees in either direction. There was a response only as the slit moved across the screen from left to right and not in the reverse direction. Moreover, the response elicited from the left (ipsilateral) eye alone was weak.

The relative strength of the responses elicited from each eye varies from one neuron to another, and the particular neuron shown in the illustration is a case of extreme contralateral dominance. The inhibitory contribution from the ipsilateral eye is far from weak, however, as can be seen by the reduction of the binocular response when the response fields are stimulated in the "wrong" spatiotemporal relationship, as for example when the prism setting is such that the response fields are side by side instead of being superimposed.

Our findings demonstrated that the binocular response of the neuron is in fact very sensitive to slight changes in the overlap of its response fields in the plane of the stimulus. Since the response fields themselves are quite small (less than half a degree), this means a high

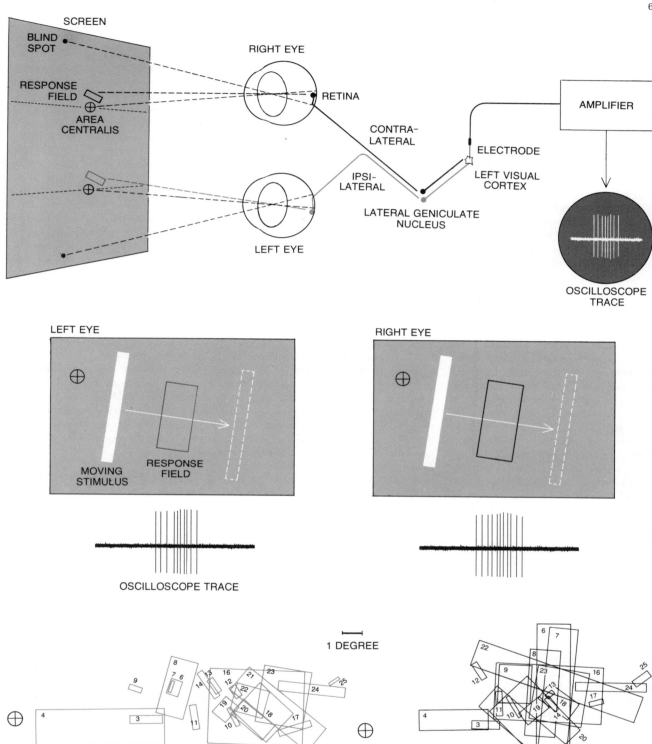

RESPONSE FIELDS FOR LEFT (IPSILATERAL) EYE

RESPONSE FIELDS FOR RIGHT (CONTRALATERAL) EYE

PAIRED RESPONSE FIELDS, one for each eye, can be plotted for a given neuron in the visual cortex of the cat (*top*). The response field of the neuron is defined as the region in the visual field of each eye where a specific stimulus will cause excitation of the cell (*middle*). In this illustration the response fields are separated on the screen because of the slightly divergent position the eyes assume in paralysis. Normally the fields would tend to overlap each other. By moving the microelectrode carefully through the cortex it is possible to record successively from a large number of different neurons; when the paired response fields of these neurons are plotted (*bottom*), those for the ipsilateral eye (the eye on the same side of the brain as the neuron in question) are more scattered than those for the contralateral eye (the eye on the opposite side). This means that it is not possible to superimpose all response fields on the same plane at the same time and that therefore different neurons would be optimally stimulated by objects in different planes.

level of disparity specificity. This particular neuron could indicate, by a marked decrease in firing rate, a disparity change as small as two minutes of arc, a feat approaching human performance. (The human threshold disparity is about 10 seconds of arc, or approximately 10 times better.)

It is perhaps not too surprising, in view of the very small size of the response fields, that the two retinal images of a binocularly presented stimulus must be very precisely located in order to produce a good response from the neuron. More surprising is the almost total suppression of the strong response from an appropriately located image in one eye if the image is inappropriately located in the other. This inhibition persists when the image is moved (for example by inserting the prism or by changing the distance of the stimulus) more than one degree of arc in either direction from the optimal position with respect to its correctly located partner in the other eye. In other words, binocular inhibition extends for more than one degree of retinal disparity on each side of the optimal disparity for a given neuron. The significance of this conclusion can be seen when one considers how nearby neurons behave with respect to one another in binocular vision; for those binocular neurons concerned with central vision the total range of optimal disparities is also a couple of degrees.

Let us now look at another disparity-specific binocular neuron recorded from the same column of tissue in the cortex as the one just described. Its stimulus requirements were quite similar (a slowly moving slit of light with the same orientation) except that the optimal disparity was 1.7 degrees more convergent because of the different position of its ipsilateral response field. Thus an oblique slit, in spite of the fact that it stimulates the contralateral response fields of both neurons, will under binocular viewing conditions excite one of them and inhibit the other, depending critically on its distance from the cat.

This binocular inhibition, operating over the same range as the range of disparity from one neuron to another, may be part of the explanation for the phenomenon of binocular fusion. A binocularly viewed target can be seen as being single in spite of the fact that it appears to lie in two different directions when the views from each eye alone are compared. In the upturned-bucket example, if the disparity between the retinal images of the larger circles is not too great, then one sees not two large circles but

a single (fused) large circle floating in depth. It is reasonable to suppose that the failure to see a second large circle is due to the binocular inhibition of those neurons that were activated monocularly by such a circle. The narrowing down of the amount of activity among different neurons narrows down in turn the number of stimulus possibilities from which the brain has to choose. In this case groups of binocular neurons associated with the same contour but with different retinal disparities are narrowed to one group and therefore a particular disparity.

Both of the neurons described above belong to Hubel and Wiesel's class of simple neurons, that is, neurons that respond only to stimuli on narrowly defined areas of the retina. It was particularly interesting to examine the binocular properties of complex neurons, since they are thought to receive an input from a number of simple neurons and therefore to respond over a wider area of retina. Would they also respond over a wider range of disparity?

Two types of disparity-specific complex neuron were found. In one group there was a high degree of specificity in spite of the large size of the response field. One binocular complex neuron had response fields six degrees across but could still detect changes of disparity as accurately as most simple neurons (which have fields less than one degree across). This astonishing precision means that the neuron would signal with a change in firing rate that a stimulus moving anywhere over a six-degree area had produced a change of just a few minutes of arc in retinal disparity. With the eyes in a constant position a disparity-specific complex neuron "looks" at a thin sheet suspended in space and fires if a stimulus with the correct orientation and speed of movement appears anywhere on the sheet (but not in front of or behind it).

Disparity-specific complex neurons behave as if they receive an input from a number of simple neurons with different absolute response-field positions in each eye but with the same relative position, so that they all have the same optimal disparity. In fact, we noticed groups of such neurons in the Berkeley experiments, and Hubel and Wiesel have recently shown that binocular neurons with the same disparity specificity in the monkey's cortex appear to be grouped in cortical columns similar to the columns for orientation specificity. We therefore have another example of the

cortical column as a system for extracting information about one specific type of stimulus while generalizing for others. A disparity-specific complex neuron can accordingly respond to a vertical edge moving over a wide region of the retina but over a very narrow depth in space. Directional specificity is lost but orientation and disparity information are retained.

There is some evidence for another type of binocular cortical column where all the neurons have response fields in the same position for the contralateral eye but have scattered fields for the ipsilateral eye. Blakemore calls these structures "constant direction" columns, because the neurons associated with them appear to respond at different disparities but to stimuli that are in the same direction from the contralateral eye. The output cell from such a column would presumably generalize for disparity but would be specific for the orientation and direction of the object.

Other complex binocular neurons responded over a wide range of disparity as well as of visual field. Since these neurons are active over the same range in which one observes binocular inhibition, they may be the source of the inhibition for simple neurons.

Once small residual eye movements had been accounted for and disparity specificity had been demonstrated, we were able to go ahead and compare the response-field pairs of a large number of different binocular neurons. In that way we could assess the total range of disparity variation. This was of particular interest because of a large body of observations obtained in psychophysical experiments on humans showing the range of disparity over which there is binocular fusion and the range of disparity over which stereopsis operates, both for central (foveal) vision and as one moves into the lower-resolution, peripheral visual field. The measurements were tedious because of the great length of time it takes to characterize a disparity-specific cortical neuron. In a typical experiment it took us three days to accumulate the 21 disparity-specific neurons whose response fields are shown in the illustration on the preceding page. All the neurons were recorded from the left striate cortex, and inspection of their response fields reveals a greater scatter in the fields of the left eye than in the fields of the right. This general observation that the ipsilateral receptive fields show more horizontal scatter is of interest in view of the fact that the ipsilateral

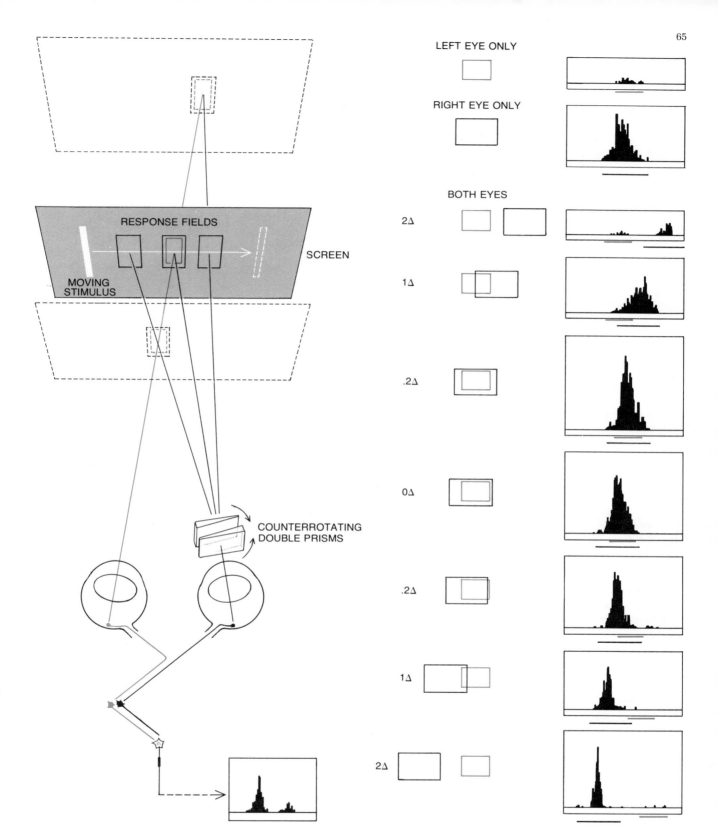

LEFT EYE ONLY

RIGHT EYE ONLY

BOTH EYES

2Δ

1Δ

.2Δ

0Δ

.2Δ

1Δ

2Δ

RESPONSE FIELDS

SCREEN

MOVING STIMULUS

COUNTERROTATING DOUBLE PRISMS

SPECIFICITY of a given binocular neuron for varying degrees of retinal disparity can be studied with the aid of counterrotating double prisms of variable power. The slight shifts of the two response fields with respect to each other in the plane of the moving stimulus are equivalent to setting that plane nearer to or farther from the animal (*left*). In this particular example, a case of extreme contralateral dominance, the response to a moving slit of light elicited from the left (ipsilateral) eye alone was weak; the inhibitory contribution from the ipsilateral eye is far from weak,

however, as can be seen from the reduction of the binocular response when the prism setting is such that the response fields are side by side instead of being superimposed (*right*). The response for this particular neuron falls off rapidly for disparities on the order of tenths of a degree; hence there would be good discrimination among neurons whose optimal disparities cover a range of several degrees. A prism setting of one diopter (Δ) is equal to a retinal disparity of one centimeter at a distance of one meter; expressed as an angle, a disparity of one Δ equals .57 degree.

fibers are the ones that have arisen most recently in the evolution of binocular vision.

One can get a measure of the range of disparity in the response fields by shifting each pair of fields horizontally so that all the left-eye fields are superimposed. It is clear that if there were no disparity between different pairs of response fields, then that would lead to superimposition of the right-eye fields also. The degree to which the fields do not superimpose can be measured, and in this case there was a range of six degrees of horizontal disparity and two degrees of vertical disparity. It is not immediately obvious why the neurons should cover a range of vertical disparity, since only the horizontal component can be used for stereopsis. The psychophysical studies show, however, that although the visual system cannot make use of vertical disparity, allowance must be made for such disparities so that the system can still operate when they are introduced. Vertical disparities arise at close viewing distances (where the image of a given object may be significantly larger on one retina) and also in the course of eye movements (where the two eyes may not remain perfectly aligned vertically).

The total range of disparity surveyed by a given cortical area varies according to retinal eccentricity. Binocular neurons concerned with the area centralis (the high-resolution part of the cat's retina that corresponds to the human fovea) cover a disparity range of two degrees compared with six degrees for those neurons dealing with the visual field about 10 degrees away from the midline. The small total range for the area centralis not only allows fine discrimination within that range but also requires fine control of eye movements so that the target being examined can be kept within the range. The range of disparities for central vision appears to be even narrower in humans and monkeys, where there is exquisite control of convergent and divergent eye movements so that the midpoint of the range can be varied. The fineness of the range is attested by the double vision that occurs if there is the slightest imbalance in the muscular system.

The preliminary results described here provide some insight into the initial operations performed by the visual cortex in extracting the information about disparity between small elements of the two retinal images. Much remains to be determined about how these first steps are utilized by the brain to yield our

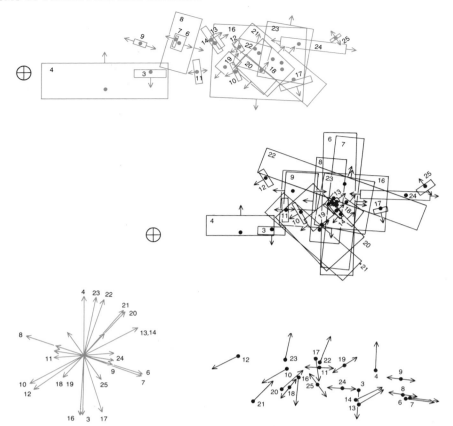

RANGE OF OPTIMAL RETINAL DISPARITIES for the 21 binocular neurons whose response fields are plotted in the illustration on page 63 (and reproduced at the top of this illustration) can be calculated by shifting each pair of response fields horizontally so that the binocular centers (*black dots*) of all the left eye's fields are superimposed (*bottom*). The scatter of the right eye's response fields then gives the range of disparities. For those fields located away from the central area there is a range of six degrees of horizontal disparity and two degrees of vertical disparity. For neurons with fields closer to the center of the retina the range is smaller and hence the neurons are capable of finer discrimination.

complete three-dimensional view of the world. Here are two examples of the kind of problem that remains to be solved: (1) Since convergent and divergent eye movements themselves produce changes in retinal disparity, how are these movements taken into account so that an absolute depth sense results that does not change with eye position? (2)

How is a synthesis achieved from the disparity information about the myriad contours of a visual scene? The answers to these and many more perplexing questions about the brain may be best answered by the combination of the approaches of psychophysics and neurophysiology that has proved fruitful thus far.

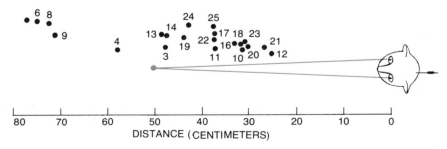

DEPTH DISCRIMINATION attributable to binocular vision is represented by this plot of the points in space at which a correctly oriented contour would optimally stimulate the 21 binocular cortical neurons whose response fields are shown in the illustration at top of this page, provided that the cat's eyes are fixed on a point 50 centimeters in front (*colored dot*).

Visual Motion Perception

by Gunnar Johansson
June 1975

*The eye has no shutter, and yet a moving world
does not appear as a blur. The visual system works
not like a camera but more like a computer with a
program of specific mathematical rules*

The eye is often compared to the camera, but there is one enormous difference between the two. In all ordinary cameras a shutter "freezes" the image; even in a television camera, which has no shutter, the scanning raster of an electron beam serves the same purpose. In all animals, however, the eye operates without a shutter. Why, then, is the world we see through our eyes not a complete blur? As we walk down a street the buildings we pass seem quite stationary. We do not perceive them as the bundles of streaks they optically create on our retina. Other pedestrians and moving vehicles all seem to be traveling through the same static visual space with sharp outlines, even though they are moving in various directions and with quite different velocities. Whether we are standing still or moving through space the eye effortlessly sorts moving objects from stationary ones and transforms the optical flow into a perfectly structured world of objects, all without the benefit of a shutter. How is this remarkable feat accomplished?

From the evolutionary point of view the feat was clearly necessary for survival. The eye has evolved to function essentially as a motion-detecting system. The concept of a motionless animal in a totally static environment has hardly any biological significance; the perception of physical motion is of decisive importance. In many lower animals the efficient perception of moving objects seems to be the most essential visual function. A frog or a chameleon, for example, can perceive and catch its prey only if the prey is moving. A motionless fly, even within easy reach, goes quite unnoticed.

Evidence for a similar dependence on changes in the visual stimulus pattern can also be demonstrated in man. In experiments where a special device holds an image motionless on the retina the corresponding percept rapidly fades and disappears. Tennis and many other sports testify to man's remarkable ability to visually determine the precise spatiotemporal position of a small fast-moving object.

The traditional comparison of the eye and the camera serves the useful didactic purpose of explaining how light rays are focused to produce a two-dimensional image on the surface of the retina. Difficulties arise, however, when the photoreceptors embedded in the retina are likened to a photographic film. Unless one deliberately wants to get a blurred image on the film it must be exposed to the incident light rays for only a brief period, just enough for the photosensitive chemicals in the film to "capture" the image. Although it is true that the retinal receptors have a similar ability to capture photons, their real function is not to capture images but to mediate changes in light flux. The light impinging on the receptors (the rods and the cones) gives rise to a continuous change in the structure of photosensitive molecules. The change in structure releases a flow of ions in the receptor, culminating in a bioelectric signal that travels from the receptor into adjacent nerve cells.

The strength of the signal varies with the light flux. Within a few milliseconds the myriad changes in signal pattern over the entire retina are combined and transformed by an intricate neural network within the retina itself, by other networks at relay stations in the midbrain and finally by the neural networks within a number of receiving terminals in the cerebral cortex. The result at the conscious level is the perception of motion in visual space. Thus the eye is basically an instrument for analyzing changes in light flux over time rather than an instrument for recording static patterns. Roughly speaking, without a change in the light striking the receptor there would be no change in ion flow and no neural response.

In studies of visual perception it is often important to distinguish between monocular and binocular vision. For the range of phenomena I shall take up here, however, the contribution made by binocular perception can be ignored. In our laboratory at the University of Uppsala my colleagues and I have contrived a variety of experiments to examine how the eye deals with moving visual stimuli. We include under this heading the motion of stationary objects perceived by a moving observer as well as the motion of moving objects perceived by a stationary observer.

As an introduction to our experiments, consider what happens when you use a camera to make a picture of a friend. You look through the viewfinder and customarily take a few steps forward or backward until you have the subject properly framed and the image expanded or contracted to the desired size. As you move toward the subject every optical element in the viewfinder streams radially outward from a central point. Conversely, when you step backward, the image contracts radially toward the center. If you are a careful photographer, you probably also check the effects of moving the camera up and down and from side to side. Such movements generate optical flows considerably more complex than the radial flow produced by moving directly toward the subject. All such changes in the viewfinder, however, follow the laws of central perspective. They are continuous perspective transformations.

The optical flow of images into the

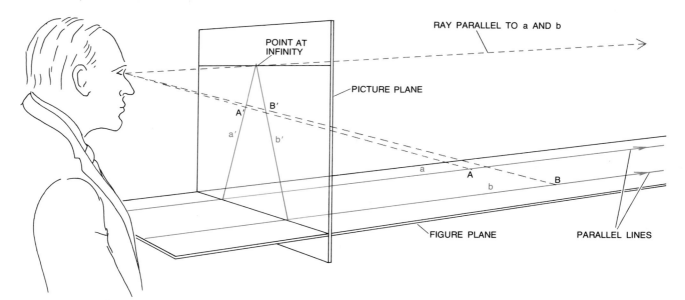

IN PERSPECTIVE DRAWING parallel lines converge at a fictitious "vanishing point" located on the viewer's horizon. The diagram shows how points *A* and *B* on parallel lines *a* and *b* are converted into their perspective equivalent on a transparent screen.

viewfinder of a camera (or into the camera itself when the lens is open) corresponds to the optical flow impinging on the retina during locomotion. From the geometrical point of view it does not matter whether it is the camera that is moving or the subject in front of the camera. It would be trivial to say that asking your friend to take a step toward you has the same effect on the size of his image as your moving a step toward him. It is significant, however, that in the first case the image of the surrounding environment remains fixed and in the second the image of the environment expands outward slightly from the optical center. To generalize, when objects move in our field of vision, they give rise to local flow patterns; when we move around in the environment, there is an optical flow across the entire retinal surface.

In everyday perception the optical flow across the retina usually represents a complex combination of patterns generated by the observer's own motion and patterns generated by the motion of moving objects. Even when the observer is simply standing still or sitting, the sway of his body or small movements of his head add a small "locomotion component" to the flow of the retinal images. Movements of the eye itself introduce a further component into the total flow; the movement can be smooth, as when an observer follows the flight of a ball, or jerky, as when your eye follows these words by a number of saccadic eye movements. The summation of all such optical flows over the retina determines the character of the incessant flow of

nerve impulses from the retinal receptors. In order to study the visual information supplied by a light-reflecting space we must consider the geometry of the optical flow reaching the retina.

A theory of the perception of visual space was outlined as long ago as 1709 by George Berkeley (later Bishop Berkeley). The theory was further developed by Hermann von Helmholtz in the 19th century and is still familiar today in a modified version known as cue theory. According to this theory, the two-dimensional image on the retina is visually interpreted as being three-dimensional by a number of cues, or signs. The cues are available not only in the image itself but also in the activity of the oculomotor apparatus. The cues include binocular disparity in the images seen by the two eyes, convergence and accommodation of the lens, size of image, interposition of figures, binocular perspective and so on. The theory also invokes visual-motor experience and learning as important supplementary factors.

Berkeley knew only Euclidean geometry (the discovery of other geometries was still in the future), and as a result he

began his study of the relation between a stimulus and a percept by analyzing the retinal image as if it could be adequately measured with a ruler and a protractor. Even today many excellent theorists stay within the tradition of measuring optical projections in millimeters and degrees of arc. This approach has given rise to many artificial problems, such as trying to explain how retinal images of different sizes and forms can evoke perception of the same object.

New geometries that have come into existence since Berkeley's day are free of the Euclidean parallel axiom, which leads to the postulate that parallel lines do not meet. One of the geometries that is not fettered by the parallel axiom is projective geometry. That geometry is of special interest for the study of vision because it is the geometry of optical paths through pinholes and lenses and provides the theoretical basis for perspective drawing. It is characterized as being a nonmetric geometry because it deals exclusively with relations rather than particular measurements.

The first comprehensive use of the principles of central perspective in the theoretical analysis of visual space perception was made by J. J. Gibson of Cor-

TWO FIGURES DANCING IN THE DARK appear on the opposite page in a sequence of 36 motion-picture frames from a film made in the author's laboratory at the University of Uppsala. Each dancer is "outlined" by 12 lights: two each at the shoulders, elbows, wrists, hips, knees and ankles. This sequence, which proceeds in vertical columns starting at upper left, consists of every sixth frame from a portion of the film. Naïve subjects shown the film can tell in a fraction of a second that they are seeing the movements of two people.

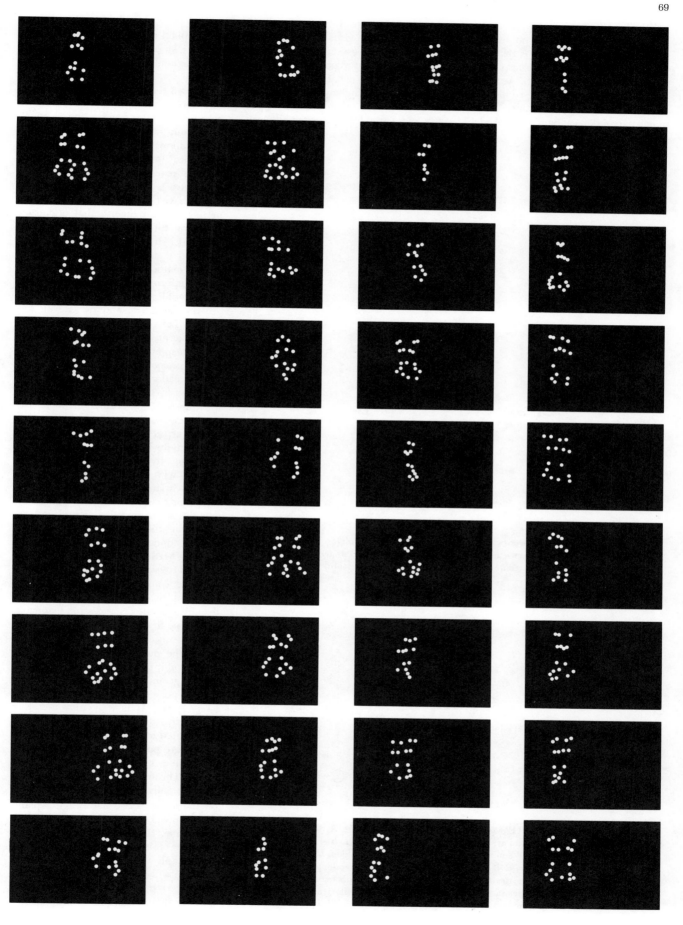

nell University in his book *The Perception of the Visual World*, published in 1950. Gibson's main thesis is that traditional cue theory is an unnecessary and even misleading construct. According to Gibson, the image itself contains all the information needed for three-dimensional perception, a fact overlooked in cue theory because of its unsophisticated description of the visual stimulus. Mathematical lawfulness in the structural change from point to point in the optical image, involving what Gibson termed "gradients" and "higher-order variables," is the effective stimulus. The gradients and variables are essentially consequences of central projection. Gibson also applied these principles to moving patterns, speaking of stimulus flow rather than stimulus images.

My own thinking closely follows Gibson's. Experimental work over the past two decades has led me to break completely with the Euclidean model and to adopt projective relations as the theoretical foundation for investigations of visual space and motion.

In retrospect it seems strange that it should have been hypothesized, as it was in the classical theory, that organisms searching for spatial information from reflected light developed an eye with a lens and then failed to take advantage of the mathematical laws determining spatial information, available in the trajectories of light through a lens. So strong are the Euclidean and Berkeleyan traditions, however, that a direct experimental approach is needed in order to gain acceptance for a model based on central projection.

The reader may ask how a geometry lacking a fixed metric can be of any use for transferring information about the rigid three-dimensional space that surrounds us, in which the Euclidean metric certainly holds true. The answer is that projective geometry is a geometry dealing with certain relations that remain invariant under perspective transformation. These invariances serve as a counterpart in terms of figural equivalence for the Euclidean figural congruence under the conditions of rigid motion. Mathematicians have also developed a special system of coordinates (homogeneous coordinates) that are determined by distance relations rather than by absolute distances and that make it possible to deal analytically with projective transformations.

For the purposes of the rest of this discussion it is sufficient to say that projective geometry underlies the rules of central perspective [*see the illustration on page 68*]. It is well known that in perspective drawing parallel lines must be pictured as converging at a fictitious "vanishing point." Thus in the perspective system the parallel axiom is abandoned. The angle between the "parallel" lines (actually converging lines) depends on the angle between the figure plane (the surface being pictured) and the picture plane. Hence we know that a rectangular tabletop in a drawing or in a photograph will be trapezoidal, a circular table will be elliptical and so on. No matter how the viewing angle or the distance to an object is changed, the object

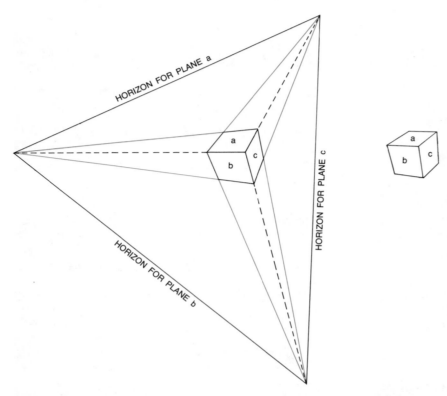

CUBE REMAINS A CUBE even when it is seen from different angles. Strictly speaking, each face of the two cubes drawn here is a trapezium. The visual system, however, automatically corrects for the distortions and delivers percept of regular solid with square faces.

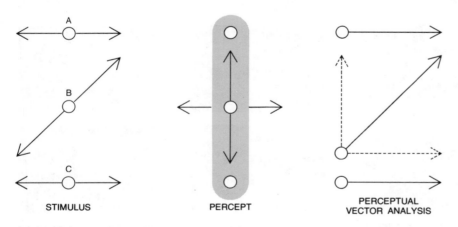

MOVING REFERENCE SYSTEM is formed by three spots of light, *A*, *B* and *C*, traveling along the paths indicated by the arrows at the left. If seen by itself, *B* simply moves back and forth on a slanting path. When the motions of *A* and *C* are added, however, the three spots form a perceptual unit (*middle*), in which the trajectory of *B* no longer seems to slant. Instead *B* seems to oscillate vertically as if bouncing back and forth between *A* and *C*. In this case the motion of *B* divides into two component vectors: one horizontal and equal to the motion of *A* and *C*, and one vertical, representing the motion of *B* relative to *A* and *C*.

is recognizable as the same object seen at different angles [*see upper illustration on preceding page*]. The forms in the pictures are equivalent because of certain invariant relations, although from a Euclidean point of view they are all different.

From recent studies of motion perception in which continuous figural changes of this type are presented without three-dimensional depth cues we have overwhelming evidence that the visual system spontaneously abstracts relational invariances in the optical flow and constructs percepts of rigid objects moving in three-dimensional space. Indeed, it has been found that continuous perspective transformations always evoke the perception of moving objects with a constant size and shape. This means that the particular projection chosen perceptually by the visual system is one that represents Euclidean invariance under the conditions of motion in rigid three-dimensional space.

A basic and well-established conclusion from a large body of experimental research dating back to the 1920's is that the visual system, in its decoding of a total optical flow, tends to extract components of projective invariances in accordance with specific rules. An example from daily life is perhaps the best way to make this rather abstract statement easier to grasp. My little granddaughter runs across the floor of my study, eager to show me a ladybug walking on her finger. The optical flow produced in my eyes by this scene includes the following components: the light reflected from (1) the floor, the walls and the furniture in my study, (2) the child's body, (3) the child's hand and finger reaching toward me and finally (4) the ladybug moving on the child's moving finger. All these components moving relative to my eyes contribute to the complex optical flow, but

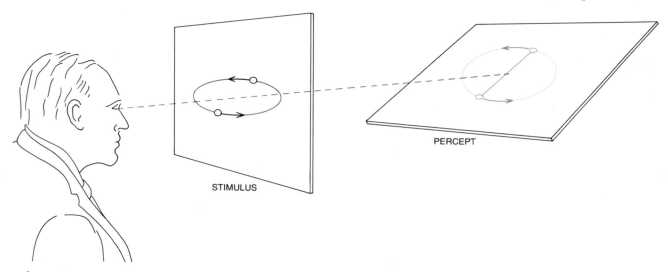

IMAGINARY ROTATING ROD is formed when the stimulus consists of two spots of light moving in an elliptical path. Because the visual system "prefers" to perceive the rod as maintaining a constant length, the viewer has the impression that the rod is rotating in a plane that is slanted either toward him or away from him, as is depicted here. The slants approximate those of projected circles.

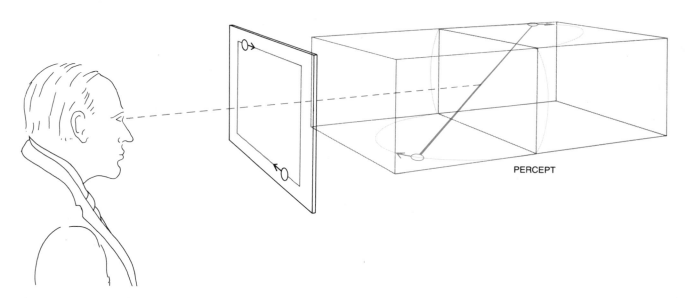

BIZARRE THREE-DIMENSIONAL FIGURE seems to be traced by an imaginary rod that is created when two spots of light move at constant speed on the opposite sides of a rectangular path. The built-in tendency for the visual system to perceive the moving spots as being connected to each other and forming a rigid structure leads to the perception of a rod that is rotating around a stationary central point in a jerky manner, executing a strange three-dimensional motion the observer quite probably has never seen before.

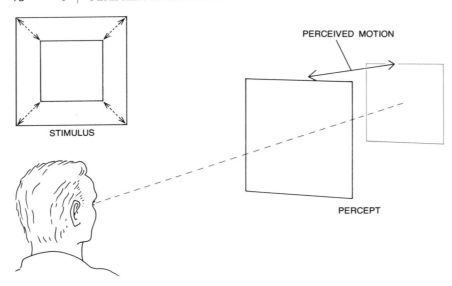

ADVANCING AND RETREATING SQUARE is perceived when the stimulus consists of a square that simply contracts and expands. The visual system interprets change in size as a perspective change produced by a figure of constant size moving back and forth in depth.

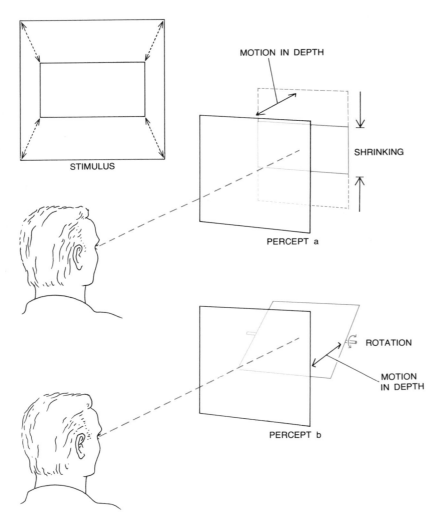

ALTERNATIVE VISUAL PERCEPTIONS are evoked if the stimulus square not only contracts and expands but also is simultaneously transformed into a rectangle as it is shrinking. One group of observers sees a figure receding and advancing while it is changing simultaneously from a square into a rectangle and back again (*percept a*). To other observers the square remains a square but one that is oscillating on its horizontal axis (*percept b*).

I quite clearly do not perceive them in this way as having a common frame of reference. Perceptually I experience the room as being static, the child as running across the floor, the child's hand and arm as moving relative to her body, the child's finger as moving relative to her hand and the ladybug as moving relative to the child's finger. Thus my visual system abstracts a hierarchical series of moving frames of reference and motions relative to each of them. The perceptual analysis of the optical flow as a hierarchical series of component motions follows closely the principles of ordinary mathematical vector analysis; hence it has been termed perceptual vector analysis. In our laboratory at the University of Uppsala we have devoted much experimental effort to a search for the basic principles underlying this perceptual function.

I shall now briefly describe some typical experiments in my laboratory involving perceptual vector analysis and its geometric basis. In most of the experiments the visual stimuli consist of computer-controlled patterns displayed on a televisionlike screen and projected into the eyes of our subjects by means of a collimating device that removes parallax as well as the possibility of seeing the screen.

Some of the fundamentals in the general principle of perceptual relativity are demonstrated in one of my earliest experiments. The stimulus pattern consists simply of three bright spots, *A, B, C*, one above the other, moving back and forth along straight paths [*see lower illustration on page 70*]. When the top and bottom spots, *A* and *C*, are displayed alone, moving horizontally to the left and to the right, they seem to be rigidly connected. When the middle spot, *B*, is presented alone, it is "correctly" seen as moving in a sloping path. When the three elements are presented simultaneously, however, we get an example of perceptual vector analysis. The entire unit *ABC* seems to be moving horizontally as a unit, but the path of *B* does not appear to be sloping; instead *B* seems to be moving vertically up and down in a straight line. This result can be generalized: Equal vectors or vector components form a perceptual unit that acts as a moving frame of reference in relation to which secondary components seem to move.

A more recent series of experiments in which a few points trace an ellipse or some other conic section provides other striking insights into the geometry of perception. If we present on our display screen two spots opposite an imaginary

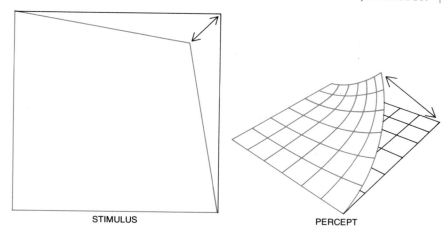

STIMULUS

PERCEPT

BENDING MOTION is perceived if one corner of a square figure is moved along a diagonal path. The perception of bending may continue until the moving corner actually touches the opposite corner. A given observer will initially perceive bending as being either toward or away from him, but with some effort he can reverse apparent direction of motion.

center point tracing an ellipse, observers always seem to see a rigid rod of which only the end points are visible [*see upper illustration on page 71*]. Even more surprising, the rod is seen as rotating in a plane that is tilted away from (or toward) the observer. The perceived plane has a slant corresponding roughly to the computed slant of a projected circle. Even though the observer is fully aware that the points on the screen are really tracing an ellipse, he is unable to see the "true" Euclidean pattern; he always sees the ellipse as a circle in perspective. Thus we meet with a convincing indication that the perceptual analysis spontaneously follows the principles of central perspective.

A still more fascinating "illusion" is created by a variation of the experiment in which the two spots of light follow a perfectly rectangular path [*see lower illustration on page 71*]. I must admit I was surprised to find that even in this case the two spots appear to be the lighted ends of a rigid rod rotating around a fixed central point. One might expect that one would simply see two spots (perhaps elastically connected) chasing each other around a rectangular track. Instead an imaginary rod is again seen; its length seems to be constant as the rod describes a curious path in which it rotates for part of the time in a nearly vertical plane and then slants rapidly away from the vertical and back again. So strong is the perceptual tendency toward abstract projective invariance that a highly complex and "unnatural" motion—one that may not have been seen before—is preferred to the simple

rectangular track traced by two moving spots. Evidently it is obligatory that the spatial relation between two isolated moving stimuli be perceived as the simplest motion that preserves a rigid connection between the stimuli. The general formula is spatial invariance plus motion.

In a related but slightly different class of experiments the display screen presents the full outline of a simple geometric figure whose shape is systematically altered in a particular way. For example, the observer may be shown a square alternately contracting and expanding [*see top illustration on opposite page*]. What the observer perceives however, is a square of fixed size alternately receding and approaching. He never perceives the square as a stationary pattern that is changing in size. The result again means that the visual system automatically prefers invariance of figure size, obtained by inferring motion in three-dimensional space.

The next experiment I shall describe is perceived two different ways by different observers. Some observers seem to see it only one way whereas for others the two types of percept alternate. In this presentation the top and bottom of a square alternately shrink and expand as in the preceding experiment while the sides of the square move in and out a smaller distance. Geometrically a large square collapses to form a somewhat smaller rectangle, then expands to its original shape [*see bototm illustration on opposite page*]. All observers have the impression that the figure is alternately advancing and retreating. For one group of observers, however, the figure seems

to change during its translatory motion from a square into a rectangle and back again. For a second group of observers the square seems to remain a square at all times, but a square that is rocking back and forth around its horizontal axis as it advances and retreats. Thus we encounter two variants of a vector analysis in the geometric framework of central projection. The first variant is particularly interesting because it represents perception of simultaneous motion and change of shape, such as one might see in a moving cloud or a ring of cigarette smoke.

A final example, taken from a set of experiments that Gunnar Jansson and I have recently published, involves a rather subtle change in the geometry of a square: one corner is made to move slowly toward the center of the square and back again [*see illustration at left*]. The result is interesting because it demonstrates a new type of perceptual invariance. The observer has the illusion that the square is a flexible surface with a corner that is bending toward him. This may seem surprising, but it is just what one would expect if the figural change is interpreted as being a continuous perspective projection.

It is a common characteristic of all the experiments I have described that the observer is evidently not free to choose between a Euclidean interpretation of the changing geometry of the figure in the display and a projective interpretation. For example, he cannot persuade himself that what he sees is simply a square growing larger and smaller in the same visual plane; his visual system insists on telling him that he is seeing a square of constant size approaching and receding. Hence he perceives rigid motion in depth, rotation in a specific slant, bending in depth and so on, paired with the highest possible degree of object constancy.

The theory of visual perception I have outlined here is based on studies with artificial and highly simplified stimulus patterns. Such experiments helped to demonstrate that the visual system uses the geometry of central perspective and enabled us to formulate the principles of perceptual vector analysis. It was natural for my colleagues and me to ask ourselves: Is there any way to show experimentally that the principles of perceptual analysis also hold true for the more complex patterns of motions encountered in everyday life? In an attempt to answer this question we began some years ago to study experimentally the complex patterns of motion generated by men and animals, patterns that might be called biological motions.

Consider, for example, all the intricate coordinations of frequencies, phase relations, amplitudes and acceleration patterns that are accomplished by one's skeletal structure when one merely walks across the floor. Even in such a simple act scores of articulated bones make precise rotations around dozens of joints.

Our simple early experiments had demonstrated that the moving end points of an otherwise invisible straight line carry enough information to convey the impression of a rigid line moving in three-dimensional space. We therefore hypothesized that if we presented the motions of the joints of a walking person in the form of a number of bright spots of light moving against a dark background, an observer might perceive that the spots represented someone walking. We attached small flashlight bulbs to the shoulders, elbows, wrists, hips, knees and ankles of one of our co-workers and made a motion-picture film of him as he moved around in a darkened room [*see illustration below*].

The results, when the motion picture was shown to naïve observers, exceeded our expectations. During the opening scene, when the actor is sitting motionless in a chair, the observers are mystified because they see only a random collection of lights, not unlike a constellation. As soon as the actor rises and starts moving, however, the observers instantly perceive that the lights are attached to an otherwise invisible human being. They are able not only to differentiate without hesitation between walking and jogging movements but also to recognize small anomalies in the actor's behavior, such as the simulation of a slight limp. In another experiment we filmed two people, similarly festooned with lights, performing a lively folk dance. When the film is projected, anyone can see immediately that the 24 swirling spots of light represent a dancing couple [*see illustration on page 69*].

The surprising ability of the human visual system to perceive a dozen or two dozen moving lights as the motions of people led us to study the minimum exposure time required for the sensory organization of such patterns. The result, recently published by our group, is that a tenth of a second (the time needed to project two motion-picture frames) is often enough to enable a naïve observer to identify a familiar biological motion. This finding, together with results not yet published, has led me to believe that the ability of the visual system to abstract invariant relations from the kind of patterns I have been describing is the product of "hard-wired," or fixed, visual pathways originating at the retina and terminating in the cortex. It is as if the hierarchies of relative invariances in the optical flow were filtered out and established before the visual signals reach the level of consciousness. And contrary to expectation the more complex a projectively coherent pattern is from the mathematical point of view, the more effective the sensory decoding is. (Witness the decipherment of the dancing lights.) Evidently as the degrees of freedom are reduced the stimuli become rich in redundant information.

From our investigations we now know that the component in the optical flow that is a consequence of locomotion generally represents a continuous perspective transformation. Generalizing further from our experiments, we conclude that

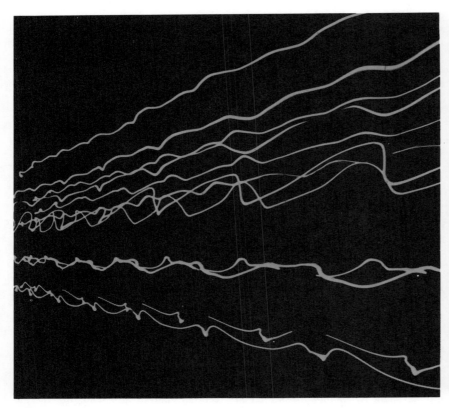 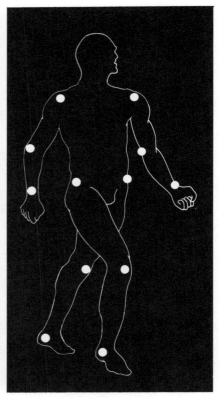

LIGHT TRACKS OF WALKING PERSON (*left*) are recorded by making a time exposure in a dark room of a subject fitted with 12 small lights at his principal joints, as is shown at the right. The continuous streaks generated in this way have no obvious interpretation. If, however, the moving-light patterns are recorded on motion-picture film, one can see instantly when the film is projected that it portrays a person walking. Motion-picture frames of two similarly lighted subjects dancing in the dark appear on page 69.

during locomotion the components of the human visual environment are interpreted as rigid structures in relative motion. In this regard the theory and our experiences are in good correspondence; there can be no doubt that we perceive the environment as being rigid.

The term relative motion can imply, however, that either the perceiver or the environment (or both) can be regarded as moving relative to the other. Both experiments and experience indicate that the environment forms the frame of reference for human locomotion. The world is perceived as being stationary and the observer as being in motion. From the point of view of theory we may nonetheless ask: Why is the eye itself not the ultimate reference? Why does one not perceive the ground to be moving instead of oneself? From the point of view of function, the answer is easy: The perceptions supplied by a "stationary" eye would be less informative. But let us ignore function, since we are considering the principles of decoding.

We recognize, of course, that visual information about locomotion does not stand alone; it interacts with signals from other sense organs that report bodily movements: organs in the joints, in the muscles, in the inner ear and so on. It is evident, however, that our consciousness of locomotion requires something more. Experiments have shown that the visual perception of locomotion is able to override conflicting spatial information from those other sensory channels. Thus it seems that the optical flow that covers the retina during locomotion takes precedence over all other sensory information.

The work I have reported, together with comparable studies from many other laboratories, provides the outlines of what one might characterize as a relativistic theory of vision. The central finding is that the geometry of the decoding of visual stimuli is a relational one similar to projective geometry. In accordance with this geometry, series of relative invariances, or perspective transformations, are abstracted from the total optical flow. This results in hierarchical systems of different components that are perceived both in common and in relative perspective transformations. As our experiments make clear, human beings tend to perceive objects as possessing constant Euclidean shapes in rigid motion in a three-dimensional world. In real life these principles of visual analysis taken together give rise to a satisfactorily close correspondence between the physical world and what we perceive that world to be.

8   Auditory Beats in the Brain

by Gerald Oster
October 1973

*Slow modulations called binaural beats are perceived
when tones of different frequency are presented
separately to each ear. The sensation may show
how certain sounds are processed by the brain*

If two tuning forks of slightly different pitch are struck simultaneously, the resulting sound waxes and wanes periodically. The modulations are referred to as beats; their frequency is equal to the difference between the frequencies of the original tones. For example, a tuning fork with a characteristic pitch of 440 hertz, or cycles per second (*A* above middle *C* on the piano), and another of 434 hertz, if struck at the same time, will produce beats with a frequency of six hertz.

In modern investigations tuning forks are replaced by electronic oscillators, which can supply tones of precisely controlled pitch, purity and intensity. Beats are produced when the outputs of two oscillators tuned to slightly different frequencies are combined electrically and applied to a loudspeaker. Alternatively, the signals can be applied individually to separate speakers and the beats will still be heard. The result is the same whether the tones are combined electrically and then converted into sound, or converted into sound separately and then combined.

A quite different phenomenon results when stereophonic earphones are used and the signals are applied separately to each ear. Under the right circumstances beats can be perceived, but they are of an entirely different character. They are called binaural beats, and in many ways they are more interesting than ordinary beats, which in this discussion will be called monaural. Monaural beats can be heard with both ears, but one ear is sufficient to perceive them. Binaural beats require the combined action of both ears. They exist as a consequence of the interaction of perceptions within the brain, and they can be used to investigate some of the brain's processes.

The physical mechanism of monaural beats is a special case of wave interference. At any instant the amplitude of the resulting sound is equal to the algebraic sum of the amplitudes of the original tones. The signals are reinforced when they are in phase, that is, when the peaks and nulls of their waves coincide. Destructive interference diminishes the net amplitude when the waves are in opposition. The pure tones used in these experiments are described by sine waves; the resulting beats are slowly varying functions similar to, but not precisely conforming to, a sine wave.

A beat frequency of about six hertz, as in the example given above, would sound something like vibrato in music (although vibrato is frequency modulation rather than amplitude modulation). If the interval between frequencies is made smaller, very slow beats can be produced, down to about one per second, but at this speed the beats may be difficult to perceive. Rapid beats, up to about 30 hertz, are heard as roughness superimposed on the sound, rather like a Scotsman's burr. With still greater intervals beats are not heard; the two tones are perceived separately.

Beats are rarely encountered in nature because in nature sustained pure tones are rare. They abound, however, in mechanical devices. In an airplane, jet engines operating at slightly different speeds may produce a very strong-beat, often recognized only as a feeling "in the pit of the stomach." Acoustical engineers can filter out the whine of the engines, but the slow vibrations are difficult to suppress. Occupants of apartment houses may be annoyed by beats produced by machinery, such as two blowers running at different speeds, but

they will have a hard time finding the source.

On the other hand, beats are used to advantage where frequencies must be determined precisely. Electrical engineers compare the output of a test oscillator with that of a standard oscillator by detecting the beats produced when their signals are combined. The tuning of pianos is another process that depends on beats. Typically the piano tuner will first listen for the beats produced by a tuning fork of 440 hertz and the *A* above middle *C*, and tighten or loosen the *A* wire until the beats slow to zero. He then strikes the *A* key and the *D* key below it and tunes the latter wire until 10 beats per second are heard. That frequency is produced by the interaction of the *A* string's second harmonic, or second multiple ($2 \times 440 = 880$), and the *D* string's third harmonic ($3 \times 290 = 870$). In this fashion, key by key, the piano is tuned; in theory it could be done even by someone who is tone-deaf.

Binaural beats were discovered in 1839 by a German experimenter named H. W. Dove, but as late as 1915 they were considered a trivial special case of monaural beats. It was argued that each ear was hearing sounds intended for the other. This extraneous result could be eliminated by placing the tuning forks in separate rooms, with the subject in a third room between them, and guiding the sounds through tubes to each ear. It was necessary to carefully seal each tube to the head, however, and another objection was raised: that sound presented to one ear could be conducted through the skull to the other. Bone conduction is well established, and indeed some hearing aids operate on this principle, although sound is attenuated a thousandfold from ear to ear.

The possible contribution of bone conduction to the perception of binaural beats is eliminated, however, by the use of modern stereophonic earphones. Such earphones have padding, often liquid-filled, to insulate the head from the sound source, and are designed explicitly to prevent conduction effects. Indeed, stereophonic recordings played through earphones can sound unnatural because the instruments seem too isolated.

The difference most immediately ap-parent between monaural and binaural beats is that binaural beats can be heard only when the tones used to produce them are of low pitch. Binaural beats are best perceived when the carrier fre-quency is about 440 hertz; above that frequency they become less distinct and above about 1,000 hertz they vanish al-together. No person I have tested re-ports hearing beats for frequencies above 900 hertz. Experimental condi-tions, particularly the intensity of the sounds and the type of earphones used, can affect the results, however, and oth-er investigators report detecting beats produced by tones up to almost 1,500 hertz. At the other end of the scale beats also become elusive. Below about 90 hertz the subject may confuse the beats with the tones used to produce them.

J. C. R. Licklider of the Massachusetts Institute of Technology developed a technique when he was working at Har-vard University to measure a spectrum

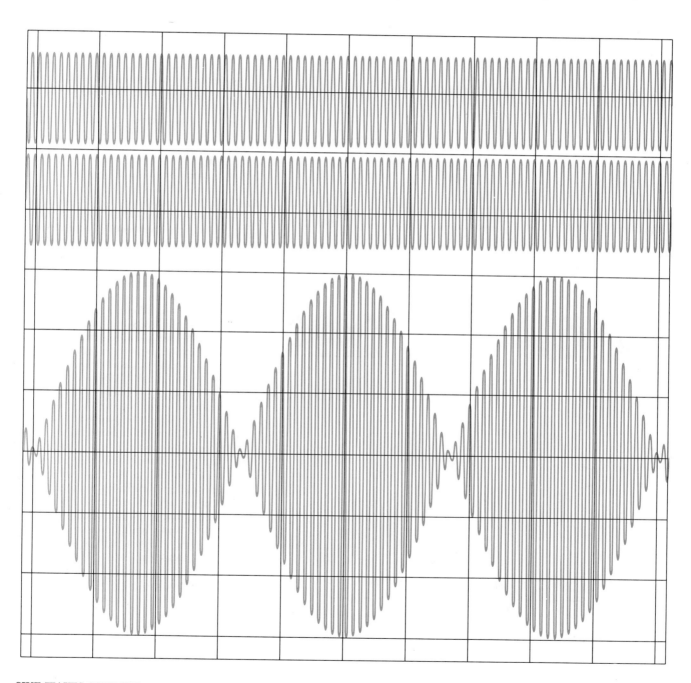

SINE WAVES COMBINE TO PRODUCE BEATS in this illustra-tion based on oscilloscope traces. The two waves at the top are of slightly different frequency; when they are combined, the result-ing wave at the bottom varies slowly in amplitude. The variations are beats and would be perceived acoustically as modulations in loudness. If the two signals were presented separately to each ear, binaural beats would be heard. These differ in character from monaural, or ordinary, beats and are generated within the brain.

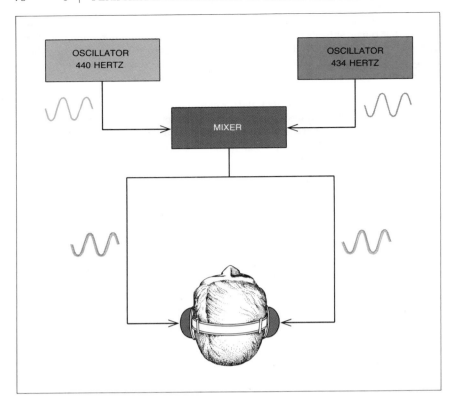

EXPERIMENTAL METHOD for generating monaural beats uses two electronic oscillators and a network, here called a mixer, to combine their outputs. Each ear hears a composite signal; the beats can be heard with one ear or both. With the oscillators tuned to the frequencies shown, six beats per second (440 hertz minus 434 hertz) would be perceived.

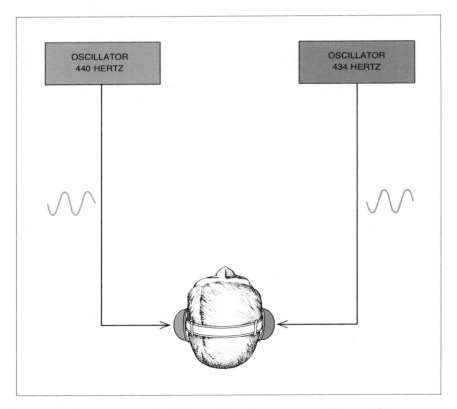

BINAURAL BEATS are produced when each oscillator is connected separately to one earphone. Again the beat frequency is six hertz, but in this mode the beats are less distinct. Whereas monaural beats are produced by the physical interference of two sound waves, binaural beats are a result of the interaction of auditory signals occurring within the brain.

of binaural beats [*see upper illustration on page 84*]. He adjusted the frequency of one oscillator until the interval was large enough so that the beats seemed "rough"; then he noted the frequency of the unchanged reference oscillator. Next he changed the setting of the reference oscillator and repeated the procedure. In this way the range of perception of each subject was recorded.

Another distinguishing characteristic of binaural beats is their muffled sound. Monaural beats produced with sounds of equal intensity pulse from loudness to silence, as their wave form would suggest. Binaural beats, on the other hand, are only a slight modulation of a loud background. I have tried to estimate the depth of the modulation, and it seems to be about three decibels, or about a tenth the loudness of a whisper. In order to help subjects recognize these relatively faint effects I usually present signals with monaural beats and then suddenly change to the binaural mode. With tones of about 440 hertz it usually takes two or three seconds for the subject to recognize the binaural beats.

To produce a monaural beat that varies from a maximum to complete silence the loudness of the two signals must be identical; if the signals are mismatched, the instantaneous amplitude of the algebraic sum will always be greater than zero. As the difference in intensity increases, the beats become less distinct. Binaural beats, on the other hand, have the same apparent strength regardless of the relative intensities of the two tones. In fact, E. Lehnhardt, a Berlin audiologist, discovered that binaural beats are perceived even if one of the signals is below the threshold of hearing. J. J. Groen of the State University of Utrecht has studied this phenomenon. Working with tones of about 200 hertz, he found that beats were perceptible when one signal had a loudness of 40 decibels and the other a loudness of minus 20 decibels, a hundredth the loudness of barely audible sound. Evidently the brain is able to detect and process the signals even though one of them is too weak to impinge on consciousness. When the experiment is attempted monaurally, only the louder sound, without beats, is heard.

A perhaps related effect is the interaction of noise and binaural beats. Noise ordinarily masks sounds one wants to hear. For example, "static" sometimes overwhelms a weak radio signal. The perception of binaural beats, however, is enhanced by noise.

When two appropriate tones are presented to the ears so that binaural beats are produced, and are accompanied in each ear by noise just loud enough to obscure the tones, the beats become more distinct. In an analogous experiment with monaural signals only the noise will be heard. In the laboratory the source of noise is an electronic device that generates a random signal called white noise, which sounds something like the swish of the wind through swamp grass. When it is added to the signals at the proper loudness, the original tones cannot be heard, but the noise seems to be modulated by the beats. The enhancement of binaural beats by noise is explained by L. A. Jeffress and his colleagues at the University of Texas in terms of chance reinforcement. At any instant the amplitude of the noise will be more likely to be reinforced if the amplitudes of the signals are in coincidence. When the amplitudes of the signals are in opposition, destructive interference is more likely.

Listening to binaural beats produces the illusion that the sounds are located somewhere within the head. This in itself is hardly extraordinary: when music is played through stereophonic earphones, the orchestra seems to be somewhere in the head rather than "out there." It is intriguing, however, that when the beats are very infrequent, fewer than about three per second, they seem to move back and forth in the head. If the intensities of the two tones are different, the motion takes an elliptical path.

This apparent movement may be explained by the connection between binaural beats and the mechanism by which the brain senses the direction of sounds. For low-frequency signals, such as those used to produce binaural beats, sound is localized primarily by detecting the difference in phase between the sounds reaching the two ears [see "Auditory Localization," by Mark R. Rosenzweig; SCIENTIFIC AMERICAN Offprint 501]. Sounds of low frequency have wavelengths much longer than the diameter of the head; as a result the sound travels around the head by diffraction. Lord Rayleigh, the 19th-century English physicist, calculated that a tone of 256 hertz (middle C) striking the head from the side would reach the far ear with 90 percent of the intensity it had at the near ear. In other words, the head is not an obstruction to sounds of low pitch, and localization by the detection of relative intensity would be inefficient for those frequencies.

Localization by detection of phase dif-

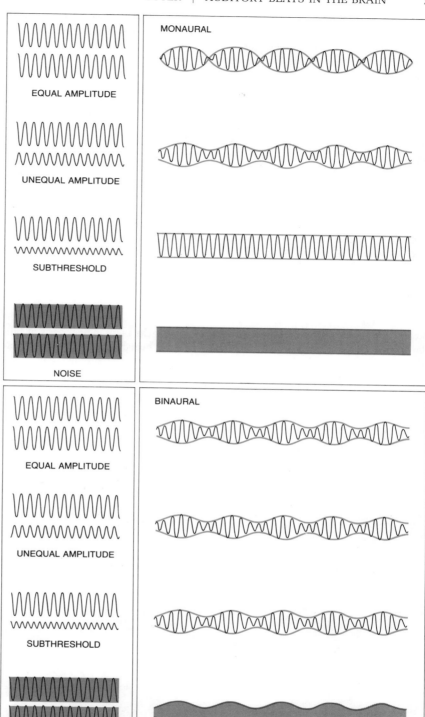

PERCEPTION OF BEATS depends on the manner in which tones are presented to the ears. In these schematic representations the applied tones at the left can be assumed to be of low pitch and separated in frequency by a small interval. The four diagrams at the top represent the monaural condition. When signals of the same intensity (*equal amplitude*) are combined, the beats vary from loudness to silence. With signals of different loudness (*unequal amplitude*) the intensity of the beats is reduced. When one tone is below the threshold of hearing (*subthreshold*), no beats are perceived. If the tones are accompanied by noise just loud enough to obscure them, again no beats are heard. In the four diagrams at the bottom, representing the binaural condition, the wave forms at the left are the same as those above but are presented to each ear separately. Under these conditions beats are heard whether the signals are of equal or of unequal amplitude and even if one is subthreshold. If noise masks the tones, binaural beats are still heard, modulating the noise.

ferences is highly efficient, however. In an open area with no reflecting structures one can locate a low-pitched sound to within 10 degrees. To do so requires detecting a phase difference of less than one millisecond, a feat accomplished without difficulty by the mechanism of binaural hearing. The same phase difference is present in the tones that produce binaural beats, which is why slow beats seem to be in motion. A source of sound revolving around the head would produce a similar sensation.

For sounds of higher pitch the wavelength is comparable to or smaller than the size of the head, and the head acts as a barrier, so that the ear in its shadow receives almost no sound. Above about 1,000 hertz sound localization is governed primarily by intensity rather than phase differences. It is significant that the ability to hear binaural beats also wanes when the tones presented approach 1,000 hertz. Direction-finding at the higher frequencies is less accurate than it is for low-pitched tones up to about 8,000 hertz, when the pinna (the external ear) becomes effective as an aid to localization.

The auditory mechanisms manifested in the perception of binaural beats aid human hearing in another way. It has often been observed that the ability to select and listen to a single conversation in a jumble of background noise is a remarkable and valuable human faculty. This phenomenon, sometimes called "the cocktail party effect," is dependent on binaural hearing. It is, in fact, an application of the enhancement of phase perception with noise also seen in the perception of binaural beats.

Hearing generally deteriorates with age. Yet I have found that older people are able to detect binaural beats and to locate sounds almost as well as the young. At 5,000 hertz the auditory acuity of a man of 60 is, on the average, 40 decibels below that of a man of 20, and the highest pitch he can hear, 8,000 hertz, is half that heard by the younger man. His acuity for low tones, however, is barely affected, and evidently his phase perception is also undiminished.

What is the neurological basis of binaural beats? The simplest explanation is that the number of nerve impulses from each ear and the route they travel to the brain are determined by the frequency of the incident sound, and that the two nerve signals interact somewhere in the brain.

One theory of the perception of pitch, called the telephone theory, was proposed by W. Rutherford in 1886. It postulated that the ear converts acoustic vibrations into electrical signals much as a microphone does, emitting one nerve impulse for each cycle of the tone. Single nerve fibers can respond to such stimuli only up to about 500 hertz, however, so that the telephone theory could describe the behavior of the ear only for the lowest frequencies. In 1865 Hermann von Helmholtz proposed the place theory, which ascribed pitch discrimination to the mechanical properties of the cochlea, or inner ear. The cochlea is a cone-shaped, fluid-filled vessel, rich in nerve endings and coiled like a snail shell. ("Cochlea" is Latin for snail.) The coiled tube of the cochlea is divided in half along its length by the basilar membrane, which vibrates in response to sound. Georg von Békésy found by direct visual observation that a sound of a certain frequency will make the basilar membrane bulge most noticeably in a certain place [see "The Ear," by Georg von Békésy; SCIENTIFIC AMERICAN Offprint 44]. This local stimulation, it is believed, excites receptor cells in the vicinity of the bulge and thus excites the nerve fibers connecting the receptor cells to the auditory area of the brain. Accord-

LOCATION OF THE SOURCE of a sound is determined for low-pitched tones by detecting the difference in phase between signals arriving at each ear. In this illustration a compression wave has reached the left ear while the right is near a maximum of rarefaction. By detecting such a phase difference the ears can find the direction of a low-frequency tone to an accuracy of about 10 degrees. At these frequencies little sound is blocked by the head; the wavelength is larger than the head and sound is diffracted around it.

ing to the place theory, the impulses transmitted by the auditory nerves reflect the intensity of the sound but not the frequency; what pitch is perceived is determined by the place on the cochlea where the nerve originates.

Above about 5,000 hertz the place theory seems to be adequate to describe pitch perception. At lower frequencies, however, the mechanical response of the basilar membrane is too unspecific to account for the precision with which the ear identifies tones. Furthermore, attempts to test the theory by excising in experimental animals those nerve fibers that should be the sole carriers of low-frequency tones have been unsuccessful.

For the frequencies between 500 and 5,000 hertz Ernest Glen Wever of Princeton University in 1939 proposed the volley theory. Although individual nerve fibers cannot fire more than 500 times per second, a group of nerve cells could exceed this rate by firing in succession, Wever suggested, much as platoons in an infantry company could fire their weapons in successive volleys. Thus while some nerve cells are in their refractory period others are producing pulses. The fading of binaural beats at frequencies between 500 and 1,000 hertz suggests that the mechanism of the beats follows the telephone theory and, at the higher frequencies, follows the related volley theory.

Interaction of the signals from the two ears probably occurs at the brain center named the superior olivary nucleus. As the messages ascend the auditory pathways to be processed and interpreted at higher centers, this is the first center in the brain to receive signals from both ears [*see illustration on page 83*]. Actually there are two superior olivary nuclei; they are arrayed symmetrically on each side of the brain, and each is a terminus for nerve fibers from both ears. They have long been considered likely sites for the neural processing of low-frequency sound impulses.

In experiments with cats Robert Galambos showed in 1959 that loud clicks stimulating both ears generate nerve impulses that meet in the superior olivary nucleus. When the clicks are simultaneous, the signals are reinforced at some site in the superior olivary nucleus. When a slight delay is introduced, however, the resulting signal is inhibited. Thus a small phase shift gives rise to a weaker perception of sound. It is presumably for this reason that one tends to turn toward the source of a sound and eliminate the phase difference. When one is listening through earphones, of course, turning the head has no effect on the phase of the signals.

Nerve potentials at the superior olivary nucleus of the cat have been measured directly. With human subjects it is possible to measure these signals by recording evoked potentials: small changes in the electrical properties of the scalp produced as a result of activity of the brain. Because they are objective indicators of certain brain functions evoked potentials have clinical applications. For example, in cases of possible hysterical blindness evoked potentials from the scalp above the occipital lobes can determine whether or not the brain is receiving visual information. Similarly, evoked potentials can be used to detect deafness in infants, which is otherwise quite difficult to diagnose. The potentials are very small (measured in microvolts) and are obscured by many random signals not associated with the stimulus. They can be measured on an oscilloscope, but special procedures must be followed.

First, the horizontal sweep of the oscilloscope must be synchronized with the stimulus; this is done by using the stimulus current to trigger the start of

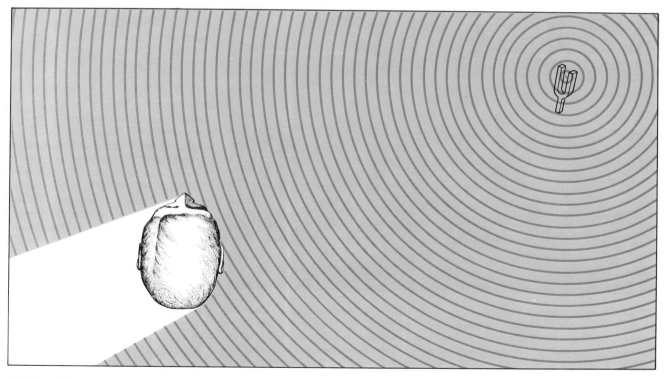

HIGH-FREQUENCY SOUND LOCALIZATION also requires binaural hearing, but differences in intensity rather than phase are detected. The wavelength of a high-pitched tone is smaller than the diameter of the head and a distinct sonic shadow is formed; thus one ear receives more sound than the other. This mode of sound localization is less accurate than phase detection except at very high frequencies. The transition takes place at about 1,000 hertz; at this frequency too the perception of binaural beats wanes.

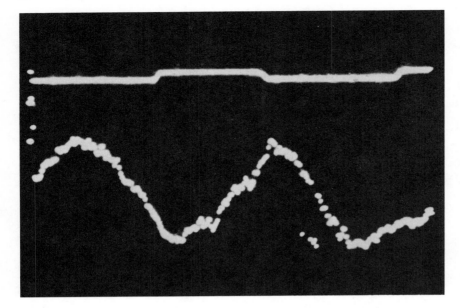

EVOKED POTENTIALS for subjects listening to monaural beats are shown in a photo-graph of an oscilloscope screen made by the author with Adam Atkin and Neil Wother-spoon at the Mount Sinai School of Medicine. Tones of 300 hertz and 303 hertz were pre-sented to each ear; an electrode attached to the scalp was used to measure electric potentials in the skin evoked by underlying electrical activity in the brain. By synchronizing the hori-zontal sweep of the oscilloscope with the beat frequency it was possible to correlate these small potentials (measured in microvolts) with the stimulus. The steplike wave form at the top of the screen is a signal used to time the oscilloscope sweep; the rise of each pulse cor-responds to the moment of maximum loudness of the beat. The periodic wave below it re-cords the evoked potentials. It consists of the average values for each point on the curve, determined by a small computer (a signal-averager) after many iterations of the procedure.

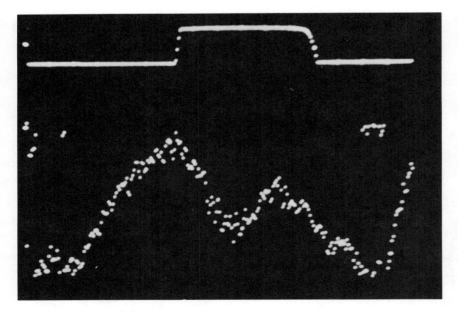

BINAURAL EXPERIMENT was conducted under the same conditions, except that the tones were presented separately to each ear. Evoked potentials were once again successfully recorded, but they differed from those detected under monaural conditions in amplitude, in wave form and in timing with respect to the stimulus. These differences suggest that binau-ral beats are processed in another way or at another site in the brain than monaural beats are. In the illustration the amplitude of the evoked potentials appears to be about the same as it is for monaural beats; it is actually much smaller. For clarity the vertical scale of the oscilloscope has been expanded, as can be seen by comparing the apparent amplitudes of the timing signals. In both illustrations bright areas not associated with the main wave form are extraneous signals produced by residual noise generated in the recording apparatus.

the sweep. In addition, a great many tracings must be made in order to obtain unambiguous data. A computer known as a signal-averager stores a series of tracings electronically, then on com-mand adds the instantaneous potentials of all the tracings to produce a com-posite signal. Because the extraneous random potentials have no fixed phase relation to the stimulus they are progres-sively suppressed as the number of trac-ings increases.

If binaural and monaural beats are in-deed processed at different sites in the brain, it should be possible to detect this difference by measuring the evoked po-tentials. With my colleagues at the Mount Sinai School of Medicine, Adam Atkin and Neil Wotherspoon, I set out to test this hypothesis. Because the stim-ulus was a continuous tone rather than a brief click, it proved particularly diffi-cult to obtain clear tracings. Eventually we learned that for effective results the subject must concentrate on the beats while in total darkness. This is a boring task, since the binaural beats are indis-tinct and many tracings must be aver-aged. Often the subject experiences auditory hallucinations imposing a spu-rious pattern on the sound, which spoils the results. Nevertheless, after many iterations of this procedure we were able to demonstrate that the evoked potentials produced by binaural and monaural beats differ qualitatively and quantitatively, indicating that they are processed differently [see illustrations at left].

Binaural beats may have clinical ap-plications. With some of my stu-dents I examined a number of neurologi-cal patients and discovered that a few could not hear binaural beats. Among these patients a few could not localize sounds (produced by the examiner's snapping his fingers). It may be signifi-cant that some of those who could not hear the beats suffered from Parkinson's disease, a disorder of the central nervous system characterized by a lack of spon-taneous muscular activity, an immobile facial expression and tremor. One pa-tient, a violinist, was unable to hear bin-aural beats when he entered the hospi-tal. As his treatment continued he be-gan to perceive the beats produced by the very lowest tones, and gradually he progressed to higher frequencies. At the end of a week, when his condition was considered satisfactory, he could hear beats produced by tones up to about 650 hertz.

A sex-related variation in the ability

to hear binaural beats has also been discovered. J. V. Tobias of the Federal Aviation Administration in Oklahoma City studied the binaural-beat spectrum of a number of volunteers and found that the upper limit of the applied frequencies is higher for men than for women [*see lower illustration on next page*]. He went on to monitor the perceptions of three women over a period of six weeks and found that the spectrum extended to the highest tones at the beginning of menstruation, then declined before reaching a second peak 15 days after the onset of menstruation. The latter peak may correspond to the time of ovulation, when a woman is most fertile.

I have tested a few women of reproductive age, with results that tend to confirm Tobias' findings. It appears that some women do show marked variations

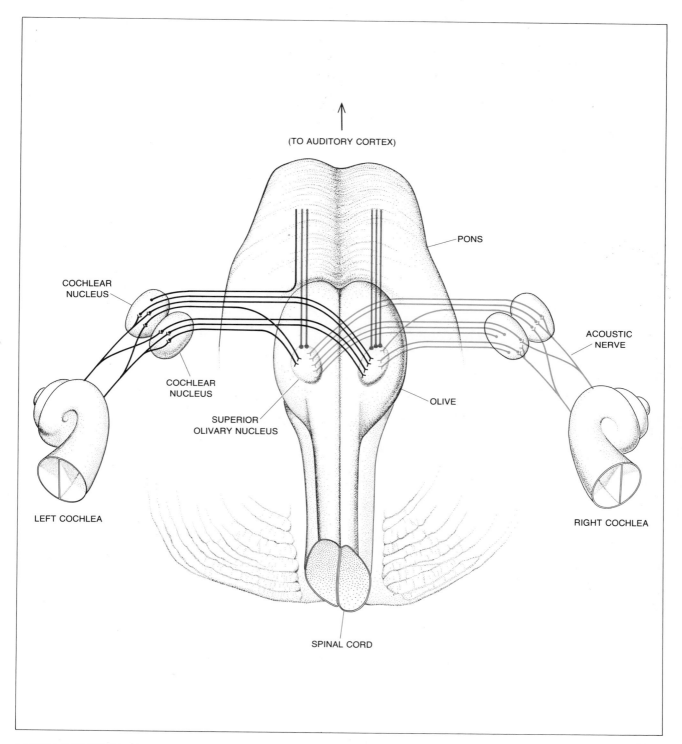

LOWER AUDITORY CENTERS of the brain are in the medulla oblongata, viewed here schematically from the back of the neck. Nerve impulses from the right (*color*) and left (*black*) ears first meet in the left or right superior olivary nucleus. These structures are part of the olive, an organ that in this view lies behind the brain stem. It is probable that binaural beats are detected here.

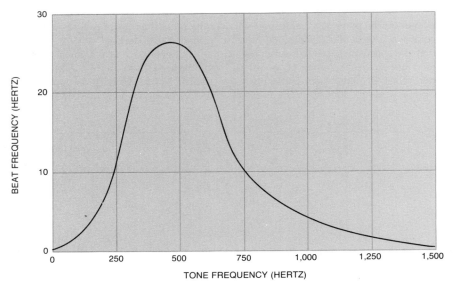

SPECTRUM OF BINAURAL BEATS was measured by J. C. R. Licklider, J. C. Webster and J. M. Hedlum. Rapid beats, up to about 26 per second, can be heard when the tones used to produce them are about 440 hertz. With tones of higher or lower pitch the maximum beat frequency declines. When the interval exceeds about 30 hertz, two tones are heard.

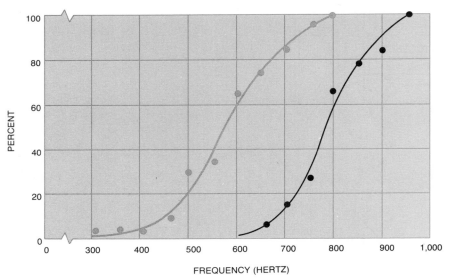

SEX-RELATED VARIATION in the perception of binaural beats is plotted from data compiled by J. V. Tobias. As the pitch of the tones used to produce beats increases, both men (*black*) and women (*color*) cease to perceive them. Women, however, lose the ability at lower frequencies. Some female subjects also report variations during the menstrual cycle.

in the perception of binaural beats during the menstrual cycle. When the beats are not heard, women often hear two separate tones. Men, on the other hand, show no variation during the month. These results suggest that the binaural-beat spectrum may be influenced by the level of estrogen in the blood.

Binaural beats have been widely regarded as a mere curiosity. A recent textbook on hearing does not mention them at all. Yet the measurement of binaural beats can explain the processes by which sounds are located, a crucial aspect of perception. The enhancement of the beats by noise is a model of the mechanism by which auditory messages are sorted from a noisy background. That subthreshold sounds are effectively rendered audible by binaural beats suggests that there may be other stimuli processed by the brain of which we are not aware. Finally, it is possible that hormonally induced physiological or behavioral changes too subtle to detect by ordinary means may be made apparent by measuring the binaural-beat spectrum.

The Superior Colliculus of the Brain

by Barbara Gordon
December 1972

The cells of this small region in the mammalian midbrain appear to help the eye detect and follow moving objects. They may do the same for the stimuli of hearing and touch

In order to survive an animal must be able to respond quickly to moving objects as soon as they enter its field of vision. The animal must rapidly determine the source of the visual stimulus and the speed and direction of its movement. Then the animal must move its head and eyes to hold the source of the stimulus in view. By the same token an animal must move its head and eyes to search for the source of a moving sound or an object brushing past its body. One might therefore predict that if one were able to identify the region of the brain involved in controlling the position of the head and eyes, one would discover that the region is responsive to different types of stimuli: visual, auditory and somatic.

Evidence is rapidly accumulating that one region of the mammalian brain intimately involved in the control of head and eye movements consists of two bumps on the upper surface of the midbrain long familiar to anatomists as the superior colliculus. (Colliculus means little hill.) By using microelectrodes to record the response of individual cells in the superior colliculus to various stimuli it has been found that this neural structure indeed receives sensory information from the animal's visual, auditory and somatic systems. In lower vertebrates the superior colliculus serves as the main visual center. In higher vertebrates much of the processing of visual information has been taken over by the visual area of the cerebral cortex. The superior colliculus, however, still receives nerve impulses directly from the optic nerve as well as impulses relayed from the visual cortex. In addition the deeper layers of the superior colliculus receive nerve inputs from the auditory and somatic systems. Recent experiments suggest that the deep layers of the superior colliculus may contain superposed topographic maps of the visual, auditory and somatic fields. Although these maps are somewhat crude, they may assist an animal in responding quickly and effectively to the ever changing stimuli presented by a complex three-dimensional environment.

In each sensory system the processing of information from the outside world begins when an electrical signal is generated in a suitable receptor by an adequate stimulus. Thus light activates the visual system, sound the auditory system and touch or joint movement the somatic system. This initial electrical signal is graded, that is, the stronger the stimulus, the larger the signal. If the electrical signal generated in the receptor is large enough, it eventually results in the generation of an action potential, or nerve impulse, in a nerve cell. Action potentials are the signals that are transmitted along the axon, the fiber of the nerve cell. Sometimes an action potential is generated in the same cell that produces the initial graded response to the stimulus. Sometimes the graded signal is transmitted across several cells before it reaches a cell that can generate an action potential. All action potentials carried by an axon are quite similar in shape and amplitude. Therefore all information about the stimulus must be coded by which cells fire and by the pattern of their firing.

Most of the complex processing of sensory information goes on not within

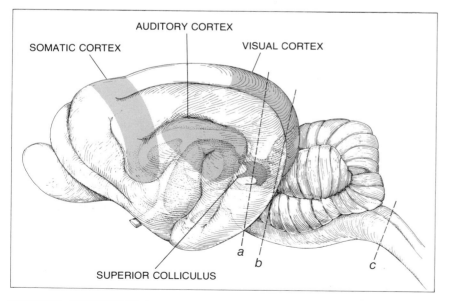

AUDITORY CORTEX

SOMATIC CORTEX

VISUAL CORTEX

SUPERIOR COLLICULUS

a *b* *c*

SUPERIOR COLLICULUS is a receiving terminal for nerve impulses from the eye, the visual cortex, the auditory cortex, the spinal cord, the brain stem and the somatic cortex. The drawing shows a cat's brain from the side. The principal nerve pathways are shown in relation to sections *a*, *b*, *c* (plus a spinal-cord section) in the illustration shown on page 87.

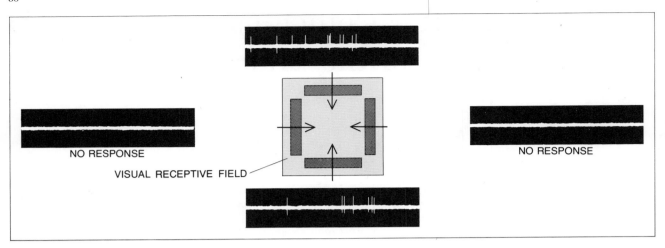

STUDIES OF VISUAL CORTEX of the cat led to the surprising finding that most of the complex cells in that part of the brain respond only to specific visual fields and only to specific stimuli entering those fields. David H. Hubel and Torsten N. Wiesel of the Harvard Medical School found, for example, that certain complex cortical cells respond strongly to a dark horizontal bar moved slowly up and down in the cell's visual receptive field (*colored square*) but not at all to same bar moved horizontally. Other cells respond to other shapes, orientations and movements. The author extended such studies to the superior colliculus (*see illustrations below*).

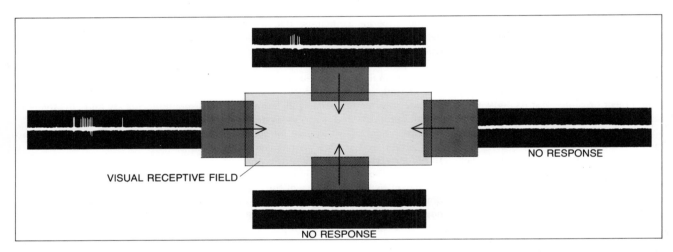

RESPONSE OF COLLICULAR CELL lying in the intermediate gray layer is distinctly different from that of a typical complex cell in the visual cortex. The cell responds strongly when a dark "tongue" is moved into the cell's visual receptive field (*colored rectangle*) from the left, responds less strongly when the tongue enters the field from above and responds not at all when it enters from either the right or the bottom. The visual receptive field is 10 degrees wide and four degrees high; tongue is three degrees wide.

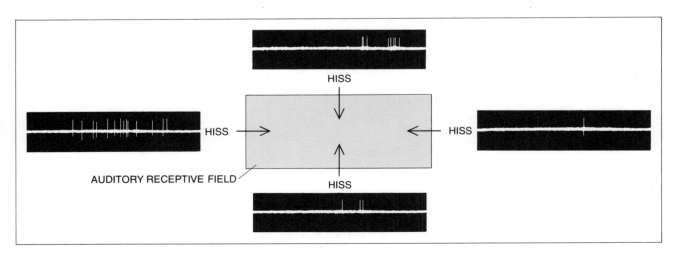

AUDITORY RESPONSE is also exhibited by the collicular cell whose response to visual stimuli is illustrated above. The sound stimulus is the hiss of a partially constricted air hose that is moved across the auditory receptive field in direction indicated by arrows.

the sense organ itself but within the brain and spinal cord. Sensory information is conveyed from the sense organ to the brain by action potentials traveling along axons. The terminal of each axon makes contact with other nerve cells in the brain at the junctions called synapses. At most synapses the arrival of an action potential results in the release of a small amount of chemical transmitter. The transmitter substance flows across the synaptic cleft onto the outer membrane of the next cell: the "postsynaptic" cell. The effect of this chemical substance on the postsynaptic cell can be either excitatory or inhibitory, that is, it can either increase or decrease the probability that the postsynaptic cell will generate an action potential.

Information from each type of sense organ is processed along a separate sensory pathway. A sensory pathway consists of peripheral sense organs and several clusters of nerve cells called nuclei. Sensory information is processed in several stages, so that each nucleus receives input from the preceding one, processes the input and sends an output to the next nucleus.

Each primary sensory pathway ends in a specific area of the cerebral cortex termed a primary sensory receiving area. For most sensory systems we know quite a lot about how stimulus properties are coded by individual cells along the pathway from the sense organ to the cortex. (The auditory system is somewhat less well understood than the visual and somatic ones.) Little is known, however, about how the outputs of the cortical receiving areas are used by the remainder of the brain. The visual system is to some extent an exception: the functioning of two visual areas beyond the primary visual cortex is fairly well understood.

Since each cell along the sensory pathway can receive excitatory and inhibitory inputs from a large variety of sensory receptors and from a large variety of other nerve cells, the precise stimulus requirements for a cell can quickly become quite complicated. For example, visual information from the receptors is processed in a rather complex way before it ever leaves the retina [see "Retinal Processing of Visual Images," by Charles R. Michael Offprint 1143]. The retinal ganglion cells, the cells sending their axons from the eye to the brain, represent the final stage in this processing. These cells receive their visual input, by way of several layers of retinal cells, from a large number of visual receptors. Retinal ganglion cells can be influenced

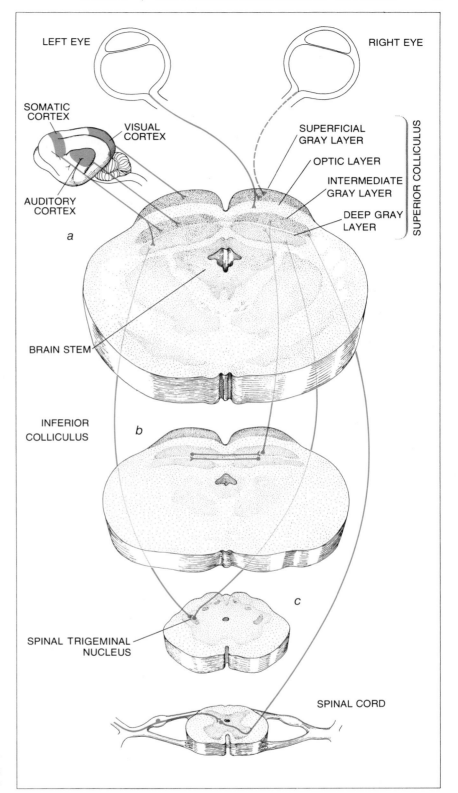

VARIETY OF SENSORY STIMULI converge on the superior colliculus, which is shown here in section (*a*). For simplicity and emphasis only one set of contralateral nerve pathways from the eyes and the spinal cord are depicted. The nerve projections from the spinal trigeminal complex (*c*), however, are bilateral and are so drawn. The retinal projection goes chiefly to the superficial gray layer and optic layer of the superior colliculus. A secondary projection from the ipsilateral eye is shown by a broken line. Nerve projections from the auditory cortex and the inferior colliculus (which is part of the auditory system) terminate chiefly in intermediate and deep gray layers. Projections from somatic cortex, somatic brain-stem nuclei and spinal cord also go mostly to intermediate and deep gray layers.

by light in a small, roughly circular region of the retina. That region is known as the cell's receptive field. The receptive field consists of two regions: a central circular region and a concentric surround. The firing of the cell is increased by a light shining on the central region and decreased by a light shining on the surround, or vice versa.

By the time visual information has reached the visual cortex, each cell has more complex stimulus requirements. For example, many cells in the visual cortex fire only when their receptive fields are stimulated by light or dark bars or edges with a specific orientation, a specific width and a specific length [see "The Visual Cortex of the Brain," by David H. Hubel; SCIENTIFIC AMERICAN, Offprint 168]. Similarly, the auditory system incorporates cells that respond to a sound only if that sound is within a specific frequency band and is within a specific portion of the auditory field. Cells in the somatic system usually respond only to one kind of stimulus (touch, hair movement or joint movement) in one region of the body.

In summary, most cells that are part of a primary sensory pathway respond only to stimuli that meet fairly rigid requirements. Such cells are well designed to determine exactly what the stimulus is, for example how big, how wide or how long. Cells with rigid stimulus requirements are not well designed, however, to help an animal orient itself to a poorly perceived stimulus so that it can better determine the precise nature of the stimulus. A significant part of this task may be performed by the superior colliculus. Not only does the superior colliculus receive a great deal of precise sensory information but also it receives each kind of information over at least two pathways.

First, it receives input from cells that are also part of the pathway leading to the cortex. Second, it receives input from the cortical sensory receiving areas. Visual input reaches the colliculus directly from the retinal ganglion cells and from the visual cortex. Auditory input originates both in the inferior colliculus and in the auditory cortex. Somatic information reaches the superior colliculus directly from the spinal cord, from the dorsal-column nuclei and from the somatic cortex [see illustration on page 87].

It has been known for a long time that the visual information received by the superior colliculus is topographically organized. Each of the two bumps of the superior colliculus receives information from the contralateral visual field.

In other words, the left colliculus sees the right visual field (that is, the entire visual field to the right of a fixation point) and the right colliculus sees the left visual field. The projections from the retina and the cortex to the colliculus are precisely organized. Each portion of the superior colliculus receives input from retinal cells and from cortical cells that respond to the same portion of the visual field. Cells in the front portion of the colliculus have receptive fields near the fixation point; cells in the rear portion of the colliculus have receptive fields in the peripheral regions of the retina. Cells in the portion of the colliculus nearest the midline of the brain have receptive fields in the upper portion of the visual field and cells in the portion of the colliculus nearest the side of the brain have receptive fields in the lower portion of the visual field. Recent experiments in my laboratory at the University of Oregon have shown that the auditory and somatic inputs to the colliculus are also topographically organized, although the topography is not as precise for these stimuli as it is for the visual input.

Many different types of experiment have been done in the attempt to find out how the superior colliculus of cats and primates processes sensory information and what kinds of information the colliculus provides to the rest of the brain. (Experiments on other species will not be discussed here.) Although most of these experiments have concentrated on the processing of visual information, they have also provided some knowledge about the way the colliculus utilizes auditory and somatic information.

Perhaps the oldest method used is the lesion method. The colliculus can be eliminated from the brain of an experimental animal by removing it surgically or by passing large amounts of electric current through it. After making such a lesion one can compare the responses of normal and lesioned animals to a large variety of stimuli. The results of these experiments are difficult to interpret in detail for several reasons. First of all, it is difficult to make precisely the same lesion twice. Second, a lesion that removes the entire colliculus frequently invades surrounding areas, whereas lesions that are strictly confined to the colliculus frequently do not succeed in removing the entire structure. Third, the fact that a particular kind of behavior remains after a collicular lesion does not mean that the colliculus has no influence on that behavior. A few clear facts have nonetheless emerged from the lesion studies.

Tauba Pasik, Pedro Pasik and Morris B. Bender of the Mount Sinai School of Medicine have shown that removing the colliculus either unilaterally (on one side of the brain) or bilaterally (on both sides of the brain) does not eliminate eye movements. Although the animals showed some deficits in eye movement immediately after the lesion, one month later all the animals could move their eyes spontaneously in all directions and exhibited normal reflex eye movements in response to a particular kind of stimulation of the ear canal (flushing the canal with cold or hot water). Apparently normal eye movements were also obtained when the animals were placed inside a rotating drum lined with vertical black and white stripes.

James M. Sprague and Thomas H. Meikle, Jr., of the University of Pennsylvania School of Medicine have done an extensive study on the effects of superior colliculus lesions in cats. They found that immediately after a unilateral lesion had been made the animals were completely unable to follow objects in the visual field contralateral to the lesioned colliculus, although they could move their eyes in all directions. (Remember that each colliculus receives visual information only from the contralateral visual field.)

A month later the animals responded to visual stimuli in the contralateral field if the stimuli were within 60 degrees of the midline. The animals rarely responded to stimuli presented beyond 60 degrees into the contralateral visual field. Immediately after the lesion had been made the animals failed to orient themselves consistently to sounds in the contralateral auditory field, and the pinna (the external ear structure) contralateral to the lesion did not move in response to sound. Although orienting responses to auditory stimuli gradually improved with time, they never became entirely normal. For the first month after the lesion had been made the animals were also unable to localize somatic stimuli on the contralateral side of the body.

Bilateral collicular lesions, like unilateral ones, did not eliminate eye movement. Even immediately after the lesions had been made the animals showed approximately normal eye movements in response to rotation of their bodies. The animals were unable, however, to visually locate small stationary objects or to follow them. They also had some difficulty in lifting their gaze above the horizontal. Although the

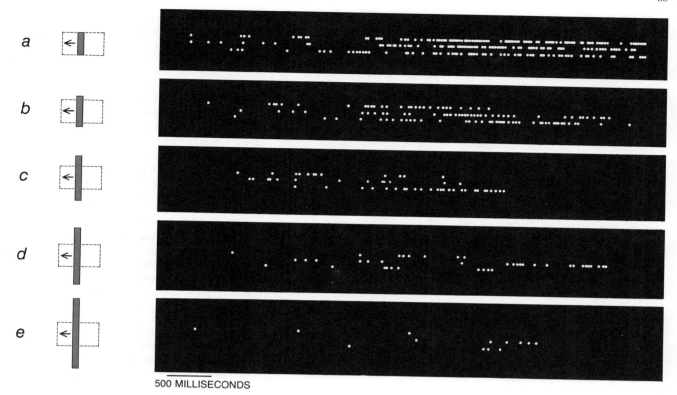

INCREASING SIZE OF STIMULUS, in this case a moving slit of light against a dark surround, evokes a smaller and smaller response from a cell in the superficial portion of the colliculus. The author has found that the maximum response results when the slit matches the width of the visual receptive field (*a*). When the slit is longer, it invades the suppressive region of the receptive field, and the response decreases. Each dot in the illustration represents a nerve impulse in three successive recordings for each stimulus.

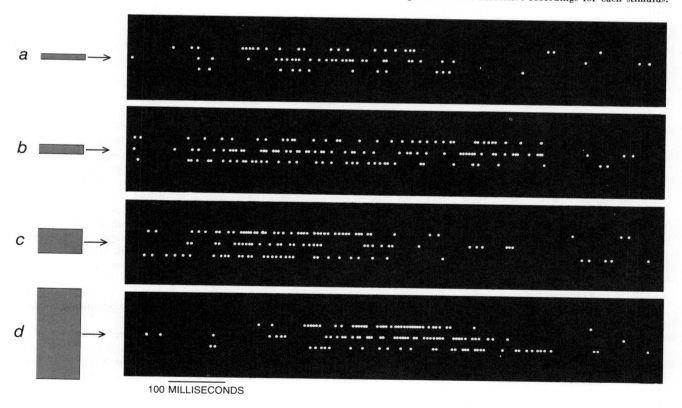

RESPONSE OF CELL DEEPER in the colliculus is not suppressed when the size of the stimulus is increased. The deep cell also has a much larger visual receptive field than the cell whose response is shown in the illustration at the top of the page. The deep cell responds to any moving stimulus in the entire contralateral visual field, beginning in a region that is 11 degrees contralateral to the center of vision. This is not a general finding; more than half of the cells in the deeper layers do have suppressive regions.

ability of the animal to localize objects in space improved greatly during the second month following the lesion, it never became entirely normal. These experiments suggest that whereas the cat's ability to make eye movements does not depend on an intact superior colliculus, the superior colliculus does contribute to the animal's ability to use head and eye movements to localize sensory stimuli accurately and to follow them.

This general interpretation is supported by some quite recent experiments conducted at the National Institute of Mental Health by Robert H. Wurtz and Michael E. Goldberg. They have trained monkeys to sit in a chair and to move their eyes from one visual target to another. The monkeys were initially trained to fixate on a small light. When the light went off and a second light went on, the monkeys learned to shift their gaze to fixate on the second target. Wurtz and Goldberg then made a lesion in the portion of the colliculus containing the cells that responded to the second target. After the lesion had been made the animals were still able to move their eyes toward the second target, but the eye movements took from 150 to 300 milliseconds longer than they had before the lesion had been made. This deficit, like other deficits following collicular lesions, waned over a period of several weeks. Although the monkeys, unlike the cats, did not lose their ability to orient themselves to visual stimuli after collicular lesions had been made, they could not do so as efficiently after the operation as before it. The collicular-lesion experiments on cats and monkeys may not be entirely comparable, however, because Sprague and Meikle removed the entire colliculus of their cats whereas Wurtz and Goldberg made large but incomplete lesions in their monkeys.

If the superior colliculus aids an animal in changing its fixation point and in responding to visual stimuli, collicular lesions might be expected to impair performance in a pattern-discrimination task, if the task requires frequent changes in fixation point. Sprague and his colleagues have shown this to be the case in another series of experiments on cats. They found that superior colliculus lesions did not impair a cat's ability to discriminate between two patterns if the task was learned before the lesion was made but greatly impaired the animal's ability to learn new discrimination tasks of the same type.

Perhaps performing a previously learned pattern-discrimination task re-

quires only a single shift of fixation point. The animal already knows what the correct stimulus looks like. If the first stimulus it inspects is incorrect, it has only to shift its gaze to the correct stimulus. When the animal is learning a new discrimination, it may have to shift its gaze from one stimulus to the other many times in order to determine what features distinguish the correct stimulus from the incorrect one. Collicular lesions seem to make the latter task much more difficult.

A second technique that has been used to elucidate the role of the colliculus in controlling eye movement is electrical stimulation. If electrodes are inserted into the colliculus and small amounts of electric current are passed through them, action potentials will be evoked in a large number of cells near the electrode. (The current must be kept small so as not to produce collicular lesions.) Electrical stimulation causes large numbers of cells to fire synchronously, whereas in response to natural sensory stimuli cells probably fire in precisely determined sequences. In spite of the abnormal firing patterns that must result from electrical stimulation, eye movements in any given direction can be evoked by stimulation of the appropriate location in the colliculus. Peter H. Schiller of the Massachusetts Institute of Technology has found that the current required to evoke eye movements by stimulating the superior colliculus is only between a third and a tenth of the current required to evoke eye movements by stimulating the visual cortex or the frontal eye fields (a more forward cortical area that may be involved in eye-movement control). This observation suggests, but does not prove, that the colliculus is more directly involved in eye movements than either the visual cortex or the frontal eye fields.

Schiller and David A. Robinson of the Johns Hopkins School of Medicine independently observed that the size and direction of eye movements evoked by the electrical stimulation of the colliculus depended on the exact location of the stimulating electrodes. The eye moved to the portion of the visual field that is mapped onto the stimulated portion of the colliculus. For example, stimulation of the medial colliculus evoked upward eye movements, and the more medial the stimulation, the larger the upward component of the eye movement. Increasing the duration of the stimulus did not increase the extent of the eye movement but resulted instead

in a series of eye movements, each having the same magnitude and direction as the others. The eye movements resulting from collicular stimulation were independent of the initial position of the eye in the socket.

This result implies that the colliculus codes eye movement rather than eye position. Presumably the activity of cells in a particular part of the colliculus indicates the position of the stimulus with respect to the current center of gaze of the animal and not with respect to the center of the head. For instance, if an animal wants to change its fixation point to fixate on an object that suddenly appears in the visual field at a position 20 degrees above and 10 degrees to the right of the current point of fixation, it will have to make an eye movement with a vertical component of 20 degrees upward and a horizontal component of 10 degrees to the right. And of course the extent and direction of the eye movement must be independent of the initial position of the center of gaze with respect to the head.

A third method of studying the superior colliculus is to examine the sensory receptive fields of collicular cells and compare them with the sensory receptive fields of cells in the primary sensory pathways. This kind of study has been pursued most intensively with collicular cells that respond to visual stimuli, although some properties of cells that respond to auditory and somatic stimuli have also been investigated. A few years ago Peter Sterling and I, working in the laboratory of David H. Hubel and Torsten N. Wiesel at the Harvard Medical School, set out to study the receptive fields of cells in the superficial layers of the superior colliculus of cats. In our experiments the cat faced a screen 57 inches away. While a microelectrode was lowered through the colliculus, patterns of light and dark stimuli, such as light and dark bars and tongue-shaped figures, were shown on the screen. We attempted to find the receptive field for each cell we recorded from and to characterize the visual stimuli that were most effective in evoking action potentials from the cell.

The first thing we noticed was that the collicular receptive fields were usually from two to four times bigger than the receptive fields of the visual cortex cells whose receptive fields are in the same portion of the visual field. We also noticed that most collicular cells responded only to moving stimuli. Stationary stimuli that were flashed on and off within the receptive field were almost completely ineffective for most cells. About three-quarters of the cells tested were also directionally selective. That means that they responded well to movement in one direction and poorly or not at all to movement in the diametrically opposite direction. Hubel and Wiesel had previously shown that many cells in the visual cortex are also directionally selective.

The directional selectivity of cells in the cortex, however, is quite different from the directional selectivity of cells in the colliculus. First, changing the orientation of the stimulus and the direction of its movement from the optimum to 20 or 30 degrees away from optimum causes a profound decrease in the response of cortical cells but caused little or no decrease in the response of collicular cells. In fact, stimuli moving 90 degrees to the preferred direction often evoked quite a vigorous response from collicular cells, although

such stimuli would be completely ineffective for cortical cells.

Hence collicular cells responded over a much wider range of directions of movement than cortical cells do. Second, for collicular cells the null direction, the direction that evokes the least response, was always diametrically opposite to the preferred direction, whereas for cortical cells the null direction is 90 degrees to the preferred direction and movement opposite to the preferred direction usually evokes some response [see two upper illustrations on page 86]. Third, there is no indication in the visual cortex that any one preferred direction is commoner than any other.

In the colliculus, however, the distribution of preferred directions was nonuniform in two respects. In the first place, for most directionally selective units the preferred direction was either parallel to the horizontal meridian of

the visual field or made an angle of less than 45 degrees to it. In the second place, for more than three-quarters of the directionally selective units the horizontal component of the preferred direction was away from the center of gaze and toward the periphery of the visual field. Therefore most units recorded in the right colliculus had receptive fields in the left field of vision and responded best to movement going from right to left. This result has been confirmed and extended by the work of M. Straschill and K. P. Hoffman of the Max Planck Institute for Psychiatry in Munich, who found that cells with receptive fields in the upper portion of the visual field had preferred directions with upward vertical components, whereas cells with receptive fields in the lower portion of the visual field had preferred directions with downward vertical components.

We also observed that cortical cells are much fussier about the size and shape of the stimulus than collicular cells. A typical complex cortical cell responds only to a slit, a bar or an edge. Cortical cells also have stringent requirements for the width and orientation of the stimulus. Hypercomplex cortical cells require that the stimulus also have a specific length.

In contrast, most collicular cells responded well to a wide range of stimulus sizes and shapes. For some 90 percent of the cells, however, the receptive field consisted of both an activating region and a suppressive region just outside the activating one. Stimuli confined to the activating region (even if they were much smaller than that region) evoked a vigorous response. If, however, the stimulus was made large enough to invade the suppressive region, the cell's firing rate began to decrease [see top illustration on page 89]. Thus cells in the superficial layers of the cat's superior colliculus tend to be more responsive to small moving objects than they are to large ones.

The relative insensitivity of collicular cells to the size, shape and orientation of stimuli suggests that the colliculus is not concerned with exactly what the stimulus is but is primarily concerned with its direction of movement. Superior colliculus cells are most likely to be activated if the stimulus is moving toward the periphery of the visual field. That is exactly the information an animal needs in order to control its head and eye movements and prevent a stimulus from leaving its visual field.

Sterling and I were puzzled about

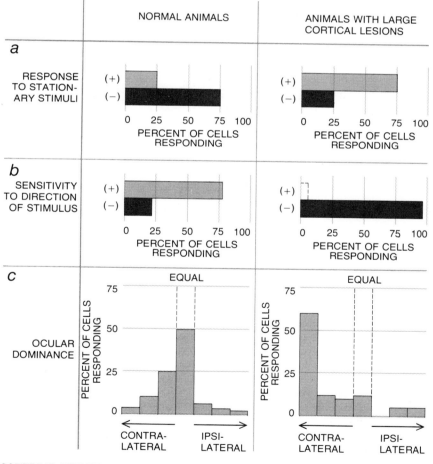

CORTICAL INFLUENCE ON COLLICULUS was studied by removing most of the visual cortex of cats. Three main effects were observed. In animals with large cortical lesions most collicular cells respond to stationary stimuli, whereas in normal animals most cells are unresponsive (a). After emplacement of lesions collicular cells are no longer sensitive to direction visual stimuli are moving (b). In animals with cortical lesions most of the collicular cells respond almost exclusively to stimulation of the contralateral eye, whereas almost all collicular cells in normal animals can be driven by stimulation of either eye (c).

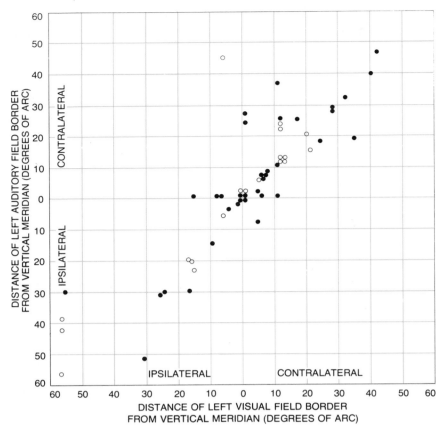

VISUAL AND AUDITORY RECEPTIVE FIELDS, when mapped for deep collicular cells, exhibit a high degree of congruence. The solid dots represent the location of the leading borders of the receptive fields for cells that responded to both visual and auditory stimuli. The open circles represent location of leading receptive-field borders for cells that respond only to auditory stimuli. The position of the visual receptive-field borders for such cells was assumed to be the field border of the nearest cell that responded to visual stimuli.

why collicular cells should exhibit such loose requirements for the size and shape of stimuli, considering that they receive sensory input from visual-cortex cells that have precise stimulus requirements. In order to investigate the function of the cortical input to the colliculus we removed the visual cortex from several cats. Two weeks after removal of the visual cortex we found three changes in the properties of collicular receptive fields [*see illustration on preceding page*].

First, we found no cells that we could be certain were directionally selective. Second, nearly all the cells were now driven only by the contralateral eye. In the normal colliculus most of the cells can be driven by either eye. This result is what one would expect from the anatomy. Most cortical cells are binocularly driven and therefore the collicular cells with which they are connected by synapses are also binocularly driven. The retinal input to the colliculus, on the other hand, is primarily from the contralateral eye; relatively little input is from the ipsilateral eye. Third, some-

what more cells could be driven by stationary stimuli flashed on and off within the receptive field in the lesioned animals than in normal animals.

Although many of the precise features of cortical receptive fields are lost when the axons of many cortical cells converge on a single collicular cell, the essential properties of collicular receptive fields depend on the presence of the cortical projection to the colliculus. Thus the colliculus cannot perform its normal function without receiving the results of the cortical processing of visual information.

When I moved to the University of Oregon, I became increasingly interested in investigating the properties of cells in the deeper layers of the cat's superior colliculus. Sterling and I had not studied these cells at Harvard because we found that in animals anesthetized with barbiturates, which we had used in our experiments, the cells simply did not respond to sensory stimulation. At Oregon I developed a procedure, similar to one used in a num-

ber of other laboratories, in which collicular cells could be studied in an unanesthetized animal.

The animals involved in these experiments were prepared several weeks before the actual recording by implantation in their skulls of four sterile bolts and a well with a screw-on cap. During the experiments the animal's head was supported by the bolts and the electrode was lowered through the well. Thus the animals had no open wounds or pressure points and did not have to be anesthetized. I found that most of the cells in the deeper layers have visual receptive fields that are quite similar to the visual receptive fields of cells in the superficial layers. The fields, however, were extremely large, sometimes covering an entire quadrant or half of the visual field. Moreover, the deep cells responded to an even wider variety of stimulus sizes and shapes than the superficial cells.

The most striking change encountered when the electrode left the superficial layers and entered the deeper layers was the presence of cells that responded to auditory and somatic stimuli. Some cells responded only to auditory stimuli or somatic stimuli, but a large number responded to both visual and auditory stimuli and a few to both visual and somatic stimuli. Cells that responded to auditory stimuli responded most vigorously to complex sounds such as the hiss made by air moving through a partially constricted hose.

The most striking characteristic of cells responding to both auditory and visual stimuli was that many of their requirements for auditory stimuli were similar to their requirements for visual stimuli. The cells had auditory receptive fields just as they had visual receptive fields. That is, they did not respond to sounds placed anywhere with respect to the cat's ears just as they did not respond to visual stimuli placed anywhere with respect to the cat's eyes. In fact, there was a striking correlation, although far from an exact correspondence, between the position of the leading edge of the visual receptive field and the position of the leading edge of the auditory receptive field. (The leading edge of the receptive field is the edge where the stimulus first evokes a response from a collicular cell as it enters the receptive field in the preferred direction.) Thus the colliculus embodies not only a topographic map of visual space but also a topographic map of auditory space.

Most of the cells that respond to sound required a moving stimulus.

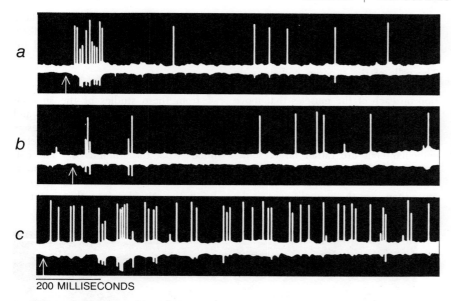

TOUCH SENSITIVITY is exhibited by cells in the colliculus of a cat. The particular cell represented here responded when something lightly touched any part of the dorsal and lateral surface of the animal's foreleg. The arrows under the traces show when the stimulus was applied. The cell responds with a short burst of impulses when touched with a camel's-hair brush (*a*). When the foreleg is pinched sharply, however, there is no evident change in the cell's random firing pattern (*b*). When the camel's-hair brush is moved lightly across the somatic receptive field (*c*), the cell responds with a sustained volley of impulses. The collicular cell also responds to visual stimuli in the lower portion of the right visual field.

Turning a stationary stimulus on and off within the receptive field was relatively ineffective. Many cells were directionally selective for both auditory and visual stimuli, and the horizontal component of the preferred direction was nearly always toward the periphery of the contralateral field for both kinds of stimulus [*see illustration on opposite page*].

Some of the cells responded to the tactile stimulation of a distinct area of the body, such as the contralateral foot or forepaw. The most effective stimulus for these cells was usually a camel's-hair brush, which ruffled the cat's hair as it was moved across the receptive field. Stationary stimuli were largely ineffective. The touch-sensitive cells were clearly not designed to detect painful stimuli because they responded no better to pressure or a pinch than to a light touch [*see illustration above*].

Although rather few of the cells responded to both visual and somatic stimuli, the position of a cell's somatic receptive field was related to the receptive-field positions of nearby cells that responded to visual stimuli. Thus the deep layers of the superior colliculus seem to embody superposed topographic maps of the visual, auditory and somatic fields. These maps are much less precise than the maps found in the nuclei of the primary sensory pathways and in the superficial collicular layers;

moreover, the receptive fields of individual cells are much larger than the receptive fields of cells in the primary sensory pathways.

Cells in the deeper layers of the superior colliculus seem to be able to integrate information about the approximate location and direction of movement of the stimuli that impinge on both the auditory and visual systems. The activity of nearby cells encodes the approximate location of the somatic stimuli. It seems reasonable to conclude that the colliculus aids in visual orienting, searching and tracking, regardless of the type of stimulus that initiates the movements.

M ost animals do not orient themselves repeatedly to repeated presentations of the same stimulus unless the animal is rewarded or punished for responding to it. This decline in response is termed habituation. One might therefore expect collicular cells to become habituated to repeated presentations of the same stimulus, and indeed that is what happens in the deep layers of the superior colliculus of heavily anesthetized cats. (Habituation also makes it frustratingly difficult for the experimenter to check his notions of the optimal stimulus for any given cell.) Wurtz and Goldberg have recently performed an ingenious experiment with monkeys demonstrating that the collicular cells

become habituated only when the stimulus has no behavioral significance for the animal. The particular cells they examined were in the superficial layers of the colliculus.

The animals were trained to fixate on a small spot of light. They were then rewarded for shifting their fixation point to a second spot of light if the second spot was turned on and simultaneously the first spot was turned off. This can be called the eye-movement condition. If both lights remained on, the animals maintained fixation on the first spot (the no-movement condition). Wurtz and Goldberg recorded from single cells in the superior colliculus of the trained animals under both conditions.

First they presented the no-eye-movement condition: the animal fixated one spot and the cell responded (as expected) to a second spot of light turned on within the cell's receptive field. When the second spot was presented repeatedly, however, the response of the cell habituated. (Monkey collicular cells, unlike those in cats, are not directionally selective and do not require moving stimuli.) Wurtz and Goldberg then presented the eye-movement condition: the fixation stimulus was turned off at the instant the receptive-field stimulus was turned on. The monkey then made a saccade (a rapid eye movement) toward the receptive-field stimulus. (After the saccade, of course, the receptive-field stimulus was no longer within the receptive field of the cell they were recording from.) The response of the cell did not habituate during repeated presentations of the eye-movement condition. In fact, the initial response was sometimes enhanced, that is, the cell fired more often during the eye-movement condition than it did in response to the first presentation of this stimulus during the no-eye-movement condition. The enhancement was specific for movement elicited by stimuli within the cell's receptive field. There was no enhancement if the eye stimulus controlling eye movements was outside the cell's receptive field.

The enhancement also did not require actual eye movement, only that the stimulus have a behavioral significance for the animal. When the animal was returned to the no-movement condition, the enhanced response of the cell was maintained for several trials [*see illustration on following page*]. Thus the enhanced response seems to be related to the animal's "paying attention" to the stimulus. Perhaps the habituation of collicular cells in the deeply anesthetized cat results from the animal's inability to move its eyes in response to sensory stimuli and its "inattention" to subsequent presentations of the same stimulus.

Perhaps the most direct demonstration that cells in the superior colliculus are intimately related to eye movement comes from experiments in which monkeys were trained to move their eyes in a specific way and the behavior of collicular cells was examined while the monkeys were making such movements. Experiments of this type have been done independently by Schiller at M.I.T. and by Wurtz and Goldberg. They found that cells in the superficial layers of the monkey superior colliculus had visual receptive fields but did not respond in relation to eye movements. The activity of many cells in the deep layer, however, was clearly related to eye movements.

In Wurtz and Goldberg's laboratory these cells were studied in experiments quite similar to those used to study the enhancement responses. The animals were trained to move their eyes when one fixation point was turned off and a second one turned on in a different part of the visual field. The cells that responded in relation to eye movements began to respond between 30 and 300 milliseconds before the beginning of the eye movement. The timing of the cells' response was more closely correlated with the onset of the eye movement than it was with the presentation of the visual stimulus eliciting the movement.

Each cell has what Wurtz and Goldberg call a movement field, that is, the cell responds only in conjunction with eye movements toward a particular area of the visual field. The notion of a movement field implies that the cells respond only in conjunction with eye movements of a particular extent. If an animal moves its eyes in the direction of the movement field but the movement stops short of the movement field or extends beyond the farthest border of the movement field, the cell does not fire. And of course if the eyes move in a direction other than toward the movement field, the cell also does not fire. Many of the cells that responded in relation to eye movement also had visual receptive fields. For any given cell the visual receptive field and the movement field were in the same portion of the visual field, but they were usually not precisely superposed.

The movement field of a single cell was independent of the initial position of the eyes in the head. This finding is just what one would expect from know-

ing that the size and direction of eye movements elicited by electrical stimulation of the colliculus are independent of the position of the eyes in the head. The cells of the superior colliculus do not code for a specific amount of tension on each of the muscles that move the eyes but may code specific changes in fixation. Wurtz and Goldberg point out that because the movement fields of collicular cells are rather large, sometimes as much as 10 or 20 degrees on a side, the active cells probably do no more than turn the animal's eyes to the

general region of the visual field where the stimulus appears; they are unlikely to provide the fine control needed for precise visual fixation.

The general conception emerging from these studies of the superior colliculus and visual cortex of cats and monkeys is that the cortex processes sensory information in order to determine "what the stimulus is." The colliculus determines "where the stimulus is and where it is going" in order to bring the stimulus into the center of

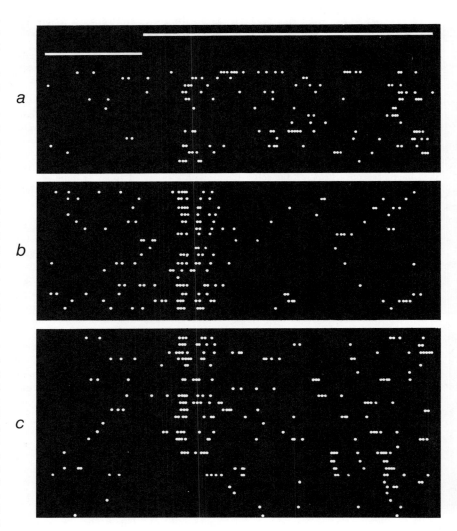

EFFECT OF REWARDING EYE RESPONSE is shown in these three sets of recordings from the superior colliculus of a monkey. The break in the horizontal line at the top shows when a visual stimulus in the receptive field of the collicular unit is turned on. Each line of dots shows how a collicular cell responds to one presentation of the stimulus. The set of traces in *a* shows the response of the unit when the stimulus has acquired no behavioral significance for the animal, that is, a fixation light is not turned off when the receptive-field light is turned on. The stimulus is then presented as the second light in a two-light sequence; the fixation light is turned off when the receptive-field light is turned on. When the animal shifts its gaze quickly to the second light, it is rewarded. Such an eye shift is called a saccade. The traces in *b* show the enhanced firing of the collicular unit after such saccades have acquired behavioral significance. The traces in *c* show a sequence when the two lights are again presented as in *a* (the no-eye-movement condition). Collicular unit fires in enhanced fashion for a short while, then its firing decreases. Experiment was performed by Robert H. Wurtz and Michael E. Goldberg of the National Institute of Mental Health.

the visual field and keep it there. Different experimental methods have nonetheless provided somewhat different types of information.

Collicular lesions in cats cause deficits in orienting to visual, auditory and somatic stimuli and in learning visual tasks that require frequent changes in fixation. Collicular lesions also decrease the speed with which monkeys can change their fixation point. Electrical stimulation of the colliculus in monkeys causes eye movements; the size and direction of the movement depend on the portion of the colliculus that is stimulated. Studies of receptive fields show that single cells in the cat colliculus respond to visual and auditory stimuli moving away from the animal. Presumably the responses of these cells cause eye movements that keep the stimuli within the visual field, but this connection has not yet been demonstrated.

The response of cells in the monkey colliculus to visual stimuli rapidly becomes habituated if the stimulus has no behavioral significance for the animal. The response is maintained and even enhanced, however, if visual tracking is rewarded. Finally, the deep layers of the monkey colliculus contain cells that respond before eye movements of a specific size and direction. It seems reasonable to suppose that the output of these cells helps to trigger the eye movement. We know little about how the output is transmitted to the motor cells that control head or eye movements. We do know that there are no monosynaptic (that is, direct) connections from the colliculus to either the motor-nerve cells that move the eyes or the motor-nerve cells in the neck that turn the head.

Thus we are still in the dark about many aspects of the role of the superior colliculus in controlling the movement of the head and the eye. It is a puzzle how the output of the colliculus can specify an eye movement independently of the initial position of the eye in its socket. Nor do we know how the colliculus receives information that a particular eye movement has been made. Does it receive sensory information indicating that the attempted tracking has been successful or does it receive feedback directly from motor-nerve cells? We know nothing about how the motor-nerve cells innervating neck and eye muscles combine information from the colliculus with information from other portions of the brain in order to determine which muscles should contract and hence how the head and eyes should move.

10

The Neural Basis
of Visually Guided Behavior

by Jörg-Peter Ewert
March 1974

Techniques from ethology and neurophysiology are combined to show how an animal localizes a visual object, discriminates its significance and then makes the appropriate motor response

Animals see things and then act on the basis of what they see. What chain of events connects some key stimulus with a specific fixed pattern of responses? In recent years workers in several laboratories have sought by many different means to analyze the nerve mechanisms by which animals interpret sensory signals and select the most appropriate response. The most effective way to understand the neural basis of behavior appears to be to apply a broad spectrum of experimental techniques: to combine ethological studies of an animal's behavior with experiments involving brain anatomy and brain-cell stimulation and the recording of individual nerve-cell activity.

For the past six years, in my laboratory first at the Technical University of Darmstadt and then at the University of Kassel, we have been taking this broad approach to learn about two kinds of visually controlled behavior in the toad: orienting (prey-catching) behavior and avoidance (escape) behavior. There are several good reasons for working with the toad. Amphibians are vertebrates, so that what we learn at their relatively low level of behavioral integration contributes to our understanding of more complex vertebrate functioning. Toads in particular have a limited and easily surveyed behavioral repertory. In response to specific stimuli one can repeatedly elicit predictable reactions, such as snapping at prey, fleeing from an enemy, clasping during courtship and making particular wiping motions after tactile stimulation. (The fickle European frog, in contrast, undergoes short-term changes in motivation and is not suitable for behavioral experiments.) Finally, the toad is not easily conditioned, so that its innate behavioral functions can be measured in successive experiments for some time without being significantly affected by accumulated experience.

Toads respond to small objects, such as a piece of white cardboard moved over a black background, with a series of prey-catching reactions. First there is orientation toward the prey, then binocular fixation, then snapping, gulping and mouth-cleaning. Two basic processes are required to produce the overall orienting reaction: the identification of a stimulus and the location of it in space. The identification process determines the type of behavior. It is dependent on specific features of the stimulus such as its angular size, the orientation of the boundaries between light and dark, its angular velocity, its contrast with the background and so on. A detection process then localizes the stimulus and, together with the result of the identification process, determines the motor response, which can be either to turn toward the stimulus if it is identified as prey or to avoid it if it appears to be an enemy. In what follows I shall attempt to analyze the neurophysiological basis of signal identification, localization and the triggering of the associated instinctive actions.

To begin one must analyze quantitatively the key stimuli for orienting and avoidance behavior. This is done by changing various characteristics of a visual stimulus in an ordered way. The toad is placed in a cylindrical glass compartment where it observes a small square of black cardboard moving against a white background at a constant angular velocity, describing a circle around the animal at a distance of seven centimeters. The toad interprets such a stimulus as prey and tries, through successive turning movements, to keep the object fixated in the center of its visual field. The degree of orienting activity is measured by counting the number of turning responses per minute.

The angular size of the stimulus—the angle it subtends—influences the orienting activity [*see illustration on page 98*]. Of a variety of square objects toads prefer those with an edge length of four to eight degrees. (The absolute size of such stimuli is five to 10 millimeters. Experiments where the distance between animal and stimulus is varied show that it is the absolute—not the angular—size that counts; in prey-catching behavior toads display "size constancy.") The toads turn away from objects larger than 30 degrees on a side, exhibiting the avoidance response. More particular information is obtained by substituting bars of various lengths for the square stimuli. As a two-by-two-degree stimulus is elongated along the horizontal axis the orienting activity increases until a saturation level is reached; wormlike objects turn out to be particularly attractive to toads. In contrast, the response decreases as a small stimulus is extended vertically, or perpendicularly to the direction of movement.

Other experiments indicate that toads discriminate prey from enemy objects through analysis of the visual stimulus in terms of point or edge configurations, also taking into consideration the direction of movement. A horizontal chain consisting of several two-by-two-degree units moving along the same path signifies prey. One such unit moving alone constitutes a prey stimulus just above the response threshold. When the horizontal chain is supplied with a separate vertical

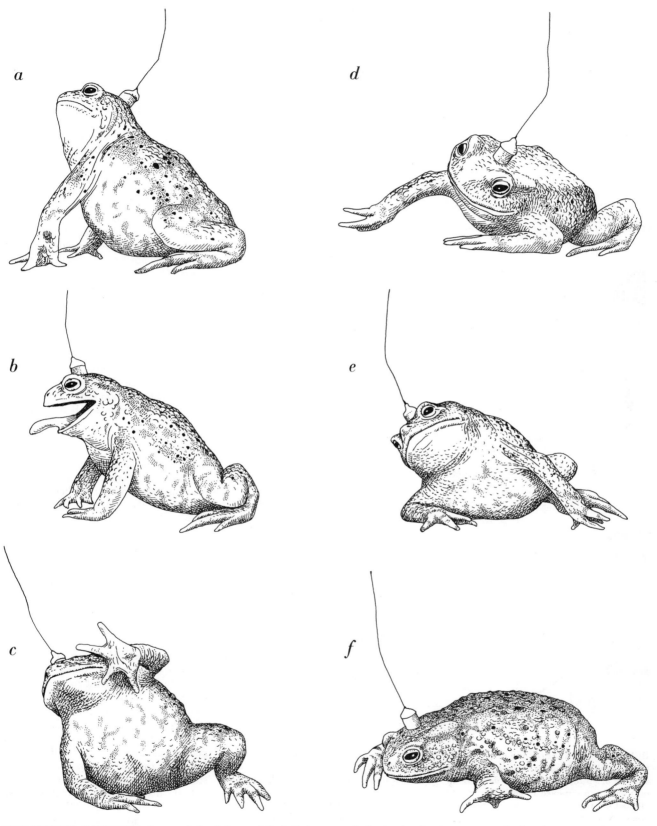

a

b

c

d

e

f

BEHAVIORAL PATTERNS characteristic of the toad *Bufo bufo* are illustrated. The actions are commonly elicited in the animal by the sight of visual objects. These drawings, however, are based on photographs of toads whose brains were being stimulated electrically as part of the author's investigation of the neural bases of visually guided behavior. The electrode on the toad's head penetrates to the brain. An electric current applied to the optic tectum, a visual center in the brain, elicits a prey-catching sequence: orienting, or turning (*a*), snapping (*b*) and mouth-cleaning (*c*). Electrical stimulation, instead, of a site in the left or right thalamus brings a "planting-down" defensive posture (*d*, *e*) and stimulation of another part of the thalamus brings a crouching avoidance response (*f*).

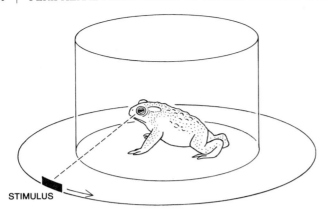

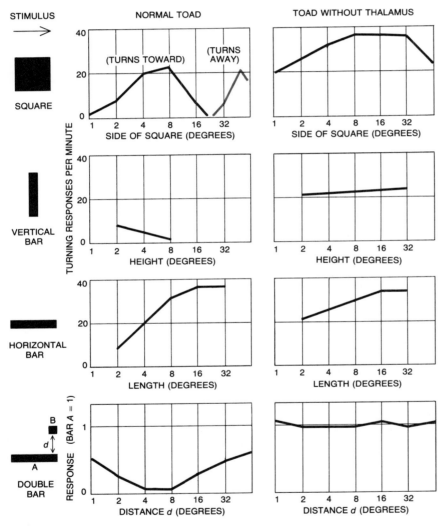

BEHAVIORAL RESPONSES of the toad to objects of various shapes and sizes were quantified. Small black objects were moved across the visual field at seven centimeters' distance and the orienting response was determined for normal toads (*left*) and those whose thalamus had been removed (*right*). Prey-catching responses (turning toward the object) were elicited most effectively in normal toads by squares with sides subtending four to eight degrees; the toads turned away from larger squares. Vertical bars were ineffective as prey objects—and increasingly ineffective with increasing height. Horizontal (wormlike) bars were increasingly effective as prey objects with increasing length, up to a limit. Double bars (a horizontal bar plus a vertical extension) were less attractive, the effect varying with distance between bars; the ratio of their effect to that of a single bar is shown (*bottom*). In toads lacking the thalamus the orienting response becomes "disinhibited." The animal tends to orient toward a target without discrimination, even if the target normally signals "danger."

extension (making it in effect an *L*-shaped structure moving on ·its long side), it loses efficiency as a prey-catching stimulus. The inhibitory effect of the vertical extension depends on its distance from the horizontal element. If a second vertical extension is introduced, in effect making the stimulus a shallow *U*-shaped structure, the total configuration signifies "enemy." The ethological interpretation is that it symbolizes a "swarm," and in the toad's brain inhibitory interactions first restrain prey-catching behavior and then induce escape behavior.

For constant form and angular velocity the behavioral activity generally increases as the amount of contrast between stimulus and background increases. White objects moving against a black background are normally more attractive as prey than black objects on white; the latter, on the other hand, are more effective in eliciting avoidance behavior. When the size and contrast are held constant, behavioral activity increases with increasing angular velocity, reaching a maximum at between 20 and 30 degrees per second. Stationary objects usually elicit no prey-catching or avoidance response. The common critical feature for key stimuli representing both prey and enemy is movement, and the two kinds of stimulus are differentiated primarily on the basis of their form: extension of the object in the horizontal direction of the movement generally means prey, whereas extension perpendicular to the direction of the movement signifies "not prey" or "enemy."

What does the toad's eye tell the toad's brain? This question was first formulated for the frog and dealt with in the fascinating research of Jerome Y. Lettvin and his colleagues at the Massachusetts Institute of Technology, and was later investigated quantitatively by O.-J. Grüsser and his co-workers at the Free University of Berlin. To ask the question is to open the "black box" of the toad's brain, or at least to examine the brain functions that participate in transforming input from visual stimuli into relevant behavioral patterns. At this point I shall describe neurophysiological findings concerning whether it is in the retina of the toad's eye that the key stimuli "prey" and "enemy" are encoded.

In the toad retina there are three types of ganglion cells that send their fibers by way of the optic nerve to the structure called the optic tectum in the midbrain. One can record the action potentials, or nerve signals, from the ends of these fibers by introducing a microelectrode into the tectum. John E. Dowling, then at

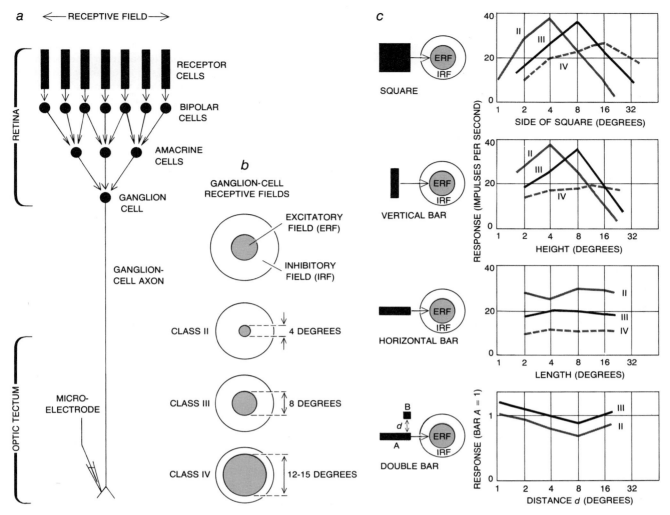

NEURAL RESPONSES of the toad to the same objects were measured with recording electrodes. The electrodes recorded impulses at the terminals in the optic tectum of fibers from individual ganglion cells, the cells in the retina of the eye on which signals from the receptor cells converge via intermediate cells (*a*). Each ganglion cell has an excitatory receptive field surrounded by an inhibitory receptive field. The diameter of the excitatory fields and the strength of the inhibitory surrounds are different for each of three classes of ganglion cells (*b*). For the square object and the vertical bar (which the ganglion cell "confuses"), maximum activity is elicited when the size of the object matches the excitatory-field size of each type of ganglion cell (*c*). Horizontal length does not much affect these cells' response. Vertical extension of a horizontal bar has less effect on these cells than on behavior (*opposite page*).

the Johns Hopkins University School of Medicine, showed through electron micrography that in the frog (or toad) retina each ganglion cell is connected to a number of receptor cells by bipolar and amacrine cells. Each ganglion cell is thus fed information from a particular part of the animal's visual field. Lateral connections established by horizontal and amacrine cells play a role in determining the properties of this receptive field. In toads as well as frogs the field consists of a central circular excitatory receptive field immediately surrounded by an inhibitory receptive field. The movement of an object through the excitatory field elicits a ganglion-cell discharge, which is inhibited if another object is simultaneously moving through the inhibitory field. The three ganglion-cell types in the toad (as in the frog) differ in several character-

istics, including in particular the diameter of their excitatory receptive fields: about four degrees for the so-called Class II ganglion cells, about eight degrees for Class III cells and from 12 to 15 degrees for Class IV cells. (Class I cells have been identified in frogs but not in toads.)

With microelectrodes we measure the rate of ganglion-cell discharge to see how it changes when objects (corresponding to those in the behavioral experiments described above) are moved through the receptive field of the cell. The impulse frequency increases with the length of the side of a square object until the length about equals the diameter of the excitatory field; then it decreases as the object becomes large enough to stimulate part of the surrounding inhibitory field. In accordance with the different sizes of the excitatory fields the maximum activa-

tion of each cell type is therefore elicited by objects of different sizes [*see illustration above*]. Extending a small square horizontally (making it a "worm") does not bring about any change in nerve-cell activation; this is in sharp contrast to the previously noted effect of extension on the behavioral response. The dependence of neuronal activation on the size of the stimulus is instead primarily a function of extension perpendicular to the direction of movement. Indeed, the discharge frequency is almost exactly the same in response to a narrow vertical bar as it is to a square with the same height as the bar. A retinal ganglion cell "confuses" the two stimuli—but the toad does not: the square excites behavioral activity and the bar inhibits it. When the object size is held constant, however, the dependence of the discharge rate on contrast between stimulus and background and on angular velocity is the same as it is in the behavioral experiments.

In summary, it is clear that the first important operations on the visual input from a prey stimulus or a threatening one are performed by the toad retina. For any particular prey or enemy stimulus the behavioral response to velocity and background contrast seems to depend on information processing in the retina. The size-dependent excitatory and inhibitory processes, however, which were noted in the behavioral experiments and which play an essential role in pattern discrimination, cannot be traced to the influence of the excitatory and inhibitory fields of retinal ganglion cells. There are no retinal "worm-detectors" as distinct from "enemy-detectors." The differential analysis, and thus the behaviorally relevant interpretation of the stimulus, must be achieved in nerve-cell populations beyond the retinal level.

Since different characteristics are coded by any one type of ganglion cell the question becomes: Where is that coding interpreted? What tells the central nervous system whether an increased rate of ganglion-cell firing stems, for example, from an increase in stimulus-background contrast or from larger size? The differentiation can be made only if separate groups of cells receive different inputs from different optic-nerve fibers. In fact they do. The fibers of the optic nerve pass from each eye through the optic chiasm to the opposite side of the brain, ending in various parts of the forebrain and midbrain. Two of these destinations are of particular interest in our work. One, to which most optic-nerve fibers project, is in the surface layers of the optic tectum in the midbrain. The other is in the thalamus and the pretectal region of the diencephalon.

The optic tectum constitutes a localization system. In the tectum there is an exact topographical mapping of the retina and hence of the entire visual field. Movement of an object in a particular part of the visual field excites a corresponding region of the tectum, where the appropriate optic-nerve fibers terminate [see illustration on these two pages]. Recording from individual tectal neurons, or nerve cells, tells one how the individual retinal ganglion cells that excite them are reacting. In certain layers, for example, there are tectal neurons with excitatory receptive fields of about 10 to 27 degrees that are activated exclusively by moving objects. These neurons probably represent a localization system. This supposition is reinforced by experiments in which we stimulate the tectum of freely moving toads with trains of impulses delivered by means of an implanted electrode. Stimulation of a given region of the tectum always causes toads to turn toward a particular part of the visual field. Presumably the neurons we are thus activating have a direct connection with the animal's motor system, since (in contrast to the natural orienting movements made in response to a prey object) the electrically induced orienting is not disrupted by simultaneous presentation of a threatening object.

If the recording electrode is driven deeper into the tectum, it encounters neurons with larger receptive fields. Some of these cover the entire visual field on the opposite side, some the entire lower part of the field and some the entire field directly in front of the animal. Interestingly enough, all three types include the fixation point: the point of maximum visual acuity near the center of the visual field. The degree of activation of these three types of neurons could provide the toad with information about the

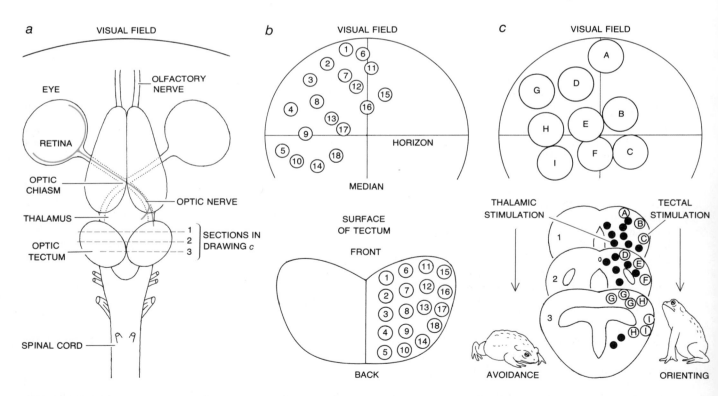

NEUROPHYSIOLOGICAL EXPERIMENTS yield data on the functions of different parts of the toad's visual system. Fibers of the retinal ganglion cells project primarily to the optic tectum and to the thalamus (a). The visual field of each eye is mapped (b), on a one-to-one basis (numbers), on the dorsal surface of the opposite side of the tectum. By the same token experimental electrical stimulation (c) of various parts of the tectum (letters) causes the toad to turn to corresponding parts of the visual field. On the other hand stimulation (black disks) of the thalamus, which partially underlies the tectum, causes the opposite action: avoidance, or turning away. As a recording electrode penetrates below the surface of the tectum it encounters successive populations of cells with differ-

location of a large object, since whenever the three types are excited simultaneously the object must be at the fixation point.

In natural situations the behavior of toads can be influenced by sensory modalities other than vision. If, for example, a beetle crosses the field of vision, the toad's orienting reaction can be either accelerated or retarded by simultaneous vibratory and tactile stimuli. Such results can be obtained in experiments if prey models are presented together with acoustic or tactile stimuli. The area for producing such changes in behavioral activity seems to be in the subtectal region, where multisensory integration is achieved. In the area below the third ventricle of the midbrain there are large-field neurons with fields similar to those of the large-field tectal cells. These subtectal neurons receive additional inputs from neurons excited by tactile and vibratory stimuli. The "mechanoreceptive" field of one of these bimodal neurons is always localized on the same side as the visual receptive field. The additional inputs from nonvisual neurons could serve to lower the threshold of a part of the visual field in which a visual stimulus is anticipated and thus

in effect to raise the level of visual alertness.

The optic tectum also comprises a neuronal system that processes behaviorally relevant aspects of moving stimuli [see illustrations on next page]. The cells have excitatory receptive fields about 27 degrees in diameter. Those designated Type I tectal neurons are activated mainly if the stimulus surface of an object moved through the receptive field is extended in the direction of movement; extension perpendicular to direction of movement does not have the same effect. Other cells, the Type II tectal neurons, differ from Type I neurons in that their discharge rate actually diminishes with surface extension perpendicular to direction of movement. The response of these neurons constitutes the key stimulus "prey." That is, they can presumably be considered the trigger system for the prey-catching response.

The thalamic-pretectal region, the second major destination of fibers from the retina, apparently provides what can be called a "caution" system. I have recently identified four main types of visually sensitive neurons in the toad's thalamus by means of single-cell recordings.

They are activated respectively by four distinct stimulus situations: (1) movement of enemy objects extended perpendicularly to the direction of motion, excitatory receptive field of about 46 degrees; (2) movement of an object toward the toad, field about 90 degrees; (3) large stationary objects, field about 45 degrees; (4) stimulation of the balance sensors in the toad's ear by tilting. In general these thalamic neurons are activated principally in situations that tend to call for evasive movements—turning away from an enemy, sidestepping or compensating for tilting of the body. Brain-stimulation experiments support our feeling that the thalamic-pretectal region is one in which reactions can be assembled that lead to protective movements. Electrical stimulation of various sites in the region elicits the following reactions: closing of the eyelids, ducking, turning away, panicky springing away or tilting of the body.

We constructed a working hypothesis involving connections between the optic tectum and the thalamic-pretectal region: Electrical triggers in the tectum mainly elicit orienting, and triggers in the thalamic-pretectal region elicit avoidance. In a natural situation trigger impulses in particular layers of the tectum are evoked by small wormlike prey. Large objects extended perpendicularly to the direction of movement stimulate particular neurons in the thalamic-pretectal region, both directly through retinal inputs and indirectly by way of the optic tectum. These thalamic-pretectal neurons in turn inhibit the tectum and can also activate avoidance behavior [see illustration on page 103].

The existence of the postulated connections between the structures in the midbrain and the diencephalon has been demonstrated physiologically in two ways. One way is by direct electrical stimulation. Thalamic neurons that are sensitive to movement can also be activated by stimulation of points in the optic tectum. When the stimulating and recording electrodes are interchanged, the response of Type II neurons in the tectum to moving objects can be inhibited by the stimulation of cells in the thalamus. The other way is by surgical operation: if the optic tectum is removed, orienting movements are lost—and so are avoidance reactions, which is evidence for pathways from the tectum to the thalamus. If the thalamic-pretectal region is removed without damage to the tectum, then avoidance behavior is lost—and the orienting response is dramatically freed from inhibition even in the presence of enemy objects; this may be

ent receptive fields (d). There are small-field cells with fields a little larger than those of ganglion cells and, lower down, three kinds of large-field cells, each with different coverage (color, horizontal hatching and vertical hatching). A drawing based on a stained brain section indicates the layers at which each of these is found. The final drawing (e) relates the various cell populations and shows another layer of large-field cells that receive inputs from visual cells above them and also from cells that respond to tactile or vibratory stimuli.

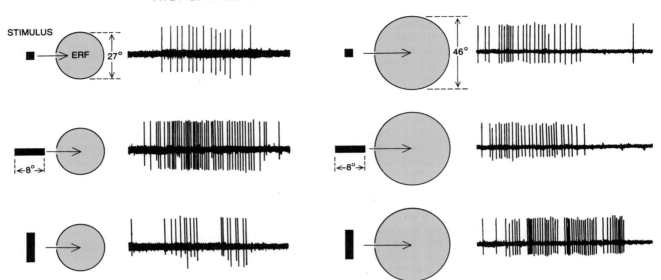

FEATURE DETECTION beyond the retinal level is accomplished by cells in the tectum and the thalamus. Recordings from individual cells indicate that tectal Type I neurons (*left*) are most activated if the object moving through the field is extended in the direction of movement. The cells in the thalamic area (*right*) respond most to an object extended perpendicularly to direction of movement.

evidence for the existence of inhibitory pathways from the thalamus to the optic tectum. In toads lacking the thalamic-pretectal region every moving stimulus elicits the orienting movements; the cautionary thalamic-pretectal system, which ordinarily allows orientation toward the stimulus only in behaviorally appropriate situations, is missing. If one lateral half of the thalamic-pretectal region is re-moved, the disinhibition extends to the entire visual field on the opposite side; small lesions in the thalamic-pretectal region affect only local small parts of the visual field. Quantitative experiments with toads lacking the thalamic-pretectal region make it clear that these animals cannot discriminate between stimuli that are behaviorally relevant and those that are irrelevant. The response of the Type II tectal cells to moving stimuli shows a similar "disinhibition" effect after thalamic-pretectal removal [*see illustrations on page 98 and below*].

The findings I have described so far suggest the following sequence of events: On the basis of retinal ganglion-cell input, the optic tectum tells the toad where in the visual field a stimulus is

TYPE II TECTAL NEURON
(NORMAL TOAD)

TYPE II TECTAL NEURON
(TOAD WITHOUT THALAMUS)

TRIGGER UNITS for the entire prey-catching response seem to be the Type II tectal neurons. In the normal toad (*left*) the cells are most activated by wormlike objects (*horizontal bar*). They are less activated (and the decrease is greater than in the case of Type I tectal neurons) by stimuli that in behavioral experiments are irrelevant for prey-catching (*vertical bar*). After removal of the thalamus, however (*right*), their response to those irrelevant stimuli is greatly increased, suggesting that the thalamic signal is inhibitory.

situated, how large it is, how strongly it contrasts with the background and how fast it is moving. The connections from the tectum to structures in the thalamic-pretectal region enable the toad to discern the significance to its behavior of the visual signals. The basic filtering process for the prey-enemy differentiation can be conceived of as passage through a series of "window discriminators" [*see illustration on next page*], each stage of which analyzes a particular aspect of the object in question. Each retinal ganglion cell acts as a vertical window that codes extension perpendicular to the direction of movement. The retinal analysis is repeated and amplified in the thalamic-pretectal region, where a neuron pool acts as another vertical window, this one with a certain minimum-response threshold. Extension in a horizontal direction is coded primarily by Type I tectal cells, which constitute a horizontal window. Type II tectal cells perform a summation, with signals arriving from the thalamic-pretectal region having an inhibitory effect and those from the Type I cells having an excitatory effect. The resultant signal acts as the trigger stimulus for the orienting movement. The triggering of avoidance behavior is probably achieved through the activation of still another pool of thalamic-pretectal neurons, the activation being proportional to an additive function of inputs from two of the window-discriminator pools.

One of the remarkable aspects of this system is a degree of plasticity, or changeability. During the summer months white prey objects moved against black backgrounds elicit orienting behavior much more effectively than do black objects against white. In fall and winter the situation is reversed, and at the same time the overall prey-catching activity of the toads decreases. Recently our recording electrodes revealed that the activation of single Class II ganglion cells in the retina exhibits this seasonal shift in white-black preference. In winter neurons with receptive fields in the lower part of the visual field are more strongly activated by black objects than by white ones; in the upper field the situation is reversed. In summer, however, the neurons whose receptive field is in the upper half of the visual field are activated primarily by black stimuli, whereas neurons receptive to the lower half of the visual field become more strongly activated by white stimuli and remain so until in the fall black stimuli again become dominant.

What is the biological significance of these observations? One can speculate that for toads, which are active at twilight, biologically important prey stimuli that appear in the lower half of the visual field are paler then their background; those in the upper part of the field, however, are for the most part relatively dark, or at least just as often dark as pale. Each of these contrast relations could be reflected in the sensitivity characteristics of the Class II retinal ganglion cells. With the approach of winter and the period of hibernation, toads stop catching prey. What makes them stop? One mechanism may be an inversion of ganglion-cell response characteristics, brought about by signals from the brain to the retina, such that the stimulus-background contrast relation is out of phase with the real world, making prey objects less visible. For the toad, in other words, identical objects appear to be dif-

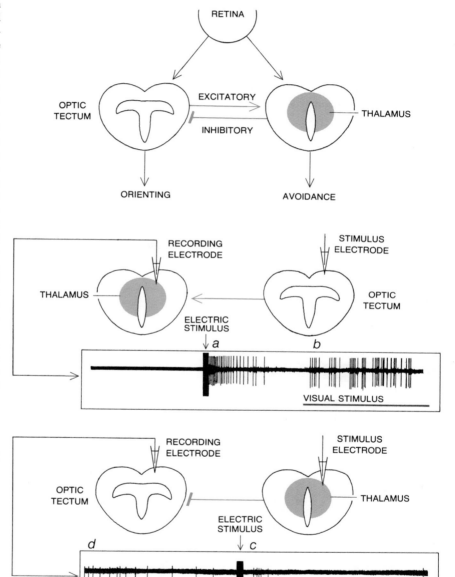

CONNECTIONS between the optic tectum and the thalamus were indicated by preceding experiments: signals from the retina excite both tectum and thalamus; subsequent impulses from Type I tectal neurons further excite cells in the thalamus, whereas signals from the thalamus inhibit activity in Type II tectal neurons. Two different kinds of motor activity are thereupon initiated by the two structures (*top*). Confirmatory evidence was obtained by electrical stimulation. Stimulation of the tectum (*middle*) elicits impulses (*a*) from cells in the thalamus that ordinarily respond to visual stimuli (*b*). Stimulation of the thalamus (*bottom*) inhibits (*c*) impulses normally elicited (*d*) in Type II neurons by moving objects.

ferent when they are seen in winter than when they are seen in summer, a reminder that an organism's picture of the environment is a product of its brain.

In contrast to the plasticity of the systems for the filtering and storage of information and for pattern recognition, brain mechanisms involved in instinctive actions are quite inflexible and do not adapt easily to changes in the stimulus situation. For each instinctive action in the behavioral repertory there is a preprogrammed "printed" neuronal circuit that coordinates the appropriate motor act—even if it becomes inappropriate! If such a circuit is triggered (either naturally or by electrode stimulation), the innate reaction proceeds automatically. Prey-catching behavior is a good example. On the basis of brain-stimulation experi-

ments we believe the sequence of events controlling a natural orientation response is about as follows: A pattern is formed by a natural stimulus on a portion of the retina that is outside the fixation region; the retinal locus has a corresponding projection locus in the optic tectum. If the filtering process described above has identified the object as prey, then the appropriate neuronal system is activated. A value corresponding to the distance between the prey's locus on the retina and the fixation point is transferred to the toad's motor system. The result is orientation: a turning movement such that the retinal representation of the prey is brought to the fixation point. That triggers a locus in the optic tectum that corresponds to the fixation point. As soon as this triggering reaches a threshold value

the rest of the prey-catching sequence is activated, quite independently of the result, or even of the short-term benefit to the animal, of such activation. For example, if an experimental prey object is removed at the instant when it is fixated by the toad, the entire normal prey-catching routine nevertheless proceeds. The toad snaps, gulps and wipes its mouth in spite of the "situational vacuum." The sequence is similar in its inevitability to what happens when the triggering region of the tectum is stimulated with an electrode.

As for avoidance behavior, the results of thalamic stimulation indicate that it is controlled by a single master program. The response consists in a firm planting of the extremities on one side of the toad's body and a gathering together of the limbs on the opposite side. With the toad in this stationary, poised position the additional behavior patterns for correcting tilting of the body or making the various evasive movements can be readily incorporated.

The evidence I have reviewed shows that in a lower vertebrate the neuronal processes for localization and identification of a visual signal and for releasing the associated instinctive motor responses are separated topographically but are intimately connected with one another. In the course of evolution the centers for two of these processes, visual localization and instinctive action, have apparently remained in about their original positions. They occupy the same areas of the brain, the tectum and the thalamus, in monkeys and cats as they do in toads. The organization of these parts of the brain, to which both neurophysiological and ethological methods have provided investigative access, shows remarkable constancy in all classes of vertebrates. That is not the case, however, for stimulus identification. In toads this process takes place primarily in the thalamic-pretectal region and also in the retina and the tectum. Mammals, however, underwent further evolution, corresponding to the importance of pattern recognition in the evolution of their behavior. A new substrate developed for two associated but highly specialized processes, filtering and storage of information: the visual cortex. From the investigations of Gerald E. Schneider at M.I.T. we learn that in this case ontogeny reflects phylogeny. In newborn hamsters subcortical pathways between the tectum and the thalamus are implicated in pattern discrimination. In adult animals, on the other hand, pattern discrimination takes place in the cortex.

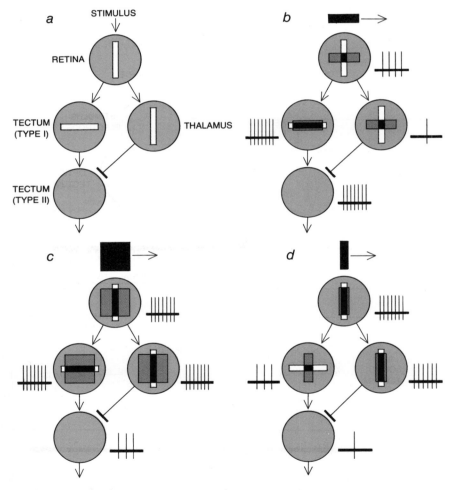

IDENTIFICATION OF AN OBJECT AS PREY OR ENEMY is symbolized as a series of operations by "window discriminators" (a). A ganglion cell in the retina codes vertical extension (perpendicular to direction of movement), in effect responding to as much of a visual object as appears in a vertical window; extension beyond the window has an inhibitory effect. Cells in the thalamus do the same thing. In the tectum Type I cells code horizontal extension (in the direction of movement). Type II tectal cells sum the excitatory signal from Type I cells and the inhibitory signal from the thalamus, and the resultant signal triggers an orienting movement. At each stage the cell discharge depends on the relation between the object and the window that senses its extension either in or perpendicular to the direction of movement (b, c, d). (The cell-discharge patterns shown here are schematic.)

Control Mechanisms
of the Eye

by Derek H. Fender
July 1964

*The control system whereby the eye tracks a target
is investigated by an engineering technique, systems
analysis, and is found to be a servomechanism
in which retinal-image motion serves as feedback*

When a biologist seeks to understand how a particular mechanism in a living organism works, he often begins by dissecting the structure and analyzing the interrelation of its parts. In the study of some biological mechanisms this approach is ineffective; it may be better to examine the mechanism "from the outside" as it performs its normal functions. Here the engineering technique known as systems analysis can be useful. The investigator measures the responses of a functional unit to some simple and well-defined stimulus, and the relation between stimulus and response reveals the presence of certain classes of elements in the unit. It thus provides a clue to the makeup of the system, and with this clue the biologist can now look for the elements of the mechanism and describe its operation with more confidence.

In this article I shall discuss an application of systems analysis to the investigation of human vision, in particular to the processes whereby the eye fixes on and tracks an object in its field

of view. I shall be considering the eye not as a camera but as a mechanical system: a servomechanism. Engineers define a servomechanism as a device that controls some variable physical quantity in a special way: by comparing its actual value with a desired reference value. It uses the difference between the two to drive an actuator that in turn adjusts the variable to correspond with the reference. The reference value is the input signal and the controlled quantity is the output signal; the basic principle of the servomechanism is a "feedback" from output to input [*see illustration below*].

The servomechanism monitors its own performance and makes corrections as required either to conform with a change in the input signal or to compensate for an external disturbance of the output. The power-steering mechanism of a modern automobile is a good example of a servomechanism. The reference, or input, signal is provided by the position of the steering wheel; the output variable is the position of the front wheels.

When input and output differ, the difference causes a hydraulic actuator to move the front wheels. When the driver rotates the steering wheel, the wheels take up a new position; when a pothole deflects the wheels, the servomechanism quickly returns them to the desired position.

The human body is a collection of servomechanisms. Feedback control systems regulate body temperature and the constitution of body fluids; they vary the flow of blood to the organs and extremities and adjust the rate of breathing to the level of physical activity. The joints have "proprioceptors" that measure the flexure of an extremity and feed back a signal to be compared with the reference, or "command," nerve signals from the brain. Some feedback loops are completed outside the body. For example, a man who wants to pick up an object observes with his eyes the closing gap between his hand and the object: the visual sense measures the "error" in hand position.

Not all of these biological control systems are equally open to investigation. Systems analysis requires that there be an input point where the stimulus can be applied and an output point where the signal regarded as the response of the system can be measured. Moreover, if it seems that the system includes a feedback loop, one must be able to change the operating conditions of that loop precisely, thus achieving the full potential of systems analysis by examining the characteristics of the "feed-forward" and feedback paths independently. These limitations have restricted the application of systems-analysis methods in human beings to a few subsystems: those in which a sensory input gives rise to motor activity. Various workers have studied feedback loops involving the control of limb

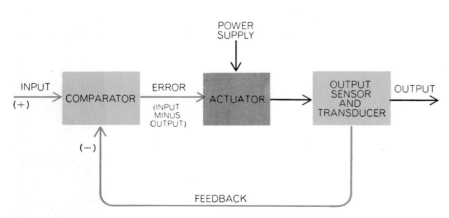

SERVOMECHANISM controls an output value by comparing it with an input, or reference, value. The sensor measures the output (a velocity, for example); the transducer states it in input terms (a voltage, perhaps) to be fed back to the comparator, where it is subtracted from the input. The resulting "error" drives the actuator to adjust the output.

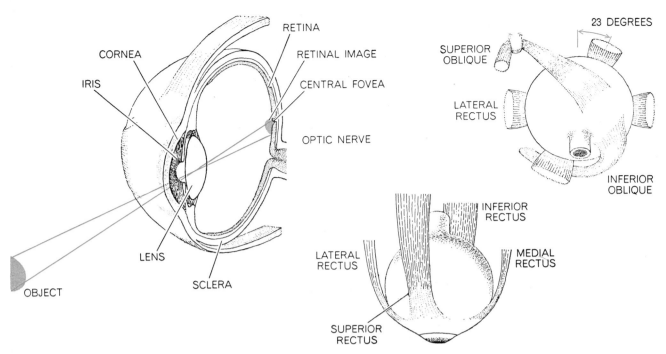

CORNEA

IRIS

RETINA

RETINAL IMAGE

CENTRAL FOVEA

OPTIC NERVE

LENS

SCLERA

OBJECT

SUPERIOR OBLIQUE

LATERAL RECTUS

INFERIOR OBLIQUE

23 DEGREES

INFERIOR RECTUS

MEDIAL RECTUS

LATERAL RECTUS

SUPERIOR RECTUS

CONTROL SYSTEM of the eye positions the image of an object on the central fovea, the most sensitive part of the retina (*left*). Three pairs of muscles move the eyeball. Two drawings show the right eyeball from above (*center*) and from the rear (*right*). The two pairs of recti move the visual axis from side to side and up and down; the oblique muscles roll the eyeball about the axis.

movements by proprioceptors, the control of manual movements by the eye and—perhaps most interesting of all—the eye's control of its own varied and richly interrelated movements.

The eye's optical components form the image of an external object on the retina, a screen of light-sensitive receptor cells that convert radiant energy into nerve impulses; these impulses pass along the optic nerve to the visual cortex of the brain and there generate the sensation of vision. The retinal receptors are not distributed uniformly; the cone cells, which are specialized for daylight and color vision, are most numerous and most closely packed in the fovea, a small depression at the center of the retina, and are intermingled with the twilight-vision reds and therefore more widely spaced toward the retina's periphery.

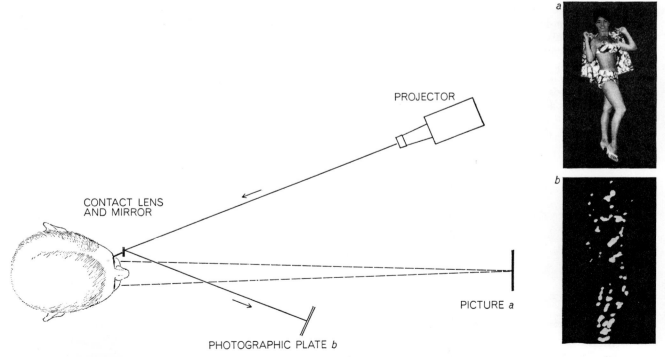

PROJECTOR

CONTACT LENS AND MIRROR

PICTURE *a*

PHOTOGRAPHIC PLATE *b*

a

b

DIRECTION OF GAZE is recorded by a beam of light reflected from the contact-lens mirror. As the eye moves and lingers over a scene (*a*) the reflected beam exposes corresponding areas on the film (*b*); the resulting light spots indicate where the eye looked.

The fovea, then, is the part of the retina capable of the sharpest vision. It is not a large area; the image of a thumbnail viewed at arm's length just about covers it. To examine an object closely a person moves his eyes so that the image of the object falls on corresponding areas of his two foveas.

Three pairs of muscles rotate the eye in its socket. The medial and lateral recti move the visual axis from side to side, the superior and inferior recti move the axis up and down and the superior and inferior obliques roll the eyeball about the visual axis. It is a servomechanism that controls these muscles to position the image of an object on the fovea. Each pair of muscles receives signals proportional to the displacement of the interesting part of the image from the fovea, and the muscles then act together to move the eyeball in such a way as to reduce the displacement to zero. Retinal-image displacement is used as a feedback signal; in this instance the eye operates as what an engineer would call a simple position servomechanism.

This is far from being the only feedback control system of the eye. Depth perception, for example, requires that images of an object be formed on corresponding areas of the retina in each eye. There is a control system that brings the eyes to the correct angle of convergence—a system that appears to be quite distinct from the mechanism governing the general direction of gaze but that operates through the same set of muscles. The image must also be focused sharply on the retina. Since the distance between the lens and the retina is fixed, focusing is achieved by changes in the thickness, and therefore in the focal length, of the lens. Here too it is a feedback control mechanism that adjusts this state of "accommodation" of the lens.

There is an interesting relation between the convergence and accommodation systems. One might expect that the angle of convergence would provide the visual system with information for calculating the distance of an object and then setting the focal length for a sharp image, rather like a coupled range finder on a camera. Instead the accommodative mechanism has a steady "hunting" motion superimposed on it that continually lengthens and shortens the focal length of the lens. Depending on the location of the object being viewed, a change in one direction will improve an out-of-focus image and a change in the other direction will worsen it; this information is fed back to steer accommodation in the direction of the sharpest focus. Once the correct lens thickness is found, information about it is fed across to the convergence mechanism. The two systems are separate and distinct in their modes of control but are cross-linked: information derived by one is fed into the other.

Still another feedback mechanism changes the diameter of the pupil. It measures the average illumination of the retina and activates the muscles of the iris to minimize variations in the brightness of the retinal image. This mechanism is linked in turn to the accommodative system, because when the focal length of the lens increases, the pupil must enlarge to keep the brightness of the image constant. Finally, there is even a control circuit that moves the eyelids out of the way when the gaze is directed upward. The visual pathway, then, is composed of a number of interconnected feedback systems. Each has been examined separately and, as I have indicated, some work has been done on the interactions among the various mechanisms. Let us now consider the eye's positioning and tracking system in some detail.

Some 60 years ago E. B. A. Delabarre of Brown University used a plaster cast of the cornea to fasten lightweight levers to his own eye and record its motion. Since then a number of less painful techniques have been developed. Large eye motions can be recorded by photographing the reflection of a light from the corneal surface. Another method relies on the fact that the eyeball has a small electric charge, and its slow movements can therefore be measured by electrodes placed around the eye socket. In 1925 Gösta Dohlman of the University of Uppsala in Sweden attached a mirror to a subject's eye with a rubber suction cup, so that a beam of light reflected from the mirror would trace the movements of the eyeball. In more recent adaptations of this technique, including those we have developed in my laboratory at the California Institute of Technology, the mirror is mounted on a contact lens.

Such a mirror, together with a simple projection system and a photographic plate, provides a record of how the eye examines a scene [see bottom illustration on opposite page]. The subject's eyes wander over the picture, hovering selectively at certain points. The mirror moves with the direction of gaze, reflecting the beam of light, which builds up exposures at corresponding points on the photographic plate. When the resulting

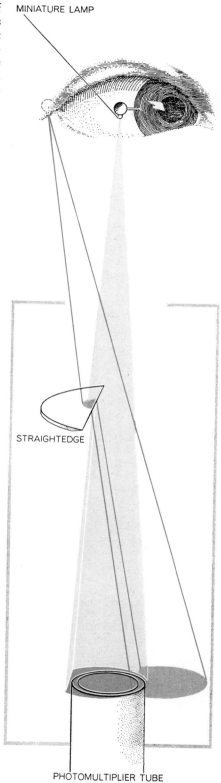

MINIATURE LAMP

STRAIGHTEDGE

PHOTOMULTIPLIER TUBE

PHOTOMULTIPLIER TUBE provides a more accurate gauge of eye movement, as shown here schematically. The apparatus is so placed that when the subject's eye is farthest to his left, maximum light strikes the tube. As the eye moves right (*colored circle*) the straightedge cuts off light from the tube. The output current of the tube therefore measures the position of the eye.

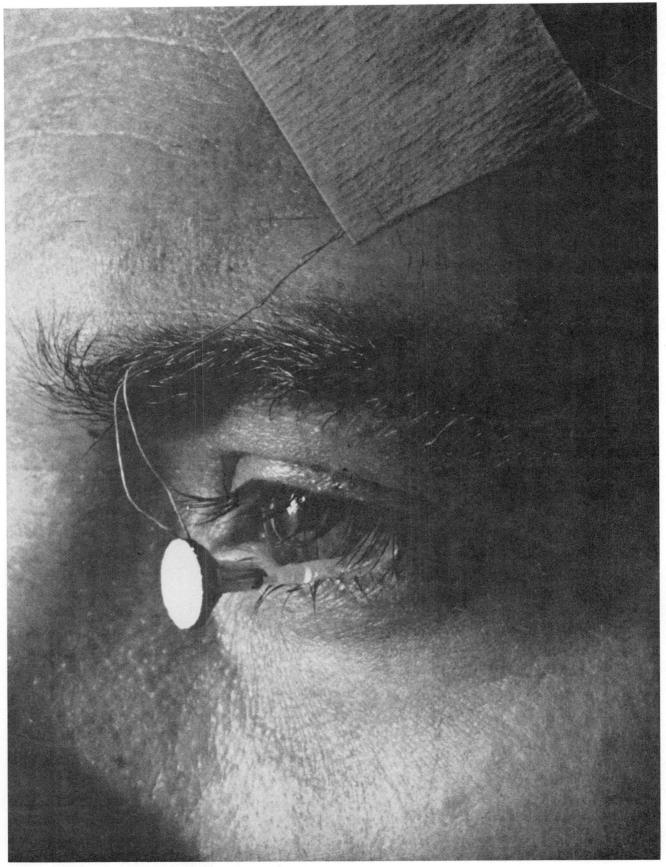

CONTACT LENS with mirror attached is mounted in the eye of George W. Beeler, Jr., one of the author's students. Light reflected from the mirror can be recorded on film to show the direction of gaze. In some experiments the mirror is made part of the optical path between the target and the eye, so that the image moves with the eye. The wires power a tiny lamp in the stem of the mirror.

negative is printed, the spots of light outline the object that was being viewed and the relative amounts of visual attention accorded to various areas.

Such measurements are quite rough. To obtain data of much higher resolution and accuracy we place a tiny medical lamp in the stem of the mirror in such a way that it shines down onto a photomultiplier tube mounted perpendicularly to the subject's line of sight [*see the illustration on page 107*]. As the eye moves, the amount of light striking the tube fluctuates and the tube's output current is therefore a measure of the motion of the eye. By combining two tubes we obtain data on both the side-to-side and the up-and-down motions of the eye.

We record these data in several ways. In one method we feed the electrical signals from the photomultipliers into a computer programed to calculate the time the eye spent in each part of the visual scene and to print the results as a sheet of numbers that can be read like a contour map. The top illustration at the left is the fixation pattern recorded as a subject stared for two minutes at a small pinhole. Although he was looking at the target as carefully as possible, involuntary eye movements carried his line of vision off the target by about 1/4 degree for short periods of time (1/4 degree is the equivalent of about 1.5 millimeters at normal reading distance, or about the width of the letters on this page). Note that the area of fixation is roughly elliptical, with its major axis canted outward from the vertical. The reason is that the muscles that move the visual axis from side to side are quite sensitive and capable of precise movement, whereas the up-and-down muscles are not capable of such fine control and do not act in a vertical plane but in a plane tilted outward at 23 degrees from the vertical. This difference in degree of precision between horizontal and vertical fixation is one of the reasons why it is easier to locate a ship by searching the horizon than it is to spot an airplane by scanning the sky in vertical sweeps.

If the signals from the photomultipliers are led to recording galvanometers instead of to a computer, the side-to-side and the up-and-down components of eye motion can be recorded separately and plotted against time, as in the bottom illustration at the left. This record too is of eye movements during fixation on a stationary target, and it is now possible to see that there are two distinct eye motions. One is a slow drift of the visual axis. The other is a

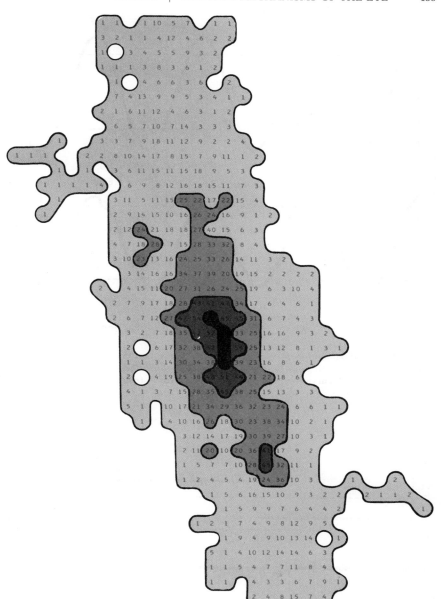

CONTOUR MAP shows how the eye wanders while staring at a very small stationary object whose position and size are shown by the black circle. The vertical extent of the fixation pattern is about 3/4 degree. The numbers give the relative period of fixation at each point.

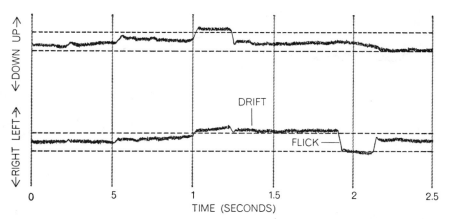

EYE MOTIONS in fixation are recorded separately. Their scale is indicated by the broken lines: distance between the two lines of each pair equals 0.1 degree of angular motion.

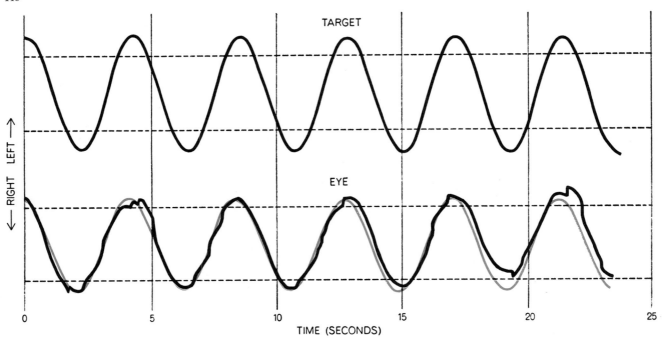

SINUSOIDAL target motion is recorded (*top*) along with the total motion of the tracking eye (*lower black curve*). "Noise" is removed from the total curve to produce a true tracking curve (*col-* *or*). Its amplitude is only eight-tenths as great as that of the target curve: the system's "gain" is 0.8. The broken lines are again for scale, the distance between them equaling two degrees of motion.

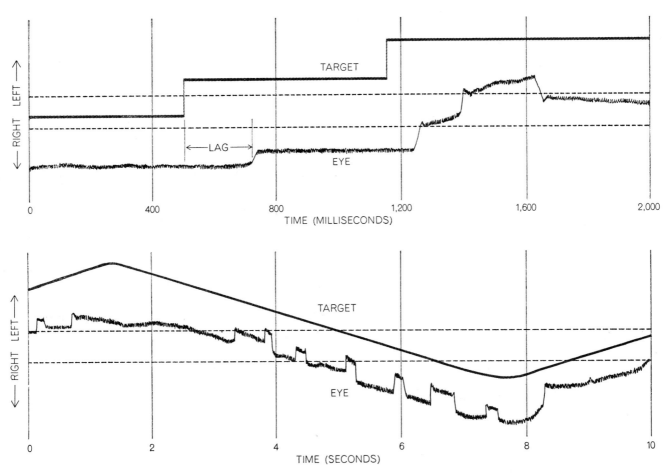

STEP AND RAMP inputs are tracked in these records. In the step input (*top*) a target is moved suddenly from one place to another; the tracking system's lag is seen clearly in this case. In the ramp input (*bottom*) the target is moved across the field and back at a constant velocity. Target and eye traces have been separated for clarity. Scale lines indicate 0.1 degree of motion.

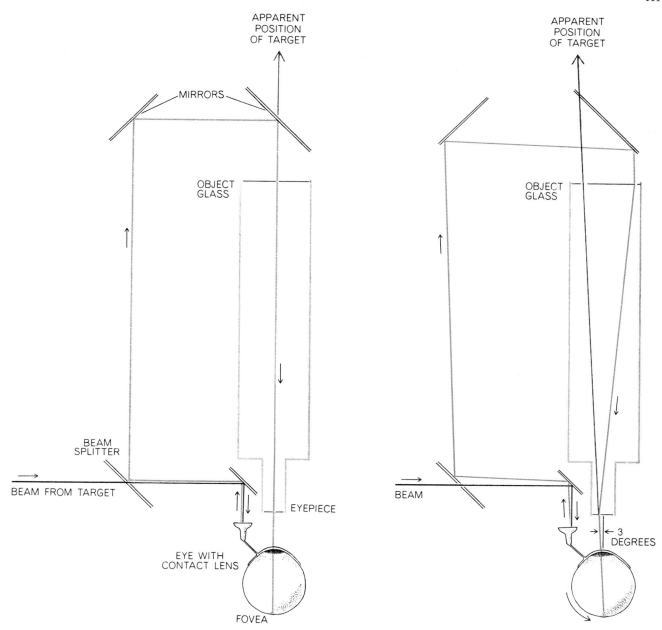

APPARENT
POSITION
OF TARGET

MIRRORS

OBJECT
GLASS

BEAM
SPLITTER

BEAM FROM TARGET

EYEPIECE

EYE WITH
CONTACT LENS

FOVEA

APPARENT
POSITION
OF TARGET

OBJECT
GLASS

BEAM

3
DEGREES

STABILIZED-IMAGE DEVICE causes the target image to remain at the same point on the retina regardless of the movements of the eye. The target, a pinpoint of light from a projector off to the left, reaches the eye only by an optical path that includes the contact-lens mirror. Here the target is stationary. The subject first sees it (*drawing at left*) in the center of his field of view. Even if he turns his eye three degrees to his left, the mirror moves the target so that it remains centered on his fovea (*right*).

sudden change of direction called a "flick," a remarkable motion that can accelerate the eyeball to an angular velocity of 5,000 degrees per second. The drift and flick are the motions by which the eye ordinarily tracks a target but, as this record shows, they are also "spontaneous" movements: they persist, along with a high-frequency tremor, even when the eye should be still. In other words, the eye has an output even when there is no input; in engineering terms, it has a lot of internal "noise." The spontaneous movements have to be cleared away before one can analyze the tracking movements of the eye and study their control mechanism. This is accomplished with standard mathematical procedures for detecting a signal buried in noise.

Systems analysis calls for varying the input to a feedback control system and measuring the response of the system. In the case of visual tracking the input is a visual stimulus and the response is eye movement. What we do is to move a target across the field of view in certain conventional ways. For a "sinusoidal" stimulus the target is moved from side to side at a fluctuating velocity. We also move the target suddenly from one location to another in what is called a "step function" or move it across the field at a constant velocity for a "ramp" input. In each case the movements of the subject's eye activate the photomultiplier device to trace a curve that can be compared with the target curve.

Consider the curves for a sinusoidal oscillating target movement [*see top il-*

lustration on page 110]. The drifting motion provides fairly smooth tracking, but from time to time a flick is required in order to catch up. We remove the noise from the curve by calculating the sine-wave component of the output that has the same frequency as the input. Comparison of this calculated curve with the target curve shows that the amplitude of the response is not so large as that of the target motion. The ratio of the two (output amplitude divided by input amplitude) is the "gain" of the system, and in this case the gain is 0.8. In other words, the eye travels only eight-tenths as far as the target does. The gain varies sensitively with the type and velocity of target motion and with the arrangement of the feedback system; it is one of the two key characteristics one deals with in analyzing a servomechanism. The other factor is the "phase lag" of the system, the lag between input and response expressed in degrees. In the case of the sinusoidal motion illustrated, the lag is five degrees, or 1/72 of a full wavelength.

The first step in analyzing the visual position servomechanism, then, is to determine typical values for the gain and the phase lag of the system in response to various inputs. The next step is to make similar measurements after disconnecting the feedback loops in the system. The loop most readily available for experiment is the feedback generated by retinal-image motion. If this loop can be opened, the subject will receive no information concerning the motion of his own eye—information he would normally get from the displacement of the retinal image.

We achieve this state of affairs with an optical system that interposes the contact-lens mirror between the target and the subject's eye, so that the target moves with every movement of the eye [*see illustration on preceding page*]. Light from a projector is focused on the contact-lens mirror and is reflected from it by a series of mirrors through telescope lenses and back to the subject's eye. The subject, with his eye relaxed, sees a spot of light apparently at an infinite distance. The angular motion of the target is doubled at the contact-lens mirror but the telescope lenses correct this, so that by the time the beam emerges from the eyepiece its angular motion is exactly the same as that of the eyeball. Now an image formed on the retina will stay there no matter how the subject moves his eye; it is a "stabilized" retinal image. When the target is actually moved by the experimenter, of course, the

retinal image will move, and that is how input to the system is generated. The servomechanism, in other words, will continue to receive input information but will presumably have lost a feedback loop. It will detect target motion but not eye motion, and it will be unable to monitor its own performance.

When the experiment is conducted with sinusoidal target motion in stabilized rather than normal vision, the movements of the eye still follow those of the target quite faithfully [*see upper illustration on this page*]. But the amplitude of the eye motion is now considerably greater than that of the target motion; the gain goes up to 1.8, whereas in normal vision it was only 0.8 at the same frequency. This confirms the assumption that retinal-image motion constitutes "negative" feedback, since disconnecting such a feedback loop in an amplifier always results in a considerable increase in gain. Feedback is normally

negative; it is subtracted from the input value. In "positive" feedback it is added to the input, magnifying the deviation of output value from input instead of correcting it. Now, if the sign of the feedback is made positive, the result, in an amplifier, is an oscillation of the output signal. We reverse the direction of retinal-image motion by substituting reversing prisms for the mirrors in the stabilized-image apparatus and the eye responds as an amplifier does: even when the target is stationary, the gaze oscillates wildly from side to side in the motion known as nystagmus.

To get more information about the visual system one can alter the frequency of target motion. If the rate at which the target goes back and forth is gradually increased, the amplitude, or gain, of the tracking motion decreases in both normal and stabilized vision [*see illustration on page 114*]. The eye cannot keep up with the target; it oscillates through a smaller distance

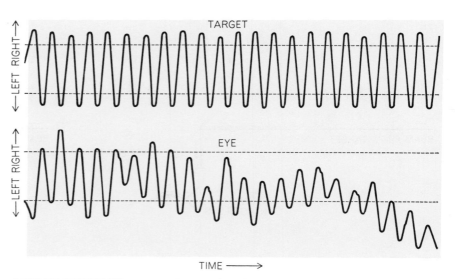

LOSS OF FEEDBACK causes an increase in gain, as in an amplifier, when retinal-image motion is eliminated in stabilized vision. (The broken lines here indicate one degree of motion.) Note that because the eye now lacks cues as to what is "straight ahead," the axis of vision drifts off to the side (this is the left eye) as the eyes do when a person faints.

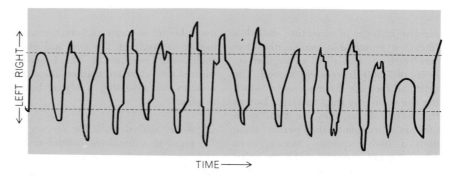

POSITIVE FEEDBACK, in which output error is exaggerated, causes wild oscillation even if the target is stationary, as it is here. The broken scale lines are two degrees apart.

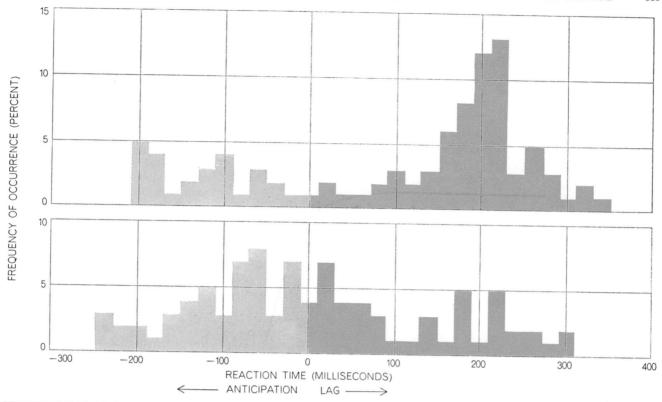

TRACKING LAG (*dark colored bars*) is the rule when the target is moved in steps at random times (*top*). When the steps come in a regular time sequence (*bottom*), however, the eye more often anticipates target motion (*light colored bars*). The anticipations in the random situation are fortuitous; the eye happened, in its "noisy" wanderings, to have been where the target was going.

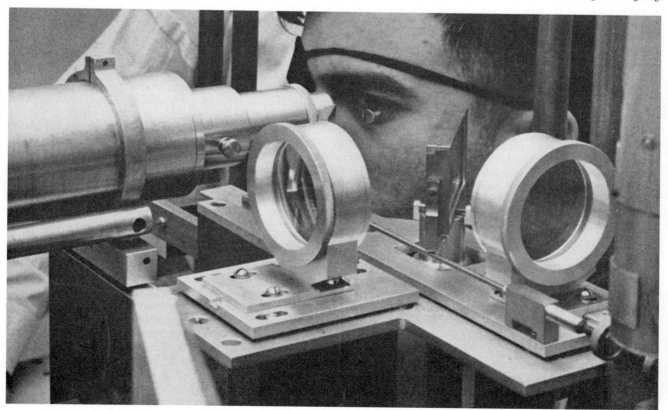

OPTICAL APPARATUS diagramed on page 110 is seen in this photograph. The target beam comes from the bottom right, strikes the mirror near the eyepiece of the telescope and is reflected to the contact-lens mirror and thence around a chain of mirrors and back through the telescope to the fovea of the subject, Park S. Nobel. The photomultiplier device is out of sight below the subject's eye.

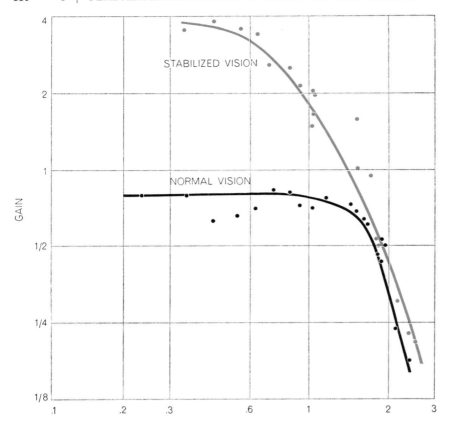

GAIN OF SYSTEM, as indicated by the amplitude of the eye-motion sine wave, decreases as the frequency of the target motion increases. The eye cannot keep up with the target.

as the target moves more quickly. (An engineer would say that the system is acting as a "low-pass filter" with a cutoff at a frequency of about three cycles per second.) This limit on the frequency attainable in tracking is not surprising; there are a number of elements in the visual pathway and each takes some time to operate. Light absorbed by the retinal receptor cells bleaches the photosensitive pigments in the cells, initiating a chemical reaction that generates electric potentials in the adjacent nerve cells; these processes take about 30 milliseconds. The potentials trigger impulses in the optic nerve that take about five milliseconds to reach the brainstem, where spontaneous eye movements are controlled. The brain takes perhaps 100 milliseconds to process the information and then sends out motor-nerve impulses that reach the eyeball muscles in another five milliseconds. So the lag between the receipt of a stimulus at the retina and the initiation of a corresponding response by the muscles is at least 150 milliseconds.

This lag is quite plain to see in the case of the step input in the lower illustration on page 110. The fact is, however,

that values as large as this occur only when the target motion is irregular or unexpected. If the movement is in any way repetitive or otherwise predictable, the eye is able to keep up with it and even to anticipate it. In one series of experiments we measured the reaction times of a number of people to step movements that occurred at random and compared these with their reaction times to steps that came at regularly spaced intervals. In the case of the regular motion most of the "responses" occurred before the target moved: they were actually anticipations. This suggests strongly that the eye's control system must be doing something more than reacting to a motion; it must be predicting. There is further evidence for prediction in the sinusoidal curves at the top of page 110. Here the lag (imperceptible in the illustration) is only about six milliseconds. A mechanical system having the same gain characteristics would lag by about 50 milliseconds at this frequency if it were a "minimum phase" system capable only of responding to an input. The eye's servomechanism, then, must contain something a minimum-phase system does not have: "active"

elements that allow it to calculate target motion and lock onto it. The system is not merely a tracking device but a predictor.

At this point systems analysis leads to physiological investigation. The response of the eye to target motion indicates that retinal-image displacement and velocity constitute feedback signals in the eye's control system. Are there elements right in the retina that extract these signals from the visual scene or is it done in the cortex of the brain? The eye also acts as a predictor; is this a retinal function or does it take place at higher levels? These questions can be tested by administering drugs that depress the activity of the central nervous system. A fairly light dose of a barbiturate or a tranquilizer interferes with a person's ability to predict target motion, so prediction is probably a function of the cortex. The drugs depress the velocity signal for targets presented in the fovea but not for targets moving at the outer periphery of the visual field—in the "corner of the eye." This suggests that the detection of objects approaching from the side (a faculty with considerable survival value) may be built right into the retina. And the image-displacement signal—the recognition that the target is no longer in the fovea—is quite unchanged by the drugs and is presumably retinal in origin. A biologist might therefore feel encouraged to examine the retina for nerve elements that detect the displacement of the retinal image and announce it to the brain.

The retina contains a number of kinds of nerve cell in addition to the light-sensitive rods and cones. These bipolar cells, amacrine cells and ganglia seem to be capable of more sophisticated functions than merely passing light signals on to the brain. Indeed, studies of lower animals have shown that their retinas do discriminate among visual signals and in effect filter information [see "Vision in Frogs," by W. R. A. Muntz; SCIENTIFIC AMERICAN, March 1964], but not much is known as yet about the processing of information in the retinas of higher animals. The microscopic structure of the retina is similar to that of the brain; in fact, the retina is a part of the brain that became detached in the course of evolution. Any information that systems analysis can provide about retinal function should therefore advance the much more difficult task of understanding how the brain works.

12

The Coordination
of Eye-Head Movements

by Emilio Bizzi
October 1974

*The sequence of events in the nervous system that
coordinates the movements of the eyes and the head
in fixating a visual target has been clarified
by recent experiments with monkeys*

How the central nervous system produces coordinated motor output has long been one of the major problems of neurophysiology. What accounts for both the graceful performance of the trained athlete and the ordinary, but hardly less remarkable, movements of everyday life? For movement to be coordinated an appropriate set of muscles must be selected, each of the contracting muscles must be activated in the proper temporal relation to the others and a precise amount of inhibition must be delivered to each of the muscles that will oppose the intended movement. In addition to triggering the contraction of a given set of muscles the nervous system must monitor the effects of its commands; it must have a way of coordinating movements of the various body parts; it must be able to decide when to terminate a given phase in a motor sequence and proceed to a new one, and so on.

For three-quarters of a century, dating back to the early studies of Charles Scott Sherrington, investigators have held different views concerning how temporally patterned sequences of neuromuscular events are programmed by the nervous system. Many workers have stressed the importance of sensory feedback in eliciting and coordinating a motor output. The feedback is viewed as originating with various types of sensors located in the muscles, the tendons and the joints. These receptors inform the central nervous system about various aspects of a movement, such as its velocity, amplitude and force. According to some investigators, sensory feedback from each phase of movement is important in eliciting each subsequent motor output. Therefore a coordinated motor performance could be described as being differentiated into many parts along the time dimension, so that each part is reflexly triggered by the sensory components of its predecessor. Thus, to use Sherrington's words, "coordination is in part the compounding of reflexes."

At the other extreme some investigators hold that the nervous system already incorporates all the information necessary for the selection of the muscles involved in a given movement and the sequential activation of those muscles. The motor system is viewed as a network capable of playing stored patterns in a predetermined manner following the presentation of an adequate input. In invertebrates, for example, the work of Cornelis A. G. Wiersma, Donald Kennedy and Donald M. Wilson has shown the importance of central, built-in mechanisms for the generation of motor patterns.

In vertebrates, however, and particularly in mammals, the contribution of centrally programmed patterns of motor command and their possible modification by feedback coming from peripheral sensors is still a matter of speculation. Hence neurophysiologists are still faced with the vexing question: What is the role of peripheral feedback? Does it provide a signal to time the release of the next phase of a movement? Does it facilitate some aspect of the motor pattern? Does it maintain or complete the next phase? Or does it add a new phase to those movements that were centrally initiated?

In an attempt to answer such questions we have been studying the coordination of eye-head movements in monkeys in our laboratory at the Massachusetts Institute of Technology. My colleagues in this effort have been Johannes Dichgans, Ronald E. Kalil, Piero Morasso and Vincenzo Tagliasco. We have investigated the spatial and temporal characteristics of the motor programs underlying the orderly sequence of eye and head movements in monkeys, and we have shown how reflex sensory feedback, generated by the turning of the head, interacts with the centrally initiated programs and thereby gives rise to "coordinated" eye-head movements.

Consider the eye and head movements that follow the unexpected presentation of a visual target. In man and monkeys the appearance of a target in the visual field is usually followed by an orderly sequence of such movements. First, a fast eye movement (called a saccade) carries the most sensitive part of the retina, the fovea, to the image of the target. Second, after a delay of between 20 and 40 milliseconds the head turns in the same direction. Since the eyes have moved first, and with a higher velocity than the head, their lines of sight reach and fixate the target while the head is still moving. Then for the duration of the head movement the eyes maintain their target fixation by performing a rotational movement that, by being counter to the movement of the head, allows the fovea to remain constantly on the target it has just acquired. This maneuver is termed compensatory eye movement [*see bottom illustration on page 116*].

To achieve this orderly sequence of movements, that is, to direct the eyes and the head toward the target and ultimately fixate the target with the fovea, the subject must make a number of computations. To begin with, the subject must compute the angular distance between the initial lines of sight and the position of the target that is to be acquired. Although we do not have a clear understanding of how the angular distance is computed by the cortical and subcortical visual areas of the brain, we do know that a signal corresponding to

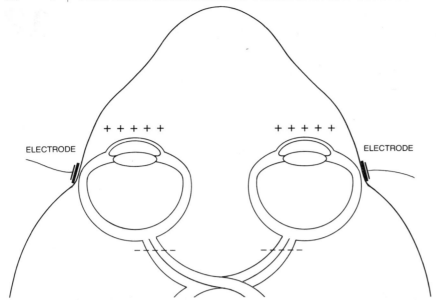

MEASUREMENT OF EYE MOVEMENT by electro-oculography takes advantage of the fact that the retina is positively charged and the choroid that lies behind it is negatively charged, even under resting conditions. The charges are kept separate by the external limiting membrane (the membrane of Bruch) that lies between the retina and the choroid. As a result the resting eye acts as a dipole in which the cornea is some 10 to 30 microvolts positive with respect to the back of the eye. Eye position can be recorded by placing a pair of electrodes on the inner and outer corner of each eye (for horizontal movements) or above and below each eye (for vertical movements). When the eyes are aimed straight ahead, the potentials between similarly placed pairs of electrodes are balanced. Any rotation of the eye, however, brings the more positive cornea closer to one electrode of each pair than to the other. Resulting difference in potential serves as an index of eye position.

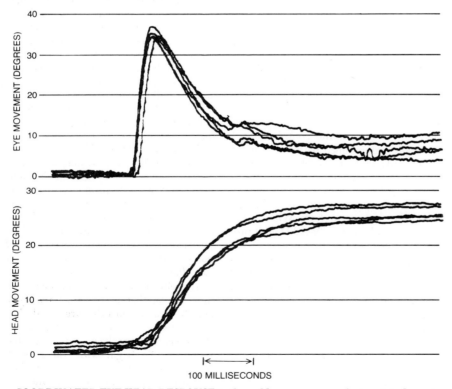

COORDINATED EYE-HEAD RESPONSE to the sudden appearance of a target is shown in five superposed tracings. The vertical scales indicate the amplitude of each movement in degrees starting from the straight-ahead position. The eyes make an initial saccade of some 30 degrees, then counterrotate as the head begins turning toward the target. As a result when the head is fully turned, the eyes are once again pointed nearly straight ahead.

that distance is translated into both the oculomotor system and the head-motor system at about the same time. In fact, the electrical activity recorded from eye-muscle and neck-muscle fibers shows that motor commands are delivered almost synchronously to those muscles. From this it follows that both the oculomotor and the head-motor control systems must be making use of the same angular-distance information at approximately the same time. As a result amplitudes of eye and head movements are produced that are well correlated with the angular distance of the target.

We have shown that this finding is valid in the case where a head movement begins from the straight-ahead position and the eyes are centered in the head at the time the target is presented. Usually, however, the eyes will not be centered when a target appears. How, then, does the head-movement control system know the position of the eye in its orbit so that a proper degree of head-turning can be generated? The head-movement control system must have access to eye-position information and then combine it with the angular-distance signal to achieve a coordinated eye-head movement. Information about the position of the eye can be supplied by sensors sensitive to stretching (muscle spindles) located in the eye muscles or by internal monitoring of the oculomotor positional commands.

The activation of eye and neck muscles leads not only to movements of the eyes and head but also to the activation of a number of sensory receptors, technically referred to as proprioceptors. These include neck-muscle spindles, neck-tendon organs, receptors located in the joints of vertebrae in the neck and receptors located in the vestibule of the inner ear. All will give rise directly or indirectly to nerve impulses whenever the head is turned. The question, then, is whether or not these sensory receptors can modify the ongoing eye and head motor programs. The following observations will make the point clear. If we compare the amplitude of the eye movement in the acquisition of a target when a monkey's head is allowed to turn and when it is held fixed, we observe that the amplitude of the eye movement is greater when the head is held fixed [*see illustration on page 118*]. Clearly the amplitude of eye movement must be less when the head is free to turn if an overshoot of the target by the combined eye-head movement is to be prevented.

Given this experimental observation,

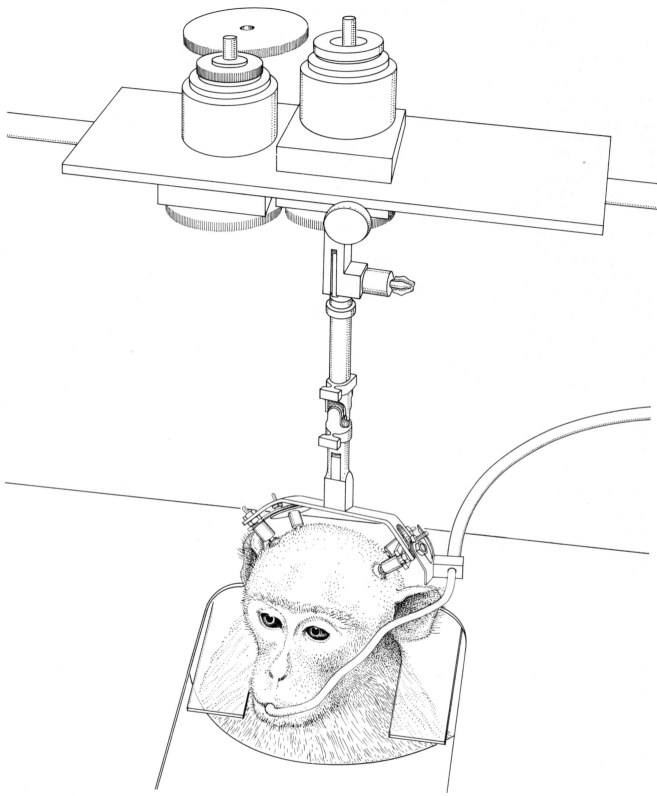

EYE-HEAD COORDINATION STUDIES are conducted in the author's laboratory at the Massachusetts Institute of Technology with the aid of the experimental apparatus illustrated here. When a visual target (*not shown*) is suddenly presented, it attracts the monkey's attention and sets in train an orderly sequence of eye and head movements. A fast eye movement, called a saccade, turns the eyes so that the target is centered on the fovea, the most sensi- tive part of the retina. Some 20 to 40 milliseconds later the mon- key's head begins turning in the same direction. During this head movement the eyes must counterrotate to keep the target fixated. The amount of head-turning is transmitted to a recorder by the lightweight apparatus clamped to monkey's head. Eye movement is recorded by electro-oculography (*see top illustration on opposite page*). Tube in monkey's mouth gives drops of water as a reward.

we must next ask what mechanism is responsible for the modulation of saccadic amplitude. Two hypotheses can be considered: Either the program responsible for fast eye saccades is modified every time the head is ready to move or reflex activities initiated by the head-turning itself apply a corrective action to the ongoing centrally programmed saccade. Our experimental evidence supports the second hypothesis. We find that afferent, or incoming, signals arising from the sensitive receptors in the vestibule of the inner ear are solely responsible for modulating the saccadic amplitude. The vestibular impulses responsible for modulation of eye movements originate when the cupula (a gelatinous cup into which hair cells protrude) in the semicircular canal is deflected by movement of the endolymph (the fluid in the canal). These impulses are first transmitted to nearby clusters of nerve cells, the vestibular nuclei. From there, by way of direct and polysynaptic pathways, they impinge on nerve cells of the oculomotor nuclei. Positive evidence of the crucial role of the vestibular afferent signals was demonstrated in monkeys by surgically interrupting the pathway linking the vestibular receptors to the vestibular nuclei. For several weeks after the operation (before the monkey had learned to compensate) the saccade amplitude during head-turning was identical with the saccade amplitude in the absence of head movement. This resulted in a remarkable overshooting of the target because the unmodulated eye movement was simply added to the head movement [*see middle illustration at top of next page*].

Having established that saccades are adjusted in scale by the vestibular activity initiated by the head movement, let us turn to the question of why this reflex-adaptive arrangement is more advantageous to the animal than one based on a centrally preprogrammed modification of saccadic parameters. Clearly the reflex mode of organization greatly simplifies the task of the motor-programming systems required for eye-head coordination. The eye and head movements can be programmed independently, since the vestibular system "automatically" nullifies any displacement of the fovea from the target as a result of head movement. Furthermore, by relying on vestibular reflexes that monitor the actual movement of the head, the resulting adjustment of eye movements will be able to compensate for all the unpredictable peripheral loads and resistances that might change the course of the centrally initiated (intended) head movement.

The modification of saccade characteristics is one aspect of the interaction of central programming and reflex activities. Although this interaction plays a decisive part in the process of target acquisition by a combined eye-head movement, the role of feedback from peripheral sensory organs (vestibular and neck afferents) extends beyond saccadic modulation to control and generate compensatory eye movements.

Since the eyes move first and with a higher velocity than the head, their lines of sight reach and fixate the target while the head is still moving. Then for the duration of the head movement the eyes maintain their fixation by executing a compensatory rotational movement that is counter to the movement of the head and compensates for it.

One can easily observe such eye movements induced by head movements by asking a friend to fixate a visual target and turn his head from side to side while maintaining fixation. You will see that, as his head moves, his eyes rotate in an equal and opposite way so that they remain on target. Such compensatory eye movements can be extremely rapid. Try fixating your index finger while rapidly turning your head, and then move your index finger with equal rapidity while keeping your head motionless. In the first case the vestibular system quickly moves the eyes in the direction opposite to that of head movement and the target is seen clearly, but in the second case the slower visual corrective loop to the eye muscles cannot compensate for the movement of the target. The target is consequently reduced to a blur as the eyes try in vain to match its velocity.

Compensatory eye movements have been studied by several investigators. Although it is generally agreed that such eye movements are strongly influenced by visual and vestibular reflexes, including feedback signals from various proprioceptors, it has been hypothesized that compensatory eye movements are initiated centrally and hence are not primarily dependent on feedback information. In our own recent work we have found no evidence for central initiation. We have been able to demonstrate, however, that compensatory eye movements result from the reflex action of the vestibular system. As a consequence of the head movement vestibular receptors are stimulated, and their activity induces a compensatory eye movement that enables the fovea to remain fixed in relation

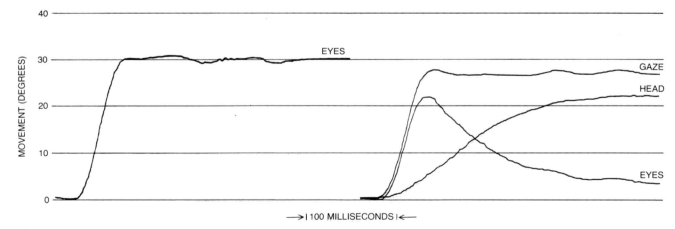

HEAD-FIXED AND HEAD-FREE RESPONSES to a suddenly appearing target are compared in two sets of traces. When the monkey's head is held fixed, the eye saccade must do the entire job of fixating the target (*left*). When the head is free to turn (*right*), fixa-tion is achieved by a combined movement, labeled "gaze," that represents the sum of the eye saccade and the head movement. Notice that the initial saccade is smaller in the second case because the turning of the head accomplishes part of the shift in the gaze.

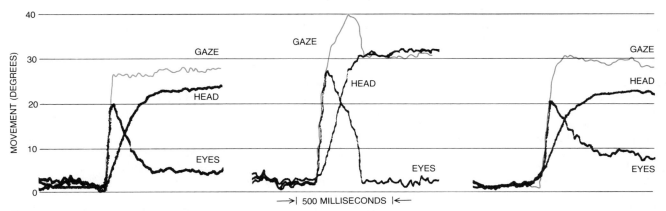

ROLE OF SENSORS IN INNER EAR in the coordination of eye-head movements was demonstrated in the author's laboratory by studies in which the vestibule of the inner ear of monkeys was surgically inactivated. The set of three traces at the left shows how a normal monkey shifts its gaze to a target by combining eye and head movements. Motion receptors in the inner ear initiate feedback signals that modulate the amplitude of saccadic eye movements and help the eyes to compensate, that is, counterrotate, smoothly as the head turns toward the target. The traces in the middle show what happens when a monkey is presented with a similar visual target 40 days after surgical removal of its vestibular apparatus. Since the initial eye saccade is uncorrected as the monkey begins turning its head, the monkey's gaze strongly overshoots the target. Even in this short period, however, some degree of compensatory eye movement has already developed. Traces at the right were made 120 days after surgery. Now, even without the help of vestibular feedback, saccadic eye movements have been "recalibrated" through experience, so that the gaze no longer overshoots.

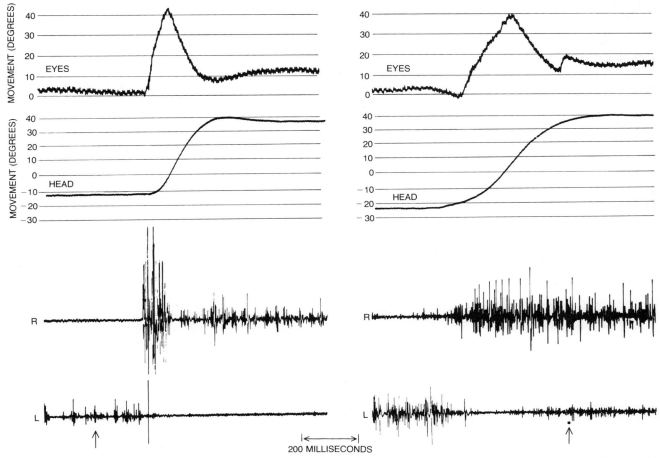

DIFFERENT STRATEGIES of eye-head coordination appear in different behavioral contexts. Whenever a visual stimulus is suddenly presented to a monkey (left), the animal first turns its eyes, then its head, in the direction of the target, which in this case appears 30 degrees to the right at eye level. The arrow indicates the time of target presentation. Trace R shows the burst of impulses that signals activation of the neck muscle (the splenius capitis) that turns the head to the right. Impulses in the antagonist muscles (L) simultaneously cease. A monkey uses a different strategy in the coordination of eye-head movements, however, when it turns toward a given position in anticipation of the appearance of a similar target (right). The author calls this mode "predictive." Now the head begins to move before the target appears and before the start of the eye saccade. Moreover, the head movement is instituted by a gradual increase in the activity of the agonist neck muscles (R) and a decrease in the activity of the antagonist muscles (L).

to a point in visual space while the head is rotating.

Summing up, we are now in a position to outline a realistic scheme for how movements of the eye and head are coordinated when a visual target is being acquired. The coordination involves a sequence of events in which feedback signals provide a closed loop, thereby making possible the correction of errors [see illustration on next page]. The sequence begins with the detection of a target somewhere in the visual field. Motor programs involving the head and the eyes are activated and respond by sending impulses to eye and neck muscles. This results in a saccadic eye movement and a head movement that activates vestibular receptors, which in turn generate a compensatory eye movement. The compensatory eye movement allows the fovea to remain fixed in relation to a point in visual space during head-turning. The fixation allows a second visual sampling, then a third and so on, with opportunities for correcting errors at each sampling.

If our hypothesized closed loop correctly describes the coordination of eye-head movements, it is clear that the role of the motor program stored in the central nervous system is simply to initiate, in an impulsive manner, movements of the eyes and head. Since there is no central programming of saccadic adjustment and of compensatory eye movement, it follows that the functional, or behavioral, coordination of head and eyes is the joint result of a central initiation (following a stored program) modified by the crucial intervention of modulating signals triggered by receptors in the vestibule of the inner ear. This conclusion somewhat simplifies our views of the neural mechanisms underlying motor coordination insofar as, contrary to common assumptions, we find no need to postulate a special central population of "executive" neurons with exclusive responsibility for coordinating the eyes and the head.

So far I have described the timing and the characteristics of the coordination of eye-head movements that are elicited by the appearance of a visual target, and have presented our evidence for the conclusion that the programs for eye-head coordination are not present in the central nervous system in their entirety. In what follows I shall take up two additional and interrelated topics. The first has to do with the fact that there are other modes or programs of the coordination of eye-head movements in addition to the one I have been discussing, and I shall indicate the relevance of

distinguishing among such modes to the continuing research on the central control of movement. The second topic is related to the impressive capacity for functional reorganization that is displayed by eye-head motor programs following lesions in key structures such as the vestibular system.

Concerning the first topic, it is well known that in primates there are several other modes of the coordination of eye-head movements, such as those observed while the animal is tracking a moving object or scanning the visual environment. In our laboratory we have recently analyzed a particularly interesting mode of coordination that we call predictive because we observe it only after the animal has memorized a set of reward contingencies and is able to make an appropriate predictive movement that anticipates the presentation of a visual stimulus.

Under these conditions the timing of eye and head movements and the pattern of neck-muscle activation are different from those found in the visually triggered mode [see bottom illustration on preceding page]. In fact, during the predictive coordination of eye-head movements the head begins to move well before the saccade of the eye is initiated. In addition the head movement is achieved by a gradual increase in activity of the agonist muscles (the muscles that initiate turning), which is accompanied by a decrease in the activity of the antagonist muscles (the muscles that oppose turning). This pattern of reciprocal, gradual agonist-antagonist activity is in marked contrast to the bursts of muscle impulses invariably recorded from the agonist muscles when a monkey is presented with an unexpected visual stimulus.

The fact that motor output subserving the coordination of eye-head movements is not fixed but instead exhibits distinctive patterns depending on the specific behavioral situation raises tantalizing questions. For instance, are there separate areas in the brain for the programming of different modes of coordination? If there are, are the various modes of coordination subserved by a totally different and separate neural network? How is the switching from one mode to another accomplished?

These are formidable questions for the neurophysiologist interested in outlining realistic models for the various kinds of motor coordination. Nevertheless, the investigation of such problems is no longer beyond reach. In fact, new

techniques of recording from a single cell in an intact trained animal such as those developed by Edward V. Evarts of the National Institute of Mental Health, combined with traditional neurophysiological and behavioral approaches, might enable us to unravel some aspects of the patterns of motor activity in the cortical and subcortical areas of the brain. I believe the possibility of bringing different strategies of motor coordination under control in the laboratory is relevant to the functional analysis of the motor system.

The notion of strategies of movement is in fact a powerful tool for interpreting single-cell recordings from cortical and subcortical motor areas. Since different strategies of movement are characterized by different spatial-temporal patterns of commands to the muscles, more compelling correlations between single-neuron activity and some aspects of motor behavior can be established. In addition the distinction between strategies of movement is an aid in the interpretation of selective brain lesions of those structures that are deemed important in the regulation of these movements.

Concerning the second topic, we were led to investigate plastic changes in the central organization of the eye-head motor system by our discovery of the decisive importance of the vestibular input in determining the nature of the coordination of eye-head movements. It was natural to wonder how that coordination would be affected if the vestibular input to the brain stem were eliminated. Are there other mechanisms that can take over the vestibular function? Our aim was not only to ascertain the degree of functional recovery of sensory-motor coordination but also to understand the mechanism underlying the recovery of the coordination of eye-head movements.

Our results have shown that a variety of several basically different mechanisms are developed and jointly brought into play. Among them are the development of new eye programs, including one that provides compensatory eye movements. We have already seen that in the normal monkey compensatory eye movements are achieved by way of vestibular impulses. Two or more months after monkeys were surgically deprived of vestibular sensors, however, centrally programmed compensatory eye movements were found to contribute to ocular stability during active turning of the head. Thus the oculomotor system is capable of taking on, albeit in a crude and in-

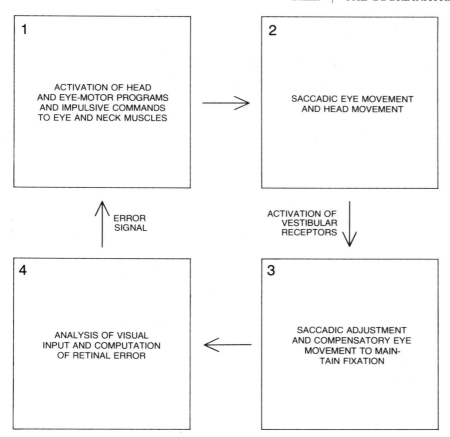

1	2
ACTIVATION OF HEAD AND EYE-MOTOR PROGRAMS AND IMPULSIVE COMMANDS TO EYE AND NECK MUSCLES	SACCADIC EYE MOVEMENT AND HEAD MOVEMENT

ERROR SIGNAL

ACTIVATION OF VESTIBULAR RECEPTORS

4	3
ANALYSIS OF VISUAL INPUT AND COMPUTATION OF RETINAL ERROR	SACCADIC ADJUSTMENT AND COMPENSATORY EYE MOVEMENT TO MAINTAIN FIXATION

CONTROL SCHEME FOR EYE-HEAD COORDINATION is believed to begin (1) with a central-nervous-system motor program that initiates the movement of the eyes and head when a visual target appears unexpectedly. The initial saccadic eye movement and head movement (2) are evidently based on a rapid computation of the target location carried out by cortical and subcortical regions of the brain in a manner not yet understood. As the head begins to turn, sensitive motion receptors in the vestibule of the inner ear initiate signals that lead to counterrotation of the eyes in order to maintain fixation of the target (3). During these coordinated eye-head movements the visual input is analyzed and an error computation is made (4). The result is an error signal that closes the control loop.

adequate form, functions previously elicited by vestibular activity.

Another mechanism contributing to the remarkable recovery in the coordination of eye-head movements that occurs within the first two to three months fol-lowing vestibulectomy entails a "recali-bration" of saccadic eye movements with respect to visual input. As I have indi-cated, immediately after vestibulectomy the gaze of a monkey whose head is free to turn will badly overshoot a visual tar-get because the saccade amplitude is no longer modulated by corrective feedback signals from the vestibular apparatus. In other words, the eye movement appro-priate for fixating the target when the head is held fixed is simply added to the head movement.

After two to three months, however, vestibulectomized monkeys learn to make saccades that are smaller than nor-mal as they turn their head in the direc-tion of a visual target, thereby reducing the tendency of the gaze to overshoot its mark [*see illustration at right at top of page 119*]. On the other hand, if the head of a vestibulectomized monkey is restrained when it is unexpectedly pre-sented with a visual target perhaps 30 degrees away from its straight-ahead axis of vision, its eyes will continue to make a saccade of 30 degrees, enabling it to fixate the target. Hence the oculomotor system is recalibrated selectively: when the head is restrained, the saccades are normal; when the head is free to turn, the saccades become smaller.

These two oculomotor functions are an important part of the mechanism un-derlying recovery of the coordination of eye-head movements. They provide a striking example of the remarkable plas-ticity of the central motor apparatus, a plasticity that comes into play whenever the organism is forced to compensate for a handicap or deficit imposed on it by events over which it has no control.

13

The Cortex
of the Cerebellum

by Rodolfo R. Llinás
January 1975

In this part of the brain the pattern of connections between nerve cells has been determined in detail. The pattern is now understood well enough to relate it to the function of the neuronal networks

In the study of the brain a perennial goal is to infer function from structure, to relate the behavior of an animal to the form and organization of the cells in its central nervous system. At the highest level this task can be equated with the tantalizing problem of identifying the mind with the brain, a problem whose solution may well elude us for some time to come. On a more modest scale the operation of certain limited regions of the brain can already be interpreted in terms of cellular anatomy. For example, the sensory nerve circuits associated with the retina of the eye and the olfactory organs of the nasal cavity have been traced in detail, and our understanding of these circuits has helped to reveal how visual and olfactory information is processed.

The region of the brain where the correlation of anatomy with function has been determined with the greatest success is the cortex, or outer sheath, of the cerebellum. The cells of this structure have been classified according to their form and their position and orientation in the tissue. The properties of each kind of cell, and in particular their response to stimulation, have been investigated. Perhaps most important, a complete "wiring diagram" of the cerebellar nerve circuit has been drawn, showing how the several types of cells are interconnected. From this knowledge of the individual cell and of the pattern of connections between cells one can begin to predict the behavior of the system as a whole.

Of course, our knowledge of the cerebellum is far from complete. To begin with, a comprehensive explanation of the cerebellum would require an equally comprehensive understanding of other parts of the brain with which the cerebellum communicates; some of those areas remain quite mysterious. Furthermore, our present model of the cerebellum is best suited to describing what happens when a single nerve impulse enters the cortex, and it must be somewhat vague in specifying the effect of a complex pattern of impulses. The model is valuable nevertheless; at the least it offers evidence that the functioning of the brain can be explained simply as the sum of the activities of its component cells, that in the final analysis all mental activity consists of known kinds of interactions between known kinds of nerve cells.

Anatomy of the Cerebellum

The cerebellum lies at the back of the skull behind the brain stem and under the great hemispheres of the cerebrum. Its name is a Latin diminutive of "cerebrum" and means simply "lesser brain." Superficially that is an adequate description of the cerebellum: it is much smaller than the cerebrum but shares certain morphological features with it. As in the cerebrum, the highest functions in the cerebellum are confined to the thin layer of gray matter that makes up the cortex and, as in the cerebrum, this layer is elaborately folded and wrinkled to increase its area. The folds are in fact much deeper and more closely spaced than those of the cerebral cortex. If the cerebellum is split down the middle, the folds form a pattern that resembles a tree, which medieval anatomists termed the *arbor vitae*, or tree of life [*see illustrations on page 125*].

Both the structure and the function of the cerebellum have been known, at least in terms of broad principles, since the end of the 19th century. The challenge to modern investigators has been in combining the two kinds of data and discovering how a particular structure generates the observed behavior.

The fundamentals of cerebellar anatomy were established in 1888 by Santiago Ramón y Cajal of Spain. He employed a staining technique that had been developed in 1873 by Camillo Golgi of Italy, in which the tissue is impregnated with salts of silver, coloring some of the nerve cells deep brown or black. By studying many stained sections of tissue Ramón y Cajal identified the principal neurons, or nerve cells, of the cerebellar cortex and described their arrangement in space. The arrangement itself is remarkable: some elements of the system are arrayed at right angles to others with extraordinary precision and delicacy. Finally, Ramón y Cajal determined the nature of the connections between the neurons and recognized in them a stereotyped pattern, repeated throughout the cortex. The essential accuracy of his observations has been repeatedly confirmed, and the neuronal circuit he described has been found to be a universal feature of the cerebellum from the most primitive vertebrates to the most advanced.

The first reliable clue to the function of the cerebellum was provided by the Italian physiologist Luigi Luciani, who discovered that experimental animals deprived of a cerebellum suffer disturbances of coordination and equilibrium. Other investigators subsequently demonstrated that the cerebellum communicates with both the motor centers of the cerebrum and the proprioceptive organs of the body, the nerves that sense the relative position and tension of the muscles. By the end of the 19th century the English physiologist Charles Sherrington was able to conclude that the cerebellum coordinates the movements of the muscles but does not initiate them. Although

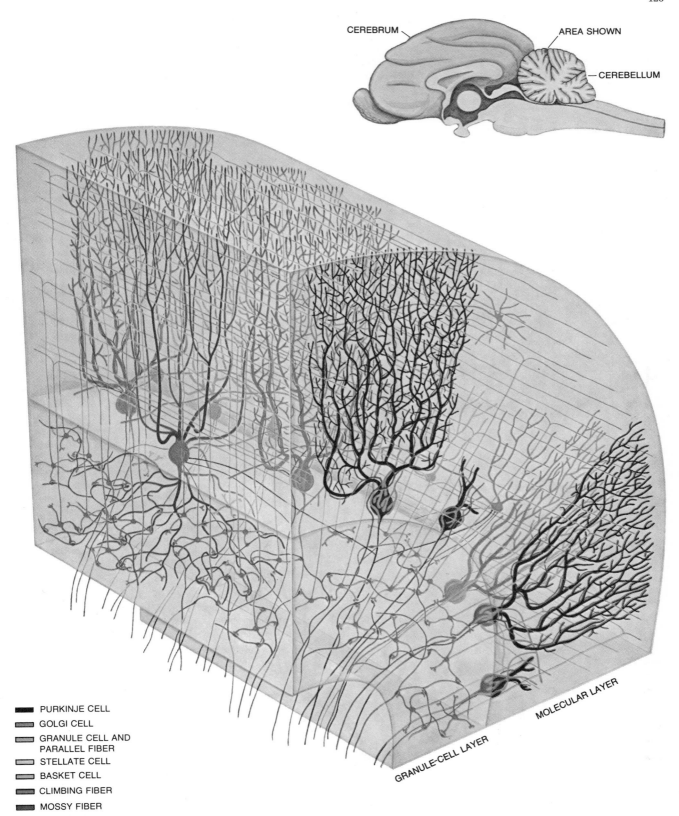

PURKINJE CELL
GOLGI CELL
GRANULE CELL AND
PARALLEL FIBER
STELLATE CELL
BASKET CELL
CLIMBING FIBER
MOSSY FIBER

ARCHITECTURE OF THE CORTEX of the cerebellum is diagrammed for a section of tissue from the brain of a cat. The location of the tissue section is indicated in the drawing at top right; the same array of cells is repeated throughout the cortex. Each cell type is identified by color in the key at bottom left. The cortex is organized around the Purkinje cells, whose somas, or cell bodies, define the border between the superficial molecular layer and the deeper granule-cell layer. In the molecular layer are the Purkinje-cell dendrites, which are arrayed in flattened networks like pressed leaves, and the parallel fibers, which pass through the dendrites perpendicularly. This layer also contains the stellate cells and the basket cells, which have similarly flattened arrays of dendrites. In the deeper layer are the granule cells, which give rise to the parallel fibers, and the Golgi cells, which are characterized by a cylindrical dendritic array. Input to the cortex is through the climbing fibers and mossy fibers; output is through the axons of Purkinje cells.

Sherrington's formulation can no longer be accepted entirely, it has been refined rather than refuted [see "The Cerebellum," by Ray S. Snider; SCIENTIFIC AMERICAN Offprint 38].

The Cerebellar Neurons

One reason the cerebellum is so well understood today is that its organization is much simpler than that of most other parts of the brain. The basic circuit of the cortex—with few modifications the circuit described by Ramón y Cajal—involves just seven nerve elements. Two of them conduct nerve impulses into the cortex; they are called the climbing fibers and the mossy fibers. Another

serves as the sole output of the system; it is the Purkinje-cell axon. The four remaining nerve elements are the granule cells, the Golgi cells, the basket cells and the stellate cells; they are entirely indigenous to the cerebellar cortex and run short distances between the other cells. The input terminals are often referred to as afferent fibers, the output cells as efferent neurons and the cells that serve as intermediaries as interneurons [see illustration below].

The discovery of a third afferent system, in addition to the climbing fibers and the mossy fibers, has recently been reported by F. E. Bloom and his colleagues at Saint Elizabeths Hospital in Washington. It consists of fibers arising

from a structure in the brain stem called the locus ceruleus. Because it is not yet clear how this system is related to the other functions of the cerebellum it will not be considered further here.

Neurons are diverse in form, but they all have certain structures in common. Each has a soma, or cell body, which contains the nucleus and usually a major portion of the cytoplasm as well. Extending from the soma are the dendrites (from the Greek for "tree"), which often branch repeatedly, and the axon, which can be quite long and may or may not branch. For the most part dendrites conduct nerve impulses toward the body of the cell and the axon conducts impulses away from it. The junction where the axon of one cell meets a dendrite of another is a synapse.

When a nerve impulse reaches the terminal point of the axon, it provokes the release of a transmitter substance, which passes across the synapse and alters the membrane of the dendrite of the next cell in the neural pathway, changing its permeability to certain ions. The resulting flow of ions across the membrane generates a small electric current, which propagates as a local electrical disturbance of the membrane down the dendrite to the soma. If the stimulating neuron is excitatory, and if the stimulation exceeds a threshold, the receiving cell will "fire" and the impulse will be conveyed through the axon to the next synapse. If the first cell is inhibitory, the probability that the receiving cell will fire is reduced.

The Purkinje cells were among the first neurons recognized in the nervous system; they are named for Johannes E. Purkinje, the Czech physiologist who described them in 1837. They are among the most complex of all neurons. Each has a large and extensive dendritic apparatus referring impulses to a bulblike soma, and a long, slender axon [see illustration on page 126]. The dendrites of a typical human Purkinje cell may form as many as 100,000 synapses with afferent fibers, more than those of any other cell in the central nervous system.

The Purkinje cells are the pivotal element in the neuronal network of the cerebellar cortex. They are found throughout the cortex, their cell bodies constituting a continuous sheath called the Purkinje-cell layer. The dendrites extend densely above the Purkinje-cell layer, toward the boundary of the cortex; this region is called the molecular layer. The axons extend in the opposite direction, into the deeper portion of the cortex called the granule-cell layer. The axons, in fact, penetrate far beyond this

PURKINJE CELL
GOLGI CELL
GRANULE CELL AND PARALLEL FIBER
STELLATE CELL
BASKET CELL
CLIMBING FIBER
MOSSY FIBER

INTERCONNECTION OF NEURONS in the cortex follows an elaborate but stereotyped pattern. Each Purkinje cell is associated with a single climbing fiber and forms many synaptic junctions with it. The climbing fiber also branches to the basket cells and Golgi cells. Mossy fibers come in contact with the terminal "claws" of granule-cell dendrites in a structure called a cerebellar glomerulus. The axons of the granule cells ascend to the molecular layer, where they bifurcate to form parallel fibers. Each parallel fiber comes in contact with many Purkinje cells, but usually it forms only one synapse with each cell. The stellate cells connect the parallel fibers with the dendrites of the Purkinje cell, the basket cells mainly with the Purkinje-cell soma. Most Golgi-cell dendrites form junctions with the parallel fibers but some join the mossy fibers; Golgi-cell axons terminate at the cerebellar glomeruli. Cells are identified in the key at lower left; arrows indicate direction of nerve conduction.

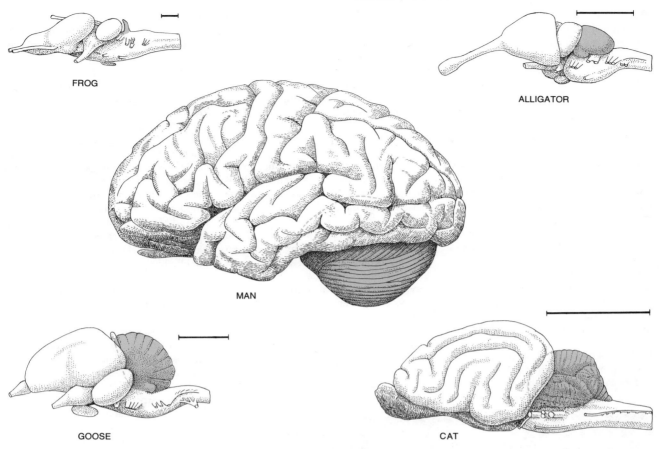

FROG

ALLIGATOR

MAN

GOOSE

CAT

EVOLUTION OF THE CEREBELLUM suggests that its function has become more important during the span of vertebrate history. From the amphibians through the reptiles and birds to the mammals it has become progressively larger, both in actual mass and in proportion to overall brain size. It has also become more convoluted, providing a greater area of cortex. In man it is a large and deeply fissured structure. The cerebellums are shown in color; the scale in relation to the human brain is indicated by horizontal bars.

region; they pass out of the cortex entirely, through the white matter in the core of the cerebellum, and eventually reach isolated lumps of gray matter called cerebellar nuclei. The nuclei are also supplied with side branches of the climbing-fiber and mossy-fiber input

systems, so that they receive all the information going to the cortex. In the nuclei the incoming messages are blended with those returning from the cortex and are relayed to other parts of the brain and down the spinal cord to the rest of the body.

The dendrites of the Purkinje cells have an unusual arrangement that is at once the most conspicuous structural element in the cerebellar cortex and an important clue to its functioning. The entire mass of tangled, repeatedly bifurcating branches is confined to a single

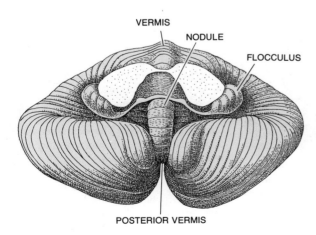

VERMIS

NODULE

FLOCCULUS

POSTERIOR VERMIS

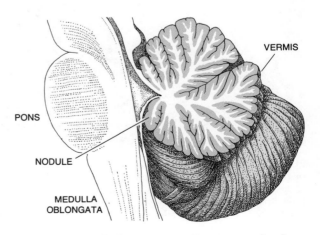

VERMIS

PONS

NODULE

MEDULLA OBLONGATA

HUMAN CEREBELLUM consists of two hemispheres separated by a narrow girdle, the vermis. At left it is viewed from below; the brain stem has been removed to reveal the vermis, flocculus and nodule, which are involved in eye movement, among other functions. At right the cerebellum is sectioned through the vermis. The pattern of cortical folds is called the *arbor vitae* ("tree of life").

plane, as if it had been flattened like a pressed leaf. Moreover, the planes of all the dendrites in a given region are parallel, so that the dendritic arrays of the cells stack up in neat ranks; adjacent cells in a single plane form equally neat, but overlapping, files.

To a large extent this orderly array determines the nature and number of contacts made with other kinds of cells. As has been pointed out by Clement A. Fox of the Wayne State University School of Medicine, the dendrites are organized like a net to "catch" as many incoming signals as possible. Fibers running perpendicular to the plane of the dendrites will intersect a great many Purkinje cells, although they will touch each cell only once or at most a few times. Fibers oriented in this way do in fact constitute one of the afferent systems in the cortex. (Geometric arrays similar to the arrangement of the Purkinje-cell dendrites appear elsewhere in biology where a large surface area must be fitted into a small volume; an example is the antennae of moths.)

The Purkinje cell represents the out-put system of the cerebellar cortex, but it is not a mere transmitter or repeater of information originating elsewhere. It is part of an indivisible system of neurons whose activity is determined entirely by the way in which the other neurons are connected with the Purkinje cells and with one another.

The Climbing Fiber

The climbing fibers and the mossy fibers, the two afferent systems that ultimately direct impulses to the Purkinje cells, are distributed throughout the cerebellar cortex in a more or less orderly array. Their presence in all parts of the cortex was demonstrated by Jan Jansen and Alf Brodal and their colleagues at the Anatomical Institute at Oslo in Norway. These workers also showed that the two systems are apparently present in all members of the vertebrate subphylum. The systems are radically different; in some properties they represent opposite extremes among the neurons of the central nervous system.

The climbing fiber is virtually a private line to a given Purkinje cell. It begins outside the cerebellum in other regions of the brain such as the inferior olive, a compact collection of nerve cells alongside the medulla oblongata. The long, ramified axons of these cells extend into the cerebellar nuclei and cortex. In embryonic development the climbing fiber is the first afferent system to reach the Purkinje cell, and once it has "mated" with its particular cell it generally enforces monogamy. The union takes place early in the development of the cerebellum, and the formation of a junction with one climbing fiber apparently discourages others from attaching themselves to the same cell. As the Purkinje cell develops its net of dendrites the climbing fiber follows, matching the intricacy of the dendrites like a vine growing on the trunk and branches of a large tree. This behavior is the root of its name.

It was once believed the climbing fiber formed synapses with the smooth surface of the Purkinje-cell dendrites. It has now been demonstrated by Luis M. H. Larramendi and his colleagues at the University of Chicago, however, that the two cells are actually in contact only where small spines protrude in groups from the surface of the Purkinje-cell dendrite [*see illustrations on opposite page*]. There are many such spines on any one Purkinje cell. Dean E. Hillman of the University of Iowa has estimated that a Purkinje cell and its climbing fiber are probably in synaptic contact at about 300 points, which is a large number of junctions to be established between a cell and a single afferent fiber.

The action of the climbing fiber on the Purkinje cell was described in 1964 by John C. Eccles, K. Sasaki and me. Working at the Australian National University in Canberra, we found that stimulating a climbing fiber produced an exceedingly powerful excitation of the corresponding Purkinje cell. The Purkinje cell responded with a prolonged burst of high-frequency action potentials, the electrically recorded evidence that a nerve cell is discharging. The intensity of the response was not unexpected, considering the large number of synapses connecting the cells. The excitation was capable of overriding any ongoing activity in the Purkinje cell.

Recordings made with electrodes implanted in Purkinje cells showed that the action potential arises very quickly, then declines slowly and irregularly [*see illustration on page 128*]. The recorded pattern represents the firing of the cell body of the neuron and the generation of

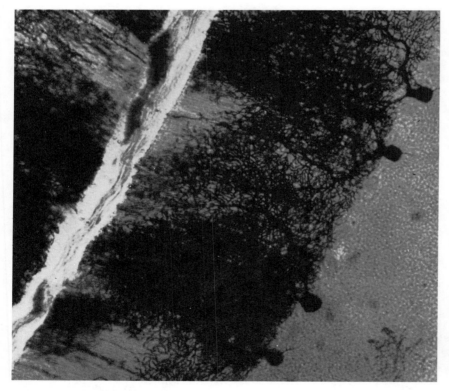

PURKINJE CELLS sprout a dense network of overlapping dendrites, all confined to a single plane and extending above the cell bodies through the molecular layer to the surface of the cortex. In this section of tissue from the brain of a monkey the surface of the cortex is the bright diagonal strip; it is inside a fold and abuts another part of the cortex with its own Purkinje cells. The parallel fibers are not visible; they run perpendicular to the plane of the page. The Purkinje-cell axons are the small fibers extending from the cell bodies toward deeper strata. The tissue was prepared by staining it with silver salts; the photomicrograph was made by Clement A. Fox of the Wayne State University School of Medicine.

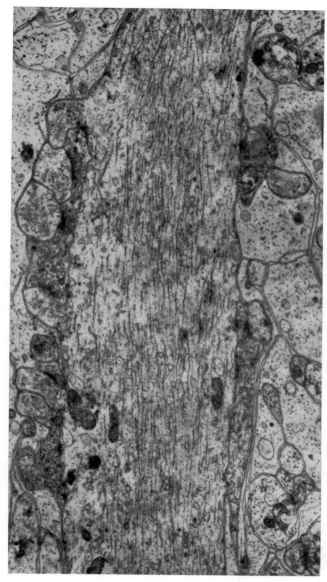

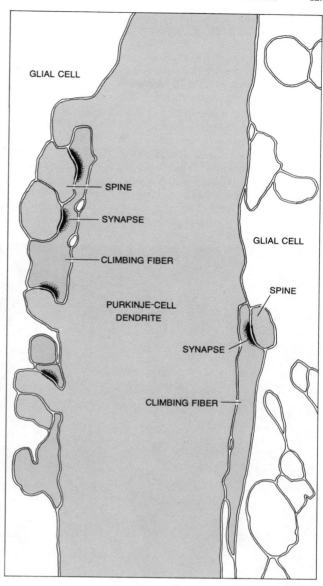

CLIMBING FIBER forms numerous synaptic junctions with a Purkinje-cell dendrite through spines that protrude in clusters from the surface of the dendrite. The structures visible in the electron micrograph at left are diagrammed and identified in the drawing at right. The several regions labeled "Climbing fiber" are segments of a single fiber that is wrapped around the dendrite. Nerve impulses are transmitted from the climbing fiber to the dendrite. Glial cells surrounding the synapse are not neurons but serve as a matrix in which the nerve cells are embedded. The photomicrograph was made by Dean E. Hillman of the University of Iowa.

many lesser action potentials in the dendrites as the cell is showered with synaptic transmitters released at many points by the climbing fiber. Because the response is provoked by a single impulse in a single afferent fiber, it is an all-or-nothing phenomenon, that is, it is present in full force or is absent altogether.

The Mossy Fiber

Whereas the climbing fiber generates many connections to a single Purkinje cell, the mossy fiber ultimately excites many Purkinje cells, but through only a few contacts with each of them. Among all the neurons of the central nervous system, the mossy fiber stimulates one of the largest numbers of cells to be activated by a single efferent fiber.

The mossy fibers do not terminate directly on Purkinje cells, as the climbing fibers do, but on small interneurons, the granule cells, which lie immediately under the Purkinje-cell layer. The granule cells serve as intermediaries, greatly increasing the number of Purkinje cells stimulated by a single afferent fiber.

One reason the granule cells can intersect so many Purkinje cells is that the granule cells are themselves exceedingly numerous. Valentino Braitenberg of the Max Planck Institute for Biological Cybernetics in Tübingen has calculated that the number of granule cells in the human cerebellar cortex may be 10 times greater than the number of cells previously believed to make up the entire brain. Sanford L. Palay of the Harvard Medical School has commented: "Of the 10^{10} cells in the brain, 10^{11} are in the granular layer of the cerebellar cortex!"

The axon of the granule cell projects upward, past the Purkinje-cell layer and into the molecular layer. There it splits, the two branches taking diametrically opposite directions, so that the axon assumes the form of a capital *T*. Fibers representing the horizontal portion of the *T* occupy all levels of the molecular layer. The orientation of these fibers is precisely determined: they are all parallel to one another (for that reason they are called parallel fibers), and they are perpendicular to the planes of the flat-turned Purkinje-cell dendrites [*see illustration on page 123*]. The arrangement of the cells is thus somewhat like an array of telephone poles (the Purkinje cells) strung with many telephone wires (the parallel fibers). The actual conformation is complicated by the curvature of the folds in the cortex.

The parallel fibers come in contact with the Purkinje cells through spines that emerge in enormous numbers from the terminal regions of the Purkinje-cell dendrites, regions called spiny branchlets [*see illustrations on opposite page*]. The junction is formed between the point of a spine and a globular expansion of the parallel fiber; the geometry of the synapse may resemble that of a ball joint, in which the spine penetrates the swollen part of the fiber.

Generally a parallel fiber comes in contact with a given Purkinje cell only once or (rarely) twice; nevertheless, most of the inputs to the Purkinje cells are through the parallel fibers. As I have noted, a single human Purkinje cell can receive as many as 100,000 parallel fibers (compared with a single climbing fiber).

Eccles, Sasaki and I have studied the effects of stimulating the mossy fibers. Like the climbing fiber, the mossy fiber is excitatory, and so is the granule cell it stimulates. Both afferent systems can therefore excite activity in the cerebellar cortex. The influence of the mossy fibers, however, is for obvious reasons diffuse and complex, in contrast to the sharply focused effect of the climbing fiber.

The Interneurons

Embedded in the matrix of the cerebellar circuitry are two sets of interneurons that, unlike the granule cells, have only short axons. One set is located in the molecular layer and consists of basket cells and stellate cells; the other is in the granule-cell layer and is represented by Golgi cells.

The basket and stellate cells are similar and can be considered members of a single class. Both receive impulses from the parallel fibers and act, through their axons, on Purkinje cells. The principal difference between the two types is that the basket cell establishes synaptic junctions with the Purkinje cell in the lower dendrites and on the soma, whereas the stellate cell is more or less confined to the dendrites. Perhaps the most significant anatomical observation on the basket and stellate cells pertains to the spatial distribution of their axons. They are perpendicular to the parallel fibers and are also perpendicular to the axis of the Purkinje cells. The network of cells in the molecular layer thus consists of three basic types of cell process all of which are mutually perpendicular.

In the granule-cell layer the remaining interneuron, the Golgi cell, also receives impulses from the parallel fibers, but its dendrites form synapses directly with the mossy fibers as well. The Golgi cells are components of a specialized synaptic linkage known as the cerebellar glomerulus, which is the basic functional unit of the granule-cell layer. It consists of a bulge or swelling in a mossy fiber, surrounded by the dendrites of granule cells, which in turn are surrounded by the axons of Golgi cells [*see illustrations on page 130*].

All three kinds of interneuron have been demonstrated to be inhibitory. The inhibitory effect of the basket cell on the soma of the Purkinje cell was initially shown by P. Andersen, Eccles and P. E.

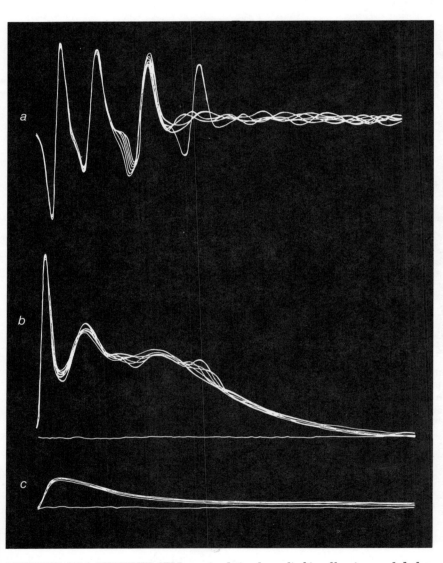

RESPONSE OF A PURKINJE CELL to stimulation by a climbing fiber is recorded electrically. Action potentials (voltages developed across the cell membrane) are measured from outside the cell (*a*) and from inside it (*b*). The response is strong and consistent; several repetitions are superposed here, revealing only small variations. It is an all-or-nothing response; if the climbing fiber fails to fire, only a straight line is recorded. Climbing-fiber stimulation provokes the firing of the Purkinje cell by depolarizing the cell membrane; the phenomenon can be recorded in isolation (*c*) in a damaged cell. The time span of the recordings is about 20 milliseconds. The voltages are not drawn to the same scale; those measured inside the cell (*b*, *c*) are actually many times larger than those measured outside (*a*).

Voorhoeve at the Australian National University in 1963; the inhibition of Purkinje-cell dendrites by stellate cells and the inhibition of granule cells by Golgi cells were demonstrated soon afterward by Eccles, Sasaki and me.

Organization of the Neurons

As we have seen, the activation of the cerebellar cortex through the climbing-fiber system is relatively straightforward: the stimulation of a single climbing fiber elicits a powerful response from a single Purkinje cell. The sequence of events that follows on the stimulation of a mossy fiber is not only more complicated but also inherently less predictable.

The initial sequence of events was first suggested by János Szentágothai of the Semmelweis University School of Medicine in Budapest: the stimulation of a small bunch of mossy fibers activates, through the granule cells and their parallel fibers, an extensive array of Purkinje cells and all three types of inhibitory interneuron. Subsequent interactions of the neurons tend to limit the extent and duration of the response. The activation of Purkinje cells through the parallel fibers is soon inhibited by the basket cells and the stellate cells, which are activated by the same parallel fibers. Because the axons of the basket and stellate cells run at right angles to the parallel fibers, the inhibition is not confined to the activated Purkinje cells; those on each side of the beam or column of stimulated Purkinje cells are also subject to strong inhibition. The effect of the inhibitory neurons is therefore to sharpen the boundary and increase the contrast between those cells that have been activated and those that have not.

At the same time the parallel fibers and the mossy fibers have activated the Golgi cells at the granule-cell level. The Golgi cells exert their inhibitory effect on the granule cells and thereby quench any further activity in the parallel fibers. This mechanism is one of negative feedback: through the Golgi cell the parallel fiber extinguishes its own stimulus. The net result of these interactions is the brief firing of a relatively large but sharply defined population of Purkinje cells.

At about the time the functional properties of these neuronal circuits were being elucidated an observation made by Masao Ito and his colleagues at the University of Tokyo changed our perspective on the behavior of the entire system. Ito and his co-workers discovered that the Purkinje cell is itself an inhibitory neuron. The entire output of the elabo-

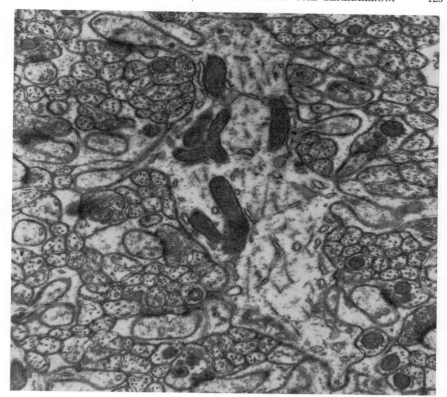

PARALLEL FIBERS attach to a Purkinje-cell dendrite in an electron micrograph made by Hillman. The dendrite is sectioned longitudinally; the parallel fibers are cut transversely.

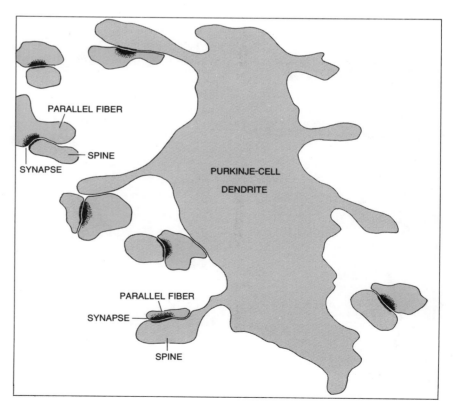

SYNAPSES between parallel fibers and the Purkinje-cell dendrite are indicated in a diagram identifying the elements of the electron micrograph at the top of the page. The region of the dendrite shown is called a spiny branchlet; the spines form junctions with the parallel fibers. Each parallel fiber ordinarily makes only one contact with a given Purkinje cell.

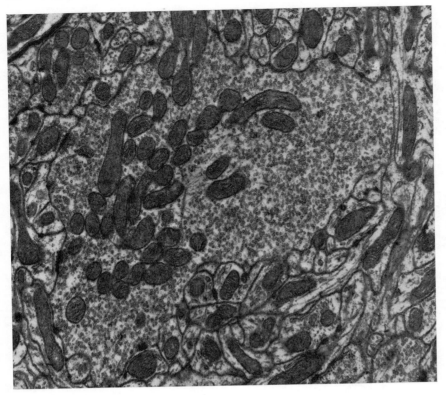

CEREBELLAR GLOMERULUS is seen in cross section in another electron micrograph made by Hillman. The cells of the mammalian tissue are identified in the diagram below.

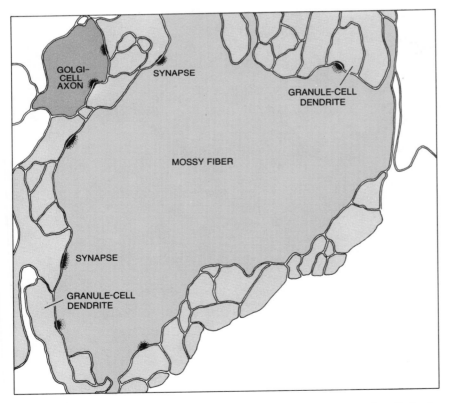

MOSSY FIBER forms synapses with the terminal dendrites of many granule cells in the cerebellar glomerulus. In addition the axons of Golgi cells make contact with the same granule-cell dendrites. The glomerulus forms on an enlarged segment of the mossy fiber.

rate neuronal network in the cerebellar cortex is therefore the organized, large-scale inhibition of other neurons in the cerebellar nuclei. Furthermore, it became evident that of the cells residing in the cortex only the granule cells are excitatory; all the rest are inhibitory. This work provided a fundamental insight into the functioning of the cortex. The firing of the nerve cells that give rise to the climbing fibers and the mossy fibers produces rapid activation of the cerebellar nuclei and through them of cerebral and spinal systems. This activity is abruptly terminated by the inhibitory signals from the cortex.

In several ways the model of the cerebellar cortex devised in these early studies was too simplistic. Although it described with some accuracy the neuronal response to an abrupt stimulus, such as an externally applied electrical potential, it was inadequate to describe the activity following the physiological stimuli constantly impinging on the cortex under ordinary circumstances. For example, the inhibitory interneurons of the molecular layer probably do not normally obliterate the activity of entire groups of Purkinje cells while allowing others to fire. It is more likely that they serve to set a threshold of excitability and thereby to regulate the dynamic range of activity in the cortex. The Golgi cell, on the other hand, is probably a central element in cerebellar organization. Through its direct contacts with the climbing fibers and the mossy fibers the Golgi cell probably "selects" what inputs reach the Purkinje-cell layer at a given time.

In spite of its limitations our study provided a foundation for constructing a theory of cerebellar function. The description of the interactions between the neuronal elements of the cortex was comprehensive and detailed, even if it was based on observations made under somewhat artificial circumstances. Furthermore, the study represented the first demonstration of a correlation between structure and function in a major lobe of the brain.

The Function of the Cerebellar Cortex

If we are finally to understand the significance of the neuronal circuits in the cerebellar cortex, we must analyze those circuits in terms of the kind of information they ordinarily receive. The techniques available for this task are necessarily less direct and less precise than dissection and staining or probing with an electrode, but they have nevertheless yielded important results. One of the most profitable techniques has been the mapping of projections onto the cerebellum. This consists in selecting a nerve fiber of known origin or destination outside the cerebellum and determining the point at which it impinges on the cerebellar cortex.

Each of the proprioceptive nerve endings in the skeletal muscles, for example, corresponds to a particular position on the surface of the cerebellum. When the sum of these positions is plotted, the result is a map such as the one that has been compiled over a period of many years by Olov Oscarsson of the University of Lund and by D. Armstrong and R. J. Harvey of the University of Bristol. By recording the projections of the climbing fibers they have discovered that these afferent cells are distributed with remarkable orderliness in the cerebellar cortex: they are organized in strips parallel to the median line and covering large areas distributed over many folds in the cortex [see bottom illustration on next page].

These maps confirm the earlier findings of Jan Voogd of the University of Leiden, who studied the effects of small lesions in the inferior olive, one of the principal sources of the climbing fibers. Nerve fibers radiating from a lesion usually degenerate, and Voogd found in this case that patterns of degenerating tissue on the cerebellar cortex assumed the form of long strips oriented from the front of the head to the back, that is, parallel to the median plane. His discovery suggests that the longitudinal strip is an important principle of organization in the projection of the climbing fibers onto the cerebellar cortex. The pattern has been detected in several vertebrate species.

A clue to the significance of this organizational pattern has recently been provided by pharmacological studies of the cortex. The experiments were performed by Y. Lamarre and C. de Montigny of the University of Montreal and by R. A. Volkind and me at the University of Iowa. They involved a drug called harmaline, derived from the herb harmal, which causes tremors; we have shown in the cat that the effects of the drug are traceable to the activation of the inferior olive. An immediate and obvious inference is that the inferior olive, with the fibers it projects to the cerebellar nuclei and the Purkinje cells, is part of a motor command system concerned with muscular movement. There is even a reasonable basis for speculation on what kind of movements are involved. When maps derived from the proprio-

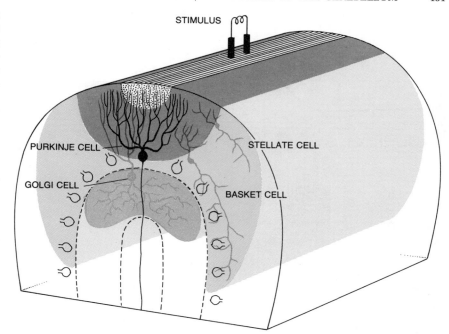

SPATIAL DISTRIBUTION of excitation in the cortex is determined largely by inhibitory neurons. When a brief electrical stimulus is applied to the surface of the cortex, a small

basket cells and Golgi cells. The firing of the Purkinje cells constitutes the sole output of the cortex; the other neurons serve to define which Purkinje cells can fire. Because the axons of basket cells and stellate cells extend at right angles to the parallel fibers in the molecular layer, they inhibit Purkinje cells in a wide area on both sides of the excited region (light color). The Golgi cells generate an area of inhibition in the granule cells directly under the activated array of parallel fibers (dark color). Because the parallel fibers are the axons of the granule cells, inhibition by Golgi cells tends to terminate the excitation.

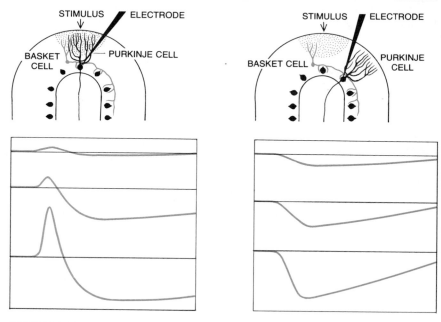

STIMULATION AND INHIBITION of Purkinje cells follow an established temporal sequence. When the response of a cell directly under the stimulated area is recorded (left), a brief period of activation is observed (upward deflection), followed by a longer period of inhibition (downward deflection). The activation results from the direct stimulation of the Purkinje cell by parallel fibers, the inhibition from the action of basket cells and stellate cells. The magnitude of the response varies with the intensity of the stimulation. When the response of a laterally located Purkinje cell is monitored (right), only the inhibition is observed, since only basket-cell axons, not stimulated parallel fibers, reach Purkinje cells.

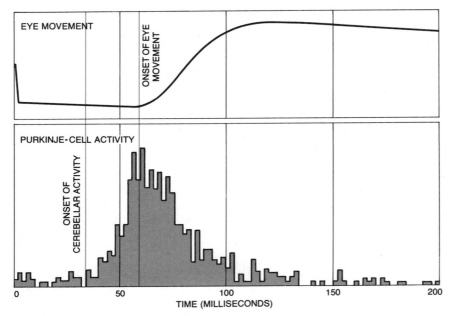

RAPID EYE MOVEMENTS called saccades are associated with activity in the cerebellar cortex. The top graph is an averaged record of 100 saccades; the bottom graph records the activity of a single Purkinje cell during the same 100 eye movements. Purkinje-cell activity begins to increase about 25 milliseconds before the movement is initiated, which suggests that the cerebellum can coordinate or correct such movements before they are generated.

ceptive sensors are superposed on the longitudinal strips that are associated with the climbing fibers, it is found that the climbing-fiber patterns overlap the projections of several areas of the body. It is the current hypothesis, therefore, that the climbing-fiber system is con-cerned with synchronous movements of groups of muscles, probably involving more than one limb. There is also reason to believe it mainly influences rapid movements. The inhibition of the cerebellar nuclei by the Purkinje cells should follow very soon after the activation of

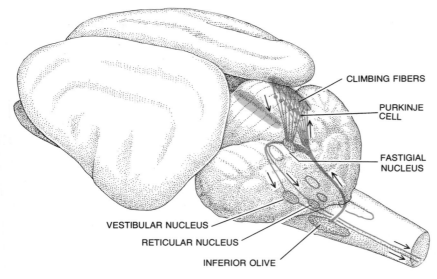

PROJECTION OF CLIMBING FIBERS onto the cerebellar cortex reveals an orderly distribution. The fibers originate in the two inferior olives of the brain stem. Fibers from each olive terminate in the opposite hemisphere of the cerebellum. There they are organized in longitudinal strips covering many cortical folds. The length and orientation of these strips suggest that the climbing-fiber system participates in the regulation of movements that involve several limbs, since each strip extends across areas known to be associated with several parts of the body. Branches of the climbing fibers also reach the cerebellar nuclei (the fastigial nucleus is shown here) and are joined there by the axons of Purkinje cells from the cortex. The output of the fastigial nucleus is applied to the vestibular and reticular nuclei.

the nuclei, generating a powerful but brief command signal.

A comprehensive analysis of the mossy-fiber system is more difficult to achieve. The effects of mossy-fiber stimulation are so different from those of the climbing fibers that it is possible the two systems are "time-sharing" the Purkinje cells, each employing them for quite different purposes. Not only do the mossy fibers activate large areas of the cortex instead of individual cells; they also enlist the aid of the inhibitory interneurons, which may modulate and detect patterns in incoming signals. The Golgi cells in particular may be involved in determining what kinds of information reach the cortex through the parallel fibers; moreover, in any time-sharing arrangement they could apportion the Purkinje cells between the two systems.

An example of a motor behavior that is linked with the mossy-fiber system has recently been encountered in studies of visual coordination. In organizing the delicate and precise movements of the eyes the cerebellum is evidently essential; cerebellar dysfunction often disrupts such movements. Two regions of the cerebellum are known to participate in these functions. One is the floccular-nodular area; it regulates the position of the eyes with respect to the orientation of the head and body, enabling one to stare at a fixed point while moving. The other is the cerebellar vermis, which is believed to control the rapid eye movements called saccades, which are important in visual tracking.

In a recent series of experiments at the Air Force School of Aerospace Medicine, James W. Wolfe and I showed that the activation of Purkinje cells by mossy fibers increases about 25 milliseconds before an eye movement begins [see top illustration at left]. The implication of this discovery is that cerebellar regulation of movement through the mossy-fiber system is capable of correcting mistakes before they have reached the muscles and have been expressed in actual movement. The cerebellum appears to correct these movements by acting as a brake.

Motor Coordination

There is no longer any doubt that the cerebellum is a central control point for the organization of movement. It does not initiate movement, and indeed movement can be generated in the absence of a cerebellum. It modulates or reorganizes motor commands, and by coordinating diverse signals it obtains the maximum efficiency from them. It is therefore an organ of regulation in the highest sense. It may in fact regulate more than motor performance. R. Nieuwenhuys and C. Nicholson of the Catholic University of Nijmegen have shown that in electric fish (family Mormyridae) employing an electric field as a sensory organ the cerebellum attains enormous size and fills most of the cranial cavity.

Without question the cerebellum is far more sophisticated than the simple control box, comparing muscle position with brain command, that Sherrington and his contemporaries supposed it to be. Israel Gelfand, M. L. Shik and their associates at the Institute of Information Transmission Systems in Moscow have shown that the cerebellum is capable of coordinating movement even in the absence of all information from the periphery of the body. They removed the forebrain and blocked proprioceptive sensation in experimental animals; as long as the cerebellum remained intact locomotion was possible, but it was disrupted when the cerebellum was removed. A series of experiments conducted by Anders Lundberg and his colleagues at the University of Göteborg provides a further indication that some cerebellar activity is concerned with the internal state of the central nervous system. They found that one of the main afferent tracts leading to the cerebellum, the ventral spinocerebellar tract, conveys information not about the state of the body or the external environment but about the activity of inhibitory interneurons in the spinal cord. Such an internal monitoring mechanism might be a necessity in a system intended to refine or revise motor commands before they reach the muscles, such as is observed in the cerebellar control of eye movement.

Excellence in motor coordination is obviously an adaptive advantage, and evidently it is enough of an advantage to sustain the development of a specialized brain center committed primarily to that purpose. The success of the motor coordination center is suggested by the calculations of Sherwood L. Washburn and R. S. Harding of the University of California at Berkeley. They report that the cerebellum has enlarged between threefold and fourfold in the past million years of human evolution.

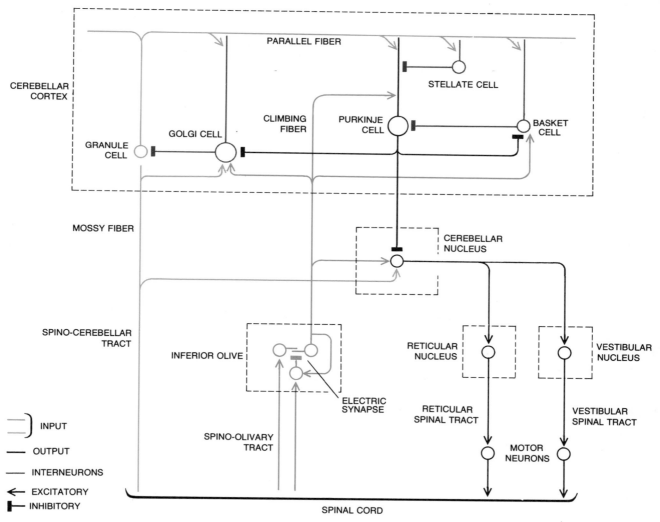

SCHEMATIC "WIRING DIAGRAM" of the cerebellar cortex and the brain centers with which it communicates relates the structure of the nerve-cell circuits to their function. The types of cells and synapses are identified in the key at lower left. Input to the cortex is through the climbing fibers and mossy fibers, both of which also send branches to the cerebellar nuclei. In the cortex both fibers ultimately act on the Purkinje cells; in addition the response of these cells is influenced by three kinds of interneurons, all of them inhibitory. Since the Purkinje cell is also inhibitory its effect on the cerebellar nuclei is to prevent the transmission of nerve impulses from the climbing fibers and mossy fibers that would otherwise reach the motor neurons and generate movement. Thus the cortex appears to be an organ of regulation, empowered to select certain motor commands for transmittal and to veto all others.

CENTRAL DETERMINANTS OF PERCEPTION

CENTRAL DETERMINANTS
OF PERCEPTION

II

INTRODUCTION

Our knowledge of perceptual processing has been acquired as a result of two opposite approaches. One approach starts with the stimulus input to receptors. The readings in Section I have dealt largely, but not entirely, with this approach. The stimulus input to receptors is defined in accord with the physics of the particular energies involved. These energies are transduced and encoded as impulses in the first- and higher-order neurons of the sensory system. The modes of processing and the constraints on this flow of information can and have been studied by analysis of the anatomical structure and physiological functioning of the successive neuronal levels. Various examples are presented in Section I. When this flow of information is constrained by early stages of processing—as it most certainly is for energy transduction at the receptor level—then all later stages must be so constrained. Consequently, any and all responses of an animal must reveal evidence for this limitation. At later stages of processing, the flow of information branches, and the effects of constraints in any one of several parallel paths need not be evident in the responses of the system unless information in that path uniquely determines a particular response. The existence of these constraints in processing at levels that control testable responses has led to many successes in our understanding of perception as a function of stimulus input and subsequent neural processing.

Whatever may be the success of this approach, it is clear that even a complete knowledge of the input to the receptors does not fully account for many examples of perception. This conclusion is nowhere more obvious than in the phenomenon of reversible figures, which may be perceived differently in the absence of any change in input. In such examples, the stimulus input constrains the percept to one of several alternatives but does not determine which one. The reversible figure, however, is but a superficial example of the pervasive determination of perception by influences intrinsic to the perceiving individual. These influences are sometimes called cognitive precisely because they do not lend themselves to explanation by the approach from analysis of the stimulus. They have frequently been ruled out of the purview of science just because of this recalcitrance. Nevertheless, they form the basis of the other main approach to the study of perceptual processing—an approach that begins with the notion that, intrinsic to the perceptual system, there are structural rules that determine relevant aspects of the environment. Moreover, we have already witnessed progress in this area, marked by the discovery of rules or laws that govern the operation of these cognitive factors. Of great influence in this regard has been the work of linguists, who have advanced our understanding of the deep structure of language. The deep structure has been convincingly characterized as unique to the working of the human mind. We should like to translate the latter into the working of the human brain, but only the barest beginning has been made in that direction.

The task for the future is reconciliation of these two approaches. At this time we can do little more than adduce the evidence on both sides. Thus the readings in this section present evidence for the role of the determinants of perception that are intrinsic to the perceiving organism.

Ambiguity

The simple reversible figure is but one member of a large class of figures that may take on more than two possible forms, as illustrated by Fred Attneave in his article "Multistability in Perception." Moreover, in figures with alternative forms, only one form may be perceived at a given moment. The forms seen in some reversible figures are recognized as familiar objects, but in others are abstract shapes. The parts of an identifiable figure must be consistent with the overall picture. An anomaly will often lead to reversal. Because of the intrinsic ambiguity of the flat representation of a three-dimensional object, depth alternations are very common. The power of the visual system to perform perspective transforms during depth alternation is impressive. Clearly, there are laws operating in this system, and the attempts at explaining them in terms of either familiarity or simplicity do little more than characterize the effects.

Marianne L. Teuber's exposition of Escher's work ("Sources of Ambiguity in the Prints of Maurits C. Escher") not only shows how rich are the possibilities of ambiguity but how a visual artist may make the perceptual processes of his viewers part of his subject matter. The author analyzes how Escher sought and found visual ideas in the psychological literature on perception. She makes it clear that there is two-way communication between the artistic and scientific approaches to perceptual processes.

Ambiguous figures are, of course, not limited to vision. Speech contains a great amount of ambiguity, ranging from homonymous words to entire sentences, such as "The organization liked paying customers." The difference lies, of course, in the fact that speech consists of a temporal sequence rather than a spatial array. As Richard and Roslyn Warren point out in "Auditory Illusions and Confusions," consistency of parts within context depends upon complete presentation of relevant material within the time interval required. The perception of speech depends greatly on the listener's linguistic knowledge.

The orientation of a figure may be an important factor in its recognition, as Irvin Rock points out in his "The Perception of Disoriented Figures." Various studies have shown that a figural stimulus by itself is insufficient to yield correct identification. The recognition of many misoriented forms may be the result of a complicated process of correction. This process is one more example of processing by a cognitive factor—actually, a rule-determined process intrinsic to the visual system.

Expectations

It is quite clear that the rate at which stimulus information is presented to sensory systems under normal conditions far exceeds that at which it may be processed. Many of the lower-level constraints on processing cut down on the flow of information, often by elimination of redundancy (see George A. Miller, "Information and Memory," in PMM). For example, certain edge analyzers in the visual cortex can be regarded as devices for encoding the presence of a line segment that, except for its endpoints, is a set of aligned and hence redundant points. That ambiguous figures may have only one interpretation at a given instant may also be regarded as a reduction of information flow.

But it is in the processes underlying what we call attention that we find the most important controls on the amount of information that undergoes perceptual processing. The process that we know by such names as "expectation," "set," "internal schemata," and other synonyms selects among partially processed sensory inputs and also produces completed percepts from fragmentary stimuli. Indeed, as some of the articles in Section II indicate, this process can result in complete confabulation.

From what is known of both the physiology and the psychophysics of sensory systems, it has been inferred that there are certain systems made up of feature extracting elements. A general question concerns the operation of these elements. Do they act as passive filters or can their filtering characteristics be changed in accord with central controls? If they have the latter function, then what we call "attention" might operate on rather low-level analyzers, producing a selective filtering out of information (see Donald E. Broadbent, "Attention and the Perception of Speech," in PMM). By this means the central processing mechanisms of the brain could be assigned selectively and sequentially only to those tasks of highest priority to the perceiver. No general answer to this question has yet emerged.

The question of what features are relevant to the perception of a complex but important entity is dealt with by Leon D. Harmon in his article "The Recognition of Faces." As Harmon points out, it is the ability to recognize and identify any one of a very large number of complex entities—faces—that is impressive. Discerning differences among faces is a much less impressive performance, since it may be done on the basis of only one or a few of the many differences among discriminable dimensions that may be sensed when faces are viewed. What are, in fact, the features that a human observer uses in order to recognize? The answer is not available, but the evidence forces us to conclude that the perceptual system somehow manages to define a small set of features that allow it to perform the recognition of a large number of faces. Previous experience with faces is important, and hence the process is inductive to some extent at least. Although a perceiver easily performs the task of recognition, he cannot define the critical features so as to program a computer to perform that task. It is precisely this inability to define for itself a set of critical features that is currently one of the shortcomings of computer-aided recognition procedures.

It is in the perception of complex human artifacts like speech, handwriting, and printed text that we find some of the most interesting examples of the operation of expectation in perception. Speech perception has previously been touched upon in reference to the article of Warren and Warren. Paul A. Kolers, in his article "Experiments in Reading," takes up the issue of reading printed text. We ordinarily think that the basic units of text are letters. But it is obvious that if the perceiver had to identify each successive letter before he could extract the meaning of a sentence, reading could never be accomplished at the speed with which it is done. What appears to happen is that the reader knows much about the properties of what he is reading before he begins to read. Moreover, he updates this knowledge during the actual scanning of the text. From a consideration of the errors made by readers, Kolers concludes that the reader constructs an internal grammatical message that is then matched with the written text by sampling at certain points. It is the skill at sampling that allows the great speed of reading.

We may regard the set of expectations that allow rapid reading and understanding of speech as theories about the nature of the messages that the perceiver will receive. Knowledge of grammatical structure and of the semantics of language are basic to such theories. But it is not only in the perception of human artifacts that the perceiver generates theories of this sort. Robert Buckhout, in his article "Eyewitness Testimony," shows how inaccurate one's perceptions are in the absence of a set to perceive certain events and how subject they are to reorganization from the experimenter's point of view. Recalled events are even more subject to this process of reorganization in the interests of logical coherence and consistency with presumed truths.

The great facility with which man perceives such things as human speech and writing suggests that he has innate capabilities for both generating and perceiving them. Such a capacity could evolve under the need for efficient social interaction, very much in the manner that the sign stimulus and releasing mechanisms have jointly evolved in birds and other animals much studied by the ethologists (see the Introduction to Section I of PMM). The role of experience, however, is not to be gainsaid in human perception, and it is this role that is explored cross-culturally by Jan B. Deregowski in his article "Pictorial Perception and Culture." He shows that conventions for the pictorial representation of objects, particularly those for depth, are not common to all cultures. Some sort of acquisition by exposure to these tricks of representation is required, but just what sort is not clear. T. G. R. Bower, in his article "The Object in the World of the Infant," explores the important problem of the development of expectations in perception. Obviously, if an expectation acts shortly after birth, before a significant amount of exposure can have occurred, then it must be innate. The study of responses of infants can result in answers to such questions, provided that the experimenter is ingenious enough to obtain them from very young infants. From his research and that of others, Bower concludes that there is a primitive unity across the senses involved in the apprehension of spatial properties of objects and their movements. His research also leads him to the surprising conclusion that very young infants fail to maintain the perceptual identification of an object that undergoes displacement. An object appears to the infant to change its identity when it is moved to a new location. As the infant grows older, however, it becomes capable of maintaining the identity of an object being displaced. This result seems to show that the development of a set of expectations requires time and perhaps a period of experience in the world.

Cerebration

The exact nature of the brain mechanisms required to perform cognitive operations is difficult to study and remains uncertain. Although major progress in our understanding of neural mechanisms has been obtained in recent years by the use of the neurophysiological technique of single-unit recording and by new methods of tracing anatomical pathways, these methods have been most successfully applied to the more peripheral parts of the nervous system, both sensory and motor. The more central parts of the system, with their multiple sensory influences, complex interconnections among nuclei, and extensive motor outputs, have so far proven rather resistant to these techniques. But the study of brain-lesioned animals and people has led to important insights, particularly about the location of certain centers for processing types of sensory information and for generating organized movements.

Using behavioral and psychophysical techniques, neuropsychologist A. R. Luria shows in his article "The Functional Organization of the Brain" how different functions may be attributed to selected parts of the brain. His overall schemata for the functions of the brain may serve as a useful way of organizing known results. The two hemispheres of the brain have been shown to differ importantly in function. Norman Geschwind, in his article "Language and the Brain," concentrates on the very important problem of language, both spoken and heard. Of great significance for clinical as well as theoretical purposes is the discovery that language disturbances, for most people, are produced only by lesions of the left hemisphere of the brain. Complete control of a function by one side of the brain is termed cerebral dominance.

Geschwind's approach is largely concerned with the neural connections among centers for processing language and gives a rather successful account of the effects of damage in relevant parts of the brain.

Does the right side of the brain have a specialized function? Doreen Kimura, in her article "The Asymmetry of the Human Brain," carefully examines the division of function between left and right halves of the human brain. She claims that the right hemisphere in most people is concerned in the analysis of information about the external environment, particularly in its spatial aspects. In that sense, it complements the work of the left hemisphere, concerned as it is with the sequential processes of the sort that are involved in speech and fine hand movements. One wonders why unilateral specialization of parts of the brain should occur. One possibility may be that functional specialization is outpacing anatomical development, with the consequence that there is an evolutionary advantage to hemispheric specialization at the expense of hemispheric duplication.

Multistability in Perception

by Fred Attneave
December 1971

*Some kinds of pictures and geometric forms
spontaneously shift in their principal aspect
when they are looked at steadily. The reason
probably lies in the physical organization
of the perceptual system*

Pictures and geometric figures that spontaneously change in appearance have a peculiar fascination. A classic example is the line drawing of a transparent cube on this page. When you first look at the cube, one of its faces seems to be at the front and the other at the back. Then if you look steadily at the drawing for a while, it will suddenly reverse in depth and what was the back face now is the front one. The two orientations will alternate spontaneously; sometimes one is seen, sometimes the other, but never both at once.

When we look steadily at a picture or a geometric figure, the information received by the retina of the eye is relatively constant and what the brain perceives usually does not change. If the figure we are viewing happens to be an ambiguous figure, what the brain perceives may change swiftly without any change in the message it is receiving from the eye. The psychologist is interested in these perceptual alternations not as a curiosity but for what they can tell us about the nature of the perceptual system.

It is the business of the brain to represent the outside world. Perceiving is not just sensing but rather an effect of sensory input on the representational system. An ambiguous figure provides the viewer with an input for which there are two or more possible representations

that are quite different and about equally good, by whatever criteria the perceptual system employs. When alternative representations or descriptions of the input are equally good, the perceptual system will sometimes adopt one and sometimes another. In other words, the perception is multistable. There are a number of physical systems that have the same kind of multistable characteristics, and a comparison of multistability in physical and perceptual situations may yield some significant clues to the basic processes of perception. First, however, let us consider several kinds of situations that produce perceptual multistability.

Figure-ground reversal has long been used in puzzle pictures. It is often illustrated by a drawing that can be seen as either a goblet or a pair of faces [*see top illustration on next page*]. This figure was introduced by the Danish psychologist Edgar Rubin. Many of the drawings and etchings of the Dutch artist Maurits C. Escher are particularly elegant examples of figure-ground reversal [*see bottom illustration on next page*]. These examples are somewhat misleading because they suggest that the components of a figure-ground reversal must be familiar objects. Actually you can make a perfectly good reversing figure by scribbling a meaningless line down the middle of a circle. The line will be seen as a contour or a boundary, and its appearance is quite different depending on which side of the contour is seen as the inside and which as the outside [*see top illustration on page 145*]. The difference is so fundamental that if a person first sees one side of the contour as the object or figure, the probability of his recognizing the same contour when it is shown as part of the other half of the field is little better than if he had never seen it at all; this was demonstrated by Rubin in a

classic study of the figure-ground dichotomy.

Note that it is quite impossible to see both sides of the contour as figures at the same time. Trying to think of the halves as two pieces of a jigsaw puzzle that fit together does not help; the pieces are still seen alternately and not simultaneously. What seems to be involved here is an attribution of surface properties to some parts of a field but not to others. This kind of distinction is of central importance in the problem of scene analysis that Marvin Lee Minsky of the Massachusetts Institute of Technology and other investigators of computer simulation have been grappling with lately. The figure made by drawing a line through a circle is actually tristable rather than bistable; the third possibility is being able to see the line as a thing in itself, as a twisted wire rather than the boundary of a figure.

PAINTING BY SALVADOR DALI on the opposite page is an example of the use of ambiguous figures by a serious artist. The illustration is a portion of "Slave Market with Apparition of the Invisible Bust of Voltaire." It is reproduced with the permission of the Dali Museum in Cleveland. When viewed at close range, the figures of people predominate; when viewed at a distance, bust of Voltaire becomes apparent.

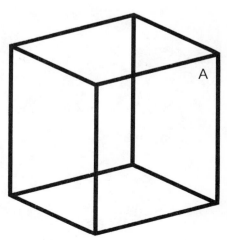

NECKER CUBE, a classic example of perspective reversal, is named after Louis Albert Necker, who in 1832 reported that line drawings of crystals appeared to reverse in depth spontaneously. Corner *A* alternates from front to back when gazed at steadily.

REVERSIBLE GOBLET was introduced by Edgar Rubin in 1915 and is still a favorite demonstration of figure-ground reversal. Either a goblet or a pair of silhouetted faces is seen.

WOODCUT by Maurits C. Escher titled "Circle Limit IV (Heaven and Hell)" is a striking example of both figure-ground reversal and competition between rival-object schemata. Devils and angels alternate repeatedly but neither seems to be able to overpower the other.

The point of basic interest in figure-ground reversal is that one line can have two shapes. Since an artist's line drawing is readily identifiable with the object it is supposed to portray, and since a shape has much the same appearance whether it is white on black, black on white or otherwise colored, many workers have suggested that the visual system represents or encodes objects primarily in terms of their contours. As we have seen, however, a contour can be part of two shapes. The perceptual representation of a contour is specific to which side is regarded as the figure and which as the ground. Shape may be invariant over a black-white reversal, but it is not invariant over an inside-outside reversal.

Under natural conditions many factors cooperate to determine the figure-ground relationship, and ambiguity is rare. For example, if one area encloses another, the enclosed area is likely to be seen as the figure. If a figure is divided into two areas, the smaller of the areas is favored as the figure [see middle illustration on opposite page].

The visual field usually consists of many objects that overlap and occlude one another. The perceptual system has an impressive ability to segregate and sort such objects from one another. Along with distinguishing figure from ground, the system must group the fragments of visual information it receives into separate sets that correspond to real objects. Elements that are close to one another or alike or homogeneous in certain respects tend to be grouped together. When alternative groupings are about equally good, ambiguity results.

For example, if a set of dots are aligned, the perceptual system tends to group them on the basis of this regularity. When the dots are in regular rows and columns, they will be seen as rows if the vertical distance between the dots is greater than the horizontal distance, and they will seem to be in columns if the horizontal distance is greater than the vertical distance. When the spacing both ways is the same, the two groupings—rows and columns—tend to alternate. What is interesting and rather puzzling about the situation is that vertical and horizontal groupings are competitive at all. Geometrically the dots form both rows and columns; why, then, does seeing them in rows preclude seeing them in columns at the same moment? Whatever the reason is in terms of perceptual mechanisms, the principle involved appears to be a general one: When elements are grouped perceptually, they are partitioned; they are not simultaneously cross-classified.

A related case of multistability involves apparent movement. Four lights are arranged in a square so that the diagonally opposite pairs of lights flash simultaneously. If the two diagonal pairs of lights are flashed alternately, it will appear to an observer as if the lights are moving. The apparent motion can take either of two forms: the observer will see motion along the vertical sides of the square, with two pairs of lights, one on the left and the other on the right, moving in opposite directions up and down, or he will see two sets of lights moving back and forth horizontally in opposite directions. If he continues to watch for a while, the motion will switch from vertical to horizontal and vice versa. When one apparent motion gives way to the other, the two perceptions are subjectively so different that the unsuspecting observer is likely to believe there has been some physical change. Apparent movement involves the grouping of events that are separated in both space and time, but the events so grouped are represented as having a common identity; specifically it appears that the same light has moved to a new place. The rivalry between the horizontal and the vertical movement is thus easier to comprehend than the rivalry between rows and columns of dots: if the representational system reflects the laws of the world it represents, the same object cannot traverse two different paths simultaneously or occupy two different places at once.

Ambiguities of grouping are also evident in fields of repetitive elements such as a floor with hexagonal tiles or even a matrix of squares drawn on paper [*see top illustration on page 149*]. If one stares at the matrix for a while, certain subsets of the squares will spontaneously organize themselves into simple figures. With voluntary effort one can attain fairly stable perceptions of rather complex figures. The most readily seen figures, however, tend to be simple, compact and symmetrical.

Some of the most striking and amusing ambiguous figures are pictures (which may or may not involve figure-ground reversal) that can be seen as either of two familiar objects, for example a duck or a rabbit, a young girl or an old woman, and a man or a girl [*see illustrations on next two pages*]. What is meant by "familiar" in this context is that the visual inputs can be matched to some acquired or learned schemata of classes of objects. Just what such class

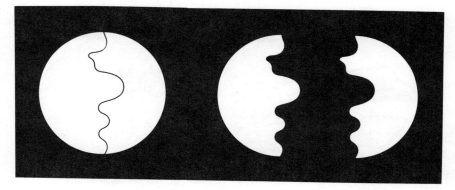

REVERSING FIGURE can be made by scribbling a line through a circle. The shape of the contour formed depends on which side of the line is regarded as part of the figure.

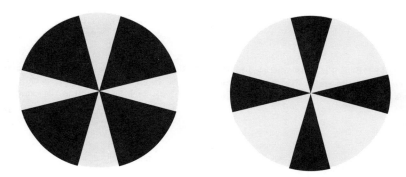

LARGER AREA of a figure is more likely to be seen as the background. Either the large crosses or the small ones may be seen as the figure, but the small crosses have the advantage.

REVERSAL AND ROTATION occur simultaneously in this ingenious design. When the stylized maple-leaf pattern alternates between black and white, it also rotates 90 degrees.

RABBIT-DUCK FIGURE was used in 1900 by psychologist Joseph Jastrow as an example of rival-schemata ambiguity. When it is a rabbit, the face looks to the right; when it is a duck, the face looks to the left. It is difficult to see both duck and rabbit at the same time.

YOUNG GIRL–OLD WOMAN was brought to the attention of psychologists by Edwin G. Boring in 1930. Created by cartoonist W. E. Hill, it was originally published in *Puck* in 1915 as "My Wife and My Mother-in-law." The young woman's chin is the old woman's nose.

schemata consist of—whether they are like composite photographs or like lists of properties—remains a matter of controversy. In any case the process of identification must involve some kind of matching between the visual input and a stored schema. If two schemata match the visual input about equally well, they compete for its perceptual interpretation; sometimes one of the objects is seen and sometimes the other. Therefore one reason ambiguity exists is that a single input can be matched to different schemata.

In certain ambiguous figures we can clearly see the nature of the positive feedback loop that accounts for the "locking in," or stabilization, of one or another aspect of the figure at any given time. For example, if in the young girl–old woman figure a certain line is tentatively identified as a nose, then a line below it must be the mouth and the shapes above it must be the eyes. These partial identifications mutually support one another to form a stable perception of an old woman. If, however, the line we started with is seen as a chin instead of as a nose, then the perception formed is that of a young woman. The identification of wholes and of parts will likewise be reciprocally supportive, contributing further to the locking-in process.

Why one aspect of an ambiguous figure, once it is locked in, should ever give way to the other is a fundamental question. Indeed, a person can look for quite a long time at an ambiguous figure and see only one aspect of it. Robert Leeper of the University of Oregon showed that if a subject was first exposed to a version of the figure that was biased in favor of one of the interpretations, he would almost always see only that aspect in the ambiguous version. Not until the other aspect was pointed out would the figure spontaneously alternate. It is only after the input has made contact with both schemata that they become competitive. Making the initial contact and the associated organization must entail a type of learning.

Ambiguities of depth characterize a large class of multistable figures, of which the cube on page 143 is the most familiar. In 1832 a Swiss geologist, Louis Albert Necker, pointed out that a drawing of a transparent rhomboid crystal could be seen in either of two different ways, that the viewer often experiences "a sudden and involuntary change in the apparent position of a crystal or solid represented by an engraved figure." Necker concluded that the aspect seen depends entirely on the point of

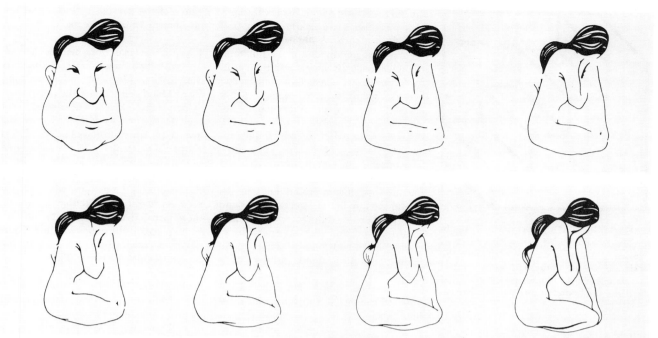

MAN-GIRL FIGURES are part of a series of progressively modified drawings devised by Gerald Fisher in 1967. He found that the last drawing in the top row has equal probability of being seen as a man or as a girl. Perception of middle pictures can be biased toward the man by viewing series in sequence beginning from top left and can be biased toward the girl by starting from bottom right.

fixation, "the point of distinct vision" being perceived as the closer. Although the fixation point is indeed important, it has been shown that depth reversal will readily occur without eye movement.

If we want to understand how depth relationships can be multistable, we must first consider the more general question of how the perceptual system can derive a three-dimensional representation from a two-dimensional drawing. A straight line in the outside world casts a straight line on the retina. A given straight line on the retina, however, could be the image of any one of an infinite number of external lines, and not necessarily straight lines, that lie in a common plane with one another and the eye. The image on a single retina is always two-dimensional, exactly as a photograph is. We should not be surprised, therefore, that depth is sometimes ambiguous; it is far more remarkable that the perceptual system is able to select a particular orientation for a line segment (or at worst to vacillate between two or three orientations) out of the infinite number of legitimate possibilities that exist.

On what basis does the system perform this feat? According to the Gestalt psychologists the answer is to be found in a principle of *Prägnanz:* one perceives the "best" figure that is consistent with a given image. For most practical purposes "best" may be taken to mean "simplest." The advantage of this interpretation is that it is easier to find objective standards for complexity than for such qualities as being "best." One observes a particular configuration of lines on paper, such as the Necker cube, and assigns a three-dimensional orientation to the lines such that the whole becomes a cube (although an infinite number of noncubical forms could project the same form) because a cube is the simplest of the possibilities. In a cube the lines (edges) are all the same length; they take only three directions, and the angles they form are all equal and right

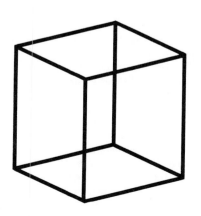
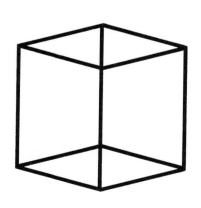
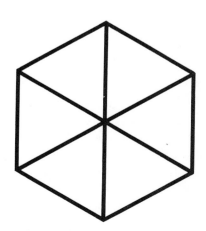

PROJECTIONS OF A CUBE onto a two-dimensional surface are nearly always seen in depth when they resemble the Necker cube *(left)*. As the projection becomes simpler and more regular it is more likely to be seen as a flat figure, such as a hexagon *(right)*.

SCHRÖDER STAIRS line drawing is another classic example of perspective reversal. Corner A is part of the rear wall when the staircase goes up to the left; when reversal occurs, corner A becomes part of the front wall and the bottom of the stairway is seen.

angles. No other interpretation of the figure, including the two-dimensional aspect itself, is as simple and regular. In cases of reversible perspective two maximally simple tridimensional constructions are permissible, each being symmetrical with the other in depth.

If this reasoning is correct, simple projections of a given solid should be perceived as being flat more often than complex projections of the same solid. Julian Hochberg and his colleagues at Cornell University studied various two-dimensional projections of a cube and other regular solids [see bottom illustra-

tion on preceding page]. Relatively complex projections are nearly always perceived in depth. A figure such as a regular hexagon divided into equilateral triangles, which is simple and regular in two dimensions, stays two-dimensional because seeing it as a cube does not make it any simpler. Intermediate figures become tristable; they are sometimes seen as being flat and sometimes as being one or another aspect of a cube. The measure of complexity devised by Hochberg and Virginia Brooks involved the number of continuous lines in the figure, the number of interior angles and the number of different angles. This measure predicted with considerable accuracy the proportion of the time that a figure was seen in depth rather than as being flat.

I have been emphasizing the importance of simplicity, but it is obvious that familiarity also plays an important role in instances of ambiguous depth. The two factors are hard to disentangle. Simple structures are experienced with great frequency, particularly in man-made environments. As Alvin G. Goldstein of the University of Missouri has shown by experiment, within limits a nonsense shape is judged to be simpler the more often it is experienced. In my view familiarity and simplicity become functionally equivalent in the perceptual system when a given input corresponds closely to a schema that is already well established by experience and can therefore be encoded or described (in the lan-

guage of the nervous system) most simply in terms of that schema.

Depth reversal does not occur only with two-dimensional pictures. As the Austrian physicist and philosopher Ernst Mach pointed out, the perspective of many real objects will reverse when the object is viewed steadily with one eye. A transparent glass half-filled with water is a particularly dramatic example, but it requires considerable effort to achieve the reversal and the stability of the reversal is precarious. Mach discovered an easier reversal that is actually more instructive. Take a white card or a small piece of stiff paper and fold it once along its longitudinal axis [see bottom illustration on this page]. Place the folded card or paper in front of you on a table so that it makes a rooflike structure. Close one eye and view the card steadily for a while from directly above. It will reverse (or you can make it reverse) so that it appears as if the fold is at the bottom instead of the top. Now view the card with one eye from above at about a 45-degree angle so that the front of the folded card can be seen. After a few seconds the card will reverse and stand up on end like an open book with the inside toward you. If the card is asymmetrically illuminated and is seen in correct perspective, it will appear to be more or less white all over, as it is in reality, in spite of the fact that the illuminated plane reflects more light than the shadowed one. When the reversal occurs, the shadowed plane looks gray instead of white and the illuminated plane may appear luminous. In the perspective reversal the perceptual mechanism that preserves the constancy of reflectance is fooled; in order to maintain the relation between light source and the surfaces the perceptual system makes corrections that are erroneous because they are based on incorrect information.

Another remarkable phenomenon involving the folded card seems to have escaped Mach's notice. Recently Murray Eden of the Massachusetts Institute of Technology found that if after you make the folded card reverse you move your head slowly from side to side, the card will appear to rock back and forth quite as convincingly as if it were physically in motion. The explanation, very roughly, is that the mechanism that makes allowance for head movements, so that still objects appear still even though the head moves, is operating properly but on erroneous premises when the perspective is reversed. The perceived rocking of the card is exactly what would

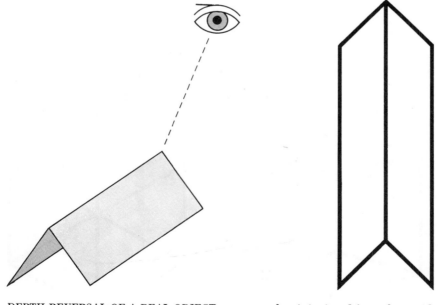

DEPTH REVERSAL OF A REAL OBJECT can occur when it is viewed from above with one eye, an effect discovered by Ernst Mach. When a folded card is viewed from above and the front, it will appear to stand on end like an open book when it reverses. The same kind of depth reversal occurs with a simple line drawing of a folded card (above right).

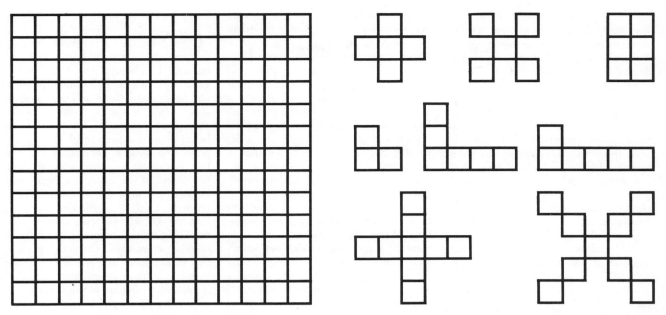

FIGURAL GROUPINGS occur when one stares at a matrix of squares. The simple figures organize themselves spontaneously and with effort more complex figures can be perceived. Some figures, however, are so complex that they are difficult to maintain.

ALIGNED DOTS fall into a regular pattern when viewed. Depending on the spacing, dots can be seen as columns (*left*) or as rows (*middle*). When vertical and horizontal spacing are equal, dots can be seen as rows or columns but not as both at the same time.

EQUILATERAL TRIANGLES appear in one of three orientations depending on the dominant axis of symmetry (*left*). Usually all point in the same direction at one time, although the direction can change spontaneously. The scalene triangles (*middle*) fluctuate in orientation even though they are asymmetrical because they can also appear as isosceles or right triangles that point down or up. The same shape can be seen as either diamonds or tilted squares (*right*) depending on the orientation of the local reference system.

have to happen objectively if the card were really reversed to account for the sequence of retinal images accompanying head movement. What is remarkable about this is not that the mechanism can be wrong but rather that it can function so efficiently as a "lightning calculator" of complex problems in projective geometry and compensate so completely to maintain the perceived orientation. It seems to me that this capacity is a good argument for the existence of some kind of working model of three-dimensional space within the nervous system that solves problems of this type by analogue operations. Indeed, the basic concept of *Prägnanz*, of a system that finds its way to stable states that are simple by tridimensional criteria, is difficult to explain without also postulating a neural analogue model of three-dimensional space. We have no good theory at present of the nature of the neural organization that might subserve such a model.

A few years ago I stumbled on a principle of ambiguity that is different from any we have been considering. While planning an experiment on perceptual grouping I drew a number of equilateral triangles. After looking at them for a time I noticed that they kept changing in their orientation, sometimes pointing one way, sometimes another and sometimes a third way [*see bottom illustration on preceding page*]. The basis for this tristable ambiguity seems to be that the perceptual system can represent symmetry about only one axis at a time, even though an equilateral triangle is objectively symmetrical about three axes. In other words, an equilateral triangle is always perceived as being merely an isosceles triangle in some particular orientation. Compare any two sides or any two angles of an equilateral triangle and you will find that the triangle immediately points in the direction around which the sides and angles are

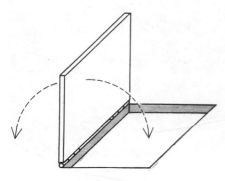

PHYSICAL SYSTEM that exhibits a simple form of multistability is a trapdoor that is stable only when it is either open or shut.

symmetrical. When a group of equilateral triangles points upward, the triangles cease to fluctuate; the perceptual system strongly prefers the vertical axis of symmetry. Indeed, any perceived axis of symmetry seems to have the character of a locally rotated vertical.

When scalene triangles (triangles with three unequal sides) are grouped together with their corresponding sides parallel, they also appear to fluctuate in orientation after a brief inspection [*see bottom illustration on preceding page*]. This is at first puzzling since they have no axes of symmetry at all. The answer to the puzzle involves the third dimension: When the triangles are seen to point in a given direction, they simultaneously go into depth in such a way that they look like isosceles triangles seen at an angle. Perspective reversal doubles the possibilities, so that there are six ways the scalene triangles can be seen as isosceles. The same triangles may also be seen as right triangles in depth, with the obtuse angles most easily becoming the right angles.

These observations begin to make sense if we suppose the perceptual system employs something quite like a Cartesian coordinate system to locate and describe things in space. (To call the system Cartesian is really putting the issue backward, since Descartes clearly took the primary perceptual directions of up-down, left-right and front-back as his reference axes.) The multistable states of triangles thus appear to involve simple relations between the figure and the reference system. The reference system may be tilted or rotated locally by the perceptual system and produce the apparent depth or orientation of the triangles.

In the same way we can explain how the same shape can appear to be so different when it is seen as a square or as a diamond. The square is perceived as having horizontal and vertical axes along its sides; the diamond is perceived as being symmetrical about a vertical axis running through opposite corners. Yet in certain kinds of grouping the perceptual axes can be locally rotated and the diamond can look like a tilted square [*see bottom illustration on preceding page*].

It should be evident by now that some principle of *Prägnanz*, or minimum complexity, runs as a common thread through most of the cases. It seems likely that the perceptual machinery is a teleological system that is "motivated" to represent the outside world as economically as possible, within the constraints of the input received and the

limitations of its encoding capabilities.

A good reason for invoking the concept of multistability to characterize figural ambiguity is that we know a great deal about multistable physical and electronic systems and may hope to apply some of this knowledge to the perceptual processes. The multistable behavior of the perceptual system displays two notable characteristics. The first is that at any one moment only one aspect of the ambiguous figure can be seen; mixtures or intermediate states occur fleetingly if at all. The second is that the different percepts alternate periodically. What accounts for this spontaneous alternation? Once the perceptual system locks into one aspect of the figure, why does it not remain in that state? An analogous physical system is a trapdoor that is stable only when it is either open or closed.

As Necker pointed out, changing the point of visual fixation may cause perspective to reverse. In the instances where the input is being matched against more than one schema visual fixation on a feature that is more critical to one representation than the other may lock perception into only one aspect of the ambiguous figure. Since the percepts can alternate without a change in the point of fixation, however, some additional explanation is needed. The most likely is that the alternative aspects of the figure are represented by activity in different neural structures, and that when one such structure becomes "fatigued," or satiated or adapted, it gives way to another that is fresher and more excitable. Several investigators have noted that a reversing figure alternates more rapidly the longer it is looked at, presumably because both alternative neural structures build up some kind of fatigue. In some respects the neural structures behave like a multistable electronic circuit. A common example of multistability in electronic circuitry is the multivibrator flip-flop circuit, which can incorporate either vacuum tubes or transistors. In the vacuum tube version [*see illustration on opposite page*] when one tube is conducting a current, the other tube is prevented from conducting by the low voltage on its grid. The plates and the grids of the two tubes are cross-coupled through capacitors, and one tube continues to conduct until the charge leaks from the coupling capacitor sufficiently for the other tube to start conducting. Once this tube begins to conduct, the positive feedback loop quickly makes it fully conducting and the other tube is cut off and becomes nonconducting. The process reverses and the system flip-flops between one state and the other.

What is "fatigued" in the multivibrator is the suppressive linkage. In other words, the inhibition of the nonconducting tube slowly weakens until it is no longer strong enough to prevent conduction. The possibility of an analogous neural process, in which the inhibition of the alternative neural structure progressively weakens, is worth considering.

Brain lesions may affect the perception of ambiguous figures. The finding most generally reported is that in people who have suffered brain damage the rate of alternation is lower, more or less independently of the locus of the lesion. On the other hand, a study of a group of brain-damaged war veterans conducted by Leonard Cohen at New York University indicated that damage to both frontal lobes increases the rate of alternation of a reversible figure, whereas damage to only one frontal lobe decreases the rate. The theoretical implications of these neurological findings are quite obscure and will doubtless remain so until we have some fundamental picture of the way the nervous system represents form and space.

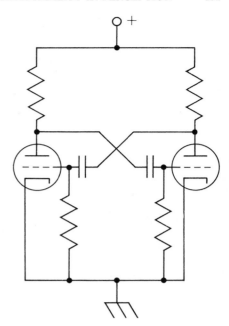

MULTIVIBRATOR CIRCUIT spontaneously alternates between two states. When one vacuum tube is conducting, the other is inhibited. A charge leaking from the coupling capacitor eventually starts the inhibited tube conducting. The positive feedback loop quickly makes it fully conducting and cuts off conduction in the first tube. The entire process is repeated in reverse, and the circuit flops from one state to the other.

15

Sources of Ambiguity in the Prints of Maurits C. Escher

by Marianne L. Teuber
July 1974

The fascinating graphic inventions of the late Dutch artist reflect a strong mathematical and crystallographic influence. Their original inspiration, however, came from experiments on visual perception

If ambiguity is a sign of our time, the late Dutch graphic artist Maurits C. Escher managed to represent it in striking visual terms. In Escher's art there is the ambiguity of figure and ground; the ambiguity of two and three dimensions on the flat surface; the ambiguity of the reversible cube; the ambiguous limits of the infinitely small and the infinitely large. In his prints visual ambiguity goes hand in hand with ambiguity of meaning. Good and evil are contemplated in the figure-ground reversal of black devils and white angels. Day changes into night; sky becomes water; fish metamorphose into fowl.

Escher's regular subdivisions of the surface have been compared to the packed periodic structures of crystals and to the mathematical transformations of topology and non-Euclidean geometry [see "Mathematical Games," SCIENTIFIC AMERICAN, April, 1961, and April, 1966]. The original inspiration for his unusual ambiguous patterns, however, can be traced to contemporary sources more familiar to the student of psychology and visual perception. Psychological studies of the relation of figure and ground—in turn encouraged by the positive and negative forms of Art Nouveau —were for Escher the primary stimulus. Only after he had mastered reversible figure-ground constructions of his own invention did he recognize their similarity to certain principles of crystallography, and his interest in mathematics was aroused.

Figure-ground designs appear at an early stage in Escher's work—as early as 1921, when he was only 23 years old. It was not until the late 1930's, however, when Escher "rediscovered" the style that made him famous, that the figure-ground ambiguity clearly became the dominant feature of his art. The well-known woodcuts *Development I, Day and Night* and *Sky and Water I,* among others, date from this period.

From Escher's own commentary on these prints in *The Graphic Work of M. C. Escher* one must conclude that he knew the pertinent psychological literature. In particular he seems to have been familiar with the early experiments on figure and ground by the Danish psychologist Edgar Rubin, with Kurt Koffka's 1935 book *Principles of Gestalt Psychology,* where Rubin's results are summarized, and with the studies of Molly R. Harrower, a student of Koffka's. Patterns related to crystallography and geometry turn out to be a later development.

One of Rubin's best-known patterns, presented in his 1915 monograph dealing with visually perceived form as a function of the relation of figure to ground, can be seen either as a vase in the center or as two profiles facing each other [*see illustration at left*]. When the profiles are seen, the vase becomes ground, and vice versa. It is impossible, as Rubin points out, to see vase and profiles simultaneously as figures.

Rubin's book was published in a German translation in Copenhagen in 1921. The following year, when the young Escher was completing his training at the School of Architecture and Ornamental Design in Haarlem, he carved a

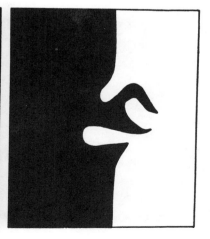

REVERSIBLE PATTERNS published originally in 1915 by the Danish psychologist Edgar Rubin in a study of the role of the figure-ground relation in visual perception were presumably familiar to Escher at an early stage. The pattern at left can be seen either as a vase in the center or as two profiles facing each other. The more abstract pattern at right can be seen either as a black figure against a white background or vice versa. In each case it is impossible, said Rubin, to see both the black and the white areas simultaneously as figures.

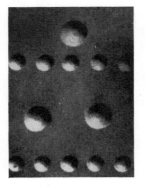 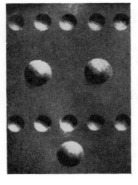 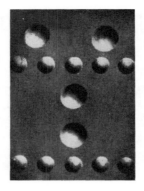 

EXPERIMENTAL PATTERNS designed to study the crater illusion were published by the Finnish psychologist Kai von Fieandt in 1938. The patterns test the changes in depth perception from concave to convex, depending on the direction of the illumination.

"CUBE WITH MAGIC RIBBONS," a 1957 Escher lithograph in the Roosevelt collection at the National Gallery, uses strips of small "buttonlike protuberances" just like those illustrated in the von Fieandt study to explore "inversions" of concave and convex.

woodcut called *Eight Heads* [*see illustration below*]. Each head fills exactly the space left between neighboring heads and acts alternately as figure and ground, depending on the viewer's attitude. Escher is quite explicit about his purpose. In *The Graphic Work of M. C. Escher* the artist himself provides an introduction and comments on his prints. These explanations reflect the technical language of his scientific sources. The wording here leaves no doubt about the

specific psychological studies that contributed to the formation of his unique style.

One can easily discern the link with Rubin's experiments when Escher classifies *Eight Heads* and his later reversible patterns of fish and bird in *Sky and Water I* or *Day and Night* under the heading "The Function of Figures as a Background." Escher comments: "Our eyes are accustomed to fixing on a specific object. The moment this happens every-

thing round about becomes reduced to background." This description is in keeping with Rubin's analysis of his ambiguous vase-profile pattern.

Whereas Escher insisted on meaningful, if fantastic, creatures for his basic reversible units, Rubin, in his attempt to find general principles of figure formation, actually preferred more abstract designs. In his 1915 book Rubin even cites Wassily Kandinsky's contemporary abstract paintings as good examples of the

"EIGHT HEADS," a woodcut carved by Escher in 1922, the year he finished his training at the School of Architecture and Ornamental Design at Haarlem in the Netherlands, bears a strong resemblance to Rubin's diagrams. Each of the four male and four female heads can act alternately as figure or ground. *Eight Heads* was Escher's first attempt at an infinitely repeating subdivision of a plane surface. This reproduction is from a print in the Escher Foundation collection in the Haags Gemeentemuseum at The Hague.

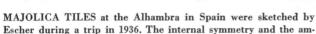

MAJOLICA TILES at the Alhambra in Spain were sketched by Escher during a trip in 1936. The internal symmetry and the ambiguous contours of the Moorish designs appear to have helped revive Escher's early fascination with the figure-ground problem.

equivalence of color fields. By means of abstract test patterns Rubin hoped to isolate basic characteristics of form perception without the distractions caused by figurative images. As he points out, it is always the form with the greater realistic or emotional appeal that tends to attract our attention; in the vase-profile pattern, for instance, the profiles will win out when the reversals are observed over prolonged periods.

To avoid these pitfalls Rubin derived the main principles of what makes for figure and what for ground from his abstract patterns. According to Rubin, one usually sees the smaller enclosed form as figure by contrast with the larger surrounding expanse of the ground. The figure has "solid-object quality," whereas the ground takes on a "film quality." The figure protrudes; the ground recedes and stretches behind the figure. The contour is seen as belonging to the figure and not to the ground.

In ambiguous patterns, however, the one-sided function of the contour is challenged. Rubin's analysis of contours can be recognized in Escher's description of the difficulties he encountered in drawing his ambiguous creatures. In discussing the borderline between two adjacent shapes having a double function Escher notes that "the act of tracing such a line is a complicated business. On either side of it, simultaneously, a recognizability takes shape. But the human eye and mind cannot be busy with two things at the same moment, and so there must be a quick and continual jumping from one side to the other. . . . This difficulty is perhaps the very moving-spring of my perseverance."

After his early exposure to Rubin's work in 1921 and 1922, Escher left his native Netherlands to live in Italy until

"METAMORPHOSIS I," a woodcut designed by Escher in 1937, represents an abrupt change in his style from the flat periodic subdivisions he had invented up to 1936 to the development of forms from flat to plastic on the two-dimensional plane. This new ap-

Unlike the Moorish artists, however, Escher continued to design his flat tessellations with contiguous human and animal forms.

Escher's original color drawings of the Alhambra tiles are part of the Escher Foundation collection in the Haags Gemeentemuseum.

1934. An extraordinarily skillful craftsman, he created a large series of woodcuts and lithographs; they represent landscapes, architecture and portraiture in brilliantly realistic style, in which the traditional Renaissance picture space prevails. Only once during his Italian period did the figure-ground problem return: in 1926 he designed some interlocking animal shapes, very similar to his later periodic structures on the picture surface. Escher claims that the departure from Italy in 1934 was responsible for his change in style. He felt that landscape in the North did not attract him as

it had in Italy; instead, he writes, "I concentrated...on personal ideas...and inner visions." He lived for more than a year in Switzerland and for five years in Belgium before settling in 1941 at Baarn in the Netherlands, where he remained until his death in 1972, except for brief visits to Britain, the U.S. and Canada.

As I have noted, the major turning point in Escher's style came in the late 1930's after he left Italy. What caused that change? It is evident that at some time between 1935 and 1938 Escher became acquainted with Koffka's *Princi-*

ples of Gestalt Psychology. That Escher was indebted to Koffka can be documented from his graphic work and written comments. Koffka, one of the three chief proponents of Gestalt psychology (with Max Wertheimer and Wolfgang Köhler), relied heavily on Rubin's work, although Rubin never counted himself among the Gestalt psychologists. In *Principles of Gestalt Psychology* an entire chapter is devoted to the topic of figure and ground. Thus, through Koffka, an old and fascinating preoccupation of Escher's was revived.

Escher's development can be appre-

proach appears to have been influenced by his reading of Kurt Koffka's 1935 book *Principles of Gestalt Psychology*. The design is

reproduced here from an original print in the National Gallery of Art in Washington, D.C. (gift of Cornelius Van Schaak Roosevelt).

ciated by considering drawings the artist made in 1936 on a trip to Spain when he copied majolica tiles at the Alhambra [*see top illustration on preceding two pages*]. These examples of Moorish art with their internal symmetry and obviously ambiguous contours must have attracted him precisely because he had been familiar with the figure-ground problem since 1921. He looked at the Alhambra tiles with eyes trained by Rubin's experiments. As in the case of Rubin's abstract patterns, however, he regretted that the Moorish artists were not allowed to make "graven images" and "always restricted themselves ... to designs of an abstract geometrical type. Not one single Moorish artist ... ever made so bold ... as to use concrete, recognizable, naturalistically conceived figures of fish, birds, reptiles or human beings as elements in their surface coverage."

Instead Escher preferred to design his flat tessellations with contiguous human and animal forms. In the course of the next year or so, however, he abruptly transformed this flat motif into three-dimensional cubes and an entire town in his woodcut *Metamorphosis I* [*see bottom illustration on preceding two pages*]. One of the new aspects noticeable in Escher's post-1937 work, in contrast with the flat periodic subdivisions he had invented up to 1936, is the development

of forms from flat to plastic on the two-dimensional plane. In *Principles of Gestalt Psychology* Koffka demonstrates the compelling three-dimensional organization of two-dimensional lines and planes under certain conditions. He shows, among other examples, how a hexagon, depending on the internal arrangement of its lines, can change from a flat pattern to a cube, just as in Escher's *Metamorphosis I*. In summarizing experiments by Hertha Kopfermann and himself, Koffka points out that it is the intrinsic tendency toward simplicity of organization that makes one see one array of forms as two-dimensional and a slightly altered one as three-dimensional.

Many of Escher's prints of the following years are based on just such a change of forms from flat to plastic. A noteworthy example is the lithograph *Reptiles,* designed in 1943 [*see illustration below*]. Escher describes this series of prints in words that echo Koffka's text: "The chief characteristics of these prints is the transition from flat to spatial and vice versa." Escher goes on to show how in such designs the individual creatures free themselves from the flat ground in which they are rigidly embedded. He writes: "We can think in terms of an interplay between the stiff, crystallized two-dimensional figures of a regular pattern and the individual freedom of three-dimensional creatures capable of mov-

ing about in space without hindrance. On the one hand, the members of the planes of collectivity come to life in space; on the other, the free individuals sink back and lose themselves in the community."

In the same manner Koffka speaks in the last chapter of his book of the embracing ground and the protruding figure as paradigms for the relation between personality and "behavioral social field." The reptiles in Escher's lithograph thus free themselves from the contiguous design on the flat page to venture into three-dimensional space, only to return to the flat surface where their individuality is again submerged. On their way they pass the paraphernalia of smoking and other ephemeral artifacts drawn in hard illusionistic style; they crawl over one of the Platonic solids (a dodecahedron). These forms fascinated Escher because, as he said, geometric shapes were timeless and not man-made.

During the same period (1936–1938) Escher also became aware of an experimental study by Harrower, who in April, 1936, published an article titled "Some Factors Determining Figure-Ground Articulation" in the *British Journal of Psychology*. She varied Rubin's pattern in the following manner. Several test cards emphasized the outline of the vase and let the profiles recede into the background; other cards emphasized the profiles and allowed the vase to become ground; the center card showed the vase and profiles as being equivalent. Two years later, in 1938, Escher created two of his most striking woodcuts, *Sky and Water I* [*see illustration at top right on opposite page*] and *Day and Night* [*see bottom illustration on opposite page*], according to the same principle; in these works the ground slowly becomes figure and the figure becomes ground; the forms in the center, however, remain equivalent. In his interpretation of *Sky and Water I* Escher employs Harrower's terminology when he says: "In the horizontal central strip there are birds and fish equivalent to each other."

This principle of equivalence, first discussed by Rubin and emphasized by Harrower, is an important ingredient of Escher's many inventive preparatory drawings for his woodcuts. When explaining his compositions, Escher would frequently refer to the fact that his forms had to be "equivalent." The crystallographic terms "distinct" and "equivalent" should not, of course, be confused with the simple notion of equivalence Escher (and Harrower) had in mind. The ingenious basic drawing of *Fish and*

"REPTILES," a lithograph designed in 1943, is a notable example of Escher's increasing preoccupation after 1937 with the transformation of forms from flat to plastic. This reproduction is from a print in the Lessing J. Rosenwald collection at the National Gallery.

"FISH AND FOWL," a preliminary drawing for the woodcut *Sky and Water I*, is a good example of Escher's interest in the "equivalence" of visual forms, a notion he adapted from Molly R. Harrower, a student of Koffka's. The original is in the Gemeentemuseum.

"SKY AND WATER I," carved in 1938, is one of Escher's best-known woodcuts. Unlike the preliminary watercolor drawing at left, the forms of the birds and the fish are equivalent only in the center. This reproduction is from a print in the Gemeentemuseum.

Fowl for *Sky and Water I* is a good example of equivalence; the surfaces of the individual birds and fish are approximately equal in extent, internal design, light-dark contrast and simplicity of contour [*see illustration at top left on this page*]. Such equivalence makes the figures ambiguous, and a rapid reversal is the result.

In her 1936 article Harrower tested the relation of figure to ground by introducing a number of variables, among them increasing and decreasing brightness contrast (or graded grays). Escher's woodcut *Development I*, made in 1937, shows how faint gray squares arranged along the periphery gain in black-and-white contrast as well as distinctness of shape until they become four black and white reptiles in the center [*see top illustration on next page*]. The two "factors"

"DAY AND NIGHT," another 1938 woodcut, represents the same slow transformation of ground into figure and figure into ground, with only the forms in the center remaining equivalent. The principle of transformation is the same as that discussed by Harrower in her 1936 article in the *British Journal of Psychology*. The original print is in the Rosenwald collection at the National Gallery.

"DEVELOPMENT I," a 1937 Escher woodcut, incorporates two basic variables from Harrower's experiments: brightness gradient and development from shapeless ground to distinct figure. This print is in the John D. Merriam collection at the Boston Public Library.

from Harrower's experiments, brightness gradient and development from shapeless ground to distinct figure, are the basic compositional principles of this impressive work. Escher's comment on the print is again couched in the technical language of Harrower's study. He writes: "Scarcely visible gray squares at the edges evolve in form and contrast toward the center."

Escher groups several additional prints under the category "Development of Form and Contrast," in keeping with Harrower's analysis. One of these is the lithograph *Liberation*, designed in 1955 [*see illustration on opposite page*]. He describes this print in terms that are reminiscent of Harrower's test cards and Koffka's text: "On the uniformly gray strip of paper that is being unrolled, a simultaneous development in form and contrast is taking place. Triangles—at first scarcely visible—change into more complicated figures, whilst the color contrast between them increases. In the middle they are transformed into white and black birds, and from there fly off into the world as independent creatures, and so the strip of paper on which they are drawn disappears."

In *Liberation* Escher presents us with a surrealist situation; the birds freed from the gray scroll are caught, nevertheless, on the surface on which the lithograph is printed. The artist reflects here on the visual absurdity of his own craft, as he had implicitly in *Reptiles*.

To summarize this important phase in Escher's artistic development, starting in 1937, he transforms his ambiguous figurative patterns in three ways: (1) from flat to plastic, derived from Koffka's *Principles of Gestalt Psychology* of 1935; (2) from shaped form to shapeless ground, derived from Harrower's study of 1936; (3) from strong black-and-white contrast to gray, also derived from Harrower.

Sky and Water I and *Day and Night*, both done in 1938, exhibit these categories of transformation of shape. In *Day and Night* the square gray fields in the foreground gain in articulation of shape and contrast; they become an equivalent pattern of distinct black birds and white birds in the upper center and from there develop into three-dimensional creatures flying off into the "real" world of day or night. In *Sky and Water I* the strongly articulated plastic single bird and single fish, above and below, evolve from the flat equivalent strip in the middle. What was bird becomes watery ground and what was fish becomes sky. Here Escher enhances the individuality, or object quality, of the figure compared with the film quality of the ground, features already emphasized by Rubin in 1915.

It is difficult to reconstruct by what route Escher came in such close contact with the technical aspects of figure-ground experiments. He may have had a mentor. The artist himself belonged to a family where professional and intellectual achievement were the rule, and he may have come across Koffka's and Harrower's experiments because of his own strong interests. The year in the French-speaking part of Switzerland (1936), near the universities of Geneva and Lau-

"SWANS," a 1956 woodcut, is a good example of how, in experimenting with space-filling tessellations on a flat surface, Escher often relied on crystallographic rules of transformation. He himself classified this print under the heading "Glide Reflexion." The print used to make this reproduction is in the Roosevelt collection at the National Gallery.

sanne, and the five years in Ukkel, not far from the University of Brussels (1937–1941), were the period of his "conversion," when he made the figure-ground problem a permanent feature of his style. Whatever his contacts may have been, by the 1930's not only was the impact of Gestalt psychology widespread at European universities but also it had become fashionable among intellectuals.

The figure-ground studies of the Gestalt psychologists were not, however, Escher's only source of inspiration. He varied his fantastic tessellations on the picture plane by following the structural principles of periodic packing in crystals. Caroline H. MacGillavry analyzed Escher's inventions in these terms in her 1965 monograph *Symmetry Aspects of M. C. Escher's Periodic Drawings*. In *Color and Symmetry*, published in 1971, A. L. Loeb selects striking instances of form and color symmetry from Escher's work to accompany his text. Escher himself recognized the similarities of his regular subdivisions on the plane to principles of crystallography. They had been pointed out to him by his brother, B. G. Escher, professor of geology at the University of Leyden. By that time, however, the artist had created his own figure-ground patterns based on Rubin's visual analyses and the Moorish tiles at the Alhambra. As the mathematician H. S. M. Coxeter has remarked, the Moors had already made use of all 17 crystallographic groups of symmetry structures, subsequently established by E. S. Fedorov in 1891.

In experimenting with space-filling creatures on the flat surface, Escher arrived at many intriguing compositions that follow crystallographic rules of transformation; a good example is his woodcut *Swans*, designed in 1956 [*see bottom illustration on opposite page*]. Again Escher writes a commentary, as he had done for his figure-ground inventions. He groups these prints under the heading "Glide Reflexion" and acknowledges the "three fundamental principles of crystallography"; they are, in his words, "repeated shifting (translation), turning about axes (rotation) and glide mirror image (reflexion)." Among

"LIBERATION," a lithograph designed in 1955, was classified by Escher under the heading "Development of Form and Contrast," in keeping with the technical terms of Harrower's analysis. This print is in Merriam collection at Boston Public Library.

scientists this aspect of Escher's graphic work is probably the best known.

Yet the origin of his compositions from playful manipulations of the figure-ground ambiguity has so far been noted only once before—by the art historian E. H. Gombrich in his article "Illusions and Visual Deadlock" (reprinted in his 1963 book *Meditations on a Hobby Horse*). This oversight is understandable, since Escher's later prints suggest mathematical prototypes as a primary source for his work. Such an interpretation is offered, for example, by Coxeter. In his essay "The Mathematical Implications of Escher's Prints" (reprinted in *The World of M. C. Escher*) Coxeter marvels at Escher's ability to extend the theory of crystallographic groups beyond Fedorov's original 17 by anticipating "through artistic intuition" the added principle of color symmetry.

Escher, however, was led to these ex-tensions by his earlier sources from the psychological literature. Thus he knew how to combine both the figurative re-versals and the crystallographic rules of regular and semiregular tessellations in one and the same composition on the flat picture surface. In *Reptiles* and in many other drawings he achieved such a feat. The fundamental region of a tes-sellation is a polygon (triangle, square or hexagon) or a combination of polygons; they must meet corner to corner. In *Rep-tiles* three heads, three elbows and three toes abut exactly at the corners of a hexa-gon, which forms the fundamental re-gion of this regular tessellation on the plane. Escher looked at these solutions, some more difficult than others, with a great deal of pride.

A similar close association between crystallographic principles and the de-sign of densely packed surfaces was rec-ognized by Paul Klee and later by Victor Vasarely. Both painters based certain pictures and diagrams on Johannes Kep-ler's humorous treatise *De Nive Sexangu-la* (*The Six-cornered Snowflake*), pub-lished in 1611. Kepler's neo-Platonic concept of an underlying order or har-mony—the belief in a mathematical structure of the universe—was shared by Escher. Occasionally one or another of his graphic works illustrates that idea, for example *Reptiles* or *Stars,* a 1948 wood engraving in the style of the early 17th century, Kepler's period [*see illus-tration on this page*]. This work depicts a star-studded sky in which the stellar bodies are composed of the Platonic sol-ids cherished by Kepler. In such prints Escher intends to draw a contrast be-tween the permanent laws of mathe-matics and the incidentals of debris or the changing colors of chameleons. "There is something in such laws that takes the breath away," Escher wrote in his essay "Approaches to Infinity." He continued: "They are not discoveries or inventions of the human mind but exist independently of us." Thus had Socrates explained the intrinsic beauty of geo-metric forms in Plato's *Philebus*. The ab-stract laws or principles of simplicity of form that attracted Escher to the per-ceptual analyses of the Gestalt psycholo-gists were also essentially Platonic in concept.

Through his new interest in mathe-matics and contact with mathematicians, Escher expanded his vocabulary of am-biguous forms. He used the Möbius strip, the Klein bottle, knots and various forms of polygons. *Circle Limit I*, a hyperbolic (non-Euclidian) construction, was devel-oped in 1958 in an exchange of letters with Coxeter [*see illustration at top left on opposite page*]. It gave Escher a chance to represent "the limits of infinite smallness," as he termed it. *Heaven and Hell*, done in 1960, belongs to the same series [*see illustration at top right on op-posite page*].

"STARS," a 1948 wood engraving done in the style of the early 17th century, celebrates Escher's identification with Johannes Kepler's neo-Platonic belief in an underlying mathe-matical order in the universe. The print is in Roosevelt collection at the National Gallery.

In the 1950's Escher returned to sour-ces from the psychology of visual per-ception in a group of prints dealing with reversible perspectives. The 1957 litho-graph *Cube with Magic Ribbons* com-bines the reversible Necker cube (a dis-covery of the 19th-century Swiss miner-alogist L. A. Necker) with the crater illusion [*see bottom illustration on page 154*]. In 1938 the Finnish psychologist Kai von Fieandt published a study on apparent changes in depth perception from concave to convex depending on different directions of light. For his ex-periments he used small knobs shaped

"CIRCLE LIMIT I," a woodcut designed by Escher in 1958, was based on a non-Euclidean mathematical construction developed in an exchange of letters with the mathematician H. S. M. Coxeter. The reproduction is made from a print in the Gemeentemuseum.

"HEAVEN AND HELL," a 1960 Escher woodcut in which the figure-ground ambiguity mirrors an ambiguity of meaning (good and evil), belongs to the same series of mathematically derived designs. The reproduction is from a print in the Gemeentemuseum.

just like those appearing on Escher's band [see top illustration on next page]. Escher must have known von Fieandt's experiments. The artist explains: "If we follow...the strips of buttonlike protuberances...with the eye, then these nodules surreptitiously change from convex to concave."

Concave and Convex [see top illustra-tion on page 164] belongs to the same group of prints where reversible perspectives, or "inversions," as Escher called them, are the topic. The cluster of cubes on the flag announces the basic visual motif of the composition. In this 1955 lithograph Escher plays with the ambiguity of volumes on the flat picture plane; they switch from solid to hollow,

from inward to outward, from roof to ceiling—like the symbol on the flag.

In 1958 Escher created *Belvedere,* an impossible building, also based on the reversible Necker cube [see bottom il-lustration on page 165]. By the end of the 19th century the Necker cube had become one of the most popular and most frequently debated optical illusions

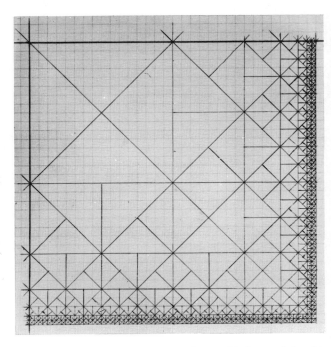

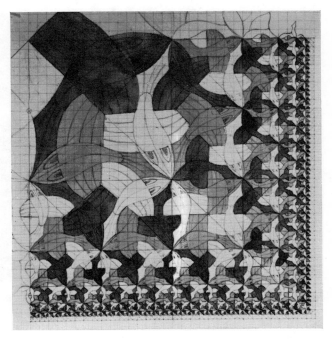

STUDIES for Escher's 1964 woodcut *Square Limit* reveal that this design was carried out by simply dividing surface after surface in

half, up to the limit of visibility at the outer edge. This repro-duction is from the original drawing in the Gemeentemuseum.

"CONCAVE AND CONVEX," a lithograph designed by Escher in 1955, also makes use of reversible perspectives to bring out the ambiguity of volumes portrayed on the flat picture plane. The original print is in the Rosenwald collection at the National Gallery.

EIGHTEENTH-CENTURY ENGRAVING by Giovanni Battista Piranesi, one of a series titled *Carceri* (*Prisons*), is distinguished by perspective aberrations of a type similar to those in Escher's prints. Escher actually owned a set of Piranesi's *Carceri*, but he discounted their influence on his own work, pointing out that he was much more inspired by experiments on visual perception. This detail of a print catalogued Plate XI, 2nd State is reproduced here by courtesy of the Museum of Fine Arts in Boston (gift of Miss Ellen Bullard).

in the psychological literature. To emphasize the theme of the fantastic piece of architecture, the boy on the bench contemplates the reversible cube in his hands and on paper. The corners that are flipping forward and backward during reversals are connected by diagonals, just as in Necker's original 1832 drawing [*see top illustration on next page*]. In *Belvedere,* however, Escher not only uses reversible perspective but also introduces perceptual impossibility, which obstructs the two perceptual interpretations of the cube simultaneously. This technique resembles the constructions of impossible figures published in 1958 by L. S. Penrose and R. Penrose in the *British Journal of Psychology,* acknowledged by Escher as a source for his 1960 lithograph *Ascending and Descending.*

The Schröder stairs, another 19th-century reversible-perspective illusion, first published by H. Schröder in 1858 [*see top illustration on page 166*], is the theme of Escher's 1953 lithograph *Relativity* [*see middle illustration on page 166*]. The stairs show the characteristic shading that facilitates reversals, so that they look either like a staircase going up or an overhang of wall coming down. For the inhabitants of this structure the stairs lead up and down at the same time.

These compositions resemble certain 18th-century engravings, particularly Giovanni Battista Piranesi's *Carceri* (*Prisons*), with their obsessional repetitions and their shifting viewpoints that break up the unity of Renaissance perspective, thus giving a hallucinatory quality to these architectural dreams [*see bottom illustration at left*]. Note in the distance in the upper left quadrant of Piranesi's print a light-shaded underside of an arch. Or is it a walkway leading to a set of stairs? In *Concave and Convex* Escher employs the same motif in both orientations. Escher actually owned a set of Piranesi's engravings, according to his son, George A. Escher, who relates the following revealing story about his father and *Belvedere:*

"One evening, it must have been late 1958, we were looking at the *Carceri* by Piranesi, which he greatly admired and of which he owned a posthumously printed set. We had been hunting for the many perspective aberrations of the same nature as occur in *Belvedere* and I asked him whether these had inspired him to make that print. No, he said, he had been aware of these oddities since long, but had always considered them as carelessness due to the reputed furious pace at which Piranesi had produced the prints during an illness. They had never awakened the particular twist of fantasy which gave birth to *Belvedere*. That, he said, was the direct consequence of noting somewhere...a picture of the reversible...cube."

Nothing could confirm more closely the essentials of Escher's art. As I have tried to show, the artist was fascinated by certain phenomena from experimental work on vision. These were the intellectual starting points for his inventions. Once gripped by one of his "visual ideas" he would spend sleepless nights, writes his son, "trying to bring some vague concept to clarity.... For weeks he would refuse to talk about what he was doing and lock his studio, whether he was there or not." The perspective displacements in Piranesi's *Carceri* or the ambiguities in the reversible patterns of the tiles of the Alhambra were exciting to him because he felt a kinship with these works reaching back over the centuries, but they were not his primary sources.

It is quite apparent that Escher's use of principles derived from the contemporary psychology of visual perception meant much more to him than a new set of themes or artistic techniques. Escher himself described the profound change that occurred in his style between 1936 and 1938 as if it had been the result of a religious conversion: "There came a moment when it seemed as though scales fell from my eyes...I became gripped by a desire the existence of which I had never suspected. Ideas came into my head quite unrelated to graphic art, notions which so fascinated me that I longed to communicate them to other people." It is no contradiction that this sudden revelation had been foreshadowed in Escher's much earlier application of Rubin's original ideas in the beginning of the 1920's. Artistic ideas, like scientific ideas, have a way of going underground only to reemerge with full force at a later stage.

Once gained, Escher's insights stayed with him into his final years. Even 30 years after his first contact with Koffka's work, when Escher was 70 years old, he expressed himself entirely in Koffka's terms (in his 1968 essay "Approaches to Infinity"): "No one can draw a line that is not a boundary line; every line splits a singularity into a plurality. Every closed contour, no matter what its shape, whether a perfect circle or an irregular random form, evokes in addition the notions of 'inside' and 'outside' and the suggestion of 'near' and 'far away,' of 'object' and 'background.'"

Here Escher refers not only to the

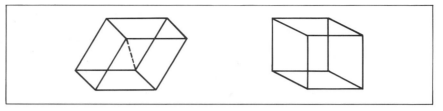

NECKER CUBE, a famous reversible-perspective illusion, was first described in 1832 by the Swiss mineralogist L. A. Necker, who noticed the reversals in his drawings of crystals.

"BELVEDERE," a 1958 lithograph by Escher, is also based on the ambiguous geometry of the Necker cube. The reversible cube, in which the corners that flip forward and backward during reversals are connected by diagonals, appears in three different forms in this print: in the impossible architecture of the building itself, in the model held by the boy sitting on the bench in front of the building and in the drawing on the piece of paper lying on the floor. The reproduction is from a print in the Roosevelt collection at the National Gallery.

SCHRÖDER STAIRS, another 19th-century reversible-perspective diagram, was first published in 1858 by H. Schröder, who pointed out that the shading facilitates the reversals.

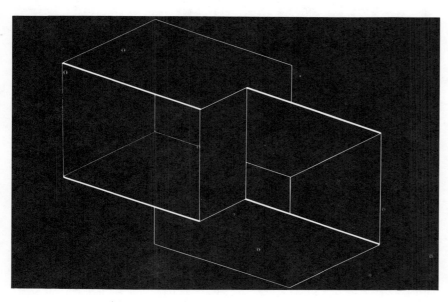

"RELATIVITY," a 1953 Escher lithograph, shows reversals similar to those in the diagram at top. The reproduction is from a print in the Rosenwald collection at the National Gallery.

"STRUCTURAL CONSTELLATION," a laminated-plastic construction by Josef Albers, can also be traced to certain reversible-perspective diagrams in the psychological literature.

principle of protruding figure and receding ground, and the double function of contours, but also to well-known Gestalt investigations on closed-contour figures and the problem of *"unum* and *duo* organization" of surface subdivisions analyzed by Wertheimer and Koffka. Regular subdivisions, as in Escher's studies for *Square Limit* of 1964 [*see bottom illustration on page 163*], could be carried out by simply dividing surface after surface in half, up to the limit of visibility at the outer edge. Therefore Escher could say with Koffka: "Every line splits a singularity into a plurality."

The figure-ground ambiguity of Rubin, Koffka and Harrower provided the decisive impetus for Escher to give up the traditional Renaissance picture space. Although he held on to the recognizable image of beast or man for his reversible units, he arrived at a new—sometimes surreal—emphasis on the flat picture surface, a development that the great innovators of 20th-century art had reached at a much earlier date. Picasso and Braque painted their first Cubist pictures between 1907 and 1909; Kandinsky's first abstract color compositions date from 1911. The interdigitation of shapes and their symbolic interpretation in Escher's graphic work, however, can be traced to a trend antedating the modern movement, namely the flat positive and negative patterns of Art Nouveau—often equally charged with meaning and in vogue just before and after the turn of the century.

Escher's contact with the visual experiments of the Gestalt psychologists is not an isolated instance. Joseph Albers' striking constructions on laminated plastic and many of his drawings can be traced to similar prototypes from the psychological literature [*see bottom illustration at right*]. Such ambiguous forms had become a focus of renewed interest at the Bauhaus in Dessau, Germany, in 1929 and 1930, when lectures on Gestalt psychology were offered at this influential school of design. Albers, first a student and then a teacher at the Bauhaus from 1920 until its closing by the Nazis in 1933, became fascinated by reversible perspectives. Beginning in 1931, abstract reversible-line constructions have continued to fascinate him throughout his artistic career.

In the 1930's (almost contemporaneously with Escher) Albers and Vasarely, both precursors of the "Op art" movement (which Albers prefers to call "perceptual art"), created paintings and woodcuts displaying the ambiguity of figure and ground. Yet it is apparent t the intellectual stimulation provided by Gestalt theory manifests itself in very different ways, depending on the artist's choice and predisposition. Albers and Vasarely continue the abstract tradition of modern art by giving it a new direction through insights gained from investigations on vision and visual perception. Escher instead extended the decorative tradition of Art Nouveau coupled with the Symbolist movement. It is perhaps no accident that Art Nouveau patterns are similarly repetitive and crowd the flat surface, just as Escher's inventions do.

Uncovering Escher's sources does not diminish the fascination of his work. Indeed, it underscores how directly the awe we experience before his compositions derives from the perplexing ambiguity of his scientific prototypes. By employing motifs from contemporary attempts at the scientific analysis of form perception, the artist plays with stripped-down mechanisms of perception and reflects on his own visual means.

Similarly, the abstract perceptual artist of the 1960's reflects on the presumed functional property of our visual apparatus by making his patterns vibrate with repetitive line and color stimuli. It is remarkable that such art culminated at the very time when physiologists of the brain began to demonstrate mechanisms for primitive "feature detection" in the cerebral visual pathways [see the article "The Visual Cortex of the Brain," by D. H. Hubel, beginning on page 19]. As the British information theorist D. M. MacKay has pointed out, complementary mechanisms of form perception (similar to complementary color perception) play a role in these scintillating patterns [see top illustration at right]. These effects were adopted by the Op-art painters in their provocative arrays of lines. Without any other visual clues to guide us, these patterns make the feature-extracting machinery in the human visual system reverberate *in vacuo*.

Escher instead clings tenaciously to meaningful, if fantastic, patterns and invites the viewer to repeat the basic figure-ground experiments of the Gestalt school. This can best be seen in the four-color woodcut *Sun and Moon*, which combines the Symbolist yearnings of the turn of the century with demonstrations of ambiguity in the perceptual process [see bottom illustration at right]. If you focus on the light birds, the crescent of the moon appears and night prevails; if you focus on the dark birds, the sun will shine.

"RAY PATTERN," published originally in *Nature* in 1957 by the British information theorist D. M. MacKay, influenced the work of the Op artists of the 1960's. A scintillating pattern of fine lines appears to run at right angles to the rays, indicating that a line-detecting mechanism of form perception complementary to the ray pattern has been stimulated.

"SUN AND MOON," a four-color woodcut designed by Escher in 1948, epitomizes, in the author's view, "the symbolist yearnings of the turn of the century with...demonstrations of ambiguity in the visual process." Reproduction is from a print in the Gemeentemuseum.

16

Auditory Illusions and Confusions

by Richard M. Warren and Roslyn P. Warren
December 1970

*These failures of perception are studied because they
isolate and clarify some fundamental processes that
normally lead to accuracy of perception and
appropriate interpretation of ambiguous sounds*

For more than a century visual illusions have been of particular interest to students of perception. Although they are in effect misjudgments of the real world, they apparently reflect the operation of fundamental perceptual mechanisms, and they serve to isolate and clarify visual processes that are normally inaccessible to investigation. Auditory illusions, on the other hand, have received little scientific attention. Until recently the fleeting nature of auditory stimuli made it difficult to create, control and reproduce sound patterns as readily as visual ones. The tape recorder made it easy to manipulate sounds, and yet for a time there was little examination of auditory illusions, perhaps because there was no historical tradition to build on—no puzzles inherited from the experimental psychologists of the past century, as there were in the case of optical illusions. Some new investigations, however, have led to the discovery of illusions in hearing that help to explain the human ability to extract information from fleeting patterns of sound. These investigations have also led to the identification of confusions in hearing that help to explain some limitations of that ability.

Consider for a moment that you are at a convention banquet. While you are still finishing your dinner the after-dinner speeches begin. The clatter of dishes masks some of the speech sounds, as do occasional coughs from your neighbors and your own munching. Nonetheless, you may be able to understand what the speaker is saying by utilizing the information that reaches you during intervals that are relatively free of these interfering noises. In order to understand how speech perception functions in the presence of transient noises, we and Charles J. Obusek did some experiments

last year in our laboratory at the University of Wisconsin at Milwaukee. First we recorded the sentence "The state governors met with their respective legislatures convening in the capital city." Then we carefully cut out of the tape recording of the sentence one phoneme, or speech sound: the first "s" in "legislatures." We also cut out enough of the preceding and following phonemes to remove any transitional cues to the identity of the missing speech sound. Finally, we spliced the recorded sound of a cough of the same duration into the tape to replace the deleted segment.

When this doctored sentence was played to listeners, we found that we had created an extremely compelling illusion: the missing speech sound was heard as clearly as were any of the phonemes that were physically present. We called this phenomenon "phonemic restoration." Even on hearing the sentence again, after having been told that a sound was missing, our subjects could not distinguish the illusory sound from the real one. One might expect that the missing phoneme could be identified by locating the position of the cough, but this strategy was of no help. The cough had no clear location in the sentence; it seemed to coexist with other speech sounds without interfering with their intelligibility. Phonemic restoration also occurred with other sounds, such as a buzz or tone, when these sounds were as loud as or louder than the loudest sound in the sentence. Moreover, phonemic restorations were not limited to single speech sounds. The entire syllable "gis" in "legislatures" was heard clearly when it was replaced by an extraneous sound of the same duration.

We did find a condition in which the missing sound was not restored. When a silent gap replaced the "s" in "legislatures," the gap could be located within

the sentence and the missing sound identified. In visual terms, it was as if an erasure of a letter in a printed text could be detected, whereas an opaque blot over the same symbol would result in illusory perception of the obliterated letter, with the blot appearing as a transparent smear over another portion of the text [*see top illustration on pages 170 and 171*]. Of course, in vision a blot can be localized readily, and even the more elusive "proofreader's illusions" can be eliminated when the reader is told in advance just where the error in the text occurs. With phonemic restorations, however, knowledge of the nature of the extraneous sound and of the identity of the missing phoneme does not prevent clear perception of the missing sound—even when the stimulus is played to the listener as many times as he wishes.

The inability to localize an extraneous sound in a sentence was first reported in 1960 by the British workers Peter Ladefoged and Donald E. Broadbent. Since they employed brief intrusive sounds (clicks and short hisses) and took care that no phoneme was obliterated, phonemic restorations did not arise. Similar short, nonmasking extraneous sounds were later used by a group at the Massachusetts Institute of Technology that included Jerry A. Fodor, Merrill F. Garrett and Thomas Bever. They have reported that systematic errors in locating the clicks are caused by various features of sentence structure, and they have used the errors to explore those features.

Perceptual synthesis of the phoneme is accomplished on the basis of verbal context. In the case of the missing "s" in "legislatures" the context prior to the absent sound suffices for identification. What about a sentence so constructed that the context necessary to identify an obliterated sound does not come until

AUDITORY ILLUSIONS are investigated in the authors' laboratory. The subject, listening through headphones to a stimulus signal generated by the equipment in the background and reproduced by the tape recorder, reports to the experimenter on what he hears.

a

| The | state | governors | met | with | their | respective | legislatures | convening | in | the | capital | city. |

b

| The | state | governors | met | with | their | respective | legi█latures | convening | in | the | capital | city. |

PHONEMIC RESTORATION is an illusion that shows the importance of context in determining what sound is heard. A sentence was recorded on tape (*a*). Then the first "s" in "legislatures" was excised and a cough of the same duration (*black rectangle*) was spliced in its place (*b*). When the altered sentence was played to subjects, the missing "s" was heard clearly (*c*) and localization of

later? With the symbol * representing a loud cough that replaces a speech sound, consider a spoken sentence beginning, "It was found that the *eel was on the ___." The context provided by the last word in the sentence should resolve the ambiguity and determine the appropriate phonemic restoration. Among the words that could complete the sentence are "axle," "shoe," "orange" and "table." Each implies a different speech sound for the preceding word fragment, respectively "wheel," "heel," "peel" and "meal." Preliminary studies by Gary

Sherman in our laboratory have indicated that the listener does experience the appropriate phonemic restoration, apparently by storing the incomplete information until the necessary context is supplied so that the required phoneme can be synthesized. We are still investigating the influence of such factors as the duration of extraneous sounds in relation to the duration of the missing phoneme and the maximum temporal separation between the ambiguous word fragment and the resolving context that will still permit phonemic restoration.

The use of subsequent context for correcting errors had been suggested on logical grounds by George A. Miller of Rockefeller University. He reasoned that unless some such strategy were available, a mistake once made while listening to spoken discourse would cause errors in interpreting the following portions of the message to pile up, until the entire system eventually stalled. The long delays in muscular activity that have been observed in the skilled transcription of an incoming message also suggest that storage of incoming lan-

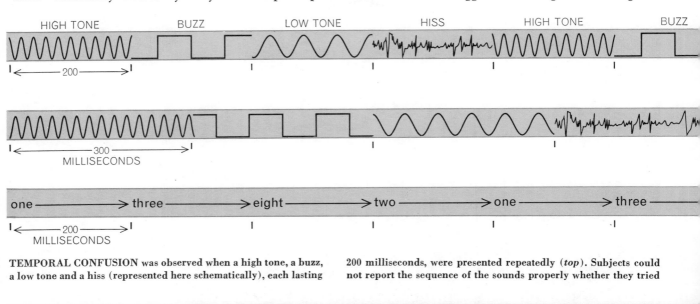

TEMPORAL CONFUSION was observed when a high tone, a buzz, a low tone and a hiss (represented here schematically), each lasting 200 milliseconds, were presented repeatedly (*top*). Subjects could not report the sequence of the sounds properly whether they tried

FOUR VOWEL SOUNDS were used in another experiment on temporal confusion. When the vowel sounds of "beet," "boot," "bit" and "but" were presented at a sustained level for 200 milliseconds, their sequence could not be determined (*top*). Deleting 50 milli-

c

| The | state | governors | met | with | their | respective | legislatures | convening | in | the | capital | city. |

d

| The | state | governors | met | with | their | respective | legi latures | convening | in | the | capital | city. |

the cough was indefinite; when required to guess the location, subjects generally missed the correct position by several phonemes, as indicated (*gray area*). When a silent gap, rather than a cough, re-

placed the "s," the gap could be located and the missing sound could be identified (*d*). This illustration, like those that follow, is necessarily an approximate representation of an auditory effect.

guage information is associated with error correction. In the 1890's William Bryan and Noble Harter noted that highly skilled telegraphers listening to Morse code did not transcribe the auditory signals that constituted a word until some six to 12 words after the signals were heard. If subsequent portions of the message could not provide helpful context, as in the case of stock quotations or transmissions in cipher, the telegraphers changed their strategy and followed the message much more closely in time. Telegraph companies charged higher

rates for sending such messages precisely because they lacked redundant context, were therefore much more difficult to receive and had to be transmitted more slowly.

This telegrapher's technique illustrates a surprising relation that one encounters again and again in perception: The development of an extremely complex procedure for data processing is necessary to achieve the deceptive impression of an "easy" perceptual task. From time to time other workers have noted the delay between language input

and motor response. In 1925 William Book observed the similarity between typewriting and code transcription, reporting that in the case of an expert typist "attention was pushed ahead of the hands as far as possible (usually four or five words)."

Inability to locate the position of extraneous sounds in sentences represents a failure in the detection of temporal order. It might be thought that this temporal confusion results from a conflict between verbal and nonverbal

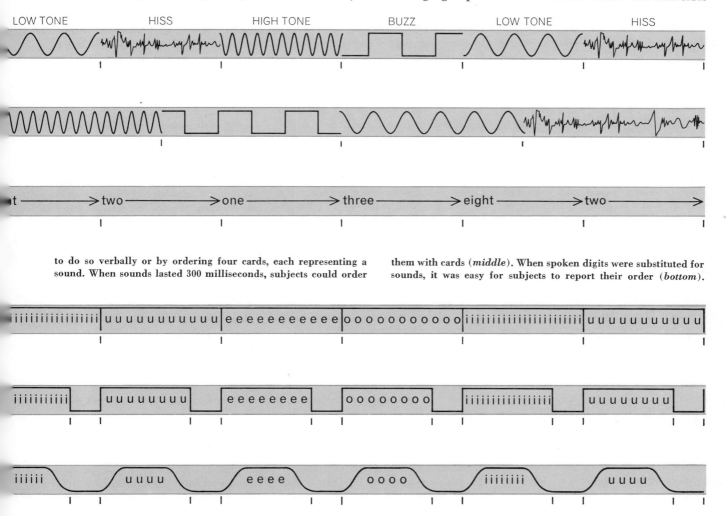

LOW TONE   HISS   HIGH TONE   BUZZ   LOW TONE   HISS

t —→ two ——————→ one ——————→ three ——————→ eight ——————→ two ——————→

to do so verbally or by ordering four cards, each representing a sound. When sounds lasted 300 milliseconds, subjects could order

them with cards (*middle*). When spoken digits were substituted for sounds, it was easy for subjects to report their order (*bottom*).

iiiiiiiiiiiiiiiii | uuuuuuuuuu | eeeeeeeeee | oooooooooo | iiiiiiiiiiiiiiiiiiiiii | uuuuuuuuuu

iiiiiiiiiii | uuuuuuuu | eeeeeeee | oooooooo | iiiiiiiiiiiiiiii | uuuuuuuu

iiiiii | uuuu | eeee | oooo | iiiiiii | uuuu

seconds of each sound and replacing it with silence (*middle*) allowed half of the subjects to determine the sequence. The se-

quence was readily determined when vowels were given normal qualities of gradual onset and decay, suggested by curves (*bottom*).

a

tresstresstresstresstresstresstresstresstresstresstresstresstresstresstresstresstresstresstresstresstresstresst

b

tress tress tress tress tress tress tress tress stress stress stress stress stress stress stress stress stress dress dress

dress dress dress dress floris floris floris floris floris florist florist florist florist florist Joyce Joyce Joyce Joyce Joyce d

VERBAL TRANSFORMATION EFFECT is noted when subjects listen to a distinct recording of a single word repeated on a loop of tape (*a*). One might expect a kind of reversal effect, with the stimulus "tress" perceived sometimes as "rest." Instead lack of context

modes of perception. Recent observations in our laboratory have indicated, however, that inability to detect sequence is not restricted to verbal-nonverbal interactions. In 1968, during an experiment on loudness, we noted to our surprise that listeners could not tell the order of three successive sounds repeated over and over without pauses. The sounds—a hiss, a tone and a buzz—each lasted a fifth of a second (200 milliseconds) and were recorded on a tape that was then spliced to form a loop. The duration of each sound was quite long compared with the 70- to 80-millisecond average for a phoneme in speech and was well within the temporal range used in music for the successive notes of melodies; the hiss, tone and buzz could each be heard clearly. Yet it was impossible to tell the order of the sounds. The pattern swirled by, the temporal structure tantalizingly just beyond one's grasp.

It might be thought that a little advance planning would make the task easy. It should be possible, for example, to concentrate on one of the sounds (say the hiss) and then decide whether the sound that follows it is a tone or a buzz; this single decision would fix the third sound in the remaining slot and solve the problem. In practice, however, the single decision cannot be made with accuracy. Out of 50 listeners we found that only 22 named the order correctly—slightly fewer than the 50 percent correct answers that would be expected by chance alone.

This seemed at first to contradict the findings of earlier studies. Results reported by Ira Hirsh of the St. Louis Central Institute for the Deaf and by others had indicated that temporal resolution of such sounds as tones, hisses and buzzes should be possible down to a separation of about 20 milliseconds—even less time than is required for accurate temporal ordering of the sounds forming speech or music. These values, however, had been based on pairs of sounds. The subjects listened to a single pair (such as a tone

and a hiss) and reported their order. It was possible, we reasoned, that subjects could say which sound came first and which last not by actually perceiving the temporal order as such but by detecting which of the sounds occurred at either the onset or the termination of the stimulus pair. In 1959 Broadbent and Ladefoged had suggested that the ability of their subjects to order pairs of sounds might be based on the "quality" of the pair as a whole. Could that "quality" be determined by which sound was present at the onset and/or the termination of the brief pair?

With threshold judgments of this kind, when subjects are working at the limit of their ability, introspection as to how they make their decisions is particularly difficult; they simply cannot say. To determine what criteria are actually being used one must rely on experiments. We returned to our recycled 200-millisecond stimuli (hiss, tone, buzz) that could not be ordered, but this time we inserted a three-second interval of silence between successive presentations of the three-sound sequence. Most listeners could now identify the first and last items in the series correctly, somewhat more accurately in the case of the last sound. This supported our suspicion that "sequence perception" with pairs of sounds represents a special case and is really perception of onset and termination.

In order to examine further the perception of temporal order in the absence of onset and termination cues, we employed a variety of repeated four-item sequences. The chance of guessing the order correctly, starting with whichever sound one chooses, is one in six. With a sequence consisting of a high tone (a frequency of 1,000 hertz, or 1,000 cycles per second), a buzz (40-hertz square wave), a low tone (796 hertz) and a hiss (2,000-hertz octave band of noise), each lasting 200 milliseconds, correct responses were only at the level of chance. It was necessary to increase the duration

of each item to between about 300 and 700 milliseconds (the exact value depending on practice and the response procedure) to obtain a correct identification of sequence from half of the subjects tested. For durations of 300 milliseconds or more, calling out the order of the sounds resulted in more errors than arranging four cards, each bearing the name of one sound, in the appropriate sequence.

We noticed a curious feature of the four-item sequences: listeners frequently could not tell at first how many different sounds were present in the series. The apparent disappearance of one or sometimes even two items could be minimized by telling the listener the number of sounds there were and by first introducing each sound alone. This illusory absence of stimuli could not account completely for the inability to perceive sequence, however: even people who heard the four sounds clearly could not report their sequence. We also found that repetition was not in itself a barrier to sequence perception. When four spoken digits, each lasting 200 milliseconds, were recorded separately (to avoid transitional cues), spliced into a loop and repeated over and over, the subjects perceived the order at once and with certainty.

This great difference between the temporal perception of verbal and of nonverbal stimuli suggested that we could use perception of sequence in an effort to establish which attributes of sounds are responsible for speechlike characteristics. We cut four 200-millisecond segments out of extended statements of separate vowels held at a fixed level for several seconds. When these tape segments were spliced into a loop and played back, the listener heard a repeated sequence of four steady vowels following one another without pauses. Since no speaker can possibly change from one vowel to another in this way, without a transition or a pause, the sequence sounded curiously artificial, like resstress

s dress dress dress dress dress dress tress tress tress tress tress tress Joyce Joyce Joyce Joyce Joyce Joyce dress

dress dress dress stress stress stress stress stress dress dress dress dress dress purse purse purse purse purse . . .

has a more profound effect: most subjects experience illusory changes involving substantial distortion of the stimulus. A man listening to "tress" repeated 360 times in three minutes heard 16 changes involving eight different words, some illustrated here (b).

crude attempts to synthesize speech sounds electronically.

Our subjects did no better than chance the first time they attempted to judge the order of the sounds. By deleting a 50-millisecond portion of each sustained vowel and replacing it with a silent gap, we made the sequence sound more like normal speech, and then identification of order was possible for half of a new group of subjects. The subjects approached a perfect score only when we presented vowels of the same duration (150 milliseconds separated by 50 milliseconds of silence) but recorded with the normal qualities of vocal onset and decay that are characteristic of separate short utterances of vowel sounds. It appears, in short, that accurate perception of temporal order may be possible only for sequences that resemble those encountered in speech and in music—special sequences in which the component sounds are linked together, following specific rules, into coherent passages.

During the 1950's Colin Cherry of the Imperial College of Science and Technology in London wrote about the "cocktail-party problem," the task of attending to one chosen conversation among several equally audible conversations. Apparently such cues as voice quality and spatial localization help the listener to keep fixed on a single voice among many. When a person attends to one of these verbal sequences, he excludes the others, so that presumably it would not be possible for him to relate the temporal position of a phoneme in one conversation (or other extraneous sounds such as coughs) to the temporal position of phonemes in the attended conversation. Such observations lead us to speculate that the inability to perceive the correct order of stimuli that do not form integrated sequences of speech or music may not represent a flaw or defect of our perceptual skills. Rather, this restriction of temporal pattern perception may be an essential step in the continual process

of extracting intelligible signals from the ubiquitous background of noise.

Musical and verbal passages have an organization based on the temporal order of their sounds; this organization furnishes a context for the individual sounds. Verbal context, as we pointed out above, can determine completely the synthesis of illusory speech sounds; phonemic restorations are heard when the context is clear but part of the stimulus is absent. Another illusion arises when the stimulus is clear but the context is absent. If one listens to a clear recording of a word or phrase repeated over and over, having only itself as context, illusory changes occur in what the voice seems to be saying. Any word or phrase is subject to these illusory changes, usually with considerable phonetic distortion and frequently with semantic linkages. These illusory words are heard quite clearly, and listeners find it difficult to believe they are hearing a single auditory pattern repeated on a loop of tape. As an example of the kind of changes heard, a subject listening to "tress" repeated without pause heard distinctly, within the course of a few minutes, such illusory forms as "dress," "stress," "Joyce," "floris," "florist" and "purse." This illusion, which we call the verbal transformation effect, has provided unexpected glimpses of hitherto unexplored perceptual mechanisms for organizing speech sounds into words and sentences.

The implications of the verbal transformation illusion were not appreciated fully in 1958, when one of us (Richard Warren) and Richard L. Gregory first reported the discovery of "an auditory analogue of the visual reversible figure." We had been looking for an auditory illusion resembling the one observed in such ambiguous figures as the Necker cube, whose faces seem to pop into different perspective orientations as one looks at it. We reasoned that ambiguous auditory patterns would undergo similar

illusory shifts; for example, the word "rest" repeated clearly over and over without pause should shift to "tress," then back to "rest" and so on. We did find such closed-loop shifts but we also found some other illusory changes—to "dress" and "Esther," for instance. At the time, although we noted that perceptual distortion of the stimulus had occurred, we considered it only a curious side effect.

Further study by the present authors has drawn attention to basic differences between the visual and auditory illusions, however. The auditory effect is not limited to ambiguous patterns; any word or phrase will do. Changes are impossible to predict, vary greatly from individual to individual and often involve considerable distortion of the stimulus pattern. A subject listening to the word "see" repeated over and over may hear a phrase as far removed from the stimulus as "lunchtime," particularly if the time is about noon! Changes occur frequently: when a single word is repeated twice a second for three minutes, the average young adult hears about 30 changes involving about six different forms.

There are some remarkable effects of age on the frequency of verbal transformations and the types of illusory changes. These age differences seem to reflect basic changes in the way in which a person processes verbal input over a life-span. Children at the age of five experience either very few or no verbal transformations. At six half the children tested heard illusory changes, and those who did experienced them at the rapid rate characteristic of older children. By the age of eight all the children tested heard verbal transformations. The rate of illusory changes apparently remains approximately constant into the twenties and then declines slowly during the middle years; for listeners over 65 the rate was found to be only a fifth the rate for young adults and was approximately equal to the rate for five-year-olds. This decrease after middle age is not due directly to any decrease in auditory acuity with aging. Actually the aged are generally more accurate in this task than the young, reporting common English stimulus words correctly and continuing to respond to the stimulus as it actually is—the same word repeated over and over without change. Moreover, if young adults hear a word played indistinctly against a background of noise (which should simulate a decrease in acuity), they still hear many more illusory changes than the aged.

Besides counting the number of changes, we have examined the groupings of speech sounds to determine the units of perceptual organization at different ages. Children respond in terms of the sounds of English but may group them in ways not found in the language. For example, with the word "tress" repeated over and over, a child might report "sreb" even though the initial "sr" sequence is not found in English words. Young adults group speech sounds only in ways that are permitted in English, but they do report nonsense syllables: given the stimulus "tress," they might report "tresh" as one of the sounds they hear. Older people, on the other hand, report only meaningful words. Presented with "tress," they tend to hear "tress" continuously, and when infrequent changes do occur, they usually are to such closely related forms as "dress." If an older person is presented with a repeated nonsense syllable, there is an

interesting result. If "flime" is the stimulus, for example, the older listener generally distorts the word into a phonetically close English word such as "slime" and tends to stay with the sense-making (but illusory) word throughout.

Our observations with verbal transformations have suggested that as people grow older they employ different perceptual mechanisms appropriate to their familiarity with language and their functional capacities, both of which change with age. We believe specific mechanisms associated with the skilled use of verbal context underlie the age differences in the frequency and nature of verbal transformations. Repeated words do not flow past us as normal components in the stream of language do; like a vortex, they move without progressing. In the absence of the semantic and grammatical confirmation ordinarily provided by verbal context, perception of repeated words becomes unstable for all but the very young and the old. And since each successive perceptual organization is subject to the same lack of stabilizing context, it suffers the fate of its predecessor.

The absence of illusory changes at age five suggests that young children have not yet reached the stage in language development where storage with skilled reorganization comes into play. The loss of susceptibility in alert and healthy elderly listeners suggests that they no longer have the functional capacity for this mechanism. It is rather well established that short-term memory is less ef-

fective in the aged when intervening activity is required between input and retrieval. Concurrent processes of coding, storing, comparing and reorganizing may therefore not be possible, so that the optimum strategy is to employ only the past context of the message as an aid to organization of the current input. The fact that in the presence of repeated stimuli the aged report only meaningful words is consistent with this view. If this interpretation is correct, one would expect that phonemic restoration for elderly people would be limited to replacement of speech sounds identified by prior context; the use of subsequent context, in the manner of young adults, would not be possible. We plan to do experiments testing this prediction.

In summary, it appears that phonemic restorations and verbal transformations provide new techniques for studying the perceptual organization of heard speech, particularly the grouping of speech sounds, the correction of the listener's errors and the resolution of acoustic ambiguities. The observations we have described for the perception of auditory sequence indicate that special perceptual treatment of the sounds of speech (and music) allow us to extract order and meaning from what would otherwise be a world of auditory chaos. It is curious that in studying illusions and confusions we encounter mechanisms that ensure accurate perception and the appropriate interpretation of ambiguities.

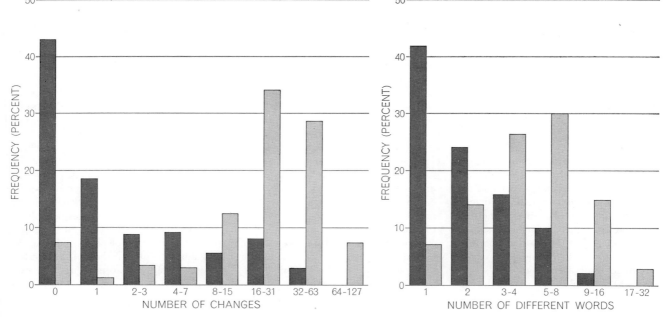

AGE DIFFERENCES in the frequency of verbal transformations are shown for two of the age groups tested. The bars indicate the number of changes from one form to another (left) and the number of different forms (right) perceived during three-minute tests by subjects 18 to 25 (gray) and 62 to 86 years old (black). Differences reflect changes in the perceptual processing of speech.

The Perception of Disoriented Figures

by Irvin Rock
January 1974

Many familiar things do not look the same when their orientation is changed. The reason appears to be that the perception of form embodies the automatic assignment of a top, a bottom and sides

Many common experiences of everyday life that we take for granted present challenging scientific problems. In the field of visual perception one such problem is why things look different when they are upside down or tilted. Consider the inverted photograph on the opposite page. Although the face is familiar to most Americans, it is difficult to recognize when it is inverted. Even when one succeeds in identifying the face, it continues to look strange and the specific facial expression is hard to make out.

Consider also what happens when printed words and words written in longhand are turned upside down. With effort the printed words can be read, but it is all but impossible to read the longhand words [*see top illustration on page 177*]. Try it with a sample of your own handwriting. One obvious explanation of why it is hard to read inverted words is that we have acquired the habit of moving our eyes from left to right, and that when we look at inverted words our eyes tend to move in the wrong direction. This may be one source of the difficulty, but it can hardly be the major one. It is just as hard to read even a single inverted word when we look at it without moving our eyes at all. It is probable that the same factor interfering with the recognition of disoriented faces and other figures is also interfering with word recognition.

The partial rotation of even a simple figure can also prevent its recognition, provided that the observer is unaware of the rotation. A familiar figure viewed in a novel orientation no longer appears to have the same shape [*see bottom illustration on page 177*]. As Ernst Mach pointed out late in the 19th century, the appearance of a square is quite different when it is rotated 45 degrees. In fact, we call it a diamond.

Some may protest that a familiar shape looks different in a novel orientation for the simple reason that we rarely see it that way. But even a figure we have not seen before will look different in different orientations [*see top illustration on page 178*]. The fact is that orientation affects perceived shape, and that the failure to recognize a familiar figure when it is in a novel orientation is based on the change in its perceived shape.

On the other hand, a figure can be changed in various ways without any effect on its perceived shape. For example, a triangle can be altered in size, color and various other ways without any change in its perceived shape [*see middle illustration on page 178*]. Psychologists, drawing an analogy with a similar phenomenon in music, call such changes transpositions. A melody can be transposed to a new key, and although all the notes then are different, there is no change in the melody. In fact, we generally remain unaware of the transposition. Clearly the melody derives from the relation of the notes to one another, which is not altered when the melody is transposed. In much the same way a visual form is based primarily on how parts of a figure are related to one another geometrically. For example, one could describe a square as being a four-sided figure having parallel opposite sides, four right angles and four sides of equal length. These features remain unchanged when a square is transposed in size or position; that is why it continues to look like a square. We owe a debt to the Gestalt psychologists for emphasizing the importance in perception of relations rather than absolute features.

Since a transposition based on rotation also does not alter the internal geometric relations of a figure, then why does it look different in an altered orientation? At this point we should consider the meaning of the term orientation. What changes are introduced by altering orientation? One obvious change is that rotating a figure would result in a change in the orientation of its image on the retina of the eye. Perhaps, therefore, we should ask why different retinal orientations of the same figure should give rise to different perceived shapes. That might lead us into speculations about how the brain processes information about form, and why differently oriented projections of a retinal image should lead to different percepts of form.

Before we go further in this direction we should consider another meaning of the term orientation. The inverted and rotated figures in the illustrations for this article are in different orientations with respect to the vertical and horizontal directions in their environment. That part of the figure which is normally pointed upward in relation to gravity, to the sky or to the ceiling is now pointed downward or sideways on the page. Perhaps it is this kind of orientation that is responsible for altered perception of shape when a figure is disoriented.

It is not difficult to separate the retinal and the environmental factors in an experiment. Cut out a paper square and tape it to the wall so that the bottom of the square is parallel to the floor. Compare the appearance of the square first with your head upright and then with your head tilted 45 degrees. You will see that the square continues to look like a square when your head is tilted. Yet when your head is tilted 45 degrees, the retinal image of the square is the same as the image of a diamond when the diamond is viewed with the head upright. Thus it is not the retinal image that is responsible for the altered appearance of a square when the square is rotated 45 degrees. The converse experiment points to the same conclusion. Rotate the square on the wall so that it becomes a diamond. The diamond viewed with your head tilted 45 degrees produces a retinal image of a square, but the diamond still looks like a diamond. Needless to say, in these simple demonstrations one continues to perceive correctly where the top, bottom and sides of the figures are even when one's posture changes. It is therefore the change of a figure's perceived orientation in the environment that affects its apparent shape and not the change of orientation of its retinal image.

These conclusions have been substantiated in experiments Walter I. Heimer and I and other colleagues have conducted with numerous subjects. In one series of experiments the subjects were shown unfamiliar figures. In the first part of the experiment a subject sat at a table and simply looked at several figures shown briefly in succession. Then some of the subjects were asked to tilt their head 90 degrees by turning it to the side and resting it on the table. In this position the subject viewed a series of figures. Most of the figures were new, but among them were some figures the subject had seen earlier. These figures were shown in either of two orientations: upright with respect to the room (as they had been in the first viewing) or rotated 90 degrees so that the "top" of the figure corresponded to the top of the subject's tilted head. The subject was asked to say whether or not he had seen each figure in the first session. He did not know that the orientation of the figures seen previously might be different. Other subjects viewed the test figures while sitting upright.

When we compared the scores of subjects who tilted their head with subjects who sat upright for the test, the results were clear. Tilted-head subjects recognized the environmentally upright (but retinally tilted) figures about as well as the upright observers did. They also failed to recognize the environmentally tilted (but retinally upright) figures about as often as the upright subjects did. In other words, the experiments confirmed that it is rotation with respect to the up-down and left-right coordinates in the environment that produces the change in the perceived shape of the figure. It is not rotation of the retinal image that produces the change, since altering the image's orientation does not adversely affect recognition and preserving it does not improve recognition.

In another experiment subjects viewed an ambiguous or reversible figure that could be perceived in one of two ways depending on its orientation. For example, when one figure that looked like a map of the U.S. was rotated 90 degrees, it looked like the profile of a bearded man. Subjects were asked to rest their head on the table when viewing the ambiguous figures. The question we asked ourselves was: Which "upright" would dominate, the retinal upright or the environmental upright? The results were decisive. About 80 percent of the subjects reported seeing only the aspect of the ambiguous figure that was environmentally upright, even though the alternative was upright on their retina [*see bottom illustration on page 179*].

Why does the orientation of a figure with respect to the directional coordinates of the environment have such a profound effect on the perceived shape of the figure? The answer I propose is that perceived shape is based on a cognitive process in which the characteristics of the figure are implicitly described by the perceptual system. For example, the colored figure at the left in the top illustration on page 178 could be described as a closed figure resting on a horizontal base with a protrusion on the figure's left side and an indentation on its right side. The colored figure to the right of it, although it is identical and only rotated 90 degrees, would be described quite differently, as being symmetrical with two bumps on the bottom and with left and right sides more or less straight and identical with each other. I am not suggesting that such a description is conscious or verbal; obviously we would be aware of the descriptive process if it were either. Furthermore, animals and infants who are nonverbal perceive shape much as we do. I am proposing that a process analogous to such a description does take place and that it is not only based on the internal geometry of a figure but also takes into account the location of the figure's top, bottom and sides. In such a description orienta-

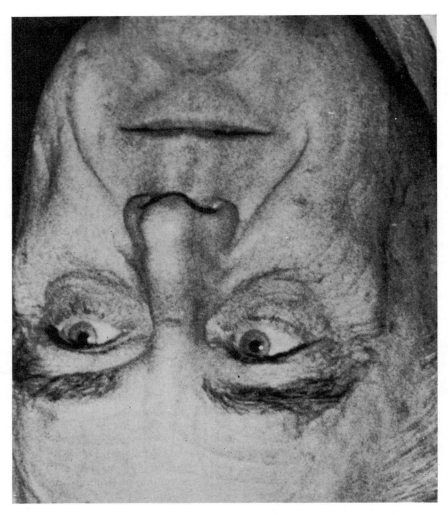

INVERTED PHOTOGRAPH of a famous American demonstrates how difficult it is to recognize a familiar face when it is presented upside down. Even after one succeeds in identifying the inverted face as that of Franklin D. Roosevelt, it continues to look strange.

orientation, say 45 or 90 degrees. Interestingly enough, inversions or rotations of 180 degrees often have only a slight effect on perceived shape, perhaps because such changes will usually not alter perceived symmetry or the perceived orientation of the long axis of the figure.

There is one kind of orientation change that has virtually no effect on perceived shape: a mirror-image reversal. This is particularly true for the novel figures we used in our experiments. How can this be explained? It seems that although the "sides" of visual space are essentially interchangeable, the up-and-down directions in the environment are not. "Up" and "down" are distinctly different directions in the world we live in. Thus a figure can be said to have three main perceptual boundaries: top, bottom and sides. As a result the description of a figure will not be much affected by whether a certain feature is on the left side or the right. Young children and animals have great difficulty learning to discriminate between a figure and its mirror image, but they can easily distinguish between a figure and its inverted counterpart.

Related to this analysis is a fact observed by Mach and tested by Erich Goldmeier: A figure that is symmetrical around one axis will generally appear to be symmetrical only if that axis is vertical. Robin Leaman and I have demonstrated that it is the perceived vertical axis of the figure and not the vertical axis of the figure's retinal image that produces this effect. An observer who tilts his head will continue to perceive a figure as being symmetrical if that figure is symmetrical around an environmental vertical axis. This suggests that perceived symmetry results only when the two equivalent halves of a figure are located on the two equivalent sides of perceptual space.

If, as I have suggested, the description of a figure is based on the location of its top, bottom and sides, the question arises: How are these directions assigned in a figure? One might suppose that the top of a figure is ordinarily the area uppermost in relation to the ceiling, the sky or the top of a page. In a dark room an observer may have to rely on his sense of gravity to inform him which way is up.

Numerous experiments by psychologists have confirmed that there are indeed two major sources of information for perceiving the vertical and the horizontal: gravity (as it is sensed by the vestibular apparatus in the inner ear, by the pressure of the ground on the body and by feedback from the muscles)

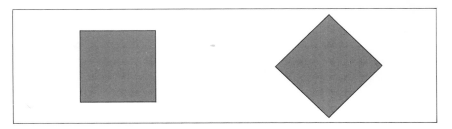

INVERTED WORDS are difficult to read when they are set in type, and words written in longhand are virtually impossible to decipher. The difficulty applies to one's own inverted handwriting in spite of a lifetime of experience reading it in the normal upright orientation.

tion is therefore a major factor in the shape that is finally perceived.

From experiments I have done in collaboration with Phyllis Olshansky it appears that certain shifts in orientation have a marked effect on perceived shape. In particular, creating symmetry around a vertical axis where no symmetry had existed before (or vice versa), shifting the long axis from vertical to horizontal (or vice versa) and changing the bottom of a figure from a broad horizontal base to a pointed angle (or vice versa) seemed to have a strong effect on perceived shape. Such changes of shape can result from only a moderate angular change of

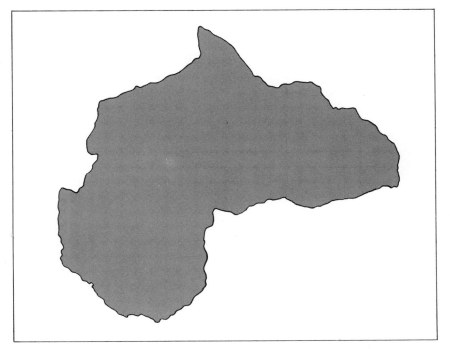

SQUARE AND DIAMOND are two familiar shapes. The two figures shown here are identical; their appearance is so different, however, that we call one a square and the other a diamond. With the diamond the angles do not spontaneously appear as right angles.

"UNFAMILIAR" SHAPE shown here becomes a familiar shape when it is rotated clockwise 90 degrees. In a classroom experiment, when the rotated figure was drawn on the blackboard, it was not recognized as an outline of the continent of Africa until the teacher told the class at the end of the lecture that the figure was rotated out of its customary orientation.

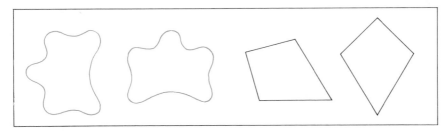

NOVEL OR UNFAMILIAR FIGURES look different in different orientations, provided that we view them naïvely and do not mentally rotate them. The reason may be the way in which a figure is "described" by the perceptual system. The colored figure at left could be described as a closed shape resting on a horizontal base with a protrusion on its left side and an indentation on its right side. The colored figure adjacent to it, although identical, would be described as a symmetrical shape resting on a curved base with a protrusion at the top. The first black figure could be described as a quadrilateral resting on a side. The black figure at right would be described as a diamondlike shape standing on end.

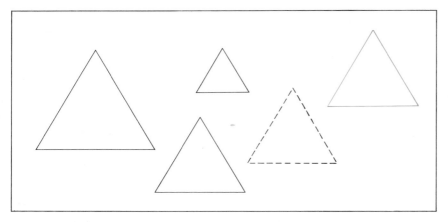

ALTERATION IN SIZE, color or type of contour does not change the perceived shape of a triangle. Even varying the location of the triangle's retinal image (by looking out of the corner of your eyes or fixating on different points) does not change perceived shape.

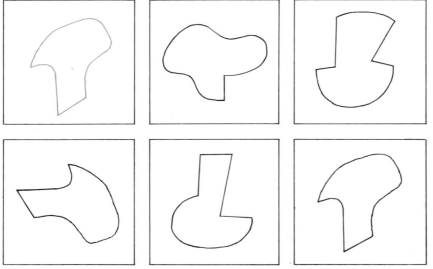

ROTATION OF RETINAL IMAGE by tilting the head 90 degrees does not appreciably affect recognition of a novel figure (color). Subjects first viewed several novel targets while sitting upright. Then they were shown a series of test figures (black) and were asked to identify those they had seen before. Some subjects tilted their head 90 degrees; others viewed the test figures with their head upright. Tilted-head subjects failed to recognize figures that were retinally "upright" (for example figure at bottom left) about as much as upright viewers did (to whom such figures were not retinally upright). Tilted-head subjects recognized environmentally upright figures (*bottom right*) as often as upright viewers did.

and information from the scene itself. We have been able to demonstrate that either can affect the perceived shape of a figure. A luminous figure in a dark room will not be recognized readily when it is rotated to a new orientation even if the observer is tilted by exactly the same amount. Here the only source of information about directions in space is gravity. In a lighted room an observer will often fail to recognize a figure when he and the figure are upright but the room is tilted. The tilted room creates a strong impression of where the up-down axis should be, and this leads to an incorrect attribution of the top and bottom of the figure [see "The Perception of the Upright," [by Herman A. Witkin; SCIENTIFIC AMERICAN Offprint 410].

Merely informing an observer that a figure is tilted will often enable him to perceive the figure correctly. This may explain why some readers will not perceive certain of the rotated figures shown here as being strange or different. The converse situation, misinforming an observer about the figures, produces impressive results. If a subject is told that the top of a figure he is about to see is somewhere other than in the region uppermost in the environment, he is likely not to recognize the figure when it is presented with the orientation in which he first saw it. The figure is not disoriented and the observer incorrectly assigns the directions top, bottom and sides on the basis of instructions.

Since such knowledge about orientation will enable the observer to shift the directions he assigns to a figure, and since it is this assignment that affects the perception of shape, it is absolutely essential to employ naïve subjects in perception experiments involving orientation. That is, the subject must not realize that the experiment is concerned with figural orientation, so that he does not examine the figures with the intent of finding the regions that had been top, bottom and sides in previous viewings of it. There are, however, some figures that seem to have intrinsic orientation in that regardless of how they are presented a certain region will be perceived as the top [*see top illustration on next page*]. It is therefore difficult or impossible to adversely affect the recognition of such figures by disorienting them.

In the absence of other clues a subject will assign top-bottom coordinates according to his subjective or egocentric reference system. Consider a figure drawn on a circular sheet of paper that is lying on the ground. Neither gravity nor visual clues indicate where the top and bottom are. Nevertheless, an observer will assign a top to that region of the figure which is uppermost with respect to his egocentric coordinate reference system. The vertical axis of the figure is seen as being aligned with the long axis of the observer's head and body. The upward direction corresponds to the position of his head. We have been able to demonstrate that such assignment of direction has the same effect on the recognition that other bases of assigning direction do. A figure first seen in one orientation on the circular sheet will generally not be recognized if its egocentric orientation is altered.

Now we come to an observation that seems to be at variance with much of what I have described. When a person lies on his side in bed to read, he does not hold the book upright (in the environmental sense) but tilts it. If the book is not tilted, the retinal image is disoriented and reading is quite difficult. Similarly, if a reader views printed matter or photographs of faces that are environmentally upright with his head between his legs, they will be just as difficult to recognize as they are when they are upside down and the viewer's head is upright. The upright pictures, however, are still perceived as being upright even when the viewer's head is inverted. Conversely, if the pictures are upside down in the environment and are viewed with the head inverted between the legs, there is no difficulty in recognizing them. Yet the observer perceives the pictures as being inverted. Therefore in these cases it is the orientation of the retinal image and not the environmental assignment of direction that seems to be responsible for recognition or failure of recognition.

Experiments with ambiguous figures conducted by Robert Thouless, G. Kanizsa and G. Tampieri support the notion that retinal orientation plays a role in recognition of a figure [see illustration on page 182]. Moreover, as George Steinfeld and I have demonstrated, the recognition of upright words and faces falls off in direct proportion to the degree of body tilt [see illustration on opposite page]. With such visual material recognition is an inverse function the degree of body tilt [see illustration on following page]. With such visual material recognizability does not hold in cases where the assignment of direction has been altered. In such cases the greatest effect is not with a 180-degree change but with a 45- or 90-degree change.

The results of all these experiments

FIGURES WITH INTRINSIC ORIENTATION appear to have a natural vertical axis regardless of their physical orientation. A region at one end of the axis is perceived as top.

IMPRESSION OF SYMMETRY is spontaneous only when a figure is symmetrical around a vertical axis. Subjects were asked to indicate which of two figures (*middle and right*) was most like the target figure (*left*). The figure at right was selected most frequently, presumably because it is symmetrical around its vertical axis. If the page is tilted 90 degrees, the figure in the middle will now be selected as being more similar to the target figure. Now if the page is held vertically and the figures are viewed with the head tilted 90 degrees, the figure at right is likely to be seen as being the most similar. This suggests that it is not the symmetry around the egocentric vertical axis on the retina but rather the symmetry around the environmental axis of the figure that determines perceived symmetry.

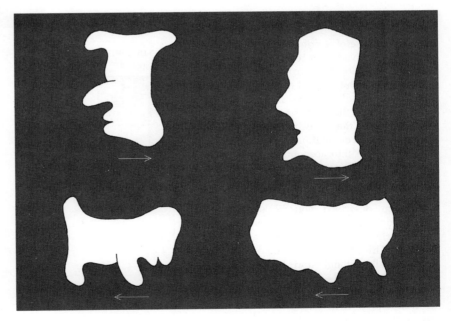

AMBIGUOUS FIGURES can be perceived in different ways depending on the orientation assigned to them. Figure at left can look like the profile of a man's head with a chef's hat (*top left*) or, when rotated 90 degrees, like a dog (*bottom left*). Figure at right can look like the profile of a bearded man's head (*top right*) or like a map of the U.S. (*bottom right*). When subjects with their head tilted 90 degrees to one side viewed these ambiguous figures (*direction of subject's head is shown by arrow*), they preferentially recognized the figure that was upright in the environment instead of the figure that was upright on the retina.

have led me to conclude that there are two distinct factors involved in the perception of disoriented figures: an assignment-of-direction factor and a retinal factor. I believe that when we view a figure with our head tilted, we automatically compensate for the tilt in much the same way that we compensate for the size of distant objects. An object at a moderate distance from us does not appear small in spite of the fact that its retinal image is much smaller than it is when the object is close by. This effect usually is explained by saying that the information supplied by the retinal image is somehow corrected by allowing for the distance of the object from us. Similarly, when a vertical luminous line in a dark room is viewed by a tilted observer, it will still look vertical or almost vertical in spite of the fact that the retinal image in the observer's eye is tilted. Thus the tilt of the body must be taken into account by the perceptual system. The tilted retinal image is then corrected, with the result that the line is perceived as being vertical. Just as the correction for size at a distance is called size constancy, so can correction for the vertical be called orientation constancy.

When we view an upright figure with our head tilted, before we have made any correction, we begin with the information provided by an image of the figure in a particular retinal orientation. The first thing that must happen is that the perceptual system processes the retinal image on the basis of an egocentrically assigned top, bottom and sides, perhaps because of a primitive sense of orientation derived from retinal orientation. For example, when we view an upright square with our head tilted, which yields a diamondlike retinal image, we may perceive a diamond for a fleeting moment before the correction goes into operation. Head orientation is then automatically taken into account to correct the perception. Thus the true top of the figure is seen to be one of the sides of the square rather than a corner. The figure is then "described" correctly as one whose sides are horizontal and vertical in the environment, in short as a "square." This correction is made quickly and usually without effort. In order to describe a figure the viewer probably must visualize or imagine it in terms of its true top, bottom and sides rather than in terms of its retinal top, bottom and sides.

If the figure is relatively simple, the correction is not too difficult to achieve. If we view an upright letter with our head tilted, we recognize it easily; it is of interest, however, that there is still something strange about it. I believe the dual aspect of the perception of orientation is responsible for this strangeness. There is an uncorrected perception of the letter based on its retinal-egocentric orientation and a corrected perception of it based on its environmental orientation. The first perception produces an unfamiliar shape, which accounts for the strange appearance of the letter in spite of its subsequent recognition. In our experiments many of the figures we employed were structurally speaking equivalent to letters, and in some cases we actually used letters from unfamiliar alphabets.

With a more complex figure, such as an inverted word or an upright word

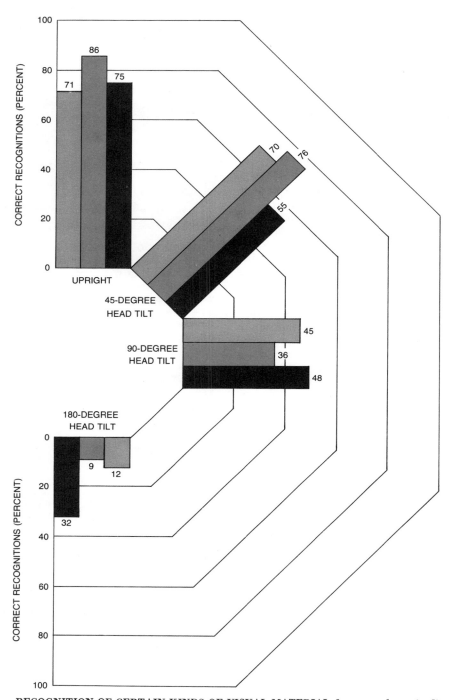

RECOGNITION OF CERTAIN KINDS OF VISUAL MATERIAL decreases almost in direct proportion to the degree of head tilt of the observer. In a series of experiments the number of correct recognitions of faces (*colored bars*), written words (*gray*) and fragmented figures (*black*) were recorded for various degrees of head tilt. Subject saw several examples of each type of test material in each of the head positions. For this visual material recognition is an inverse function of the degree of disorientation of the retinal image.

viewed by an inverted observer, the corrective mechanism may be entirely overtaxed. Each letter of the word must be corrected separately, and the corrective mechanism apparently cannot cope simultaneously with multiple components. It is true that if an observer is given enough time, an inverted word can be deciphered, but it will never look the same as it does when it is upright. While one letter is being corrected the others continue to be perceived in their uncorrected form. There is a further difficulty: letter order is crucial for word recognition, and inverting a word reverses the normal left-to-right order.

The recognition of inverted longhand writing is even more difficult. When such writing is turned upside down, many of the inverted "units" strongly resemble normal upright longhand letters. Moreover, since the letters are connected, it is difficult to tell where one letter ends and another begins. Separating the letters of the inverted word makes recognition easier. Even so, it is all too easy to confuse a *u* and an *n*. This type of confusion is also encountered with certain printed letters, namely, *b* and *q*, *d* and *p* and *n* and *u*, although not as frequently. In other words, if a figure is recognized on the basis of its upright retinal-egocentric orientation, this may tend to stabilize the perception and block the correction process. The dominance of the retinally upright faces in the illustration on the opposite page probably is an effect of just this kind.

There may be a similar overtaxing of the corrective mechanism when we view an inverted face. It may be that the face contains a number of features each of which must be properly perceived if the whole is to be recognized [see the article "The Recognition of Faces," by Leon D. Harmon, beginning on page 183]. While attention is focused on correcting one feature, say the mouth, other features remain uncorrected and continue to be perceived on the basis of the image they form on the retina. Of course, the relation of features is also important in the recognition of a face, but here too there are a great number of such relations and the corrective mechanism may again be overtaxed.

Charles C. Bebber, Douglas Blewett and I conducted an experiment to test the hypothesis that it is the presence of multiple components that creates the difficulty of correcting figures. Subjects were briefly shown a quadrilateral figure and asked to study it. They viewed the target figure with their head upright. Then they were shown a series of test

SINGLE LETTER that is tilted can be easily identified once it is realized how it is oriented. A strangeness in its appearance, however, remains because the percept arising from the uncorrected retinal image continues to exist simultaneously with the corrected percept.

INVERTED LONGHAND WRITING is difficult to decipher because many inverted units resemble written upright letters. For example, an inverted *u* will look like an *n* and an inverted *c* like an *s*. Moreover, the connection between letters leads to uncertainty about where a letter begins and ends. Several inverted units can be grouped together and misperceived as an upright letter. Separating the inverted letters makes them easier to decipher.

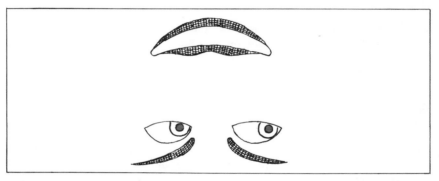

INVERTED FACIAL FEATURES are difficult to interpret because while attention is focused on correcting one feature other features remain uncorrected. For example, one might succeed in correcting the eyes shown here so that they are perceived as gazing downward and leftward, but at that very moment the mouth is uncorrected and expresses sorrow rather than pleasure. Conversely, one might correct the mouth and misperceive the eyes.

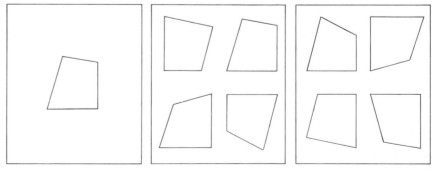

MULTIPLE ITEMS were found to have an adverse effect on recognition of even simple figures. Subjects sitting upright viewed the target (*left*). Then they were briefly shown test cards, some of which contained the target figure (*middle*) and some of which did not (*right*). The subjects were to indicate when they saw a figure that was identical with the target figure. Half of the test cards were viewed with the head upright and half with the head inverted. Recognition was poor when inverted subjects viewed the test cards. In other experiments with a single test figure head inversion did not significantly affect recognition.

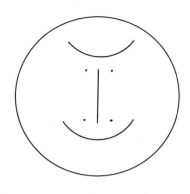

AMBIGUOUS FACES are perceived differently when their images on the retina of the observer are inverted. If you hold the illustration upright and view it from between your legs with your head inverted, the alternative faces will be perceived even though they are upside down in terms of the environment. The same effect occurs when the illustration is inverted and viewed from an upright position. Such tests provide evidence that figures such as faces are recognized on the basis of their upright retinal orientation.

cards each of which had four quadrilateral figures. The test cards were viewed for one second, and the subjects were required to indicate if the target figure was on the card.

The subjects understood that they were to respond affirmatively only when they saw a figure that was identical with the target figure both in shape and in orientation. (Some of the test figures were similar to the target figure but were rotated by 180 degrees.) Half of the test cards were seen with the subject's head upright and half with the subject's head inverted. It was assumed that the subject would not be able to correct all four test figures in the brief time that was allowed him while he was viewing them with his head down. He had to perceive just as many units in the same brief time while he was viewing them with his head upright, but he did not have to correct any of the units. We expected that target figures would often not be recognized and that incorrect figures would be mistakenly identified as the target when the subjects viewed the test cards with their head inverted.

The results bore out our prediction. When multiple components have to be corrected, retinal disorientation has an adverse effect on recognition. The observer responded to twice as many test cards correctly when he was upright than he did when he was inverted.

As I have noted, when we look at figures that are difficult to recognize when they are retinally disoriented, the difficulty increases as the degree of disorientation increases. Why this happens may also be related to the nature of the correction process. I suggested that the observer must suppress the retinally (egocentrically) upright percept and substitute a corrected percept. To do this, however, he must visualize or imagine

how the figure would look if it were rotated until it was upright with respect to himself or, what amounts to the same thing, how it would look if he rotated himself into alignment with the figure. The process of mental rotation requires visualizing the entire sequence of angular change, and therefore the greater the angular change, the greater the difficulty.

As every parent knows, children between the ages of two and five seem to be quite indifferent to how a picture is oriented. They often hold a book upside down and seem not at all disturbed by it. On the basis of such observations and the results of some early experiments, many psychologists concluded that the orientation of a figure did not enter into its recognition by young children. More recent laboratory experiments, however, do not confirm the fact that children recognize figures equally well in any orientation. They have as much difficulty as, or more difficulty than, adults in recognizing previously seen figures when the figure is shown in a new orientation. Why then do young children often spontaneously look at pictures upside down in everyday situations? Perhaps they have not yet learned to pay attention to orientation, and do not realize that their recognition would improve if they did so. When children learn to read after the age of six, they are forced to pay attention to orientation because certain letters differ only in their orientation.

In summary, the central fact we have learned about orientation is that the perceived shape of a figure is not simply a function of its internal geometry. The perceived shape is also very much a function of the up, down and side directions we assign to the figure. If there is a change in the assigned directions, the figure will take on a different per-

ceptual shape. I have speculated that the change in perceived shape is based on a new "description" of the figure by the perceptual system. The directions assigned are based on information of various kinds about where the top, bottom and sides of a figure are and usually do not depend on the retinal orientation of the image of the figure. When the image is not retinally upright, a process of correction is necessary in order to arrive at the correct description, and this correction is difficult or impossible to achieve in the case of visual material that has multiple components.

All of this implies that form perception in general is based to a much greater extent on cognitive processes than any current theory maintains. A prevailing view among psychologists and sensory physiologists is that form perception can be reduced to the perception of contours and that contour perception in turn can be reduced to abrupt differences in light intensity that cause certain neural units in the retina and brain to fire. If this is true, then perceiving form results from the specific concatenation of perceived contours. Although the work I have described does not deny the possible importance of contour detection as a basis of form perception, it does suggest that such an explanation is far from sufficient, and that the perception of form depends on certain mental processes such as description and correction. These processes in turn are necessary to account for the further step of recognition of a figure. A physically unchanged retinal image often will not lead to recognition if there has been a shift in the assigned directions. Conversely, if there has been no shift in the assigned directions, even a very different retinal image will still allow recognition.

The Recognition of Faces

by Leon D. Harmon
November 1973

*One of the subtler tasks of perception can be
investigated experimentally by asking how much
information is required for recognition and what
information is the most important*

Faces, like fingerprints and snow-flakes, come in virtually infinite variety. There is little chance of encountering two so similar they cannot be distinguished, even on casual inspection. Unlike fingerprints and snowflakes, however, faces can be recognized as well as discriminated. It is possible not only to tell one from another but also to pick one from a large population and absolutely identify it, to perceive it as something previously known, just as in reading one not only can tell that an *A* is different from a *B* but also can identify and name each letter.

Why are faces so readily recognized? In seeking the answer to this question my colleagues and I posed several related but more modest questions that we believed would be more amenable to experimental investigation: How can a face be formally described? Given a verbal description, how well can a particular face be identified? To what extent is recognition impaired when the image of a face is blurred or otherwise degraded? What kinds of image degradation most seriously affect recognition? Can faces be classified and sorted as numerical data?

This inquiry was inspired by yet another question: How can a computer be made to recognize a human face? This question remains unanswered, because pattern recognition by computer is still too crude to achieve automatic identification of objects as complex as faces. Machines can recognize print and script, craters and clouds, fingerprints and pieces of jigsaw puzzles; the recognition of human faces, however, is a much subtler task.

Even though machine recognition of faces has not been attained, the investigation of how it might be done has led to a number of related issues that in themselves are worthwhile (and tractable) areas of research. Several new approaches to problems in the manipulation of visual data have emerged. I shall recount here four series of experiments that were directed to an understanding of recognition. The first is concerned with how artists reconstruct faces from descriptions and how closely the resulting portraits resemble the person described. Next I shall comment on a set of experiments in which faces were identified from pictures that had limited information content. The third approach examines the recognition of faces from formal numerical descriptions. Finally, I shall describe a system in which man and computer interact to identify faces more efficiently than either could alone.

If one could devise an objective formulation of the criteria used by an artist in drawing a portrait, a set of properties useful for automatic recognition might emerge. One kind of art that we thought might provide useful information is the sketches drawn by police artists (called face-reconstruction artists) from descriptions provided by witnesses. (Another promising possibility is the caricature, but we have not yet studied it.)

Verbal descriptions are rarely used in the drawing of police sketches. Few observers, unless they are specially trained, can give satisfactory clues to appearance in words. Most can point to features similar to those they remember, however, and that is how the reconstruction artist usually begins. Our initial experiments were intended to test the effectiveness of this procedure and to gain some preliminary notions of what features are considered important in describing or recognizing a face.

Frontal-view photographs were shown to an experienced artist, who compiled a written description of each face; the description included references to facial features in a catalogue of faces made up of photographs of various head shapes, eye spacings, lip thicknesses and so on, organized by feature type. Thus a large part of the description consisted of "pointing to" similar features on other portraits. The completed description was given to another artist, whose task was to reconstruct the face from the written description [*see illustration on next page*].

The first attempt, although obviously resembling the original photograph, differed from it in the depiction of important features and proportions. When limited feedback was allowed, however, there was rapid improvement. The describing artist, with the initial sketch in hand, provided simple verbal corrections, such as "The hair should be bushier at the temples"; with this information the reconstructing artist was able to draw a much more accurate likeness. Finally, to find the limit of improvement, that is, to discover just how faithful a portrait could be drawn, the reconstructing artist was given the photograph to work from. Under those conditions he was able to produce a strikingly realistic representation. Some sketches, in fact, were judged to look more like the person than the photograph did. Presumably the artist enhanced recognition by in some way emphasizing significant detail.

All the sketches were shown to test subjects who, as fellow employees, had seen the "suspect" often. Almost half of the sketches drawn from descriptions were correctly identified and about 93 percent of the drawings made directly from photographs were recognized.

Our work with face-reconstruction artists was a pilot experiment we hoped would lead, through informal observation, to a better understanding of the problems confronted in the recognition of faces and to the formulation of further experiments. Some of the incidental information derived from the study was indeed interesting. For example, we found that several of the faces were outstandingly easy to recognize in the sketches. Presumably those subjects were more easily described than the others, or perhaps they possessed certain features that are conspicuous or rare. Several subjects remarked that the nose and eyes in one sketch were important to identification, yet for the same face other subjects observed that although the nose, mouth and hair were well drawn, the eyes were not and did not aid recognition.

Another way to study recognition is to ask how little information, in the informal sense of "bits," or binary digits, is required to pictorially represent a

face so that it can be recognized out of a finite ensemble of faces. We explored this "threshold" of recognition with portraits that had been precisely blurred.

The type of blurring commonly encountered in photographs is caused by an improperly focused optical system; it reduces the information content of the picture, but it proved unsuitable as a technique in our investigations because the degree of blurring cannot be precisely specified or controlled. A more measurable method degrades the image in quantifiable steps through a relative-

LEONARDO'S "MONA LISA," rendered as a "block portrait," consists of 560 squares, each of which is roughly uniform in color and brightness throughout its area. The degraded image was produced by an optical process from a photographic copy of the painting. In spite of its low resolution the picture can be easily identified. Recognition is enhanced by squinting at the image, by rapidly jiggling it, or by viewing it from a distance of 10 to 15 feet

———————————→

ly simple computer process.

In our experiments a 35-millimeter transparency of a conventional portrait photograph is scanned by a beam of light moving in a raster pattern of 1,024 lines. The variations in the intensity of the beam caused by the varying transparency of the film are detected by a photomultiplier tube. The analogue signals produced by the photomultiplier are converted into digital form by sampling each line in the raster at 1,024 points and assigning a brightness value to each point, so that the completed image consists of $1,024^2$ (or 2^{20}) discrete points, about four times the resolution of the commercial television image. Each of the points may have 1,024 brightness values, or tones of gray. The dissected image is stored in the magnetic-tape memory of a digital computer.

To create the degraded image the computer divides the picture into $n \times n$ squares of uniform size and averages the brightness values of all the points within each square. For example, if a photograph is to be made into an array of 16×16 squares, each square will contain 64×64, or 4,096, points; the brightness to be assigned to the entire square will be found by averaging the values of these points. In a final step the number of brightness values is reduced to eight or 16 by assigning to each square the gray tone closest to its original averaged value.

The computer stores the digital information comprising the picture on magnetic tape and the tape controls a cathode-ray-tube monitor, which then displays the completed portrait. A photograph of this display constitutes the finished product. Alternatively, the magnetic tape can be used to control a facsimile printer that produces a print of the processed image without the intermediary cathode ray tube [see bottom illustration on page 187].

Viewed from close up, these "block portraits" appear to be merely an assemblage of squares. Viewed remotely, from a distance of 30 to 40 picture diameters, faces are perceived and recognized.

Preliminary experiments were made to select the coarsest image that might be expected to yield about 50 percent accuracy of recognition. For some kinds of picture, resolution of only a few thou-

SKETCHES FROM DESCRIPTIONS were made by a "face-reconstruction artist" skilled in drawing portraits from information provided by witnesses. At top left is the photograph from which the three sketches are derived. For the first drawing (top right) a written description of the face, including references to illustrations in a catalogue of facial features, was presented to the artist. A better likeness was produced (bottom left) when simple verbal corrections were provided. For the final version (bottom right) the artist was given the photograph; the resulting portrait represents the limit of accuracy of the process.

sand elements provides acceptable quality; the limits of recognition for photographs of faces, however, have not been reported. Our informal investigation revealed that a spatial resolution of 16 × 16 squares was very close to the minimum resolution that allows identification.

Tests were also made to determine the useful limits of gray-scale representation. The relation between gray-scale and spatial resolution is an interesting one: either factor can serve as a limit to recognition. It was not the object of our experiments to document this relation, however, and so only a few gray-scale tests were made once the 16 × 16 spatial pattern was decided on. For 16 × 16

portraits gray scales of either eight or 16 levels yielded eminently recognizable portraits; consequently our experiments used those levels exclusively. (The allowed gray levels can be expressed in terms of bits. A gray scale of eight levels requires three bits of information; a scale of 16 levels calls for four bits.)

Fourteen of the block portraits were shown to 28 subjects. Each subject was given a list of 28 names, including the names of the 14 persons depicted. The experiment was intended to investigate the effects of changing the gray scale from a three-bit to a four-bit one, as well as to test identification performance.

Overall recognition accuracy was found to be 48 percent. (Random guess-

ing would produce such a result only four times in a million trials.) The result was essentially indifferent to the resolution of the gray scale. Thus the number of bits required for approximately 50 percent accuracy of recognition was no more than 16 × 16 squares times three bits, or 768 bits. None of the portraits, however, filled all the squares in the 16 × 16 grid; therefore fewer than 256 squares made up each face. An average of 108 squares was needed.

Recognition of particular faces ranged from 10 percent to 96 percent. In these experiments too some faces were always easy to identify, although, as will be seen, the reasons are peculiar to the conditions of the experiment. Two portraits received outstanding recognition and four were rarely identified correctly.

Two possible explanations of these disparities were suggested. First, some faces, because of the peculiar arrangement of their features, respond notably well or particularly poorly to coarse spatial presentation. Second, the grid, arbitrarily positioned over a given face by the scanning process, may land luckily or unluckily for adequate representation. For example, a square might just bracket an eye, or it might land half on and half off. The latter possibility was judged to be the more likely. I hypothesized that those pictures that were recognized well probably had a fortuitously placed grid.

To test the hypothesis each portrait was reprocessed by shifting the 16 × 16 matrix with respect to the original block portrait. Three new pictures were made: one shifted a half-square to the right, one a half-square down and a third a half-square to the right and down [see illustration at left].

Recognition of the sets of four shifted pictures was tested. The subjects were given the identity of each photograph; their task was to rank the four portraits in each set in order of pictorial accuracy. My hypothesis predicted that in these tests those pictures that were readily identified in the earlier experiment would be ranked first in their set and that those scoring worst initially would be ranked near the bottom. So it turned out; both correlations were confirmed.

This result led us to believe that if the best grid positions had been found and used in the earlier experiments, the average accuracy of recognition might have been closer to 100 percent than to 50 percent. A new experiment confirmed this: performance rose to 95 percent.

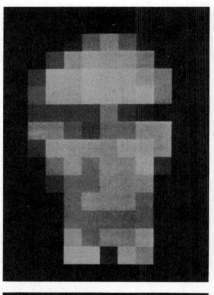
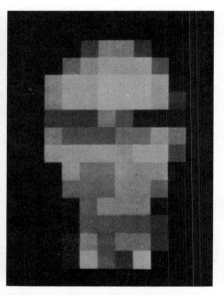
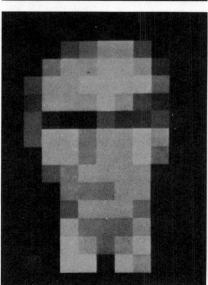
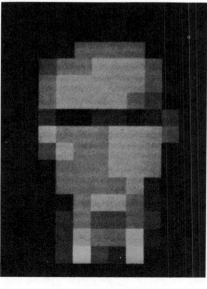

EFFECTS OF GRID PLACEMENT on recognition are illustrated by four block portraits of the same face. The original is at top left. Alternative versions were made by shifting the grid placement one half-block to the right (*top right*), one half-block down (*bottom left*) and one half-block right and down (*bottom right*). When portraits made with optimum placement replaced those made with random placement, recognition accuracy doubled.

An interesting and provocative characteristic of block portraits is that once recognition is achieved more apparent

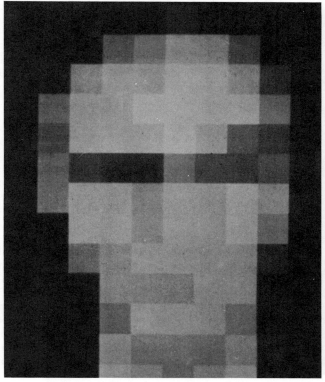

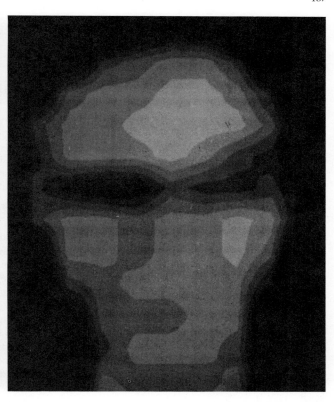

REDUCED-INFORMATION-CONTENT PORTRAITS were generated by a computer. The picture at left is a block portrait; it is an array of 16 × 16 squares, each one of which can assume any one of 16 levels of gray. Not all the 256 squares are required to represent the face. The contoured representation at right was produced by filtering the block portrait to remove high frequencies.

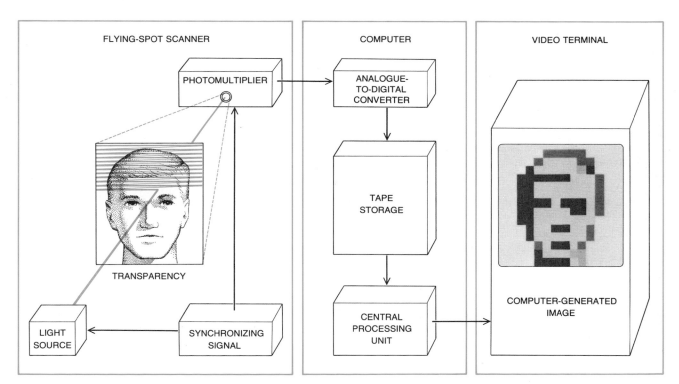

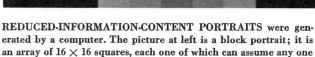

SYSTEM FOR MAKING BLOCK PORTRAITS uses a flying-spot scanner, a device similar to a television camera. The image, usually in the form of a 35-millimeter photographic transparency, is scanned in a raster pattern of 1,024 lines. In the analogue-to-digital converter each line is sampled at 1,024 points and the brightness of each point is assigned one of 1,024 values. Using this information stored on magnetic tape, the central processing unit divides the image into $n \times n$ squares and averages the brightness values of all the points within each square. The number of permissible brightness values is then reduced to eight or 16. The resulting image is displayed on a video terminal (a television screen) and photographed. The computer can also be made to operate a facsimile printer, which produces a finished picture directly. Most of the portraits used in these experiments were made by the latter process.

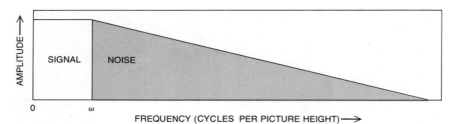

BLOCK-PORTRAIT SPECTRUM consists of a signal that extends to some finite spatial frequency ω, corresponding to the block-sampling frequency and noise of frequencies above ω. The amplitude of the noise typically decreases with increasing spatial frequency.

detail is noticed. It is as though the mind's eye superposes additional detail on the coarse optical image. Moreover, once a face is perceived it becomes difficult not to see it, as if some kind of perceptual hysteresis prevented the image from once again dissolving into an abstract pattern of squares. The observation that is most intriguing, however, is that recognition can be enhanced by viewing the picture from a distance, by squinting at it, by jiggling it or by moving the head while looking at it. The effect of all these actions is to blur the already degraded image.

Why should recognition be improved by blurring? The explanation almost certainly lies in the "noise" that tends to obscure the image.

A picture, like a sound, can be described as the sum of simple component frequencies. In acoustical signals pressure varies with time; in the optical signals discussed here the frequencies are spatial and consist of variations of "density" (or darkness) with distance. Just as a musical note consists of a fundamental frequency and its harmonics, so an optical image consists of combinations of single frequencies, which make up its spatial spectrum. The spectral representation exists in two dimensions. This spectrum refers only to spatial frequen-

cies; the color spectrum describes another aspect of the image.

When pictures are considered combinations of spatial frequencies, they can be manipulated in the same ways as other frequency-dependent signals are. For example, Fourier analysis can be used to determine the component frequencies of an image, or low-pass filtering can be used to remove the high frequencies that represent fine detail. Signal-frequency bands, the signal and noise spectrum and other terms usually associated with discussions of acoustical phenomena can be applied to the processing of visual images.

The description of a two-dimensional image as a signal of various spatial frequencies leads to a possible explanation of the enhancement of block portraits with blurring. Whenever a signal with a spectrum running from zero to some frequency designated ω is reduced by sampling to discrete frequency components, noise artifacts whose spectrum extends above ω are introduced. The noise is a product of the sampling procedure. In two-dimensional signals it appears as patterns not present in the original image.

Because the noise in these pictures is ordinarily of higher frequency than the signal it can be readily eliminated by a

low-pass filter, that is, a filter that preserves only the low frequencies, eliminating the high frequencies that represent fine detail. This operation too is performed by the computer; all spectral components above ω are removed while the desired signal is retained [see top illustration on this page].

In block portraits the most obvious noise is that introduced by the sharp edges of the squares. Although Fourier analysis shows that the energy content of these high frequencies is relatively small, one might speculate that because the eye is particularly sensitive to straight lines and regular geometric shapes such square-patterned noise masks particularly well. That is, such image-correlated noise might mask more effectively than randomly distributed noise of equal energy. If so, low-pass filtering should enhance perception. This explanation would seem to be confirmed by the fact that recognition is improved by progressive defocusing or distant viewing, since the effect of both of these actions is to filter out high frequencies.

This hypothesis, however, is not the only candidate; another possibility is called critical-band masking. In both hearing and vision the spectral proximity of noise to a signal drastically influences the detection threshold of the signal. For example, the threshold for detecting a single sinusoidal wave anywhere in the spectrum is elevated when a noise signal is introduced if the noise lies within about two octaves of the signal. If the noise lies outside this "critical band," masking does not occur [see bottom illustration on this page].

This phenomenon has been tested and confirmed by others for relatively simple visual presentations such as sine-wave and square-wave gratings in a single dimension. My colleague Bela Julesz and I reasoned that similar masking might occur in more complicated two-dimensional patterns.

If critical-band masking is the mechanism that hinders the recognition of block portraits, then those components of the noise that fall within about two octaves of the sampling frequency ω would be primarily responsible. The rest of the noise spectrum, including the high-frequency signals contributing to the sharp edges of the blocks, should cause little or no masking.

To resolve this question we prepared a series of block portraits that were spectrally manipulated by the computer. The original image was transformed to obtain its Fourier spectrum, filtered to specification, then transformed back and

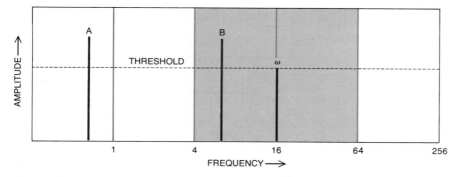

CRITICAL-BAND MASKING is known to occur in presentations of simple visual or audio signals, such as single sinusoidal waves. The test signal ω, at the threshold of perception, would be masked by signal B, within the band, but not by signal A. The critical band (colored area) extends for about two octaves above and below the test frequency. The author's investigations indicate the critical-band masking also affects two-dimensional signals.

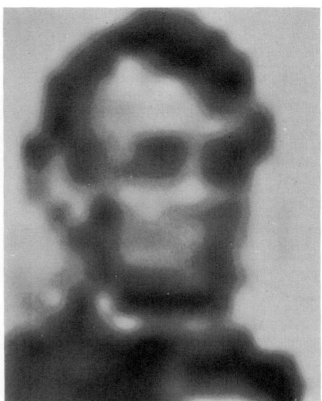

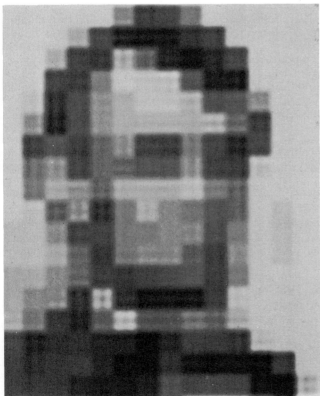

SELECTIVE FREQUENCY FILTERING influences the ease with which block portraits are recognized. The original block portrait of Abraham Lincoln is at top left. It consists of the photographic "signal," whose highest spatial frequency is 10 cycles per picture height, and noise frequencies extending above 10 cycles. As was anticipated, filtering out all spatial frequencies above 10 cycles (*top right*) greatly enhances recognition. Selective removal of only part of the noise spectrum, however, reveals which frequencies most effectively mask the image. At bottom left all frequencies above 40 cycles have been removed; even though the sharp edges of the squares are eliminated, perception is improved only slightly. When the two-octave band from 10 to 40 cycles is removed (*bottom right*), the face is more readily recognized. The phenomenon apparently responsible for this effect is critical-band masking.

printed out. This technique provides precise control of spatial frequencies. We were able to remove all signals above a specified frequency, or to remove only a band of frequencies adjacent to ω.

In our first attempt to evaluate the relative importance of high-frequency and critical-band noise masking we prepared a series of filtered block portraits [*see illustration on page 189*]. The result looked promising: removal of the very high frequencies did little to change the block aspect, and some effort was still required to perceive the face. Removal of only the frequencies adjacent to the signal produced pictures that were much closer in appearance to the original photographs. That is, the very high frequencies did not seem to be the most important in masking.

Although the results of this experiment suggest that noise spectrally adjacent to the signal is most effective in masking recognition, the point is not proved. There are three reasons why the experiment is not conclusive. First, the noise generated by the block-sampling process is spatially periodic, at the block frequency and at higher harmonics. Second, the noise amplitudes are correlated with picture information: the magnitude of the noise in any block depends on the density of the image in that block. Finally, the energy of the noise spectrum is greatest at the block-sampling frequency, and it decreases with increasing frequency. Hence the adjacent band noise may mask more effectively simply because its amplitude is higher, not because of the critical-band effect.

There is a straightforward way to avoid these difficulties. We can simply add random noise of the proper frequency to a picture that is smoothly blurred rather than block-sampled. We added random noise of constant spectral energy to a portrait that had been low-pass filtered to the same bandwidth as that used in the first recognition studies. When such a picture containing adjacent-frequency noise is compared with one masked by remote-frequency noise, the result is unequivocal: critical-band masking is responsible for the suppression of recognition [*see illustration on this page*].

The discovery that critical-band masking affects complex pictures as well as simple sinusoidal presentations raises additional questions. How effective in masking are noises of equal energy and bandwidth but of various spectral shapes? When noise is added to a signal, is the shape of the noise signal or its location in the spectrum more important?

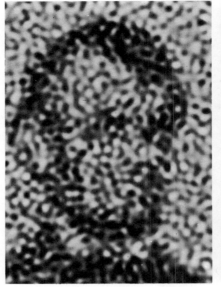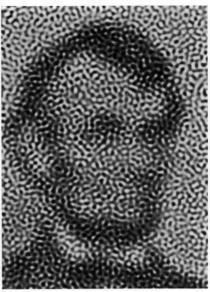

RANDOMLY DISTRIBUTED NOISE of uniform amplitude is added to smoothly blurred portraits of Lincoln. When the noise is in the band adjacent to the signal frequencies (*left*), it obscures the picture more effectively than when it is at least two octaves removed from the picture frequencies (*right*), confirming that critical-band masking is the most important mechanism limiting the recognition of degraded or blurred images such as block portraits.

What are the relative effects of spatial disposition and spectral disposition? That is, if equal amounts of noise energy are added to visual scenes, is the placement with respect to position or with respect to frequency more important for masking? These and related questions remain for future investigation. Their answers will provide new insights into the psychophysics of vision.

A more conventional means of blurring pictures is continuous smearing. In optical systems one can simply project the image out of focus; as I have noted, however, this operation cannot be precisely controlled. The analogous operation performed by a digital computer is intrinsically discrete, but by using sufficiently numerous sample points to represent an image, blurring can be made arbitrarily smooth and extremely precise.

Pictures made up of 256×256 elements (about one-fourth the resolution of television) produce fairly sharp portraits. Such pictures can be blurred by selecting for each point a brightness value computed by averaging the brightness of the points surrounding it. An "averaging window" of $n \times n$ points is used to compute a new value for each point in the 256×256 array; after a new point is written the window is moved over one element and a new average is made.

Through this process the computer can rapidly and accurately blur a picture to a specified degree. The size and shape of the averaging window and the relative weight given to each element in the array can be selected at will. For example, the average could be uniformly weighted or computed on a Gaussian, or bell-shaped, curve. In our experiments we used a square window of varying size with uniform weighting; each element contributed equally to the average value assigned the new point.

We have used portraits made in this way to study the limits of face recognition. Fourteen portraits were shown to subjects who were given a list of 28 names, including the names of the 14 "target" individuals. All 28 persons were known to the test subjects. Several degrees of blurring were tested [*see illustration on next page*]. Some subjects were shown the most blurred pictures first, some the least blurred, and so on, in order to simultaneously test for the effects of learning. The experiments were conducted by Ann B. Lesk, John Levinson and me.

Contrary to what we had expected, recognition scores were quite good. For photographs blurred by a 27×27-point averaging window the recognition was 84 percent. As the degree of blurring increased, the scores declined to about 65 percent for those portraits made with a 43×43-point window, which represents severe blurring. (The expected score for random guessing is 3.5 percent.)

Even more surprising were the results

of trials with photographs blurred with a 51×51-point window. Here the width of the window is 20 percent of the picture's width, and blurring is so extreme that facial features are entirely washed out. Nevertheless, the accuracy was almost 60 percent. (This level of recognition cannot continue with much more extensive blurring. When the averaging window includes all the picture elements, the field will be smeared to a uniform gray and pictures will differ only in the level of that gray.)

Recognition of the most strongly blurred of these portraits cannot depend on the identification of features. The high-frequency information required to represent the eyes, the ears and the mouth is lost. Although some intermediate frequencies remain, their representa-

tion of the chin, the cheeks and the hair is not clear. The low-frequency information that relates to head shape, neck-and-shoulder geometry and gross hairline is all that remains unimpaired, yet this alone seems to be adequate for rather good recognition among individuals in a restricted population.

Again, some faces were consistently well recognized. This time the responsible cues were easy to see. One portrait, for example, was distinguished by a round, bald head, and the picture was consistently recognized, even when it was badly blurred.

Some learning apparently took place in these experiments; it would appear that practice at struggling with the task improved performance.

Determining exactly how one recog-

nizes a face is probably an intractable problem for the present. It is possible, however, to determine how well and with what cues identification can be achieved. Similarly, although machine recognition is not yet possible, search for and retrieval of faces by machine is a problem suitable for research. My colleagues and I approached these matters by investigating how effectively one can identify an individual face from a group of faces by using verbal descriptions.

It should be noted that successful identification of faces by feature descriptions does not suggest that the normal processes of recognition regularly detect and assess such features. All we can determine from experiments of this kind is how effectively people can perform a certain recognition task on the basis of certain assigned measures.

The problems of the automatic analysis of faces have received little attention. The work begun by W. W. Bledsoe and his colleagues is one of the few attempts I know of to automate the recognition of faces; the method uses a hybrid man-machine system in which a computer sorts and classifies faces on the basis of fiducial marks entered manually on photographs. The technique is called the Bertillon method, after Alphonse Bertillon, a French criminologist, and is better known for its application to fingerprint classification. A similar method has been developed by Makoto Nagao and his colleagues in Japan in an attempt to devise an automated system that would produce simple numerical descriptions of faces.

I was led to this line of inquiry by wondering if one could play a "20 questions" game with faces. (In games of this kind one player thinks of a person and the other asks him up to 20 questions, which must be answered yes or no, until the subject is guessed.) An informal, preliminary experiment began with 22 portraits; they were shown to subjects who were asked to list features they thought striking or extreme in order of decreasing extremeness. If a face displayed very wide-set eyes, for example, that statement was put at the top of the list. Or if the chin jutted extremely, that fact was listed first. A consensus list was compiled for each of the 22 faces, then new experimental subjects were selected.

Each subject was given the pile of pictures and a list of features, derived from the earlier work, describing one of the faces. He was asked to do a binary sorting, one feature at a time, starting with the most extreme and working down the

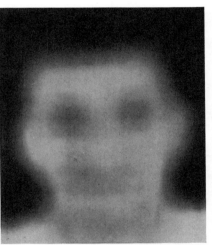

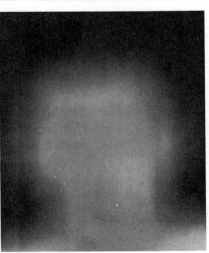

PRECISELY BLURRED PORTRAITS were constructed by a computer using an "averaging window." At top left is the original picture; it is not a continuous-tone photograph but an array of 256×256 dots. The averaging window determines a new value for each of the dots by averaging the values of those that surround it in some $n \times n$ field. When the window is set at 27×27 points (*top right*), basic facial features are still discernible. A 43×43-point window (*bottom left*) produces severe blurring and a 51×51-point window (*bottom right*) eliminates almost all information except gross forms. Accuracy of identification declined as blurring increased but even with the worst pictures approached 60 percent.

	1	2	3	4	5
HAIR					
COVERAGE	FULL		RECEDING		BALD
LENGTH	SHORT		AVERAGE		LONG
TEXTURE	STRAIGHT		WAVY		CURLY
SHADE	DARK	MEDIUM	LIGHT	GRAY	WHITE
FOREHEAD	RECEDING		VERTICAL		BULGING
EYEBROWS					
WEIGHT	THIN		MEDIUM		BUSHY
SEPARATION	SEPARATED		MEETING		
EYES					
OPENING	NARROW		MEDIUM		WIDE
SEPARATION	CLOSE		MEDIUM		WIDE
SHADE	LIGHT		MEDIUM		DARK
EARS					
LENGTH	SHORT		MEDIUM		LONG
PROTRUSION	SLIGHT		MEDIUM		LARGE
CHEEKS	SUNKEN		AVERAGE		FULL
NOSE					
LENGTH	SHORT		MEDIUM		LONG
TIP	UPWARD		HORIZONTAL		DOWNWARI
PROFILE	CONCAVE		STRAIGHT		HOOKED
MOUTH					
LIP THICKNESS (UPPER)	THIN		MEDIUM		THICK
LIP THICKNESS (LOWER)	THIN		MEDIUM		THICK
LIP OVERLAP	UPPER	NEITHER	LOWER		
WIDTH	SMALL		MEDIUM		LARGE
CHIN					
PROFILE	RECEDING		STRAIGHT		JUTTING
	1	2	3	4	5

list. The first sorting, therefore, produced a pile of pictures that the subject believed satisfied the first statement on the list and a pile of rejected pictures. The "accept" pile was then sorted for the second feature and for additional features until the pile was reduced to one portrait.

Two interesting questions arose: How often is the remaining portrait the correct one? How many sortings are required to reduce the population to a single member?

In this preliminary study the remaining portrait was always the correct one, and the average number of sortings required for the isolation was 4.5. We were led to wonder how the accuracy would decline as the population size increased and how rapidly the number of sortings required would grow. If the number of sortings increased linearly with population size, the process would soon become too cumbersome to be effective. (It is difficult to enumerate more than a few tens of features.) If the number of feature sortings grew, say, logarithmically, however, the process could remain useful for quite large populations.

A theoretical model devised by A. Jay Goldstein, Ann Lesk and me indicated that the feature set could indeed be expected to grow logarithmically. Under the experimental conditions we planned to employ, the feature set would grow to 5.4 for a population of 256 faces, to about 6.5 for 1,000 faces and to about a dozen features for a population of a million faces. We decided to test this model in a series of experiments using a population of 256 faces.

To make these studies it was necessary to find a pool of features that could be judged quantitatively and reliably. It was also necessary that these features be independent of one another, so that each one carried useful information.

Portraits were made of 256 faces. Each consisted of three views: frontal, three-quarter and profile. The population was deliberately made homogeneous in order to make the subsequent tasks more difficult. All the subjects were white males between 20 and 50 years

FACES WERE CLASSIFIED in the author's system by numerical judgments of 21 selected features. The population of 256 portraits was examined by a panel of 10 observers, who rated each face according to the 21 criteria shown in the chart at right. The judgments of the panel became the "official" values used as standards in later experiments.

old, wearing no glasses, having no beards and displaying no unusual facial marks or scars.

Starting with a tentative set of 35 features, a panel of 10 trained observers filled out questionnaires describing the 256 faces. Each feature was assigned a numerical measure, usually on a scale of from 1 to 5. After a week of tedious labor the resulting data were analyzed statistically for reliability and independence. Twenty-one features were found to be the most useful and were preserved for all further experiments [*see illustration on preceding page*]. The "official" value of each feature was taken as the average of the values assigned by the 10 observers.

With these measures of features it is possible to program a computer to sort a population of faces. If the value of each feature is considered a coordinate in 21-dimensional space, each face will represent a point in that space, the collection

of features providing its 21 coordinates. The distinction between any pair of faces can be calculated simply as the Euclidean distance between the points [*see illustration below*].

With this technique one can produce listings of, say, the 100 most similar pairs of faces or the 100 least similar pairs. When the computer was instructed to name the face whose feature values were closest to the average values of those in the population, "Mr. Average" was identified through a procedure that required the nontrivial comparison of 32,640 pairs of 21-dimensional items.

While seeking the most similar faces, we discovered that the Euclidean distance separating one pair was extremely small, much smaller than the distance between the faces chosen as the authentic closest pair. When we checked the photographs, we found that the same person was shown in both. One of our colleagues had visited the studio twice,

and none of the subjects examining the photographs had discovered the duplication until the computer analysis revealed it. For all subsequent study the population was reduced to 255.

Once the feature judgments were classified in the computer memory a number of simulation experiments were conducted in which the computer modeled human performance in sorting the portraits. Given a description, the computer sorted through the population, starting with the most extreme feature. It decided for each feature whether to accept or reject a given portrait on the basis of several different judgment thresholds. For the criteria and conditions that seem most reasonably to replicate human judgments the computer required about six sortings to isolate a photograph.

When human subjects were given the same task, 7.3 sortings were needed; the remaining portrait was the correct one in 53 percent of the trials. If one does not insist on absolute identification but asks only for a reduction of the population, the performance was fairly good. The population was reduced to no more than 5 percent in three-fourths of the trials. That is, 75 percent of the time the "target" face was included in a reduced group of no more than 13 faces.

One of the factors that limits the reliability and accuracy of this procedure is a characteristic of the binary sorting process itself: a mistake made in any decision can lead to the irretrievable loss of the target photograph. Once a portrait has been rejected it can no longer even be considered in later decisions.

A more forgiving process is rank ordering. If at each step the photograph is ranked according to how well it fits the description but is never discarded entirely, then any reasonably accurate description can be expected to place the correct portrait high in the resulting rank-ordered list. Again, even if the accuracy of the individual judgments is not extremely high, and even if a few judgments are clearly wrong, we can expect the procedure to focus attention on a small subset of the population that has a high probability of containing the target. (Population-reduction techniques of this kind are useful in many sorting tasks, such as handwriting recognition and document retrieval.)

The rank-ordered sorting leads to the fourth study to be discussed here: a system in which man and machine interact to identify faces by feature descriptions.

A subject at a computer terminal was given frontal, three-quarter and profile

THREE-DIMENSIONAL ANALOGUE of the 21-dimensional face-classification system makes each face a point inside or on the surface of a cube. For this simplified illustration three features are judged so that the assigned values become the coordinates of the point representing the face. Face *A*, for example, has a hair length of 4, eye separation of 3 and chin profile of 3. The distinction between any two faces can be measured simply as the Euclidean distance between the points. Thus the distinction between face *A* and face *B* in the drawing is $(2^2 + 2^2 + 1^2)^{1/2}$, or 3. In the 21-dimensional model each point is described by 21 coordinates and the equation for the distance between two points has 21 terms.

photographs of one member of the population. He was instructed to describe this target face to the computer, using the numerical feature values. After each description is entered on the keyboard the computer assigns a goodness-of-fit measure, called a "weight," to each member of the population. The weight represents the similarity of the subject's description to the official description. The population is ranked by weight and the list is revised each time a new feature is described. No portraits are rejected, but the target face is expected to climb through the ranks and eventually, if the process is effective, to be listed in first place.

The questions of interest are the same as those in the manual studies: How many feature steps are required and after a specified number of steps how often is the top-ranking face the correct one?

In addition to rank ordering we introduced another procedure to improve performance. In the earlier experiments the subject had chosen features to describe in descending order of extremeness. This technique takes advantage of the human ability to detect and describe conspicuous features, a process beyond the capabilities of machines. Eventually, however, and usually after finding only three or four extreme features, the observer is unable to identify more; few faces have more than four features that could be described as extreme. At this point the machine can contribute to identification in a way that would be difficult for a man.

Rather than the subject's being asked to choose features at random after he has exhausted his judgments of extreme features, he is instructed to invoke "automatic feature selection." The subject possesses exhaustive knowledge of the face he is describing, yet he knows very little about the characteristics of the population stored in the machine. The computer, on the other hand, does not know who the target is but does have the official descriptions of all the faces and their goodness-of-fit to the description that has been given so far. Automatic feature selection enables the computer to ask for a description of the feature that will be most discriminating at any stage of the identification process.

For example, if all members of the population have close-set ears, a description of that feature would not discriminate between faces. The most discriminating feature is the one that has the most uniform distribution of judged values over the permitted range. The

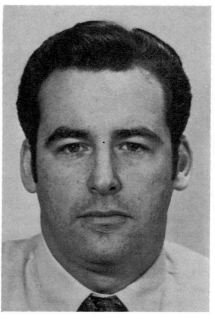

MOST SIMILAR PAIR of faces was found by comparing the 21 judged values of the features of the 32,640 possible combinations. The operation was performed by a computer.

computer, having knowledge of these statistics, can select the sequence of features that will most efficiently separate the members of the population.

After a few feature-description steps, directed by the human subject, the probability is high that the target face has risen in the rank-ordered list. The computer can therefore confine its search for discriminating features to some subset of the population that the portrait thus far describes well. This has the effect of enhancing discrimination of the target.

In our experiments subjects were told to describe conspicuous features until no more were apparent and then to invoke automatic feature selection. The procedure was terminated after 10 steps, since theory and previous experience predicted that this should be sufficient for good accuracy.

Performance was excellent. The subjects' votes and the official values were in good agreement. In spite of the vaga-

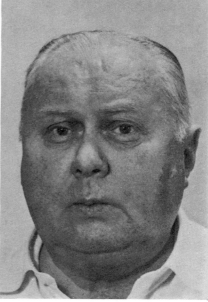

LEAST SIMILAR PAIR of faces was determined by the same procedure. The population was deliberately made homogeneous: all members were white males from 20 to 50 years old.

ries of subjective judgment the difference between the experimental and the official values, in a scale typically ranging from 1 to 5, was less than one in more than 95 percent of the trials. Accuracy of identification was also impressive. The population was reduced to less than 4 percent 99 percent of the time, that is, the correct face was in 10th place or better in 99 of every 100 trials. By the 10th sorting the target was in first place in 70 percent of all trials.

In control experiments features were selected by the human operator only and by the computer only; in both cases performance was poorer than when both man and machine participated.

This last exercise has more general applications than the identification of faces. It is a technique for the retrieval of any multidimensional vectors by information obtained from imprecise descriptions. Such probabilistic file searches are important in answering telephone-directory assistance inquiries, in medical diagnosis and in law-enforcement information retrieval.

Our studies have touched on a host of questions about human perception, automatic pattern recognition and procedures for information retrieval. Although the ultimate question of how a face is recognized remains unanswered, a few promising lines of inquiry have emerged. It has once again been clearly shown that the human viewer is a fantastically competent information processor. In some recognition tasks a synergy of man and machine is effective, but in further explorations of the identification of complex images both by men and by machines there is much to learn.

```
DESCRIBE NEXT PICTURE.

FEATURE
        EYEBROW WT.
THIN      MEDIUM        BUSHY
    1     2     3     4     5
=1
    93   244   183   223   159
   1.00  1.00  1.00  1.00  0.82


FEATURE
        EAR LENGTH
SHORT     MEDIUM        LONG
    1     2     3     4     5
=1
    72   244   175    93    43
   1.00  1.00  0.82  0.67  0.66


FEATURE
        LIP OVERLAP
UPPER       NEITHER       LOWER
    1           2           3
=1
    72   226   114   122    76
   1.00  0.73  0.66  0.61  0.60


FEATURE
        HAIR TEXTURE
STRAIGHT   WAVY         CURLY
    1     2     3     4     5
=4
    76   122    32   244    52
   1.00  0.74  0.56  0.55  0.50


FEATURE

        AUTOMATIC FEATURE SELECTION
******EYE SHADE
LIGHT     MEDIUM        DARK
    1     2     3     4     5
=3
    76    52    72   221   191
   1.00  0.56  0.45  0.38  0.36


******EYEBROW SEP.
SEPARATE   MEDIUM      MEETING
    1          2           3
=2
    76   147    52    84    72
   1.00  0.50  0.42  0.37  0.34
```

```
******EYE OPENING
NARROW    MEDIUM        WIDE
    1     2     3     4     5
=2
    76    72   226    26   191
   1.00  0.51  0.40  0.38  0.36


******UPPER LIP
THIN      MEDIUM        THICK
    1     2     3     4     5
=3
    76   191    72   221    52
   1.00  0.33  0.28  0.23  0.21


******HAIR SHADE
DARK  MED.  LT.   GRAY  WHT.
    1     2     3     4     5
=2
    76   221    72   226   191
   1.00  0.34  0.34  0.33  0.25


******LOWER LIP
THIN      MEDIUM        THICK
    1     2     3     4     5
=1
    76    72   221    84   191
   1.00  0.19  0.13  0.12  0.11


PLEASE TYPE TARGET NUMBER.
=76
```

ORDER	FEATURE	DESCRIPTION YOU	DESCRIPTION AVG.	RANK NO.	RANK %
1	EYEBROW WT.	1	2.2	27	10.2
2	EAR LENGTH	1	2.3	8	2.7
3	LIP OVERLAP	1	1.2	5	1.6
4	HAIR TEXTURE	4	3.0	1	0.
5	EYE SHADE	3	2.7	1	0.
6	EYEBROW SEP.	2	1.3	1	0.
7	EYE OPENING	2	2.6	1	0.
8	UPPER LIP	3	2.9	1	0.
9	HAIR SHADE	2	1.5	1	0.
10	LOWER LIP	1	2.3	1	0.

DIALOGUE WITH A COMPUTER records a search for a "target" face. The computer "speaks" first and requests a description; the subject replies by announcing that he will describe eyebrow weight. The computer then prints the range of allowable values. The subject selects "1" for "thin" and the computer ranks each member of the population according to how well it fits this value. The five members that best fit the description are printed in the next line, followed by their relative "weights." The first four faces here are tied with weights of 1.00. The target face in this trial was No. 76; by the third step it was in fifth place and by the fourth step in first place. After the fourth feature description the subject called for "automatic feature selection," which enables the computer to request descriptions of those features that would be most discriminating. After the 10th step No. 76 had a weight of 1.00 and its nearest neighbor a weight of .19. The correct face was clearly identified even though the first two descriptions were in error. Following the dialogue is a summary comparing the subject's judgments with the "official" values (*AVG.*) and showing the rank of the target at each step and the percent of the population with a higher rank. The procedure was stopped after 10 steps; 21 steps were possible.

19   Experiments in Reading

by Paul A. Kolers
July 1972

Unusual presentations of printed matter suggest that reading is not simply stringing symbols together. A better description is that it is generating hypotheses about the meaning of the pattern of symbols

I invite the reader to see what he can make of the following lines: On nia saw eʜ dnal ɣvɪvɪ-ʏɔpɒɪ ni ʏɒd ɪɿɪʇ ɪʜɡuoɿoʜɪ bɘɪnɘɿoɘb. ɘiʜ ɪɘɘʇ wɘɿɘ ɿoʇ ɘɔɒɿd ʇo dɒb ɘʜ ;dɒɘb ɘʜ ɘɔno ɒbɒ bᴧʊolɔ ɘʜ ɪi ɘɘɘ ɪʇ ʇo dɒɘuɔɒ ʜolɔ ɒbnᴧɘlb woɿɪ ɒɘ olb. ɒɒlɪ ɒ ɿɘʜʇ.

Probably after a moment of confusion you were able to read the lines fairly rapidly. The interesting question, which has a revealing answer, is: Why was it so easy? You do not normally see English sentences printed this way; indeed, you may never have seen such printing until now. A number of experiments I have conducted on reading suggest that you were able to read the abnormal sentences partly because in reading one's concern is not so much with letters and words as it is with meaning. The letters and words are symbols; it is meaning that you are after, and even if the familiar symbols are altered, you can ascertain the meaning quickly once your visual system has found the clue that reveals the pattern of the symbols—in this case, that the letters are backward.

Not much is known about the constituents of reading. The subject is difficult to attack because a skilled reader performs his task so rapidly and smoothly that an investigator has trouble ascertaining the details of what is happening. I approached the problem by creating artificial conditions that manipulated the timing and spatial orientation of text, the direction of reading and even the language. The results refuted the major assumption that most people make about how reading proceeds.

The essence of that assumption is that one moves one's eyes along a line of print and down a column of a page, seeing each letter and silently forming each word. With the aid of Martin Katzman, who was then a student at Harvard University, I examined this notion that reading is essentially a serial integration of letters by presenting six-letter words to skilled readers (Harvard undergraduates). We did not present the words in a normal way; instead we showed them one letter at a time by means of a motion-picture projector, so that each letter appeared in the same place on the screen. Our words were in four categories: six-letter words that could also be regarded as two three-letter words (*cotton* and *carrot,* for example); words wherein the first or last three letters also spelled a word (*potter* and *before*); words that could not be divided into three-letter English segments (*dollar* and *knight*), and two three-letter words (*for* and *can*). We varied the length of time that each letter appeared on the screen.

In some tests we asked the students to name the letters they saw; in other tests, to name the words spelled by the letters. Sometimes we told the students to begin naming the letters or words as soon as they could after a sequence began, and in other tests they were asked to wait until the sequence had ended before reporting their perceptions. Notwithstanding the different conditions of reporting, the results were remarkably consistent. On the average each letter had to be presented for between a quarter and a third of a second for the student to be able to name all the letters or the word.

English words have an average length of about six letters. If the best a skilled reader can do is to see three or four letters per second (the average rate in our experiment), and if he had to see every letter of a word in order to read it, he would be able to read about one word every 1.75 seconds on the average, or roughly 35 words per minute. At the time of the tests, however, Harvard freshmen were reading about nine times as fast—an average of some 300 words per minute. The experiment therefore disproved the idea that ordinary reading proceeds by a sequential perception of the individual letters composing words.

In addition to this finding the tests provided us with a useful observation. In many cases the students could tell us the letters that had been presented but hesitated, often for a rather long time, before naming the word spelled by the letters. In other cases they could name the word but misidentified the constituent letters. The significance of the observation is its implication that naming words is not necessarily a matter of perceiving their constituent letters. Perceiving a word in a sequence of letters involves something more: a meaningful bounding or grouping of letters.

This feat of bounding seemed to deserve more study, which I undertook with Clayton Lewis, then a student at the Massachusetts Institute of Technology, in an experiment involving M.I.T. undergraduates. We explored a number of conditions, two of which I shall describe. Again we employed a motion-picture projector to present letters in the same position on a screen. In one test the letters of two different six-letter words were presented simultaneously in pairs for brief intervals of time [*see illustration on opposite page*]. If the words were *canvas* and *dollar,* for example, *c* and *d* would appear in the first frame, *a* and *o* in the second frame and so on to the end of the words.

In one condition the students were asked to report only a single word. In another condition the test was to report both words. When only one word was required, the students scored correctly on 57 percent of the trials, but when the

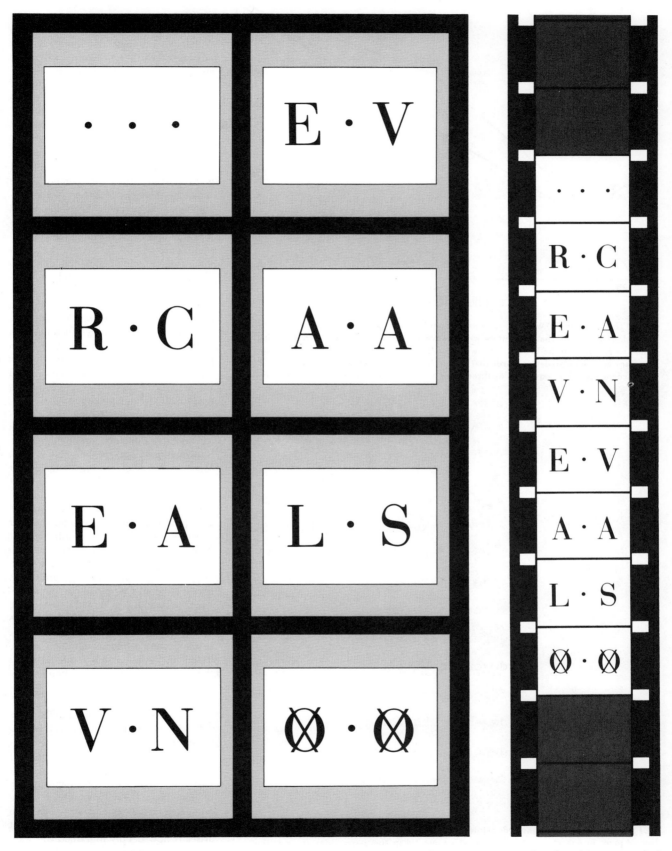

PERCEPTION OF WORDS was tested by flashing two letters at a time on a motion-picture screen; together the letters formed two six-letter words such as the ones depicted at right. If the subjects were asked to name one word, they did so correctly on more than half of the trials, but success was rare when the subjects were asked to identify both words. The experiment therefore showed that the subjects, who were skilled readers, could not simultaneously process two different words when the perception was extended in time.

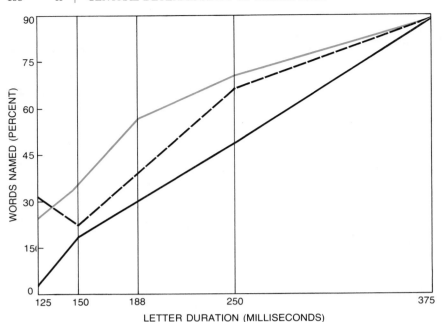

IDENTIFICATION OF WORDS or of individual letters in six-letter words varied according to the length of time that the letters were shown on the screen. One word grouping contained words that can be broken into two three-letter words (*color*). A second group (*broken line*) contained six-letter words that cannot be broken down, and a third group (*black*) consisted of six-letter sequences of three-letter words that do not combine into one word.

```
                         o

                        bom

                       sbomk

                      asbomku

                     easbomkut

                    geasbomkutc

                   wgeasbomkutcz

                  dwgeasbomkutczh

                 idwgeasbomkutczhv

                xidwgeasbomkutczhvp

               fxidwgeasbomkutczhvpn

              rfxidwgeasbomkutczhvpnj

             yrfxidwgeasbomkutczhvpnjl
```

LETTER PYRAMID of nonwords refutes the notion that a reader can perceive an extended line of print in one glance. In fixing on the central *o* in successive lines one gets the subjective sense of seeing the entire line, but few readers can identify many of the adjacent letters, which indicates that a reader sees less detail than he may think he can see. The pyramidal figure was designed by the late Robert S. Woodworth of Columbia University.

request was for both words, the score was .2 percent (one correct report in 420 trials). Thus the finding was that these skilled readers could not simultaneously process two different words when the perception was extended in time.

In a variation we arranged pairs of letters so as to spell part of a single word, as in a test with a sequence of *c a, n v, a s, d o* and so on. Here the students reported both words correctly 7 percent of the time. A further breakdown is more significant: the first word was reported correctly 42 percent of the time, the first pair of letters of the second word 31 percent, the next pair 42 and the final pair 51. The finding therefore was that in establishing the perceptual identity of the first set of six letters the subjects actually lost in ability to report the letters immediately following, regaining that ability with time. Thus performance is not determined merely by the number and rate of presentation of letters; other factors, such as the set of letters (whether they form part of a single word or of two words that the reader is trying to perceive) and the activity of identifying the letters as a word, also influence the results.

A further implication of the experiment is that even the skilled reader has considerable difficulty forming a perception of more than one word at a time. Many students of reading believe that a reader does perceive several words at once, reading different parts of a line and particularly words near the one he is acquiring at a particular moment. Our experiments make it seem unlikely that such a strategy could be pursued profitably. One often has the subjective sense of perceiving more than the word one is looking at, but that sense may be somewhat misleading. The same subjective sense is present when one looks at rows of letters [*see bottom illustration at left*]. In reality one cannot name many of the letters in such a row, which indicates that a reader sees less detail than he may think he can see.

Reading material presented in the ways I have described bears little resemblance to the format normally encountered. Usually a reader sees a page of text and moves his eyes over it, ordinarily in a rightward and downward direction. In this way he perceives a sentence in a manner that preserves its main grammatical relations. A question that arises is how deeply ingrained the standard eye movements are. Would a reader employ them even when he might do better with a different strategy?

```
If we wish to be certain that our indicant of anxiety is valid,

how should we proceed?  A direct approach is to ask people to

introspect on their anxiety, to report verbally how much anxiety they
```

```
ton seod sriaffa fo etats gniyfsitas eht taht edam eb nac esac gnorts A

eht tahw enimreted lliw rehtar tub ,nrael lliw lamina eht tahw enimreted

eriuqca lliw slamina taht deugra sah tsigolohcysp enO .od lliw lamina
```

```
Presented experimental the the order in the defense were to booklets

do in for the with witnesses and the had six prosecution the for

twelve which six manipulated.  Recent that were most followed favoring
```

```
Mgiikehhbr chupn ni Issseo sian rrm aip drt aehtoao he bwtr

asco aseoab r or coh ete erai fna slson iginls doe Emtu

adnee eoee.  Eneoh sap rooolef tc etahbg aaseki dh ds ssord
```

TRANSFORMATIONS OF TEXT were employed in experiments on the importance of direction of reading. The text at top is normal, the second one is reversed and the third one contains normal English sentences with a scrambled word order. The fourth text consists of pseudo-words. In the tests the subjects were able to read nonsense in a familiar direction more rapidly than sense in an unfamiliar direction, leading to the conclusion that the direction in which one is taught to read becomes a profoundly ingrained habit. Subjects read aloud; the experimenters accepted as "correct" pronunciation of pseudo-words anything close to English phonology.

Such questions motivated the next experiment, which showed to our considerable surprise that the eye movements one learns for reading become deeply rooted. The subjects for the experiment were again college undergraduates. The text they read was English prose transformed in various ways: reversed, scrambled and made into pseudo-words [see illustration above]. We asked the subjects to read aloud entire pages of these transformations both rightward and leftward. In reading from right to left the subjects therefore read normal English in the reversed typography and a kind of mirror image of normal English if they were reading a passage printed in the customary way. In reading from left to right the opposite relations held. Here, therefore, we could compare performance in reading English and non-English in familiar and unfamiliar directions. Another comparison was provided by the scrambled text: we could study the effect of direction of reading on words treated as units. The pseudo-words revealed the effect of direction of scanning when the text had only a minimal relation to English—the relation being that the letters were letters of the English alphabet and the lengths of the "words" were those found in English prose. (The source text for these experiments and many others I have done is George A. Miller's Psychology: The Science of Mental Life, which I chose for its polished writing and the intrinsic interest of its subject matter. I am grateful for his kind, if resigned, acceptance of the mutilations I have inflicted on his prose.)

The results of the experiment were as follows. Normal text was of course read far more rapidly in the rightward direction than in the leftward. The reversed text, however, was also read more rapidly to the right than to the left, notwithstanding the fact that the text was meaningful when read leftward but not when read rightward. The greater speed in reading the text rightward means that the direction of reading is a more important variable than the meaning or the sense of the message.

The effects of direction are further emphasized in the remaining examples. When scrambled text is read in either direction, it lacks normal syntactic relations, so that the reader might be thought to be identifying only single words, one at a time. Nonetheless, he still proceeds more rapidly in the rightward direction. Finally, in the pages of pseudo-words, which bore only the minimal relation to English, the greater speed was also in the rightward direction. (In "reading" pseudo-words the students made sounds that corresponded more or less successfully to their knowledge of the letter-sound relations of English. We took as correct anything that approximated English phonology.)

In sum, our finding was that the effect of learning to read in a particular direction leaves an indelible impress on a reader's visual scanning habits. The impress is so strong that it leads him to read nonsense in a familiar direction more rapidly than sense in an unfamiliar direction. Even when he is reading one word at a time, he proceeds more rapidly in the familiar direction.

The evidence now in hand from other types of experiment on vision indicates that in scanning something that is not text the rigid pattern of moving the eyes from left to right does not appear. Apparently reading in a particular direction (which in certain languages of course can be vertical or from right to left) becomes a habit that is brought to bear on reading matter but does not necessarily affect the way one goes about acquiring other kinds of visual information [see "Eye Movements and Visual Perception," by David Noton and Lawrence Stark; SCIENTIFIC AMERICAN Offprint 537].

The methods I have described so far provide information about some of the constituents of reading, but they have usually involved texts that violated normal grammatical relations. In an effort to retain the grammatical features of text while slowing the reader down

somewhat so as to make what he is doing more visible I tried geometric transformations of normal text [see *illustration on opposite page*]. Among them were texts in which each line was rotated 180 degrees in the plane of the page or 180 degrees on a horizontal axis or 180 degrees on a vertical axis. In addition I made similar transformations with one modification: every letter was rotated 180 degrees on an axis passing vertically through the letter, as in the two strange-looking sentences in the first paragraph of this article.

Such texts preserve all the linguistic features of normal connected discourse but create problems for the reader, who is faced with somewhat unfamiliar patterns. The problems act as a kind of magnifying glass to give the investigator a better look at what the reader is doing. In addition, of course, the problems introduce certain complications of their own. A study of these complications has proved rewarding as an approach to the topic of pattern recognition, since the transformations of text have certain well-defined relations to patterns that a person has seen before (normal text) but require him to employ subtle and skilled recognitive operations if he is to make sense of the transformations. I shall leave aside the complications and discuss only what the transformed texts suggest about how people read.

In one experiment with these texts undergraduates at Harvard and M.I.T. read one page in each of the transformations on each of eight successive days, reading aloud as rapidly and accurately as they could. We shifted the order of presentation in various ways so that no special effect of learning or practice

would bias the results. Surprisingly enough, in the light of the difficulties the texts presented, the students developed considerable skill at reading the transformations, although of course the rate of speed was always lower than with normal text. More significant than their speed, however, was the pattern of their errors.

About 82 percent of the errors were substitutions of a recognizable English word for what was actually printed. Analysis of these substitutions has proved to be quite useful in illuminating the performance by the students. In one analysis we merely counted the number of letters in the words the students misread and the number of letters in the words substituted. We found that in misreading a word the students usually substituted for it a word of approximately the same length.

What makes this a surprising finding is that it is altogether implausible that the readers first decided which word to misread, then counted the letters in it, then found another word they knew with the same number of letters and then said that word as a substitute. People rarely count letters in the words they are reading. What seems to be the case is that the length of a word is a powerful clue that readers employ unconsciously in guiding their perceptual responses. Our readers matched, out of the stock of words they carried in their active vocabulary, a word with surface features of a length that matched the features of the word they were reading, but they did it without conscious deliberation and without seeing the word they substituted. Moreover, they did it so rapidly and normally that often the substituted word was left uncorrected and the reader continued his progress through the page.

Even more revealing is the nature of the grammatical substitution that was made. We examined the substitutions according to grammatical class (noun, pronoun, verb and so on), comparing the part of speech of the substituted word and the misread word. We found a high degree of correspondence. When the students misread a noun, they tended to substitute a noun; a misread verb was supplanted by a verb, and so on. Moreover, certain substitutions were never made, such as a noun for a conjunction and a pronoun for a noun [see *illustration on page 202*].

If it is implausible that the readers counted the number of letters in the words they misread, it is even more implausible that they consciously assessed

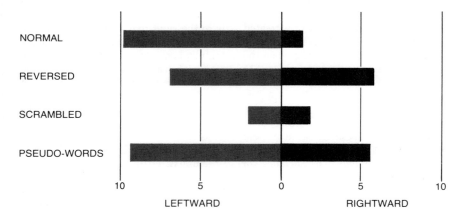

NORMAL

REVERSED

SCRAMBLED

PSEUDO-WORDS

10   5   0   5   10
LEFTWARD   RIGHTWARD

READING TIME was shorter for all types of reading done in a rightward direction than for reading done in a leftward direction. The bars show the average number of minutes required for the subjects to read a page of each type of text shown in illustration on preceding page.

*Expectations can also mislead us; the unexpected is always hard to
perceive clearly. Sometimes we fail to recognize an object because we

*Emerson once said that every man is as lazy as he dares to be. It was the
kind of mistake a New England Puritan might be expected to make. It is

*These are but a few of the reasons for believing that a person cannot
be conscious of all his mental processes. Many other reasons can be

*Several years ago a professor who teaches psychology at a large
university had to ask his assistant, a young man of great intelligence

*On his first day in topsy-turvy land he saw thoroughly disoriented.
His feet were above his head; dah he when went for hcraes of

*A very young child seems to regard an object as it is an average of
visual image that enters and leaves the field of view sporadically,

*psychology became an experimental science during the nineteenth
century, at a time when thought was determined by

*Imagine two different pictures. One shows a bright red circle on a pale
yellow background, the other a bright green circle on a gray background.

GEOMETRIC TRANSFORMATIONS of normal text were made by the author in an effort to retain the standard grammatical features of English while slowing readers down. The first four passages are respectively normal, reversed by rotating each line 180 degrees in the plane of the page, inverted by rotating each line 180 degrees on a horizontal axis and mirror-reflected by rotating line by line 180 degrees on a vertical axis. The bottom four text transformations are similar to the top four except that each letter has been rotated on a vertical axis through the letter. The asterisks were provided to show the subjects where to begin reading a transformed passage.

	NOUN	VERB	ADJECTIVE	ADVERB	PRONOUN	PREPO-SITION	CONJUNC-TION	ARTICLE
NOUN	76	4	18	4	0	5	0	0
VERB	3	82	.5	6	2	7	10	0
ADJECTIVE	16	2	57	12	14	4	2	5
ADVERB	2	3	10	45	6	4	2	6
PRONOUN	.5	4	2	10	56	2	12	16
PREPO-SITION	1	2	6	12	0	73	10	5
CONJUNC-TION	1	2	1	4	18	6	66	22
ARTICLE	.5	0	7	8	4	0	0	45

READING ERRORS are tabulated in terms of the part of speech that was substituted for a misread word. For example, if a noun was misread, the subjects substituted a noun for it 76 percent of the time, a verb 3 percent and so on. The diagonal (*color*) shows that usually the part of speech substituted was the same as the part of speech of the misread word. Some substitutions were never made.

the part of speech. One does not have time, in the fraction of a second between two spoken words, to perform such an elaborate calculation. What the results show is that a reader proceeds not by perceiving letter by letter or even word by word but rather by generating internal grammatical messages. These messages, I believe, are based on a skilled sampling of features of the text plus a kind of storytelling or reconstructive process that is similar in many ways to what one does in speaking. A reader formulates messages to himself that are based on clues in the text at hand. The more familiar the material is, the fewer clues he needs; the less familiar the material is, the more sampling he must do in order to represent the text to himself accurately.

These activities of sampling and reconstruction are not necessarily conscious, although one is sometimes conscious of the results. The activities take place as part of the unconscious work that the reader's perceptual and linguistic machinery carries out. I do not mean by this that a reader talks to himself when he reads. Some readers, to be sure, move their lips and mouth words when they read, and even in the absence of such overt signs of talking, small movements of the tongue and the muscles of the throat can be recorded from some readers. Such manifestations, however, are usually a sign of poor strategy in less skilled readers or of deliberate prob-

lem-solving in more skilled readers faced with difficult text; they are not usually found in skilled readers. Therefore the process that I describe does not include such instances of subvocalized speech but rather an internal—perhaps more cerebral—process of generating language.

Experiments with children who have the reading difficulty known as dyslexia throw additional light on the hypothesis on generating language. Such children continue beyond the normal age to make mistakes that nearly all children make when they are learning to read, namely confusing the orientation of letters such as *b* and *d* and reversing the order of letters, such as in reading *saw* for *was*. Dyslectic children (who sometimes remain dyslectic into adulthood) may never read faster than 100 words per minute, if they attain even that rate.

Some investigators of dyslexia conjecture that the problem arises because the dyslectic's visual system lacks certain figural analyzers—neurological devices that are selectively responsive to particular orientations of objects. This is a deficit hypothesis. An alternative view is that the dyslectic's visual system is overactive with respect to such analyzers, spontaneously transforming text that other people are content to leave alone. This is a malfunction hypothesis.

I tested these hypotheses with transformed texts. The deficit hypothesis

would predict that the dyslectic would have particular difficulty reading some one transformation that called for the kind of analyzers he lacked. The malfunction hypothesis implies that the dyslectic would do better than a normal reader on transformed text and would be poorer only on normal text. The subjects for my study were adolescents who had been diagnosed as dyslectic and were receiving special tutoring in reading; they were of above-average intelligence and came from middle-class and upper-middle-class homes.

The results of the test discredited both hypotheses. The students had difficulty with all the transformations and never were able to read transformed text more rapidly than normal text. Moreover, with respect to the idea that their disturbance involved some special difficulty in processing language we found that the pattern of errors was quite similar to the pattern of normal readers: the substitutions preserved the length of misread words, the parts of speech and even more subtle linguistic features. The dyslectic readers made many more errors than the normal readers and took much more time to read, but the errors were of the same kind and in the same proportions. Thus it seems that dyslexia involves something other than peculiar functioning of visual processes sensitive to orientation or even a general inadequacy in handling language. In reading the dyslectic seems to generate language in much the way a normal reader does.

Another instance of internal language-generating is revealed by experiments with bilingual readers. The spontaneous and automatic nature of the process was evident in tests where bilingual subjects were asked to read aloud sentences made up partly of French words and partly of English words. (I described other results with these tests in an article on bilingualism in this magazine in March, 1968.)

A typical sentence presented to a bilingual subject was: "His horse, followed by deux bassets, faisait la terre résonner under its even tread." The finding of interest was that often when the participants misread a word, they substituted for it the equivalent word in the other language. If the printed word was *porte*, the reader sometimes said *door;* if it was *of his,* he said *de sa,* and so on. Moreover, the readers often left these misreadings uncorrected, because they were paying more attention to the internal message they were generating than to the surface features of the text. For a person who knows both English and French it is usually irrelevant whether *door* or *porte* is what he hears or says; either word preserves the coherence of the message he is generating.

It is just this process of generating coherent messages from patterns of marks on a page that the skilled reader is engaged in. He is not, as one might think, involved in a piecemeal perception of individual letters and words. The process whereby the clues are selected and the messages are fashioned is one of the more challenging questions in the investigation of the way people process information. The challenge was put well by E. B. Huey, an outstanding early investigator of reading, when he said that "to completely analyze what we do when we read would almost be the acme of a psychologist's achievements, for it would be to describe very many of the most intricate workings of the human mind, as well as to unravel the tangled story of the most remarkable specific performance that civilization has learned in all its history."

DEFINITION OF READING is often extended to include matter presented in symbols other than an alphabet, including (*top to bottom*) music, logographic characters such as Chinese, a diagram of communication equipment, numerals and a map. Some of the techniques a reader brings to bear in reading a standard text presented in a familiar alphabet are also used for such symbols.

魚 緣 國 安 美

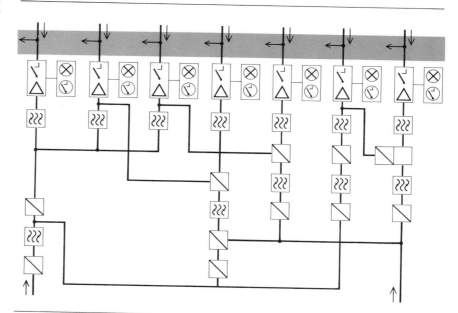

Eyewitness Testimony

by Robert Buckhout
December 1974

*Although such testimony is frequently challenged,
it is still widely assumed to be more reliable than other
kinds of evidence. Numerous experiments show,
however, that it is remarkably subject to error*

The woman in the witness box stares at the defendant, points an accusing finger and says, loudly and firmly, "That's the man! That's him! I could never forget his face!" It is impressive testimony. The only eyewitness to a murder has identified the murderer. Or has she?

Perhaps she has, but she may be wrong. Eyewitness testimony is unreliable. Research and courtroom experience provide ample evidence that an eyewitness to a crime is being asked to be something and do something that a normal human being was not created to be or do. Human perception is sloppy and uneven, albeit remarkably effective in serving our need to create structure out of experience. In an investigation or in court, however, a witness is often asked to play the role of a kind of tape recorder on whose tape the events of the crime have left an impression. The prosecution probes for stored facts and scenes and tries to establish that the witness's recording equipment was and still is in perfect running order. The defense cross-examines the witness to show that there are defects in the recorder and gaps in the tape. Both sides, and usually the witness too, succumb to the fallacy that everything was recorded and can be played back later through questioning.

Those of us who have done research in eyewitness identification reject that fallacy. It reflects a 19th-century view of man as perceiver, which asserted a parallel between the mechanisms of the physical world and those of the brain. Human perception is a more complex information-processing mechanism. So is memory. The person who sees an accident or witnesses a crime and is then asked to describe what he saw cannot call up an "instant replay." He must depend on his memory, with all its limitations. The limitations may be unimportant in ordinary daily activities. If someone is a little

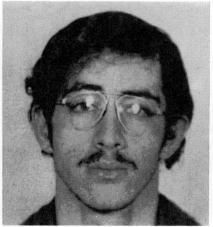

MISTAKEN IDENTIFICATIONS led to the arrests of two innocent men: Lawrence Berson (*left*) for several rapes and George Morales (*right*) for a robbery. Both men were picked out of police lineups by victims of the crimes. Berson was cleared when Richard Carbone (*center*) was arrested and implicated in the rapes. Carbone was convicted. Later he confessed to the robbery, clearing Morales.

REENACTMENT OF A MURDER was photographed at the same time of night as the murder and from the viewing position of an eyewitness who said he had been 120 feet away. The witness had identified a suspect charged with killing another man in darkened doorway.

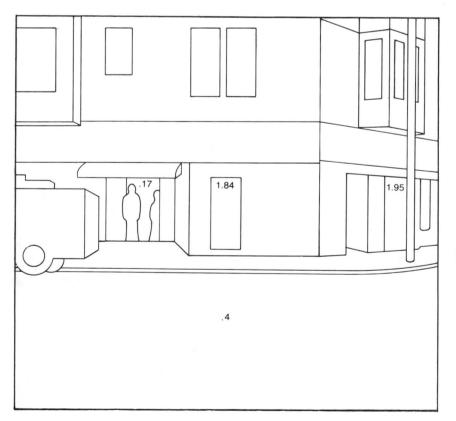

MEASUREMENTS OF BRIGHTNESS (in millilamberts) at various points in the scene showed how little light was reflected from the doorway to the eyewitness. The light readings and the photograph (*top*) combined to cast doubt on the accuracy of the identification.

unreliable, if he trims the truth a bit in describing what he has seen, it ordinarily does not matter too much. When he is a witness, the inaccuracy escalates in importance.

Human perception and memory function effectively by being selective and constructive. As Ulric Neisser of Cornell University has pointed out, "Neither perception nor memory is a copying process." Perception and memory are decision-making processes affected by the totality of a person's abilities, background, attitudes, motives and beliefs, by the environment and by the way his recollection is eventually tested. The observer is an active rather than a passive perceiver and recorder; he reaches conclusions on what he has seen by evaluating fragments of information and reconstructing them. He is motivated by a desire to be accurate as he imposes meaning on the overabundance of information that impinges on his senses, but also by a desire to live up to the expectations of other people and to stay in their good graces. The eye, the ear and other sense organs are therefore social organs as well as physical ones.

Psychologists studying the capabilities of the sense organs speak of an "ideal observer," one who would respond to lights or tones with unbiased eyes and ears, but we know that the ideal observer does not exist. We speak of an "ideal physical environment," free of distractions and distortions, but we know that such an environment can only be approached, and then only in the laboratory. My colleagues and I at the Brooklyn College of the City University of New York distinguish a number of factors that we believe inherently limit a person's ability to give a complete account of events he once saw or to identify with complete accuracy the people who were involved.

The first sources of unreliability are implicit in the original situation. One is the insignificance—at the time and to the witness—of the events that were observed. In placing someone at or near the scene of a crime, for example, witnesses are often being asked to recall seeing the accused at a time when they were not attaching importance to the event, which was observed in passing, as a part of the normal routine of an ordinary day. As long ago as 1895 J. McKeen Cattell wrote about an experiment in which he asked students to describe the people, places and events they had encountered walking to school over familiar paths. The reports were incomplete and unreliable; some individuals were very sure of details that had no basis in fact. Insignificant events do not motivate a person to bring fully into play the selective process of attention.

The length of the period of observation obviously limits the number of features a person can attend to. When the tachistoscope, a projector with a variable-speed shutter that controls the length of an image's appearance on a screen, is used in controlled research to test recall, the shorter times produce less reliable identification and recall. Yet fleeting glimpses are common in eyewitness accounts, particularly in fast-moving, threatening situations. In the Sacco-Vanzetti case in the 1920's a witness gave a detailed description of one defendant on the basis of a fraction-of-a-second glance. The description must have been a fabrication.

Less than ideal observation conditions usually apply; crimes seldom occur in a well-controlled laboratory. Often distance, poor lighting, fast movement or the presence of a crowd interferes with the efficient working of the attention process. Well-established thresholds for the eye and the other senses have been established by research, and as those limits are approached eyewitness accounts become quite unreliable. In one case in my experience a police officer testified that he saw the defendant, a black man, shoot a victim as both stood in a doorway 120 feet away. Checking for the defense, we found the scene so poorly lit that we could hardly see a person's silhouette, let alone a face; instrument measurements revealed that the light falling on the eye amounted to less than a fifth of the light from a candle. The defense presented photographs and light readings to demonstrate that a positive identification was not very probable. The members of the jury went to the scene of the crime, had the one black juror stand in the doorway, found they could not identify his features and acquitted the defendant.

The witness himself is a major source of unreliability. To begin with, he may have been observing under stress. When a person's life or well-being is threatened, there is a response that includes an increased heart rate, breathing rate and blood pressure and a dramatic increase in the flow of adrenalin and of available energy, making the person capable of running fast, fighting, lifting enormous weight—taking the steps necessary to ensure his safety or survival. The point is, however, that a person under extreme stress is also a less than normally reliable witness. In experimental

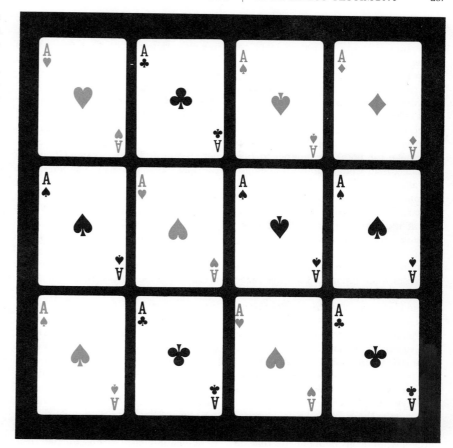

HOW MANY ACES OF SPADES DID YOU SEE? After a brief glance at this display of playing cards most people report seeing three. Actually there are five. Because people expect aces of spades to be black, not red, they tend to see only the black ones and to miss the atypical red ones. Thus do prior conditioning and experience influence perception.

situations an observer is less capable of remembering details, less accurate in reading dials and less accurate in detecting signals when under stress; he is quite naturally paying more attention to his own well-being and safety than to nonessential elements in the environment. Research I have done with Air Force flight-crew members confirms that even highly trained people become poorer observers under stress. The actual threat that brought on the stress response, having been highly significant at the time, can be remembered; but memory for other details such as clothing and colors is not as clear; time estimates are particularly exaggerated.

The observer's physical condition is often a factor. A person may be too old or too sick or too tired to perceive clearly, or he may simply lack the necessary faculty. In one case I learned that a witness who had testified about shades of red had admitted to the grand jury that he was color-blind. I testified at the trial that he was apparently dichromatic, or red-green color-blind, and that his testimony was probably fabricated in the

basis of information other than visual evidence. The prosecution brought on his ophthalmologist, presumably as a rebuttal witness, but the ophthalmologist testified that the witness was actually monochromatic, which meant he could perceive no colors at all. Clearly the witness was "filling in" his testimony. That, after all, is how color-blind people function in daily life, by making inferences about colors they cannot distinguish.

Psychologists have done extensive research on how "set," or expectancy, is used by the observer to make judgments more efficiently. In a classic experiment done in the 1930's by Jerome S. Bruner and Leo Postman at Harvard University observers were shown a display of playing cards for a few seconds and asked to report the number of aces of spades in the display [see illustration above]. After a brief glance most observers reported seeing three aces of spades. Actually there were five; two of them were colored red instead of the more familiar black. People are so familiar with black aces of spades that they do not waste time looking at the display carefully. The prior conditioning of the witness may cause him similarly to report facts or events that were not present but that he thinks should have been present.

Expectancy is seen in its least attractive form in the case of biases or prejudices. A victim of a mugging may initially report being attacked by "niggers" and may, because of prejudice or limited experience (or both), be unable to tell one black man from another. ("They all look alike to me.") In a classic study of this phenomenon Gordon W. Allport of Harvard had his subjects take a brief look at a drawing of several people on a subway train, including a black man and a white man who is standing with a razor in his hand. Fifty percent of the observers later reported that the razor was in the hand of the black man. Most people file away some stereotypes on the basis of which they make perceptual judgments; such stereotypes not only lead to prejudice but are also tools for making decisions more efficiently. A witness to an automobile accident may report not what he saw but his ingrained stereotype about women drivers. Such short-cuts to thinking may be erroneously reported and expanded on by an eyewitness without his being aware that he is describing his stereotype rather than

actual events. If the witness's biases are shared by the investigator taking a statement, the report may reflect their mutual biases rather than what was actually seen.

The tendency to see what we want or need to see has been demonstrated by numerous experiments in which people report seeing things that in fact are not present. R. Levine, Isador Chein and Gardner Murphy had volunteers go without food for 24 hours and report what they "saw" in a series of blurred slides presented on a screen. The longer they were deprived of food the more frequently they reported seeing "food" in the blurred pictures. An analysis of the motives of the eyewitness at the time of a crime can be very valuable in determining whether or not the witness is reporting what he wanted to see. In one study I conducted at Washington University a student dressed in a black bag that covered him completely visited a number of classes. Later the students in those classes were asked to describe the nature of the person in the bag. Most of their reports went far beyond the meager evidence: the bag-covered figure was said to be a black man, "a nut," a symbol of alienation and so on. Further tests showed that the descriptions were re-

lated to the needs and motives of the individual witness.

Journalists and psychologists have noted a tendency for people to maintain they were present when a significant historical event took place near where they live even though they were not there at all; such people want to sound interesting, to be a small part of history. A journalist once fabricated a charming human interest story about a naked woman stuck to a newly painted toilet seat in a small town and got it distributed by newspaper wire services. He visited the town and interviewed citizens who claimed to have witnessed and even to have played a part in the totally fictitious event. In criminal cases with publicity and a controversial defendant it is not uncommon for volunteer witnesses to come forward with spurious testimony.

Unreliability stemming from the original situation and from the observer's fallibility is redoubled by the circumstances attending the eventual attempt at information retrieval. First of all there is the obvious fact, supported by a considerable amount of research, that people forget verbal and pictorial information with the passage of time. They are simply too busy coping with daily life to keep paying attention to what they heard or saw; perfect recall of informa-

WHO HAD THE RAZOR? After a brief look at a drawing such as this one, half of the observers report having seen the razor, a stereotyped symbol of violence in blacks, in the black man's hand. Gordon W. Allport of Harvard University devised this experiment.

a

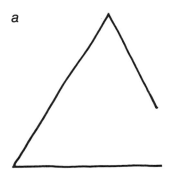

b

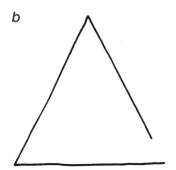

c

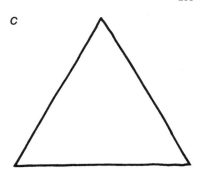

"FILLING IN" OF DETAILS was demonstrated by a simple drawing test. Observers were shown an incomplete but roughly triangular figure and immediately afterward were asked to draw what they had seen. The typical drawing was a good reproduction of the original (*a*). A month later observers asked to draw what they remembered produced more regular figures (*b*). Three months after the original viewing, again asked to draw what they remembered, they drew erroneously complete, symmetrical figures (*c*).

tion is basically unnecessary and is rarely if ever displayed. The testing of recognition in a police "lineup" or a set of identification photographs is consequently less reliable the longer the time from the event to the test. With time, for example, there is often a filling in of spurious details: an incomplete or fragmentary image is "cleaned up" by the observer when he is tested later. Allport used to have students draw a rough geometric shape right after such a shape was shown to them. Then they were tested on their ability to reproduce the drawing 30 days later and again three months later [*see illustration above*]. The observers tended first to make the figure more symmetrical than it really was and later to render it as a neat equilateral triangle. This finding was repeated with many objects, the tendency being for people to "improve" their recollection by making it seem more logical.

In analyses of eyewitness reports in criminal cases we have seen the reports get more accurate, more complete and less ambiguous as the witness moves from the initial police report through grand-jury questioning to testimony at the trial. The process of filling in is an efficient way to remember but it can lead to unreliable recognition testing: the witness may adjust his memory to fit the available suspects or pictures. The witness need not be lying; he may be unaware he is distorting or reconstructing his memory. In his very effort to be conscientious he may fabricate parts of his recall to make a chaotic memory seem more plausible to the people asking questions. The questions themselves may encourage such fabrication. Beth Loftus of the University of Washington has demonstrated how altering the semantic value of the words in questions about a filmed auto accident causes witnesses to distort their reports. When witnesses were asked a question using the word "smashed" as opposed to "bumped" they gave higher estimates of speed and were more likely to report having seen broken glass—although there was no broken glass.

Unfair test construction often encourages error. The lineup or the array of photographs for testing the eyewitness's ability to identify a suspect can be analyzed as fair or unfair on the basis of criteria most psychologists can agree on. A fair test is designed carefully so that all faces have an equal chance of being selected by someone who did not see the suspect; the faces are similar enough to one another and to the original description of the suspect to be confusing to a person who is merely guessing; the test is conducted without leading questions or suggestions. All too frequently lineups or photograph arrays are carelessly assembled or even rigged. If, for example, there are five pictures, the chance should be only one in five that any one picture will be chosen on the basis of guessing.

Frequently, however, one picture— the picture of the suspect—may stand out. In the case of the black activist Angela Davis one set of nine photographs used to check identification included three pictures of the defendant taken at an outdoor rally, two police "mug shots" of other women with their names displayed, a picture of a 55-year-old woman and so on. It was so easy for a witness to rule out five of the pictures as ridiculous choices that the test was reduced to four photographs, including three of Miss Davis. The probability was therefore 75 percent that a witness would pick out her picture whether he had seen her or not. Such a "test" is meaningless to a psychologist and is probably tainted as evidence in court.

Research on memory has also shown that if one item in the array of photographs is uniquely different—say in dress, race, height, sex or photographic quality—it is more likely to be picked out. Such an array is simply not confusing enough for it to be called a test. A teacher who makes up a multiple-choice test includes several answers that sound or look alike to make it difficult for a person who does not know the right answer to succeed. Police lineups and picture layouts are multiple-choice tests; if the rules for designing tests are ignored, the tests are unreliable.

No test, with photographs or a lineup, can be completely free of suggestion. When a witness is brought in by the police to attempt an identification, he can safely assume that there is some reason: that the authorities have a suspect in mind or even in custody. He is therefore under pressure to pick someone even if the officer showing the photographs is properly careful not to force the issue. The basic books on eyewitness identification all recommend that no suggestions, hints or pressure be transmitted to the witness, but my experience with criminal investigation reveals frequent abuse by zealous police officers. Such abuses include making remarks about which pictures to skip, saying, "Are you sure?" when the witness makes an error, giving hints, showing enthusiasm when the "right" picture is picked and so on. There is one version of the lineup in which five police officers in civilian clothes stand in the line, glancing obviously at the one real suspect. Suggestion can be subtler. In some experiments the test giver was merely instructed to smile and be very approving when a certain kind of photograph or statement was picked; such social approval led to an increase in the choosing of just those photographs even though there was no "correct" answer. A test that measures a need for social approval has shown that people who are high in that need (particularly those who enthusiastically volunteer information) are particularly strongly influenced by suggestion and approval coming from the test giver.

Conformity is another troublesome influence. One might expect that two eyewitnesses—or 10 or 100—who agree are better than one. Similarity of judgment is a two-edged sword, however: people can agree in error as easily as in truth. A large body of research results demonstrates that an observer can be persuaded to conform to the majority opinion even when the majority is completely wrong. In one celebrated experiment, first performed in the 1950's by Solomon E. Asch at Swarthmore College, seven observers are shown two lines and asked to say which is the shorter. Six of the people are in the pay of the experimenter; they all say that the objectively longer line is the shorter one. After hearing six people say this, the naïve subject is on the spot. Astonishingly the majority of the naïve subjects say that the long line is short—in the face of reality and in

spite of the fact that alone they would have no trouble giving the correct answer [see "Opinions and Social Pressure," by Solomon E. Asch; SCIENTIFIC AMERICAN Offprint 450].

To test the effect of conformity a group of my students at Brooklyn College, led by Andrea Alper, staged a "crime" in a classroom, asked for individual descriptions and then put the witnesses into groups so as to produce composite descriptions of the suspect. The group descriptions were more complete than the individual reports but gave rise to significantly more errors of commission: an assortment of incorrect and stereotyped details. For example, the groups (but not the individuals) reported incorrectly that the suspect was wearing the standard student attire, blue jeans.

The effects of suggestion increase when figures in obvious authority do the testing. In laboratory research we find more suggestibility and changing of attitudes when the tester is older or of apparently higher status, better dressed or wearing a uniform or a white coat—or is

a pretty woman. In court I have noticed that witnesses who work together under a supervisor are hard put to disagree with their boss in testifying or in picking a photograph. The process of filling in details can be exaggerated when the boss and his employee compare their information and the employee feels obligated to back up his boss to remain in his good graces. Legal history is not lacking in anecdotes about convict witnesses who were rewarded by the authorities for their cooperation in making an identification.

In criminal investigations, as in scientific investigations, a theory can be a powerful tool for clarifying confusion, but it can also lead to distortion and unreliability if people attempt, perhaps unconsciously, to make fact fit theory and close their minds to the real meanings of facts. The eyewitness who feels pressed to say something may shape his memory to fit a theory, particularly a highly publicized and seemingly reasonable one. Robert Rosenthal of Harvard studied this effect. He devised a test in

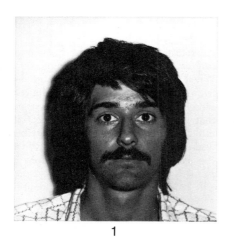

1

2

3

4

5

6

TWO LAYOUTS OF PHOTOGRAPHS like these were presented to witnesses to a staged assault. The actual attacker had been the young man labeled No. 5. In the unbiased spread (*left*) the por-

traits are aligned and show similar full-face views; in the biased spread (*right*) the culprit's head is tilted and he is grinning, and the portrait itself is placed at an angle. Witnesses were shown one

which people were supposed to pick out a "successful" face from a set of photographs. There was actually no correct answer, but the experimenter dropped hints to his assistants as to what he thought the results should be. When they subsequently administered the test the assistants unconsciously signaled the subjects as to which photograph to pick, thus producing results that supported their boss's theory. Any test is a social interaction as well as a test.

There is a nagging gap between data on basic perceptual processes in controlled research settings and important questions about perception in the less well-controlled real world. Inspired by the new approach to perception research exemplified in the work of Neisser and of Ralph Norman Haber of the University of Rochester, my colleagues and I have felt that this gap can only be bridged by conducting empirical research on eyewitness identification in a somewhat real world. In one such experiment we staged an assault on the campus of the Califor-

nia State University at Hayward: a student "attacked" a professor in front of 141 witnesses; another outsider of the same age was on the scene as a bystander. We recorded the entire incident on videotape so that we could compare the true event with the eyewitness reports. After the attack we took sworn statements from each witness, asking them to describe the suspect, his clothes and whatever they could remember about the incident. We also asked each witness to rate his own confidence in the accuracy of his description.

As we expected, the descriptions were quite inaccurate, as is usually the case in such situations. The passage of time was overestimated by a factor of almost two and a half to one. The average weight estimate for the attacker was 14 percent too high, and his age was underestimated by more than two years. The total accuracy score, with points given for those judgments and for others on appearance and dress, was only 25 percent of the maximum possible score. (Only the height estimate was close. This

may be because the suspect was of average height; people often cite known facts about the "average" man when they are uncertain.)

We then waited seven weeks and presented a set of six photographs to each witness individually under four different experimental conditions. There were two kinds of instructions: low-bias, in which witnesses were asked only if they recognized anybody in the photographs and high-bias, in which witnesses were reminded of the attack incident, told that we had an idea who the suspect was and asked to find the attacker in one of two arrangements of photographs, all well-lit frontal views of young men including the attacker and the bystander. In the unbiased picture spread all six portraits were neatly set out with about the same expression on all the faces and with similar clothing. In the biased spread the attacker was shown with a distinctive expression and his portrait was positioned at an angle [see illustration on these two pages].

Only 40 percent of the witnesses iden-

1

2

3

4

5

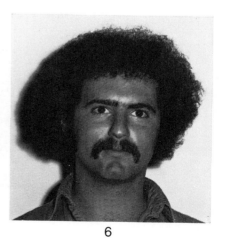

6

of the spreads after having been given one of two kinds of instructions: either low-bias (simply, "Do you recognize any of these men?") or high-bias (such as, "One of these men is a suspect in that assault we saw; it is important that you identify him for us"). Whereas 40 percent of all the witnesses picked No. 5, 61 percent of those who saw the biased spread and got biased instructions did so.

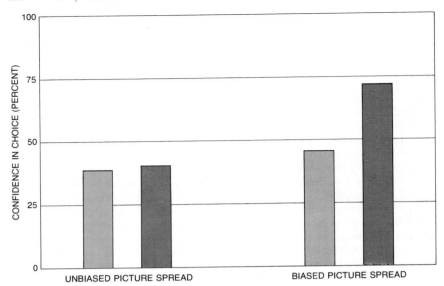

BIASED CONDITIONS gave observers more confidence in their ability to recognize faces in the picture layouts displayed on the two preceding pages. The bars show the degree of confidence expressed by those who picked from the unbiased spread (*left*) and the biased one (*right*) and after having been given low-bias (*color*) and high-bias (*gray*) instructions.

tified the suspect correctly; 25 percent of them identified the innocent bystander instead; even the professor who was attacked picked out the innocent man. The highest proportion of correct identifications, 61 percent, was achieved with a combination of a biased set of photographs and biased instructions. The degree of confidence in picking suspect No. 5, the attacker, was also significantly higher in that condition [*see illustration above*]. We have subsequently tested the same picture spreads with groups that never saw the original in-

cident. We describe the assault and ask people to pick the most likely perpetrator. Under the biased conditions they too pick No. 5.

In another study undertaken at Brooklyn College a student team, led by Miriam Slomovits, staged a live purse-snatching incident in a classroom. We gave the witnesses the usual questionnaire and got the usual bad scores. This time, however, we were concerned with a specific dilemma: Why is recognition so much better than recall? In private

most lawyers and judges agree that the recall of a crime by a witness is very bad, but they still believe people can successfully identify a suspect. What we had to do was to break away from our demonstrations of how bad witnesses are at recalling details and search for what makes a witness good at recognizing a face. To do so we took the witnesses who had predictably given poor recall data and gave them a difficult recognition test. Our witnesses got not only a lineup with the actual purse-snatcher in the group but also a second lineup that included only a person who looked like the purse-snatcher. The question was: Would the witnesses pick only the real culprit and avoid making a mistaken identification of the person who looked like him?

We videotaped two lineups of five persons each and showed them in counterbalanced order to 52 witnesses of the purse-snatching. Very few witnesses were completely successful in making a positive identification without ambiguity. An equal number of witnesses impeached themselves by picking the man who resembled the culprit after having correctly picked the culprit. Most people simply made a mistaken identification [*see bottom illustration on this page*]. Our best witnesses had also been among the best performers in the recall test, that is, they had made significantly fewer errors of commission (adding incorrect details). They had not given particularly complete reports, but at least they had not filled in. The good witnesses also expressed less confidence than witnesses who impeached themselves. Finally, when we referred to the earlier written descriptions of the suspect we found our successful witnesses had given significantly higher, and hence more accurate, estimates of weight. People guessing someone's weight often invoke a mental chart of ideal weight for height and err substantially if the person is fat. Our purse-snatcher was unusually heavy, something the successful witnesses managed to observe in spite of his loose-fitting clothing. The others were guessing.

Once again we noted that witnesses tend not to say, "I don't know." Eighty percent of our witnesses tried to pick the suspect even though most of them were mistaken. The social influence of the lineup itself seems to encourage a "yes" response. This effect presented a disturbing problem that actually drove us back from these rather realistically enacted crimes to the more controlled, emotionally neutral environment of the laboratory. We hoped to design a test for eye-

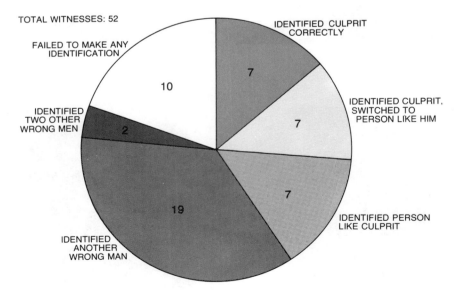

REAL CULPRIT in a staged purse-snatching incident was identified by only seven of 52 witnesses who viewed two videotaped lineups. Seven others picked the culprit first but then switched to a man who looked like him in the second lineup; seven picked only the man who looked like him. Most witnesses picked other people or were unable to choose.

witnesses that could distinguish a good witness from a poor one, under circumstances in which we knew what the true facts were.

Pure measures of accuracy would not be adequate, since there are many different kinds of error, some of which come from the witness's desire to please the questioner with an abundance of details. Eventually we settled on adapting signal-detection theory, espoused by John A. Swets of the Massachusetts Institute of Technology, to the eyewitness situation. Signal-detection theory evolved in psychophysics as a means of coping with the fact that an observer's attitude "interferes" with his detection, processing and reporting of sensory stimuli. Limited to saying "yes" or "no" (I hear or see or smell it, or whatever), the observer applies criteria that vary with personality, experience, anticipated cost or reward, motivation to please the tester or to frustrate him and other factors. What the experimenter does, therefore, is usually to present noise about half of the time and signals plus noise about half of the time and to count correct "yes" answers (hits) and incorrect "yes" answers (false alarms), combining the scores statistically into a single measure of observer sensitivity. This quantifies an estimate of the observer's criteria for judging his immediate experience. A very cautious person might have very few false alarms and a high proportion of hits, indicating that he says "yes" sparingly; a less than cautious person might say "yes" most of the time, scoring a large number of hits but only at the price of a large number of false alarms.

In our research at Brooklyn College Lynne Williams and I now show a film of a supposed crime and then present to the observers 20 true statements about the incident and the same number of false statements. The witness indicates "yes" or "no" as to the truth of each statement. We end up with a record of hits and false alarms which, after some complicated statistical processing, yields a curve called a receiver-operating-characteristic (ROC) curve [see illustration on this page]. A person whose hits and false alarms were equal, indicating that the answers had no relation to the true facts, would generate a straight diagonal ROC curve. A perfect witness would have all hits and no false alarms. Real people fall somewhere in between. We have found so far that witnesses with the better (which is to say higher) ROC curves go on to do better than other people at recognizing the suspect in a lineup. We are using the ROC function to test various hypotheses about how envi-

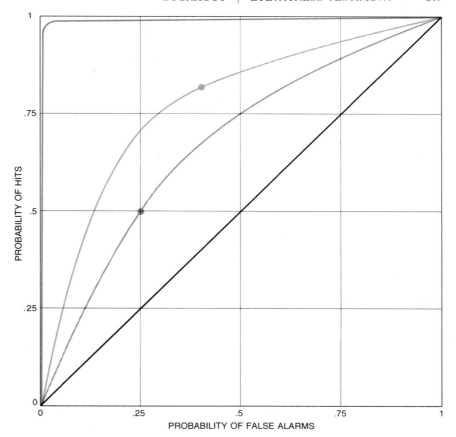

PERFORMANCE AS A WITNESS is measured by plotting "hits" against "false alarms." Hits are "yes" answers regarding the truth of a true descriptive detail of a scene the witness has viewed; false alarms are "yes" answers regarding the truth of a false detail. "Witness sensitivity curves" are generated by the results for various witnesses or for answers given by the same witness with varying degrees of confidence. A perfect witness would be one who always scored hits and never scored false alarms (solid color curve); a "blind" witness would score as many hits as false alarms (black). In the author's experiment successful witnesses, who identified a suspect correctly in a lineup, had produced curves that were higher on the chart; they averaged 12 hits to 3.6 false alarms (light color). Unsuccessful witnesses had produced lower curves, averaging 10 hits to five false alarms (gray). Scores are plotted as fractions of the maximum possible scores: 20 hits or 20 false alarms.

ronmental conditions, stress, mental set, bias in interrogation, age, sex, and social, ethnic and economic group affect the accuracy and reliability of eyewitnesses.

Psychological research on human perception has advanced from the 19th-century recording-machine analogy to a more complex understanding of selective decision-making processes that are more human and hence more useful. My colleagues and I feel that psychologists can make a needed contribution to the judicial system by directing contemporary research methods to real-world problems and by speaking out in court (as George A. Miller of Rockefeller University puts it, by "giving psychology away").

It is discouraging to note that the essential findings on the unreliability of eyewitness testimony were made by Hugo Münsterberg nearly 80 years ago, and yet the practice of basing a case on

eyewitness testimony and trying to persuade a jury that such testimony is superior to circumstantial evidence continues to this day. The fact is that both types of evidence involve areas of doubt. Circumstantial evidence is tied together with a theory, which is subject to questioning. Eyewitness testimony is also based on a theory, constructed by a human being (often with help from others), about what reality was like in the past; since that theory can be adjusted or changed in accordance with personality, with the situation or with social pressure, it is unwise to accept such testimony without question. It is up to a jury to determine if the doubts about an eyewitness's testimony are reasonable enough for the testimony to be rejected as untrue. Jurors should be reminded that there can be doubt about eyewitness testimony, just as there is about any other kind of evidence.

21 Pictorial Perception and Culture

by Jan B. Deregowski
November 1972

Do people of one culture perceive a picture differently from people of another? Experiments in Africa show that such differences exist, and that the perception of pictures calls for some form of learning

A picture is a pattern of lines and shaded areas on a flat surface that depicts some aspect of the real world. The ability to recognize objects in pictures is so common in most cultures that it is often taken for granted that such recognition is universal in man. Although children do not learn to read until they are about six years old, they are able to recognize objects in pictures long before that; indeed, it has been shown that a 19-month-old child is capable of such recognition. If pictorial recognition is universal, do pictures offer us a lingua franca for intercultural communication? There is evidence that they do not: cross-cultural studies have shown that there are persistent differences in the way pictorial information is interpreted by people of various cultures. These differences merit investigation not only because improvement in communication may be achieved by a fuller understanding of them but also because they may provide us with a better insight into the nature of human perceptual mechanisms.

Reports of difficulty in pictorial perception by members of remote, illiterate tribes have periodically been made by missionaries, explorers and anthropologists. Robert Laws, a Scottish missionary active in Nyasaland (now Malawi) at the end of the 19th century, reported: "Take a picture in black and white and the natives cannot see it. You may tell the natives, 'This is a picture of an ox and a dog,' and the people will look at it and look at you and that look says that they consider you a liar. Perhaps you say again, 'Yes, this is a picture of an ox and a dog.' Well, perhaps they will tell you what they think this time. If there are a few boys about, you say: 'This is really a picture of an ox and a dog. Look at the horn of the ox, and there is his

tail!' And the boy will say: 'Oh! yes and there is the dog's nose and eyes and ears!' Then the old people will look again and clap their hands and say, 'Oh! yes, it is a dog.' When a man has seen a picture for the first time, his book education has begun."

Mrs. Donald Fraser, who taught health care to Africans in the 1920's, had similar experiences. This is her description of an African woman slowly discovering that a picture she was looking at portrayed a human head in profile: "She discovered in turn the nose, the mouth, the eye, but where was the other eye? I tried by turning my profile to explain why she could only see one eye but she hopped round to my other side to point out that I possessed a second eye which the other lacked."

There were also, however, reports of vivid and instant responses to pictures: "When all the people were quickly seated, the first picture flashed on the sheet was that of an elephant. The wildest excitement immediately prevailed, many of the people jumping up and shouting, fearing the beast must be alive, while those nearest to the sheet sprang up and fled. The chief himself crept stealthily forward and peeped behind the sheet to see if the animal had a body, and when he discovered that the animal's body was only the thickness of the sheet, a great roar broke the stillness of the night."

Thus the evidence gleaned from the insightful but unsystematic observations quoted is ambiguous. The laborious way some of these Africans pieced together a picture suggests that some form of learning is required to recognize pictures. Inability to perceive that a pattern of lines and shaded areas on a flat surface represents a real object would render all pictorial material incomprehensible. All drawings would be perceived as being meaningless, abstract patterns until the viewer had learned to interpret and organize the symbolic elements. On the other hand, one could also argue that pictorial recognition is largely independent of learning, and that even people from cultures where pictorial materials are uncommon will recognize items in pictures, provided that the pictures show familiar objects. It has been shown that an unsophisticated adult African from a remote village is unlikely to choose the wrong toy animal when asked to match the toy to a picture of, say, a lion. Given a photograph of a kangaroo, however, he is likely to choose at random from the array of toys. Yet one can argue that this sample was not as culturally remote as those described above. It is therefore probably safer to assume that utter incomprehension of pictorial material may be observed only in extremely isolated human populations.

Conventions for depicting the spatial arrangement of three-dimensional ob-

PICTORIAL DEPTH PERCEPTION is tested by showing subjects a picture such as the top illustration on the opposite page. A correct interpretation is that the hunter is trying to spear the antelope, which is nearer to him than the elephant. An incorrect interpretation is that the elephant is nearer and is about to be speared. The picture contains two depth cues: overlapping objects and known size of objects. The bottom illustration depicts the man, elephant and antelope in true size ratios when all are the same distance from the observer.

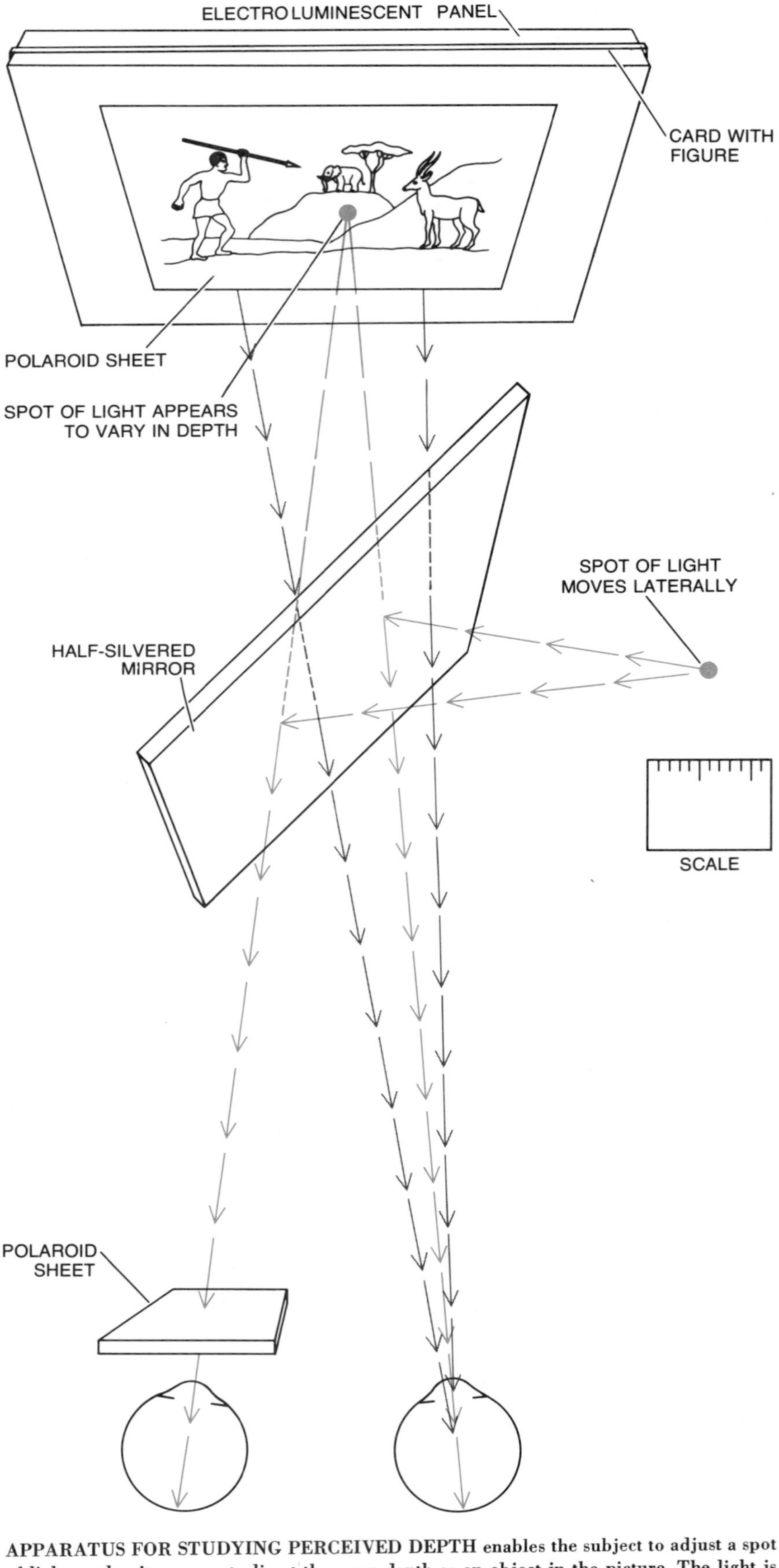

ELECTROLUMINESCENT PANEL

CARD WITH FIGURE

POLAROID SHEET

SPOT OF LIGHT APPEARS TO VARY IN DEPTH

SPOT OF LIGHT MOVES LATERALLY

HALF-SILVERED MIRROR

SCALE

POLAROID SHEET

APPARATUS FOR STUDYING PERCEIVED DEPTH enables the subject to adjust a spot of light so that it appears to lie at the same depth as an object in the picture. The light is seen stereoscopically with both eyes but the picture is seen with only one eye. Africans unfamiliar with pictorial depth cues set the light at the same depth on all parts of the picture.

jects in a flat picture can also give rise to difficulties in perception. These conventions give the observer depth cues that tell him the objects are not all the same distance from him. Inability to interpret such cues is bound to lead to misunderstanding of the meaning of the picture as a whole. William Hudson, who was then working at the National Institute for Personnel Research in Johannesburg, stumbled on such a difficulty in testing South African Bantu workers. His discovery led him to construct a pictorial perception test and to carry out much of the pioneering work in cross-cultural studies of perception.

Hudson's test consists of a series of pictures in which there are various combinations of three pictorial depth cues. The first cue is familiar size, which calls for the larger of two known objects to be drawn considerably smaller to indicate that it is farther away. The second cue is overlap, in which portions of nearer objects overlap and obscure portions of objects that are farther away; a hill is partly obscured by another hill that is closer to the viewer. The third cue is perspective, the convergence of lines known to be parallel to suggest distance; lines representing the edges of a road converge in the distance. In all but one of his tests Hudson omitted an entire group of powerful depth cues: density gradients. Density gradients are provided by any elements of uniform size: bricks in a wall or pebbles on a beach. The elements are drawn larger or smaller depending on whether they are nearer to the viewer or farther away from him.

Hudson's test has been applied in many parts of Africa with subjects drawn from a variety of tribal and linguistic groups. The subjects were shown one picture at a time and asked to name all the objects in the picture in order to determine whether or not the elements were correctly recognized. Then they were asked about the relation between the objects. (What is the man doing? What is closer to the man?) If the subject takes note of the depth cues and makes the "correct" interpretations, he is classified as having three-dimensional perception. If the depth cues are not taken into account by the subject, he is said to have two-dimensional perception [*see illustration on preceding page*]. The results from African tribal subjects were unequivocal: both children and adults found it difficult to perceive depth in the pictorial material. The difficulty varied in extent but appeared to persist through most educational and social levels.

Further experimentation revealed that the phenomenon was not simply the result of the pictorial material used in the test. Subjects were shown a drawing of two squares, one behind the other and connected by a single rod [*see top illustration at right*]. They were also given sticks and modeling clay and asked to build a model of what they saw. If Hudson's test is valid, people designated as two-dimensional perceivers should build flat models when they are shown the drawing, whereas those designated as three-dimensional perceivers should build a cubelike object. When primary-school boys and unskilled workers in Zambia were given Hudson's test and then asked to build models, a few of the subjects who had been classified as three-dimensional responders by the test made flat models. A substantial number of the subjects classified as two-dimensional perceivers built three-dimensional models. Thus Hudson's test, although it is more severe than the construction task, appears to measure the same variable.

The finding was checked in another experiment. A group of Zambian primary-school children were classified into three-dimensional and two-dimensional perceivers on the basis of the model-building test. They were then asked to copy a "two-pronged trident," a tantalizing drawing that confuses many people. The confusion is a direct result of attempting to interpret the drawing as a three-dimensional object [*see top illustration on next page*]. One would expect that those who are confused by the trident would find it difficult to recall and draw. The students actually made copies of two tridents: the ambiguous one and a control figure that had three simple prongs. To view the figure the student had to lift a flap, which actuated a timer that measured how long the flap was held up. The student could view the figure for as long as he wanted to, but he could not copy it while the flap was open. After the flap was closed the student had to wait 10 seconds before he began to draw. The delay was introduced to increase the difficulty of copying the figure. The results confirmed that the students who were three-dimensional perceivers spent more time looking at the ambiguous trident than at the control trident, whereas the two-dimensional perceivers did not differ significantly in the time spent viewing each of the two tridents.

Do people who perceive pictorial

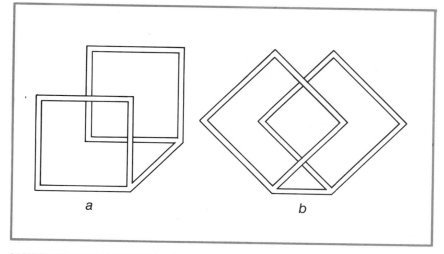

CONSTRUCTION-TASK FIGURES consist of two squares connected by a single rod. Most subjects from Western cultures see the figure *a* as a three-dimensional object, but when the figure is rotated 45 degrees (*right*), they see it as being flat. Subjects from African cultures are more likely to see both figures as being flat, with the two squares in the same plane.

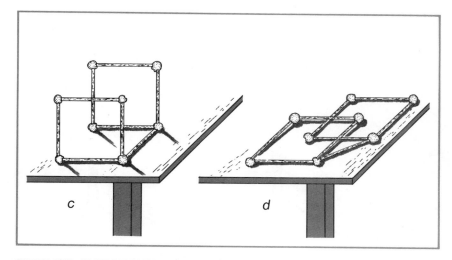

STICK-AND-CLAY MODELS of the figure *a* in the top illustration were made by test subjects. Almost all the three-dimensional perceivers built a three-dimensional object (*left*). Subjects who did not readily perceive depth in pictures tended to build a flat model (*right*).

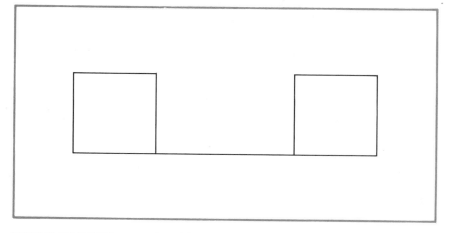

"SPLIT" DRAWING was preferred by two-dimensional perceivers when shown a model like figure *c* and given a choice between the split drawing and figure *a* in top illustration.

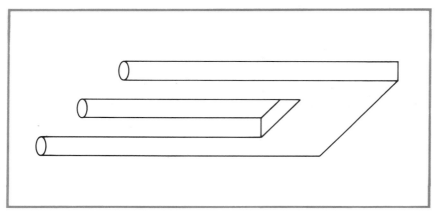

AMBIGUOUS TRIDENT is confusing to observers who attempt to see it as a three-dimensional object. Two-dimensional perceivers see the pattern as being flat and are not confused.

depth really see depth in the picture or are they merely interpreting symbolic depth cues in the same way that we learn to interpret the set of symbols in "horse" to mean a certain quadruped? An ingenious apparatus for studying perceived depth helped us to obtain an answer. This is how the apparatus is de-scribed by its designer, Richard L. Gregory of the University of Bristol:

"The figure is presented back-illuminated, to avoid texture, and it is viewed through a sheet of Polaroid. A second sheet of Polaroid is placed over one eye crossed with the first so that no light from the figure reaches this eye. Be-tween the eyes and the figure is a half-silvered mirror through which the figure is seen but which also reflects one or more small light sources mounted on an optical bench. These appear to lie in the figure; indeed, optically they *do* lie in the figure provided the path length of the lights to the eyes is the same as that of the figure to the eyes. But the small light sources are seen with both eyes while the figure is seen with only *one* eye because of the crossed Polaroids. By moving the lights along their optical bench, they may be placed so as to lie at the same distance as any selected part of the figure."

A Hudson-test picture that embodied both familiar-size and overlap depth cues was presented in the apparatus to a group of unskilled African workers, who for the most part do not show perception of pictorial depth in the Hudson test and in the construction test [*see illustration on page 216*]. The test picture showed a hunter and an antelope in the foreground and an elephant in the distance. The subjects set the movable light at the same apparent depth regardless of whether they were asked to place it above the hunter, the antelope or the elephant. In contrast, when three-dimensional perceivers were tested, they set the light farther away from themselves when placing it on the elephant than when setting it on the figures in the foreground. The result shows that they were not simply interpreting symbolic depth cues but were actually seeing depth in the picture.

When only familiar size was used as the depth cue, neither group of subjects placed the movable light farther back for the elephant. The result should not be surprising, since other studies have shown that familiar-size cues alone do not enable people even in Western cultures to see actual depth in a picture, even though they may interpret the picture three-dimensionally.

The fact that depth was seen in the picture only in the presence of overlap cues is of theoretical interest because it had been postulated that a perceptual mechanism for seeing depth cues where none are intended is responsible for certain geometric illusions, for example overestimating the length of the vertical limb of the letter *L*. If the mechanism is the same as the one for the perception of pictorial depth in Hudson's tests, then one would expect a decrease in the perception of geometric illusions in people who have low three-dimensional scores.

Do people who find pictures of the

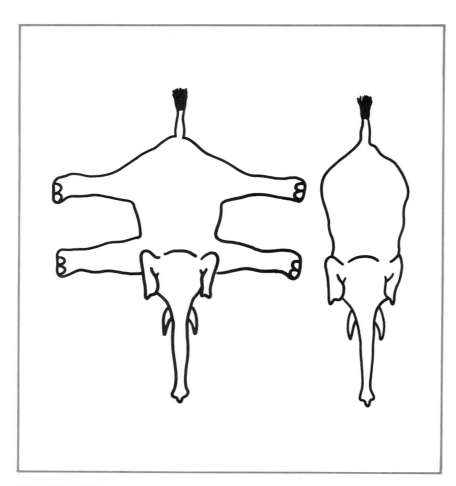

SPLIT-ELEPHANT DRAWING (*left*) was generally preferred by African children and adults to the top-view perspective drawing (*right*). One person, however, did not like the split drawing because he thought the elephant was jumping around in a dangerous manner.

perspective type difficult to interpret tend to prefer pictures that depict the essential characteristics of an object even if all those characteristics cannot be seen from a single viewpoint? Here again the first systematic cross-cultural observations were carried out by Hudson. He showed African children and adults pictures of an elephant. One view was like a photograph of an elephant seen from above; the other was a top view of an elephant with its legs unnaturally split to the sides. With only one exception all the subjects preferred the drawing of the split elephant [*see bottom illustration on opposite page*]. The one person who did not prefer the drawing said that it was because the elephant was jumping about dangerously.

Other studies have shown that preference for drawings of the split type is not confined to meaningful pictures but also applies to geometric representations. Unskilled Zambian workers were shown a wire model and were asked to make a drawing of it. Only an insignificant proportion of them drew a figure that had pictorial depth; most drew a flat figure of the split type [*see bottom illustration on page 217*]. They also preferred the split drawing when they were shown the model and were asked to choose between it and a perspective drawing. Then the process was reversed, and the subjects were asked to choose the appropriate wire model after looking at a drawing. Only a few chose the three-dimensional model after looking at the split drawing; instead they chose a flat wire model that resembled the drawing. Paradoxically the split drawing had proved to be less efficient than the less preferred perspective drawing when an actual object had to be identified.

Although preference for drawings of the split type has only recently been studied systematically, indications of such a preference have long been apparent in the artistic styles of certain cultures, for example the Indians of the northwestern coast of North America. Other instances of the split style in art are rock paintings in the caves of the Sahara and primitive art found in Siberia and New Zealand. What art historians often fail to note is that the style is universal. It can be found in the drawings of children in all cultures, even in those cultures where the style is considered manifestly wrong by adults.

Perspective drawings and drawings of the split type are not equally easy to interpret. Even industrial draftsmen with a great deal of experience in interpreting engineering drawings, which are essentially of the split type, find it more difficult to assemble simple models from engineering drawings than from perspective drawings.

One theory of the origin of the split style was put forward by the anthropologist Franz Boas. His hypothesis postulated the following sequence of events. Solid sculpture was gradually adapted to the ornamentation of objects such as boxes or bracelets. In order to make a box or a bracelet the artist had to reduce the sculpture to a surface pattern and include an opening in the solid form, so that when the sculptured object was flattened out, it became a picture of the split type. It is possible that this development led to the beginnings of split drawings and that the natural preference of the style ensured its acceptance. There is no historical evidence that this evolution actually took place, however, and it does seem that the hypothesis is unnecessarily complicated.

The anthropologist Claude Lévi-Strauss has proposed a theory in which the split style has social origins. According to him, split representation can be explored as a function of a sociological theory of split personality. This trait is common in "mask cultures," where privileges, emblems and degrees of prestige are displayed by means of elaborate masks. The use of these mask symbols apparently generates a great deal of per-

STYLIZED BEAR rendered by the Tsimshian Indians on the Pacific coast of British Columbia is an example of split drawing developed to a high artistic level. According to anthropologist Franz Boas, the drawings are ornamental and not intended to convey what an object looks like. The symbolic elements represent specific characteristics of the object.

sonality stress. Personalities are torn asunder, and this finds its reflection in split-style art.

Both Boas' and Lévi-Strauss's hypotheses ignore the universality of the phenomenon. If one accepts the existence of a fundamental identity of perceptual processes in all human beings and extrapolates from the data I have described, one is led to postulate the following. In all societies children have an aesthetic preference for drawings of the split type. In most societies this preference is suppressed because the drawings do not convey information about the depicted objects as accurately as perspective drawings do. Therefore aesthetic preference is sacrificed on the altar of efficiency in communication.

Some societies, however, have developed the split drawing to a high artistic level. This development occurs if the drawings are not regarded as a means of communication about objects or if the drawings incorporate cues that compensate for the loss of communication value due to the adoption of the split style. Both of these provisions are found in the art of the Indians of the Pacific Northwest. These pictures were intended to serve primarily as ornaments. They also incorporate symbolic elements that enable the viewer to interpret the artist's intention. Every such code, however, carries the penalty that communication is confined to people familiar with the code. Highly stylized art is not likely to be easily understood outside of its specific culture. Thus whereas the same psychological processes under the influence of different cultural forces may lead to widely different artistic styles, the styles arrived at are not equally efficient in conveying the correct description of objects and evoking the perception of pictorial depth.

What are the forces responsible for the lack of perception of pictorial depth in pictures drawn in accordance with the efficacious conventions of the West? At present we can only speculate. Perhaps the basic difficulty lies in the observers' inability to integrate the pictorial elements. They see individual symbols and cues but are incapable of linking all the elements into a consolidated whole. To the purely pragmatic question "Do drawings offer us a universal lingua franca?" a more precise answer is available. The answer is no. There are significant differences in the way pictures can be interpreted. The task of mapping out these differences in various cultures is only beginning.

The Object in the World of the Infant

by T. G. R. Bower
October 1971

*At what stage of development does an infant begin
to associate qualities such as solidity with objects
that he sees? Experiments with infants reveal that
this occurs much earlier than expected*

According to most traditional theories of how we come to perceive the world around us, the quality of solidity belongs to the sense of touch in the same way that the quality of color belongs to the sense of vision or the quality of pitch to the sense of hearing. Only the sense of touch has the intrinsic ability to distinguish solids from nonsolids. The ability to identify solid objects visually is the result of learning to associate visual clues with tactile impressions, or so the traditional arguments have asserted. The classic version of the theory was presented by Bishop Berkeley. It was espoused in the 19th century by Hermann von Helmholtz and more recently by J. McV. Hunt, Burton White and Richard L. Gregory.

If the ability to associate touch and sight is learned, then at what stage of human development does the learning occur? Since young children clearly exhibit a unity of the senses, such learning must take place at some early stage of infancy. The infant who has not yet made the association must therefore live in a world of clouds, smoke puffs and insubstantial images of objects rather than in a world of solid, stable objects.

A similar situation holds when we observe an object move behind another object and disappear from sight. An adult knows that the object is still there, that it has not ceased to exist. This can be verified simply by removing the obstructing object or looking around it. It is hard to understand how an infant could know that the object is still there by using vision alone; how can vision provide information about the location of an invisible object? Touch must play a critical role in the development of the ability to deal with hidden objects. The hand can go around obstacles to reach such objects, and only as a result of such

explorations can an infant come to know that the object is still there. So, again, goes the traditional argument, and very plausible it seems.

These aspects of objects—solidity and permanence—present deep problems to the student of human development. Not the least formidable of the problems is finding ways to measure a naïve infant's response to objects. The infant, with his limited repertory of responses, is a refractory subject for psychological investigation. Recent advances in techniques of studying space perception and pattern recognition in infants are inherently unsuitable. These methods mostly determine whether or not the infant discriminates between two presentations, for example a regular pattern and an irregular one. One could present a solid object and, say, a bounded air space with the same external contour to an infant. Undoubtedly an infant of any age could discriminate between the two objects. The mere fact of discrimination would not tell us that the infant knew the object was solid, tangible and would offer resistance to his touch. There are visual differences between solids and nonsolids, and the infant could pick up these differences without realizing that they signify solidity. Indeed, according to some theories there must be such a stage, where the infant does perceive differences but is not aware of their significance.

The methods I adopted to measure the infant's expectation of solidity involve the element of surprise and the use of an optical illusion. The illusion is produced with a binocular shadow-caster, a device consisting of two light projectors with polarizing filters and a rear-projection screen. The object, made of translucent plastic, is suspended be-

tween the lights and the screen so that it casts a double shadow on the rear of the screen. The small subject sits in front of the screen and views the shadows through polarizing goggles that have the effect of making only one shadow visible to each eye. The two retinal images are combined by the normal processes of binocular vision to yield a stereoscopic percept of the object. This virtual object appears in front of the screen and looks very real and solid. It is nonetheless an illusion and is therefore intangible. When the infant attempts to grasp it, his hand closes on empty air. To reach out for a seemingly solid object and come in contact with nothing is startling for anyone. The surprise clearly is a consequence of the nonfulfillment of the expectation that the seen object will be tangible.

Since even very young infants display the startle response, it can serve as an indicator of surprise. If the infant is startled by the absence of solidity in the virtual object, that can be taken as an index of an expectation that the seen object will be tangible. In contrast, a startle response on contact with the real object could be taken as an indication that the seen object is not expected to be tangible.

In the first experiment the infant sat before a screen and was presented with the virtual object or the real object. The two situations were presented several times, always beginning with the virtual object. We looked for evidence of startle behavior. The startle response can be measured in numerous ways, some of which are sophisticated and expensive, but in this experiment we used very simple indicators: facial expression and crying. These measures, so simple as to seem unscientific, are in fact as reliable as the more complex ones we used later.

Our subjects were infants between 16 and 24 weeks old. The results were quite unambiguous. None of the infants showed any sign of surprise when he touched the real object in front of him. Every infant showed marked surprise when his hand failed to make contact with the perceived virtual object. Whenever the infant's hand reached the place where the virtual object seemed to be, within a fraction of a second he emitted a coo, a whoop or a cry, accompanied by a change in facial expression so marked as to seem a caricature. The older infants reacted even more: they stared at their hand, rubbed their hands together or banged their hand on the chair before reaching again for the virtual object. All of this supports the idea that the infants expected to be able to touch a seen object and were very surprised when their attempts to do so produced no tactile feedback.

Although these results are interesting,

they do not resolve the problem under investigation. They merely indicate that learning to coordinate vision and touch must take place, if it takes place at all, before the age of 16 weeks. We therefore attempted to study coordination between vision and touch in even younger infants, hoping to find a period of noncoordination. The communication problem is intensified in very young infants, since their behavioral repertoire is even more limited than that of older infants.

Some investigators have reported that an infant less than six weeks old will not show defensive or avoidance behavior when an object approaches him. Other studies, however, have shown that an infant can discriminate changes in the position of objects in space well before the age of six weeks [see "The Visual World of Infants," by T. G. R. Bower; SCIENTIFIC AMERICAN Offprint 502]. The lack of defensive behavior

may indicate the absence of the expectation that the seen object would produce tactile consequences, and it seemed to us that the infant's response to approaching objects would be a promising area to investigate.

Our preliminary investigations were highly encouraging. We took infants in their second week of life, placed them on their back and moved objects toward their face. We used objects of a wide variety of sizes and a wide variety of speeds. Some objects were moved noisily, some silently. All of this was to no avail. The infants, more than 40 of them, did not even blink. These two-week-old infants certainly did not seem to expect a seen object to have tactile consequences. It appeared that we had indeed found a period when vision and touch were not coordinated.

At this point in the research I became aware of the work of Heinz Prechtl, who

INTANGIBLE OBJECT is produced by a shadow-caster, in which two oppositely polarized beams of light cast a double shadow of an object on a rear-projection screen. An infant views the double shadows through polarizing goggles that make a different shadow visible to each eye. The innate processes of stereopsis fuse the two images to make the infant think he is seeing a solid object in front of the screen. When the infant tries to grasp the virtual image, he is startled when his hand closes on empty air; within a fraction of a second he cries and his face expresses marked surprise. When a real object is placed in front of the screen, none of the infants show any signs of surprise when they touch it. These results indicate that the infants expect a seen object to be solid and tangible.

had gathered evidence that implied infants under two weeks old are never fully awake while they are lying on their back. Since one could not expect defensive behavior from infants who were half-asleep, we repeated the experiment with infants of the same age who were held in an upright or semiupright position. With this modification the results were totally different. The infants clearly showed a defensive response to an approaching object. They pulled their head back and put their hands between their face and the object. These responses were accompanied by distress and crying so intense that the experiment had to be terminated earlier than had been planned. We were nonetheless able to try a few variations. We found that the defensive behavior was specific to an approaching object; if an object moved away, it produced neither defensive behavior nor crying. Moreover, the response was specific to a seen object. A moving solid object displaces air, which presumably causes pressure changes at the surface of the skin. In order to rule out the possibility that such pressure changes were the effective stimulus, we had a group of infants view an approaching virtual object produced by a

shadow-caster. An object behind a translucent screen was moved away from the infant toward a projector. When the infant is placed at the same distance in front of the screen as the projectors are behind it, a shadow on the screen produces an image on the infant's retina that is identical with the image produced by a real object moving toward the baby, without the displacement of air and other nonvisual changes that accompany the movement of a real object.

The results were that seven out of seven infants in their second week of life exhibited defensive behavior when they saw the approaching virtual object. In our study the intensity of the infant's response to the virtual object seems somewhat less than the response to the real object, but a replication of the experiment by E. Tronick and C. Ball of Harvard University showed that the two responses are not that different. As a further check on the role of air movement another group of infants was presented with air displacement alone (produced by an air hose) with no object in the field of vision. None of these infants exhibited any defensive behavior or marked distress.

Taken together, these results suggest

that by the second week of life an infant expects a seen object to have tactile consequences. The precocity of this expectation is quite surprising from the traditional point of view. Indeed, it seems to me that these findings are fatal to traditional theories of human development. In our culture it is unlikely that an infant less than two weeks old has been hit in the face by an approaching object, so that none of the infants in the study could have been exposed to situations where they could have learned to fear an approaching object and expect it to have tactile qualities. We can only conclude that in man there is a primitive unity of the senses, with visual variables specifying tactile consequences, and that this primitive unity is built into the structure of the human nervous system.

In an effort to further test this hypothesis we repeated the original virtual-object experiment with a group of newborn infants. It was not easy to do this, since the infants had to meet the criterion that they would wear the polarizing goggles without fussing. Newborn infants do not reach for objects in the same way that older infants do. They will, however, reach out and grasp ob-

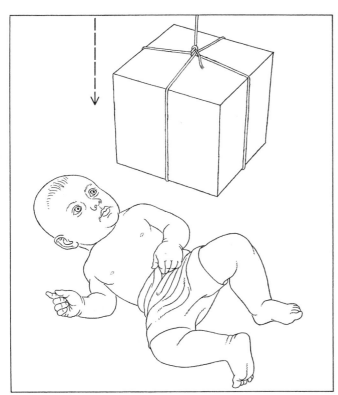

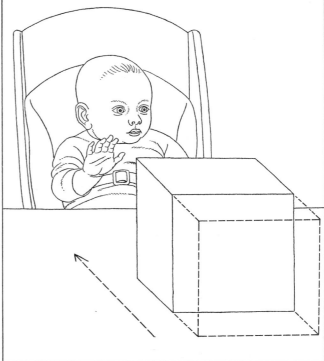

NO RESPONSE was observed when objects were moved toward the face of two-week-old infants who were lying on their back. At first this was taken to mean that infants at this age do not expect seen objects to have tactile qualities, but the author learned later that very young infants are never fully awake when on their back.

DEFENSIVE RESPONSE and marked distress to an approaching object was exhibited by upright two-week-old infants, even when the approaching object was an illusion produced by a shadow-caster. This evidence contradicts the theory that the perception of solidity is learned by associating tactile impressions and vision.

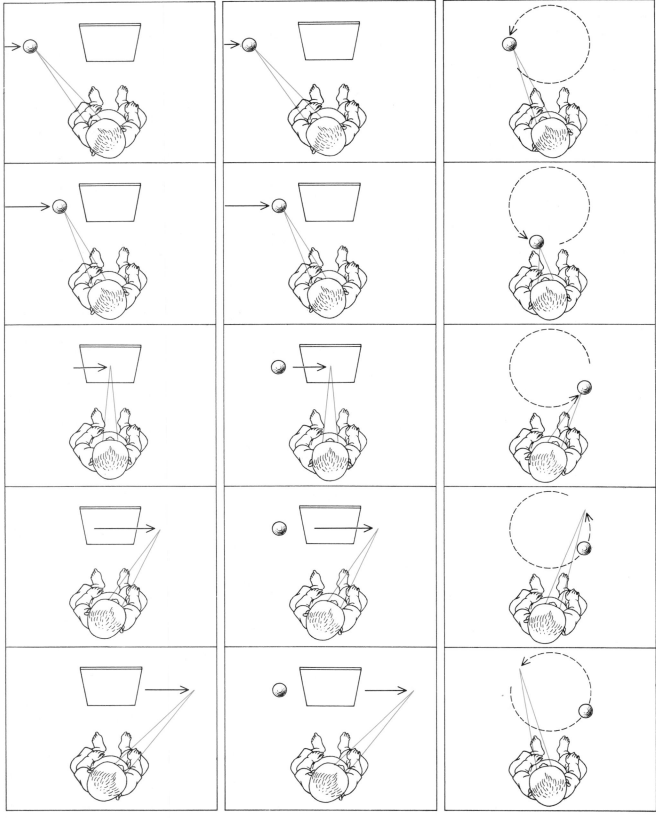

INFANT'S ANTICIPATION of the reappearance of an object that moves behind a screen and stops (*left*) seems to prove that the infant knew the object was still behind the screen. When the object stops before it reaches the screen, however, the infant continues to track the path of motion as if he could not arrest his head movement (*middle*). Next the infant was shown an object moving in a circle. If inability to arrest head movement were responsible for the continuation of tracking, then when the object stops halfway up the arc (*right*), the infant's gaze should continue tangentially to the circular path. Instead the infant's gaze paused on the stopped object for half a second and then continued along the circular path. It seems that the eight- and 16-week-old infants did not identify an object as being the same object when it was moving and when it was stationary and so they continued to look for the moving object.

jects if they are supported so that their hands and arms are free to move to the objects in front of them. (They also reach out and grasp at empty air, but that does not affect the argument.)

We found that all the newborn infants touched and grasped real objects without any sign of being disturbed. The virtual object, however, produced a howl as soon as the infant's hand went to the intangible object's location. Here too, then, in dealing with the absence of tactile input in a situation where it normally would be expected, we have evidence of a primitive unity of the senses. This unity is unlikely to have been learned, given the early age and the history of the infants studied.

These results were surprising and interesting. They showed that at least one aspect of the eye-and-hand interaction is built into the nervous system. If it is built in, might not a more complex aspect of objects, namely permanence, also be built in? Is it possible that inborn structural properties ensure that an infant knows an object moving out of sight behind another object is still there? In order to find out we again used the startle response as an indicator of surprise. We sat an infant in front of an object. A screen moved in from one side and covered the object. After various intervals (1.5, 3, 7.5 or 15 seconds) the screen moved away. In half of the trials the object was still there when the screen moved away. In the other trials the object was no longer there when the screen moved away. If the infant knew that the object was still there behind the screen, its absence when the screen moved away should have surprised him. If, on the other hand, the infant thought the object had ceased to exist when it was covered by the screen, its reappearance when the screen moved away should have been surprising.

In this experiment surprise was determined by a more quantitative index: a change in the heart rate. It is well known that the heart rate of an adult changes when he is surprised, and the same is true of infants. We measured the change in the heart rate of an infant by comparing his average heart rate over the 10 seconds after the moment of revelation with the average heart rate over the 10 seconds before the object was covered with the screen. Our subjects were infants who were 20, 40, 80 and 100 days old.

The results revealed an interesting pattern. When the object had been occluded for 1.5 seconds, all the infants manifested greater surprise at its nonreappearance than at its reappearance.

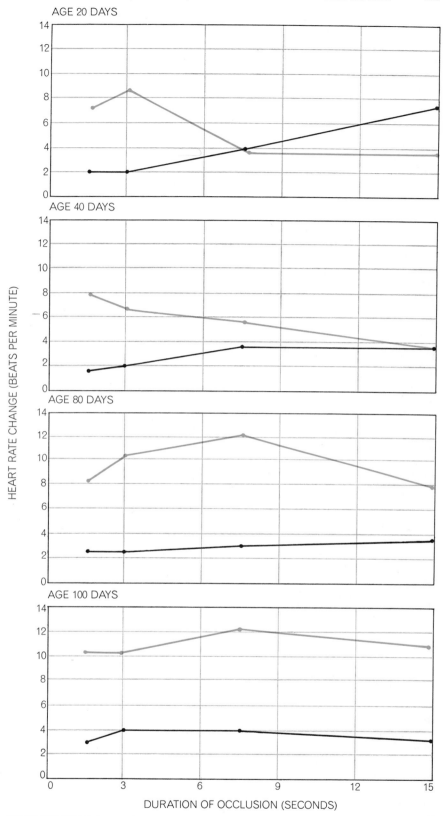

CHANGES IN HEART RATE reveal the degree of surprise in infants at the reappearance or disappearance of an object after it has been covered by a moving screen for various periods of time. Older infants are not surprised at the reappearance (**black curves**) of the object when the screen moves on, regardless of the duration of occlusion, and show little change in their heart rate. They are surprised when the object does not reappear (**colored curves**) from behind the moving screen. The youngest infants also are surprised by the object's failure to reappear when the occluding period is brief; when the time is increased to 15 seconds, they seem to forget about the object and show surprise at its reappearance.

In short, they expected the object to still be there. When the object failed to reappear, the change in the heart rate was about seven beats per minute; when the object did reappear, the change was very slight.

The oldest infants expected the object to reappear even after the longest occlusion period; when the object did not reappear, the change in their heart rate was 11 beats per minute. Curiously, the youngest infants exhibited a reverse effect after the longest occlusion period. They showed more surprise at the object's reappearance than at its nonreappearance. It seems that even very young infants know that an object is still there after it has been hidden, but if the time of occlusion is prolonged, they forget the object altogether. The early age of the infants and the novelty of the testing situation make it unlikely that such a response has been learned.

If object permanence is a built-in property of the nervous system, then it should show up in other situations. If the object was moved behind a stationary screen instead of the screen's moving to cover a stationary object, the same neural process should inform the infant that the object was behind the screen. We tested this assumption by having an eight-week-old infant watch an object that could be moved from side to side in front of him. A screen hid the center segment of the object's path. We reasoned that if the infant knew that the object had gone behind the screen rather than disappearing into some kind of limbo, he should be able to anticipate its reappearance on the other side of the screen. On the other hand, if the infant did not know that the object was behind the screen, he should not look over to the place where it would reappear; his eye movement should be arrested at the point of disappearance.

Two television cameras were lined up with the infant's face in order to record what side of the screen the infant was looking at. In the first part of the experiment the object would begin at one side, move slowly toward the screen, go behind it, emerge and continue to move for some distance. Then on random trials the object stopped behind the screen. Would such eight-week-old infants look over to the side where the object was due to emerge, or would they halt their gaze at the point of disappearance? The answer was quite straightforward: all the infants anticipated the reappearance of the object. Their behavior supported the hypothesis that a built-in neural process had informed them the object was behind the screen.

Unfortunately this result might have been an artifact of the experiment. Perhaps the infant following the object could not stop the movement of his head and the movement simply continued after it had begun. In order to test this possibility we ran a comparison series of experiments in which the object stopped in full view before it reached the screen. We reasoned that if the infant's apparent anticipation of the object's reappearance had been the result of the continuing movement of his head, the movement should continue after the object had stopped. On the other hand, if the infant had been genuinely anticipating the reappearance of the object, he would not look at the other side of the screen for an object he had just seen stop before reaching the screen. To our great disappointment the infants all looked over to the other side of the screen. This result seemed to rule out the hypothesis that eight-week-old infants seeing an object go behind a screen know that the object is still there and will reappear. Further studies indicated that infants up to 16 weeks old also were likely to look for the object to reappear in both experimental situations.

The inability to arrest head movement is an intrinsically unsatisfying explanation, particularly since it does not explain the results from the experiment with the stationary object and the moving screen. We therefore tried a variety of other experiments. In one test infants were presented with an object that moved in a circular trajectory at right angles to their line of sight. After a time the object stopped in full view at a point halfway up the arc. If the continuation of tracking was the result of an inability to arrest ongoing movement, a pause in the object's movement on a circular path should have produced head movements tangential to the path. Every infant, however, continued to look along the circular trajectory. Furthermore, frame-by-frame analysis of motion pictures of the head movements and eye movements revealed that the infant's fixation on the object was held for about half a second before the tracking movement continued. This bizarre behavior, continuing to track a moving object after seeing it stop, cannot be the result of an inability to arrest head movement. Every infant was able to momentarily hold his gaze on the object when it stopped. Therefore the infants must at least have noticed that the object had stopped. Yet they continued to track the path the object would have taken had it continued to move.

The explanation of this behavior was not, and is not, obvious. Superficially the infant's behavior appears to reflect an inability to identify a stationary object with the same object when it is moving. It was as if the infants had been tracking a moving object, had noticed the stationary object that the moving object had become, had looked at it for a while and then had looked farther on to find the moving object again. It seems that they had not been aware that the stationary object was in fact the same as the moving object.

Could the converse be true? Would infants look for an object in the place where it had been stationary after seeing it move off to a new location? In order to find out we seated an infant in front of a toy railroad track that had a train on it. The train carried flashing lights to attract the infant's attention. At the beginning of the experiment the train was stationary in the middle of the track. After 10 seconds the train moved slowly to the left and stopped at a new position, where it remained for 10 seconds, and then returned to its original position. The cycle was repeated 10 times.

How would this simple to-and-fro movement be seen by a three-month-old infant? Our hypothesis was that an infant of this age fails to recognize the identity of a moving object and the same object standing still. Initially the infant should see a stationary object in a particular place. Then the object would disappear and a new moving object would appear. Then the moving object would disappear and a stationary object would appear in a new place. After a time that too would disappear and a new moving object would appear, which in turn would give way to the original object in the original place again. To the infant the cycle would seem to involve perhaps four objects, whereas in reality there is only one. An infant quickly learns to look from one place to another as an object moves between them. If our hypothesis is correct, the infant is not following an object from place to place; rather he is applying a rule in the form, "Object disappears at A, object will reappear at B."

Suppose now that after the 10th cycle the train moves to the right to an entirely new position instead of moving to the left as usual. A subject who was following a single object would have no trouble. If an infant is applying the rule above, he should make an error. Specifically, when the stationary object moves to the right for the first time, thereby disappearing at the middle, the infant should look for the stationary object to the left in the place where it has reappeared before. When we tested three-month-old infants, every infant made the error predicted by our hypothesis. That is, when the train moved to the right, the infant looked to the left and

stared at the empty space where the train had stopped before. Meanwhile the train with its flashing lights was in full view in its new place to the right.

This last result, together with those from our earlier studies, confirms the hypothesis that three-month-old infants do not recognize the identity of an object at a standstill and the same object in motion, and vice versa. Note that I am using "identity" in a rather special

sense, meaning to recognize an object as being the same object rather than another identical object. If an infant does not identify a stationary object with a moving object when they are the same object, how does he identify a stationary object with itself when it is stationary in the same place later? How does he identify a moving object with itself when it is moving along a continuous trajectory? We began a new series of experiments to answer this fundamental question. The most obvious features of an object are its size, shape and color. These seem to serve as identification elements for adults. For an infant their role would seem to be somewhat different.

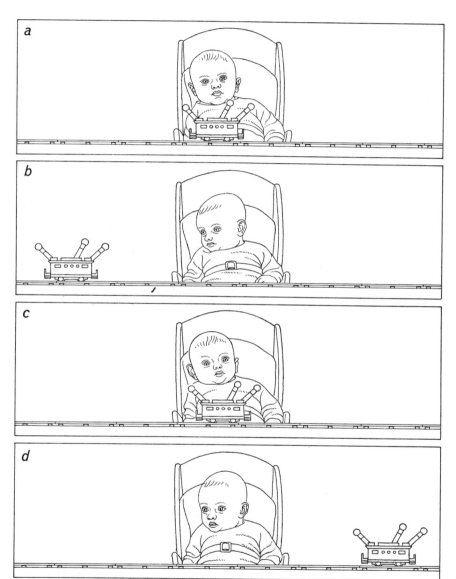

DISAPPEARING TRAIN confirms the hypothesis that infants 12 weeks old do not watch a single object when the object is at first stationary, then moves and stops. They do not follow the moving object from place to place but rather apply a cognitive rule that can be stated: "Object disappears at A; object reappears at B." In the experimental test the infant sat watching a toy train with flashing lights at rest in the middle of the track (a). After 10 seconds the train moved to the left and stopped (b) and remained there for 10 seconds before returning to the center again. The cycle was repeated 10 times. On the next cycle (c, d) the train moved slowly to the right and stopped. If the infant had been following the moving object, he would have looked to the right, but if he had been following the hypothesized cognitive rule, he would have looked to the left in the place where the train had stopped before. Every 12-week-old infant tested made the error predicted by the hypothesis.

We presented infants with four situations: (1) An object (a small white mannikin) moved along a track, went behind a screen, emerged on the other side, moved on for a short distance, stopped and then returned to its original position. (2) The object moved along the track, went behind a screen and at the moment when the object should have emerged on the other side of the screen a totally different object (a stylized red lion) emerged, moved on for a short distance before reversing and repeating the entire cycle in the opposite direction. In this sequence there were differences of size, shape and color between the two objects, but there was only one kind of movement in any one direction. (3) The object moved along a track as before, except that at a time when, according to its speed before occlusion, it should still have been behind the screen, an identical object moved out. Here the objects were identical but there were two kinds of movement and evidence that there were two different objects since a single object could not have moved quickly enough to get across the screen in such a short time. (4) The object moved along a track as before, and at a time when it still should have been behind the screen a totally different object moved out. Here there were two kinds of difference in movement and features to indicate that there were two different objects. In all the situations only one object was visible at a time.

We conducted the experiment with groups of infants between six and 22 weeks old. The older infants tracked the moving object in Situation 1 quite happily; when the object stopped, they stopped tracking it. In Situation 2, where a different object emerged, they also followed the object in motion, although some glancing back and forth between

MOVEMENT AND FEATURES mean different things in the perceptual worlds of young and older infants. Infants less than 16 weeks old tracked a moving object (*left*) until it went behind a screen and anticipated its reappearance; when a different object emerged, they continued to track its motion with no sign of surprise. Older infants also tracked the object in motion when a different object emerged from behind the screen (*right*), but when the object stopped, the older infants often glanced to the other side of the screen as if they were looking for the first object. This indicates that the younger infants do not respond to moving objects but to movements, and not to stationary objects but to places. Older infants have learned to recognize an object by its features rather than by its place or movement.

the sides of the screen was noticeable. When the object stopped, at least 25 percent of the time they looked to the other side of the screen as if they were looking for the object that had disappeared. Their responses in Situation 3 and Situation 4 were similar, with the difference that when the object stopped, on every trial the infants looked to the other half of the track in apparent anticipation of the appearance of the other object.

Infants less than 16 weeks old showed a complete contrast in behavior. In Situation 1 they followed the moving object with no sign of being disturbed. When the object stopped, they continued to follow its path of movement. In Situation 2, when a different object emerged, they also continued to track it with no sign of being disturbed. When the object stopped, they continued to track it. In Situation 3, however, where the object came out from behind the screen sooner than it should have, they were upset and refused to look any more. They also refused to look in Situation 4. In both cases when the object stopped, the infants did not continue to follow its path as they had in the first two situations. This was largely due to their refusal to track at all.

These results show that younger infants are not affected by feature differences. For them movement is predominant. They respond to a change in motion but not to a change in size, shape or color. They ignore features to such an extent that I would suggest they respond not to moving objects but to movements. Similarly, I would suggest that they respond not to stationary objects but to places. In contrast, older infants have learned to define an object as something that can go from place to place along pathways of movement. They identify an object by its features rather than by its place or movement. For them different features imply different objects that can move independently, so that the stopping of one does not imply the stopping of the other.

This attainment is obviously one of tremendous significance. It transforms the perceptual world of the infant at one stroke into something very close to the perceptual world of the adult. According to these studies it seems that infants less than 16 weeks old live in a world articulated in terms of solids that are stably arranged in space according to their location, with a constancy of existence when they occlude one another. It is, however, a grossly overpopulated world. An object becomes a different object as soon as it moves to a new location. In this world every object is unique. The infant must cope with a large number of objects when only one is really there.

In the last experiment I shall describe infants sat in front of an arrangement of mirrors that produced two or three images of a person. In some instances the infant was presented with two or three images of his mother; in others he would see his mother and one or two strangers who were seated so that they were in a position identical with the earlier additional images of his mother.

In the multiple-mother presentation infants less than 20 weeks old happily responded with smiles, coos and arm-waving to each mother in turn. In the mother-stranger presentation the infants were also quite happy and interacted with their mother, and they normally ignored the strangers. This demonstrates that young infants can recognize features in recognizing their mother, but they recognize the mother as one of many identical mothers. They do not recognize the identity of the multi-

ple mothers in the special sense in which I have used the word "identity," that is, they do not identify the multiple images of the mother as belonging to one and the same person.

Infants more than 20 weeks old also ignored the strangers and interacted with their mothers. In the multiple-mother situation, however, the older infants became quite upset at the sight of more than one mother. This shows, I would argue, that the younger infants do identify objects with places and hence think they have a multiplicity of mothers. Because the older infants identify objects by features, they know that they have only one mother, and this is why they are upset by the sight of multiple mothers.

The discovery of the object concept must simplify the world of the infant more than almost any subsequent intellectual advance. Two pressing questions arise from this research. We do not know why the object concept must be discovered rather than being built into the neural system (as so many other kinds of perceptual knowledge are), nor

do we know how the discovery is made. There are indications that built-in analyzers are limited to the initial input areas of the brain and their cross-connections. It is known that place and movement are separately coded in the visual system. Moreover, errors of the kind made by young infants persist in adults in some form. The late Baron Albert Michotte of the University of Louvain found that adults who are shown an impossible sequence such as the one described in Situation 3, where an object reappears from behind the screen sooner than it should, will say something like, "It looks as if it is the same object, but I know. . . ." This kind of response indicates that the infant's error persists in the adult's perceptual system and is overcome by a cognitive rule. We do know that particular environments can speed or slow the acquisition of such conceptual behavior. In line with this fact there is evidence that nonhuman primates never overcome perceptual errors and remain much like the young infants we studied. The object concept may thus be outside the limits of intrinsic neural specification.

MULTIPLE MOTHERS were presented to infants by an arrangement of mirrors. In other instances the infant would see his mother and two unfamiliar women seated in the same position as the mirror images of the mother. Infants less than 20 weeks old waved their arms, smiled and called to each of the mother images in turn. Older infants, however, became quite disturbed by the sight of more than one mother. All the infants ignored the strangers and interacted only with the mother. It seems that the younger infants think they have a multiplicity of mothers because they identify objects with places. Older infants identify objects by features and know they have only one mother. Learning to identify objects by features is one of the major intellectual advances made by infants.

23

The Functional Organization of the Brain

A. R. Luria
March 1970

The sensory and motor functions of the human brain are well localized, but more complex functions such as speech and writing remain obscure. Injuries to the brain provide clues to how such systems are organized

The functional organization of the human brain is a problem that is far from solved. I shall describe in this article some recent advances in the mapping of the brain. They open up a new field of exploration having to do with the structures of the brain involved in complex forms of behavior.

So far as sensory and motor functions are concerned, the brain, as is well known, has been mapped in precise detail. Studies by neurologists and psychologists over the past century have defined the centers that are responsible for some elementary functions such as seeing, hearing, other sensory functions and the control of the various muscular systems of the body. From outward symptoms or simple tests disclosing a disturbance of one of these functions it is possible to deduce the location of the lesion (a tumor or a hemorrhage, for example) causing the disturbance. Such a finding is of major importance in neurology and neurosurgery. The sensory and motor centers, however, account for only a small part of the area of the cerebral cortex. At least three-quarters of the cortex has nothing to do with sensory functions or muscle actions. In order to proceed further with the mapping of the brain's functions we must look into the systems responsible for the higher, more complex behavioral processes.

It is obvious that these processes, being social in origin and highly complex in structure and involving the elaboration and storage of information and the programming and control of actions, are not localized in particular centers of the brain. Plainly they must be managed by an elaborate apparatus consisting of various brain structures. Modern psychological investigations have made it clear that each behavioral process is a complex functional system based on a plan or program of operations that leads to a definite goal. The system is self-regulating: the brain judges the result of every action in relation to the basic plan and calls an end to the activity when it arrives at a successful completion of the program. This mechanism is equally applicable to elementary, involuntary forms of behavior such as breathing and walking and to complicated, voluntary ones such as reading, writing, decision-making and problem-solving.

What is the organizational form of this system in the brain? Our present knowledge of neurology indicates that the apparatus directing a complex behavioral process comprises a number of brain structures, each playing a highly specific role and all under coordinated control. One should therefore expect that lesions of the structures involved might result in changes in the behavior, and that the nature of the change would vary according to the particular structure that is damaged.

A New Approach

This concept forms the basis of our new approach to exploration of the functional organization of the brain—a study we call neuropsychology. The study has two objectives. First, by pinpointing the brain lesions responsible for specific behavioral disorders we hope to develop a means of early diagnosis and precise location of brain injuries (including those from tumors or from hemorrhage) so that they can be treated by surgery as soon as possible. Second, neuropsychological investigation should provide us with a factor analysis that will lead to better understanding of the components of complex psychological functions for which the operations of the different parts of the brain are responsible.

The human brain can be considered to be made up of three main blocks incorporating basic functions. Let us examine the responsibilities of each block in turn.

The first block regulates the energy level and tone of the cortex, providing it with a stable basis for the organization of its various processes. The brilliant researches of Horace W. Magoun, Giuseppe Moruzzi, Herbert H. Jasper and Donald B. Lindsley located the components of the first block in the upper and lower parts of the brain stem and particularly in the reticular formation, which controls wakefulness. If an injury occurs in some part of the first block, the cortex goes into a pathological state: the stability of its dynamic processes breaks down, there is a marked deterioration of wakefulness and memory traces become disorganized.

I. P. Pavlov observed that when the normal tone of the cortex is lowered, the "law of force" is lost and much of the brain's ability to discriminate among stimuli suffers. Normally the cortex reacts powerfully to strong or significant stimuli and responds hardly at all to feeble or insignificant stimuli, which are easily suppressed. A weakened cortex, on the other hand, has about the same response to insignificant stimuli as to significant ones, and in an extremely weakened state it may react even more strongly to weak stimuli than to strong ones. We all know about this loss of the brain's selectivity from common experience. Recall how diffuse and disorganized our thoughts become when we are drowsy, and what bizarre associations the mind may form in a state of fatigue or in dreams.

Obviously the results of injury to the first block in the brain, namely the loss of the selectivity of cortical actions and of normal discrimination of stimuli, will bring about marked changes in behavior. The control of behavior becomes deranged. In our common work with Macdonald Critchley of England such disturbances have been observed in patients who had tumors of the middle parts of the frontal lobes, and other investigators in our laboratory in Moscow have since reported similar effects from lesions in deep parts of the brain.

The Second Block

The second block of the brain has received much more study, and its role in the organization of behavior is better known. Located in the rear parts of the cortex, it plays a decisive role in the analysis, coding and storage of information. In contrast to the functions of the first block, which are mainly of a general nature (for example controlling wakefulness), the systems of the second block have highly specific assignments.

We can easily identify areas in the second block that are respectively responsible for the analysis of optic, acoustic, cutaneous and kinesthetic stimuli. Each of these cortical areas has a hierarchical organization: a primary zone that sorts and records the sensory information, a secondary zone that organizes the information further and codes it and a tertiary zone where the data from different sources overlap and are combined to lay the groundwork for the organization of behavior.

Injuries to the parts of the second block produce much more specific effects than lesions in the first block do. An injury in a primary zone of the second block results in a sensory defect (in seeing or hearing, for example); it does not, however, bring about a marked change in complex forms of behavior. A lesion

in a secondary zone produces more complicated disturbances. It interferes with analysis of the sensory stimuli the zone receives and, because the coding function is impaired, the lesion leads to disorganization of all the behavioral processes that would normally respond to these particular stimuli. It does not disturb any other behavioral processes, however, which is an important aid for locating the lesion.

Of the various lesions in the second block of the brain those in the tertiary zones are particularly interesting to us as neuropsychologists. Since these zones are responsible for the synthesis of a collection of information inputs from different sources into a coherent whole, a lesion of a tertiary zone can cause such complex disturbances as visual disorientation in space. The lesion seriously im-

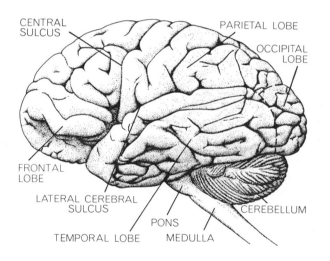

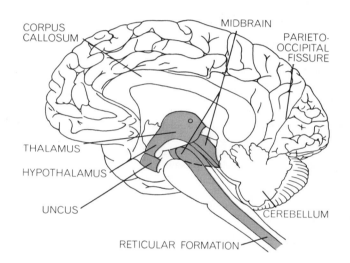

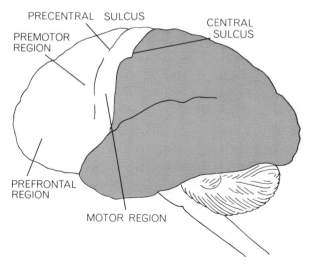

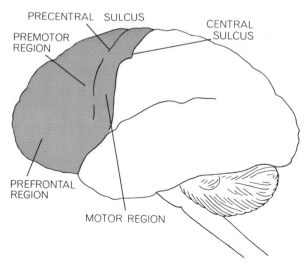

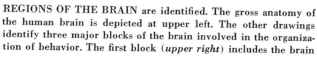

REGIONS OF THE BRAIN are identified. The gross anatomy of the human brain is depicted at upper left. The other drawings identify three major blocks of the brain involved in the organization of behavior. The first block (*upper right*) includes the brain stem and the old cortex. It regulates wakefulness and the response to stimuli. The second block (*lower left*) plays a key role in the analysis, coding and storage of information. The third block (*lower right*) is involved in the formation of intentions and programs.

pairs the ability to handle complex problems that entail an organization of input in simultaneous matrixes. That is why these lesions may render a person incapable of performing complex operations with numbers or of coping with a complexity in grammar logic or language structure.

The Third Block

The third block of the brain, comprising the frontal lobes, is involved in the formation of intentions and programs for behavior. Important contributions to elucidation of the functions of the frontal lobes have been made by S. I. Franz, L. Bianchi, Karl H. Pribram and Jerzy Konorski through studies of animals and by V. M. Bekhterev, C. Kleist and Derek E. Denny-Brown through clinical observations. We have devoted much study to the roles of the third block in our laboratory.

The frontal lobes perform no sensory or motor functions; sensation, movement, perception, speech and similar processes remain entirely unimpaired even after severe injury to these lobes. Nevertheless, the frontal lobes of the human brain are by no means silent. Our findings make it clear that they participate to a highly important degree in every complex behavioral process.

Intimately connected with the brain stem, including its reticular formation, the frontal lobes serve primarily to activate the brain. They regulate attention and concentration. W. Grey Walter showed a number of years ago that the activity of the brain could be measured by the appearance of certain slow brain waves in an electroencephalogram; these waves are evoked when a subject is stimulated to active expectancy and disappear when the subject's attention is exhausted [see "The Electrical Activity of the Brain," by W. Grey Walter; SCIENTIFIC AMERICAN Offprint 73]. At about the same time M. N. Livanov, a Russian investigator, found that mental activity is signaled by a complex of electrical excitations in the frontal cortex and that these excitations disappear when the subject subsides to a passive state or is lulled with tranquilizers.

Functional Systems

Now that we have reviewed the functions of the brain's basic blocks, let us see what we can learn about the location of specific parts of the various functional systems. It is clear that every complex form of behavior depends on the joint operation of several faculties located in different zones of the brain. A disturbance of any one faculty will affect the behavior, but each failure of a specific factor presumably will change the behavior in a different way. We have explored these effects in detail with a number of psychological experiments.

To illustrate our findings I shall discuss the results of a neuropsychological analysis of two processes. One is voluntary movement; the other is speech and in particular one of its forms, namely writing.

It was long supposed that voluntary movements are a function of the motor cortex, that is, the large pyramidal cells of the cortex of the anterior convolution of the brain. These cells, discovered by the Russian anatomist V. A. Betz more than 100 years ago, have exceptionally long axons that conduct the excitation toward the roots of the spinal cord. Impulses from these cells result in the constriction of muscles and are supposed to be the neurophysiological basis of voluntary movement.

Up to a certain point this is true, but the mechanism of the formation of a voluntary movement is much more complicated. To think that a voluntary action is formed in the narrow field of the motor cortex would be a mistake similar to an assumption that all the goods exported through a terminal are produced in the terminal. The system of cortical zones participating in the creation of a voluntary movement includes a complex of subcortical and cortical zones, each playing a highly specific role in the whole functional system. That is why lesions of different parts of the brain can result in the disturbance of different voluntary movements.

Let us examine the components of voluntary movement and see how it is affected differently by lesions in different parts of the brain. The first component is a precisely organized system of afferent (sensory) signals. The Russian physiologist N. A. Bernstein has shown in a series of studies that it is impossible to regulate a voluntary movement only by way of efferent impulses from the brain to the muscles. At every moment of the movement the position of the limb is different, and so is the density of the muscles. The brain has to receive feedback from the muscles and joints to correct the program of impulses directed to the motor apparatus. One can recognize the nature of the problem by recalling how difficult it is to start a leg movement if

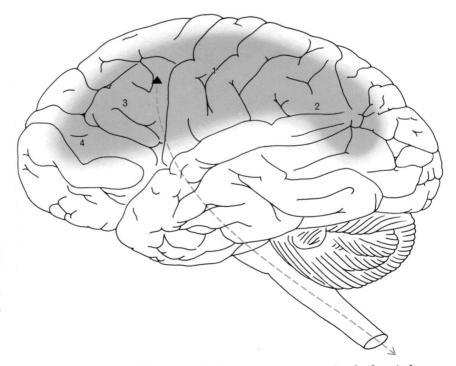

VOLUNTARY MOVEMENT is controlled by a complex of cortical and subcortical zones. The classical theory was that voluntary movement originated with the large pyramidal cells (*arrowhead*) of the cortex; they have long axons that conduct impulses to the spinal cord. It is now known that other zones participating in voluntary movement are the postcentral zone (*1*), which deals with sensory feedback from the muscles; the parieto-occipital zone (*2*), which is involved in the spatial orientation of movement; the premotor zone (*3*), which deals with the separate links of motor behavior, and the frontal zone (*4*), which programs movements. Lesions in different zones give rise to different behavioral aberrations.

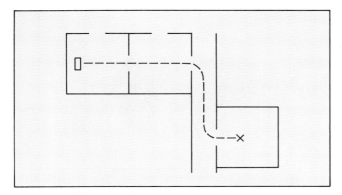

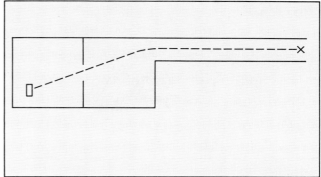

SPATIAL DISORGANIZATION is evident in a patient who had a gunshot wound of the right parieto-occipital part of the brain. The patient was asked to depict the layout of his hospital ward. His visualization is at right and the actual layout of the ward is at left.

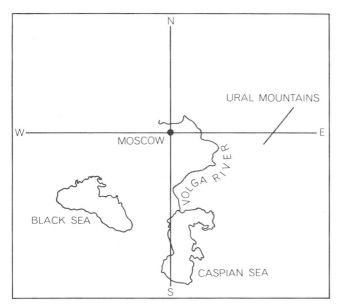

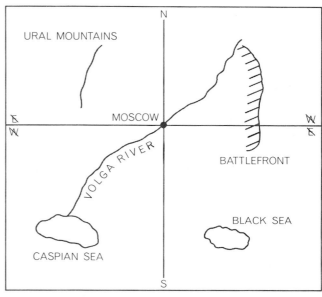

CONFUSION OVER DIRECTIONS was manifested by another patient with a gunshot wound of the right parieto-occipital zone. He was asked to draw a map of the region of the U.S.S.R. where he had been involved in fighting during World War II. The actual geographical relations are shown at left; the patient's view is at right. The line of battle represented on his map was in fact west of Moscow. In addition to reversing most of the locations, the patient could not make up his mind on the labeling of east and west.

the leg has become numb. This sensory or proprioceptive base is provided by a special part of the brain: the postcentral sensory cortex. If this part of the cortex is destroyed by a wound or other injury, the patient not only loses sensation in the limb but also is unable to fulfill a well-organized voluntary movement.

One of our co-workers has studied the physiological mechanism of such a disturbance and has shown that in lesions of the sensory part of the cortex every voluntary impulse loses its specific "address" and arrives equally at all muscles, both flexors and extensors. No organized movement can be elicited in such conditions. That is why neurologists have called this kind of motor disturbance afferent paresis.

A second component of voluntary movement is the spatial field. The movement has to be precisely oriented toward a certain point in space. Spatial analysis is done in another zone of the cortex: the tertiary parts of the parieto-occipital areas. Lesions of these highly complicated parts of the cortex result in a different kind of disturbance of voluntary movement. The sensory base of the movement remains intact, but the patient fails in a precise spatial organization of the movement. He loses the ability to evaluate spatial relations and confuses left and right. Such a patient may be unable to find his way in a familiar place or may be confused in such matters as evaluating the position of the hands of a watch or in distinguishing east and west on a map.

The sensory and spatial factors in the organization of a movement are basic but still insufficient to allow the completion of the movement. A voluntary movement is the result of a sequence of events. A skilled movement is really a kinetic melody of such interchangeable links. Only if one already fulfilled part of the movement is blocked and the impulse is shifted to another link can an organized skilled movement be made.

An important finding, first described by Karl S. Lashley and John F. Fulton and carefully studied in our laboratory for many years, is that a totally different part of the brain—the premotor cortex—is responsible for sequential interchanges of separate links of motor behavior. A skilled movement disintegrates when this part of the brain is injured. Such a patient still has sensory feedback and spatial orientation, but he loses the ability to arrest one of the steps of the movement and to make a transition from one step to the next.

Even now I have not fully described the brain's organization of a voluntary

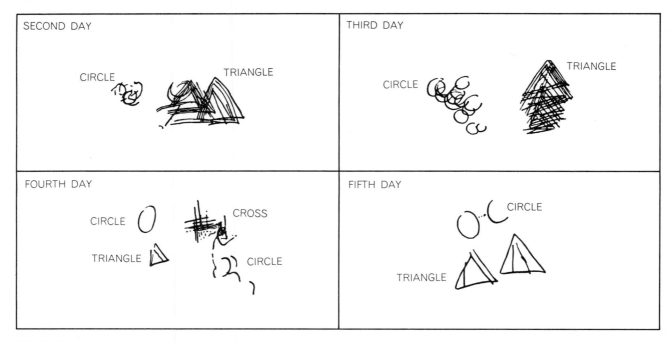

INFLUENCE OF PREMOTOR REGION on the organization of movement appears in drawings made by a patient after surgery for removal of a meningioma, which is a tumor arising from the me-ninges, from the left premotor region. On each of the days represented in the illustration the patient was asked to draw simple figures such as those shown here. Performance improved steadily.

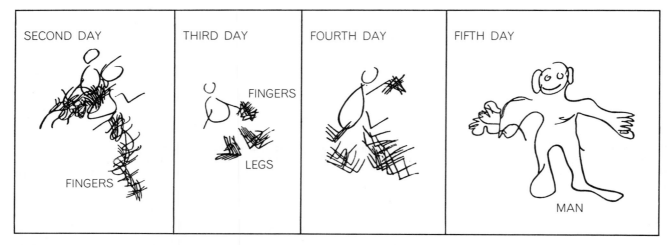

DRAWINGS OF A MAN were attempted by the same patient during the postoperative period. At first he drew a head and body, represented by the circles at top center in the drawing at left. Then he drew a second man, whose head is to the right of the first man's body. Then he made a series of stereotyped pen strokes. The ones that trail off at lower right in the first drawing were made on moving paper. On successive days the patient's work improved. Difficulty in stopping a movement often appears in premotor lesions.

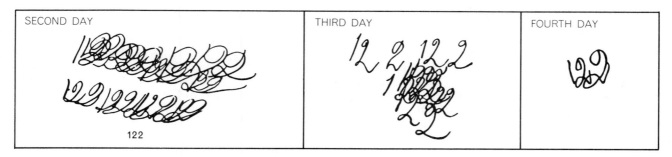

WRITING OF NUMBERS was attempted by the same patient on the second, third and fourth day after the operation. As in the other cases the patient at first showed a tendency to repeat part of the task, but the repetition diminished on the following days.

movement. Every movement has to be subordinated to a stable program or a stable intention. They are provided in the prefrontal lobes of the brain (included in the third block). If the frontal lobes are injured, the sensory base, spatial organization and plasticity of the movement remain but goal-linked actions are replaced by meaningless repetitions of already fulfilled movements or impulsive answers to outside stimuli. The whole purposive conduct of the patient is disturbed.

Speech and Writing

Let us now analyze a more complex psychological process: the ability to speak, and particularly the ability to write. It used to be thought that the operation of writing is controlled by a certain area (called Exher's center) in the middle of the premotor zone of the brain's left hemisphere (for a right-handed writer). It has since been learned, however, that this is not the case, and that a broad area of the left hemisphere is involved. We must therefore consider the effects of lesions in all parts of this region on writing.

Let us start by a psychological analysis of the processes involved in writing something in response to an instruction. Suppose one is asked to write a given word. The interpretation of the oral request turns out to be in itself a complex process. A word is composed of individual sounds, or phonemes, each coded by a letter or combination of letters. The recognition of a word may depend on the perception of very slight differences between phonemes, or acoustic cues. Consider, for example, "vine" and "wine," "special" and "spatial," "bull" and "pull," "bark" and "park." The practiced brain readily distinguishes between similar sounds, and to a person brought up in the English language the two words in these pairs sound quite different from each other. Obviously the brain must perform a sharp analysis of phonemes on the basis of learning. We become impressed with this fact when we see how difficult it is to sense distinctions in listening to a foreign language. To an English-speaking or French-speaking person, for example, three words in the Russian language—*pyl*, meaning "ardor," *pyl'* (with the *l* palatalized), meaning "dust," and *pil* (with a hard *l*), meaning "he drank"—sound almost exactly the same, yet a Russian has no difficulty distinguishing these words. Much more remarkable instances of subtle distinctions the mind is called on to make can be

cited in other languages. In Chinese *ma* and *ma* have the opposite meaning ("to buy" and "to sell"), although the only difference is in the tone of the vowel. In the Vietnamese language the phoneme *tü* has at least six different meanings, depending on the pitch of the voice!

What part of the brain is responsible for recognizing phonemes? Our observations on many hundreds of patients with local brain wounds or tumors who underwent word-writing tests established clearly that the critical region lies in the secondary zones of the left temporal lobe, which are intimately connected with other parts of the brain's speech area. People with lesions in this region cannot distinguish *b* from *p* or *t* from *d*, and they may write "pull" instead of "bull" or "tome" instead of "dome." Moreover, they may make unsuccessful attempts to find the contents of the sounds of words they try to write. Interestingly enough, Chinese patients with severe injury of the acoustic region have no such difficulty, because their writing is based on ideographs instead of on words that call for the coding of phonemes.

Continuing our dissection of the process of word recognition, we must note that people commonly pronounce an unfamiliar word before writing it, and in the case of an unfamiliar name they are likely to ask the person to spell it. Articulation of the sounds helps to clarify the word's acoustic structure. A class of Russian elementary schoolchildren during a lesson in the early stages of learning to write is generally abuzz with their mouthing of the words. To find out if this activity was really helpful, I asked one of my co-workers to conduct an ex-

periment. The children were instructed to hold their mouths open or to immobilize their tongues with their teeth while they wrote. In these circumstances, unable to articulate the words, the children made six times as many spelling mistakes!

It turns out that a separate area of the brain cortex, in the central (kinesthetic) region of the left hemisphere, controls the articulation of speech sounds. People with lesions in this area confuse the sound of *b* with that of *m* (both made with similar tongue and lip movements) and often cannot distinguish between *d, e, n* and *l*. A Russian with such a lesion may write *ston* ("groan") instead of *stol* ("table") and *khadat* (meaningless) instead of *khalat* ("dressing gown").

After evaluation of the speech sounds and recognition of the word, the next step toward writing the word is the coding of the sound units (phonemes) into the units of writing (letters). We find that this step calls into play still other parts of the brain cortex, in the visual and spatial zones. Patients with lesions in these zones (in the occipital and parietal lobes) have a perfectly normal ability to analyze speech sounds, but they show marked difficulty in recognizing and forming written letters. They find it difficult to visualize the required structure of a letter, to grasp the spatial relations among the parts of the letter and to put the parts together to form the whole.

The mental process for writing a word entails still another specialization: putting the letters in the proper sequence to form the word. Lashley discovered many years ago that sequential analysis

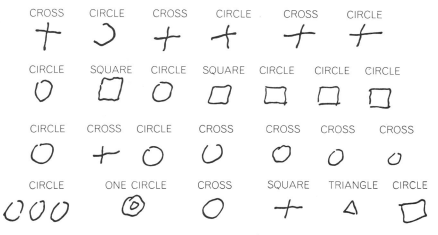

LESIONS OF FRONTAL LOBES interfere with the programming of actions and cause errors such as repetition. On each line of the illustration are drawings made by patients; printed words show what they were asked to draw. The first, second and fourth patient had tumors of the left frontal lobe; the third patient had an abscess of the right frontal lobe.

involved a zone of the brain different from that employed for spatial analysis. In the course of our extensive studies we have located the region responsible for sequential analysis in the anterior region of the left hemisphere. Lesions in the prefrontal region disturb the ability to carry out rhythmic movements of the body, and they also give patients difficulty in writing letters in the correct order. Such patients transpose letters, are unable to proceed serially from one let-ter to another and often replace the required letter with a meaningless stereotype. If the lesion is located deep in the brain where it interrupts connections between the basal ganglia and the cortex, the patient becomes incapable of writing words at all; he may merely repeat fragments of letters. Yet such a patient, with the higher parts of the cortex undamaged, can recognize phonemes and letters perfectly well.

Finally, there is an overall require-ment for writing that involves the apparatuses of the third block of the brain as a whole. This is the matter of writing not merely letters or words but expressing thoughts and ideas. When the third block is damaged by severe lesions of the frontal lobes, the patient becomes unable to express his thoughts either orally or in writing. I shall never forget a letter written to the noted Russian neurosurgeon N. N. Burdenko by a woman with a severe lesion of the left frontal lobe. "Dear Professor," she wrote, "I want to tell you that I want to tell you that I want to tell you ..." and so on for page after page!

The analysis of the writing process is just one of the tracers we have used in our psychological exploration of the functional organization of the brain. Over the past three decades investigators in our laboratory and our clinical associates have carried out similar analyses of the brain systems involved in perception, bodily movements, performance of planned actions, memorization and problem-solving. All these studies have demonstrated that detailed investigation of the nature of a behavioral disturbance can indeed guide one to the location of the causative lesion in the brain.

Factor Analyses

Obviously the neuropsychological approach provides a valuable means of dissecting mental processes as well as diagnosing illness. It is enabling us to search out the details of the brain's normal operations and capacities. A generation ago L. L. Thurstone of the University of Chicago and C. E. Spearman of the University of London learned some of the details by the statistical technique of factor analysis based on batteries of tests administered to great numbers of subjects. With the neuropsychological technique we can now make factor analyses in individual subjects. When a particular factor is incapacitated by a brain lesion, all the complex behavior processes that involve the factor are disturbed and all others remain normal. We find, for example, that an injury in the left temporal lobe causes the patient to have serious difficulty in analyzing speech sounds, in repeating verbal sounds, in naming objects and in writing, but the person retains normal capacities in spatial orientation and in handling simple computations. On the other hand, a lesion in the left parieto-occipital region that destroys spatial organization does not affect the patient's fluency of speech or sense of rhythm.

Sorting out the various factors and

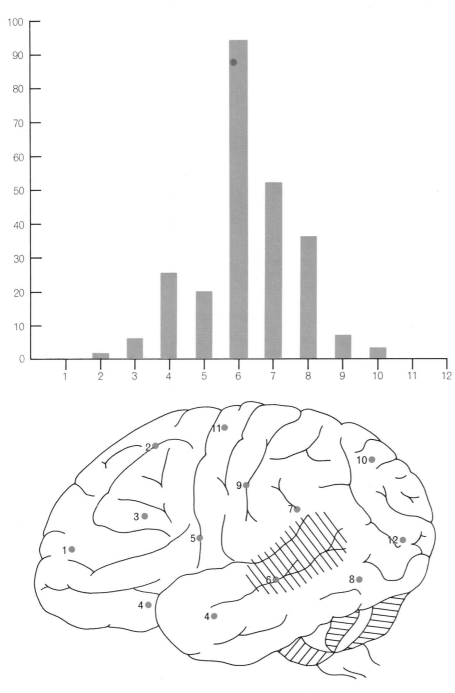

DISRUPTION OF HEARING in patients with bullet wounds in the left hemisphere of the cerebral cortex is charted. Affected areas of the brain are numbered, and the correspond-ingly numbered bars show the percent of patients who had difficulty recognizing sounds.

their effects, we arrive at some surprising findings. One is that behavioral processes that seem very similar or even identical may not be related to one another at all. For example, it turns out that the mechanism for perception of musical sounds is quite different from that for verbal sounds. A lesion of the left temporal lobe that destroys the ability to analyze phonemes leaves musical hearing undisturbed. I observed an outstanding Russian composer who suffered a hemorrhage in the left temporal lobe that deprived him of the ability to understand speech, yet he went on creating wonderful symphonies!

On the other hand, behavioral processes that seem to have nothing in common may actually be related through dependence on a particular brain factor. What can there be in common between the capacities for orientation in space, for doing computations and for dealing with complexities in grammar logic? Yet all three of these abilities are affected by the same lesion in the lower part of the left parietal lobe. Why so? A close analysis of the three processes suggests an explanation. Computation and the ability to handle language structure depend, like orientation, on the ability to grasp spatial relations. In order to subtract 7 from 31, for example, one first performs the operation $30 - 7 = 23$ and then adds the 1 to this preliminary result. There is a spatial factor here: one indicates unambiguously that the 1 is to be *added* by placing it to the right of the 23. A patient with a lesion disturbing his capacity for spatial organization is unable to cope with the problem because

he is at a loss whether to place the 1 to the left or the right—in other words, whether to add it or subtract it.

The same principle applies to understanding complex grammatical constructions. In order to grasp the difference between "father's brother" and "brother's father" or between "summer comes after spring" and "spring comes after summer," for example, one must make a clear analysis of the quasi-spatial relations between the elements in each expression.

Finally, the neuropsychological approach gives us a new insight into the effects of learning on the brain's processes. There is a well-known story of a patient of the 19th-century English neurologist Sir William Gowers who, after many unsuccessful attempts to repeat the word "no" in response to his instruction, at last burst out: "No, doctor, I can't say 'no.'" We have observed many cases of automatic performances of this kind in brain-injured patients who could not achieve a given task when they thought about it. One was an old lady who was unable to write a single word on instruction, but when she was asked to write a whole sentence quickly (a kinetic skill), she did so without hesitation. Patients who cannot write from dictation are often able to sign their names readily. It appears, therefore, that training or habituation changes the organization of the brain's activity, so that the brain comes to perform accustomed tasks without recourse to the processes of analysis. That is to say, the task may invoke a stereotype based on a network of cortical zones quite different from the one that was

(OKHO = OKŃO)
(WINDOW)

(ИВАН = IVAN)

WRITING ABERRATION was shown by a patient with a tumor in the deep part of the brain's left premotor zone. He was asked to write the Russian words for window and Ivan, which are printed in Russian and in English transliteration below each example. Arrows show repetition or fragments.

called on originally when the performance required the help of the analytical apparatus.

Neuropsychology has put us on a new path in the investigation of how the brain functions, and we can suppose that it is likely to lead the way to substantial changes in the design of psychological research in the future.

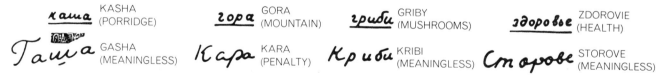

каша KASHA (PORRIDGE)
Гаша GASHA (MEANINGLESS)

гора GORA (MOUNTAIN)
Кара KARA (PENALTY)

грибы GRIBY (MUSHROOMS)
Криби KRIBI (MEANINGLESS)

здоровье ZDOROVIE (HEALTH)
Старове STOROVE (MEANINGLESS)

WRITING DISTURBANCES appear in a patient with a lesion of the left temporal area. The patient was writing to dictation; the dictated Russian word, its transliteration and its English meaning are on the top line. The written response of the patient in each case appears below with its transliteration and English meaning in the single instance (*kara*) where the patient wrote a meaningful word.

т m   *л* l

л l   *н* n

халат KHALAT (SMOCK)
канат KHANAT (MEANINGLESS)
хадат KHADAT (MEANINGLESS)

большой BOLSHOI (BIG)
Бониши BONISHOI (MEANINGLESS)
Бониш BONISH (MEANINGLESS)

ERRORS IN WRITING also were shown by a patient with a lesion of the left parietal area. Again the dictated letter or word appears on the top line; the bottom lines show the written response by the patient. None of the words that the patient wrote were meaningful.

24 Language and the Brain

by Norman Geschwind
April 1972

*Aphasias are speech disorders caused by brain damage.
The relations between these disorders and specific kinds
of brain damage suggest a model of how the language
areas of the human brain are organized*

Virtually everything we know of how the functions of language are organized in the human brain has been learned from abnormal conditions or under abnormal circumstances: brain damage, brain surgery, electrical stimulation of brains exposed during surgery and the effects of drugs on the brain. Of these the most fruitful has been the study of language disorders, followed by postmortem analysis of the brain, in patients who have suffered brain damage. From these studies has emerged a model of how the language areas of the brain are interconnected and what each area does.

A disturbance of language resulting from damage to the brain is called aphasia. Such disorders are not rare. Aphasia is a common aftereffect of the obstruction or rupture of blood vessels in the brain, which is the third leading cause of death in the U.S. Although loss of speech from damage to the brain had been described occasionally before the 19th century, the medical study of such cases was begun by a remarkable Frenchman, Paul Broca, who in 1861 published the first of a series of papers on language and the brain. Broca was the first to point out that damage to a specific portion of the brain results in disturbance of language output. The portion he identified, lying in the third frontal gyrus of the cerebral cortex, is now called Broca's area [see illustration on page 240].

Broca's area lies immediately in front of the portion of the motor cortex that controls the muscles of the face, the jaw, the tongue, the palate and the larynx, in other words, the muscles involved in speech production. The region is often called the "motor face area." It might therefore seem that loss of speech from damage to Broca's area is the result of paralysis of these muscles. This explana-tion, however, is not the correct one. Direct damage to the area that controls these muscles often produces only mild weakness of the lower facial muscles on the side opposite the damage and no permanent weakness of the jaw, the tongue, the palate or the vocal cords. The reason is that most of these muscles can be controlled by either side of the brain. Damage to the motor face area on one side of the brain can be compensated by the control center on the opposite side. Broca named the lesion-produced language disorder "aphemia," but this term was soon replaced by "aphasia," which was suggested by Armand Trousseau.

In 1865 Broca made a second major contribution to the study of language and the brain. He reported that damage to specific areas of the left half of the brain led to disorder of spoken language but that destruction of corresponding areas in the right side of the brain left language abilities intact. Broca based his conclusion on eight consecutive cases of aphasia, and in the century since his report his observation has been amply confirmed. Only rarely does damage to the right hemisphere of the brain lead to language disorder; out of 100 people with permanent language disorder caused by brain lesions approximately 97 will have damage on the left side. This unilateral control of certain functions is called cerebral dominance. As far as we know man is the only mammal in which learned behavior is controlled by one half of the brain. Fernando Nottebohm of Rockefeller University has found unilateral neural control of birdsong. It is an interesting fact that a person with aphasia of the Broca type who can utter at most only one or two slurred words may be able to sing a melody rapidly, correctly and even with elegance. This is another proof that aphasia is not the result of muscle paralysis.

In the decade following Broca's first report on brain lesions and language there was a profusion of papers on aphasias of the Broca type. In fact, there was a tendency to believe all aphasias were the result of damage to Broca's area. At this point another great pioneer of the brain appeared on the scene. Unlike Broca, who already had a reputation at the time of his first paper on aphasia, Carl Wernicke was an unknown with no previous publications; he was only 26 years old and a junior assistant in the neurological service in Breslau. In spite of his youth and obscurity his paper on aphasia, published in 1874, gained immediate attention. Wernicke described damage at a site in the left hemisphere outside Broca's area that results in a language disorder differing from Broca's aphasia.

In Broca's aphasia speech is slow and labored. Articulation is crude. Characteristically, small grammatical words and the endings of nouns and verbs are

LOCATION OF SOME LESIONS in the brain can be determined by injecting into the bloodstream a radioactive isotope of mercury, which is taken up by damaged brain tissue. The damaged region is identified by scanning the head for areas of high radioactivity. The top scan on the opposite page was made from the back of the head; the white area on the left shows that the damage is in the left hemisphere. The bottom scan is of the left side of the head and shows that the uptake of mercury was predominantly in the first temporal gyrus, indicating damage to Wernicke's speech area by occlusion of blood vessels. David Patten and Martin Albert of the Boston Veterans Administration Hospital supplied the scans.

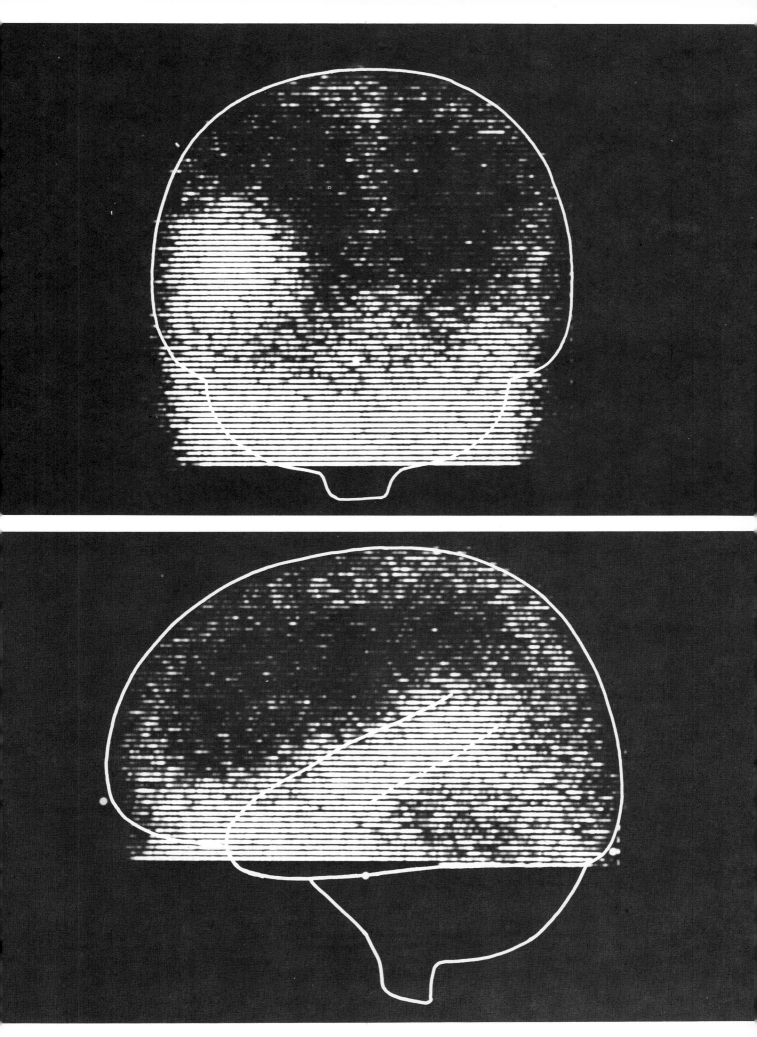

omitted, so that the speech has a telegraphic style. Asked to describe a trip he has taken, the patient may say "New York." When urged to produce a sentence, he may do no better than "Go... New York." This difficulty is not simply a desire to economize effort, as some have suggested. Even when the patient does his best to cooperate in repeating words, he has difficulty with certain grammatical words and phrases. "If he were here, I would go" is more difficult than "The general commands the army." The hardest phrase for such patients to repeat is "No ifs, ands or buts."

The aphasia described by Wernicke is quite different. The patient may speak very rapidly, preserving rhythm, grammar and articulation. The speech, if not listened to closely, may almost sound normal. For example, the patient may say: "Before I was in the one here, I was over in the other one. My sister had the department in the other one." It is abnormal in that it is remarkably devoid of content. The patient fails to use the correct word and substitutes for it by circumlocutory phrases ("what you use to cut with" for "knife") and empty words ("thing"). He also suffers from paraphasia, which is of two kinds. Verbal paraphasia is the substitution of one word or phrase for another, sometimes related in meaning ("knife" for "fork") and sometimes unrelated ("hammer" for "paper"). Literal or phonemic paraphasia is the substitution of incorrect sounds in otherwise correct words ("kench" for "wrench"). If there are several incorrect sounds in a word, it becomes a neologism, for example "pluver" or "flieber."

Wernicke also noted another difference between these aphasic patients and those with Broca's aphasia. A person with Broca's aphasia may have an essentially normal comprehension of language. Indeed, Broca had argued that no single lesion in the brain could cause a loss of comprehension. He was wrong. A lesion in Wernicke's area can produce a severe loss of understanding, even though hearing of nonverbal sounds and music may be fully normal.

Perhaps the most important contribution made by Wernicke was his model of how the language areas in the brain are connected. Wernicke modestly stated that his ideas were based on the teachings of Theodor Meynert, a Viennese neuroanatomist who had attempted to correlate the nervous system's structure with its function. Since Broca's area was adjacent to the cortical region of the brain that controlled the muscles of speech, it was reasonable to assume, Wernicke argued, that Broca's area incorporated the programs for complex coordination of these muscles. In addition Wernicke's area lay adjacent to the cortical region that received auditory stimuli [see illustration below]. Wernicke made the natural assumption that Broca's area and Wernicke's area must be connected. We now know that the two areas are indeed connected, by a bundle of nerve fibers known as the arcuate fasciculus. One can hypothesize that in the repetition of a heard word the auditory patterns are relayed from Wernicke's area to Broca's area.

Comprehension of written language

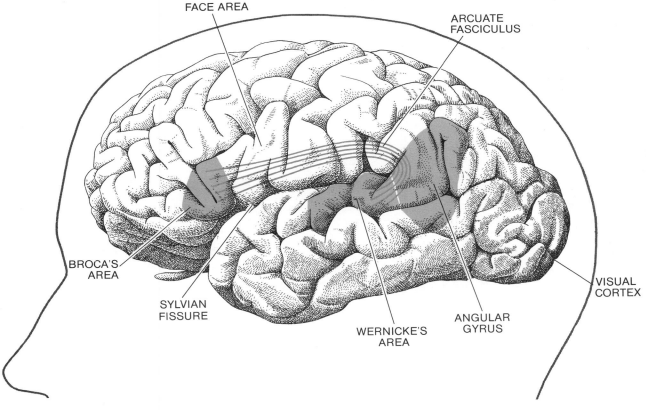

PRIMARY LANGUAGE AREAS of the human brain are thought to be located in the left hemisphere, because only rarely does damage to the right hemisphere cause language disorders. Broca's area, which is adjacent to the region of the motor cortex that controls the movement of the muscles of the lips, the jaw, the tongue, the soft palate and the vocal cords, apparently incorporates programs for the coordination of these muscles in speech. Damage to Broca's area results in slow and labored speech, but comprehension of language remains intact. Wernicke's area lies between Heschl's gyrus, which is the primary receiver of auditory stimuli, and the angular gyrus, which acts as a way station between the auditory and the visual regions. When Wernicke's area is damaged, speech is fluent but has little content and comprehension is usually lost. Wernicke and Broca areas are joined by a nerve bundle called the arcuate fasciculus. When it is damaged, speech is fluent but abnormal, and patient can comprehend words but cannot repeat them.

would require connections from the visual regions to the speech regions. This function is served by the angular gyrus, a cortical region just behind Wernicke's area. It acts in some way to convert a visual stimulus into the appropriate auditory form.

We can now deduce from the model what happens in the brain during the production of language. When a word is heard, the output from the primary auditory area of the cortex is received by Wernicke's area. If the word is to be spoken, the pattern is transmitted from Wernicke's area to Broca's area, where the articulatory form is aroused and passed on to the motor area that controls the movement of the muscles of speech. If the spoken word is to be spelled, the auditory pattern is passed to the angular gyrus, where it elicits the visual pattern. When a word is read, the output from the primary visual areas passes to the angular gyrus, which in turn arouses the corresponding auditory form of the word in Wernicke's area. It should be noted that in most people comprehension of a written word involves arousal of the auditory form in Wernicke's area. Wernicke argued that this was the result of the way most people learn written language. He thought, however, that in people who were born deaf, but had learned to read, Wernicke's area would not be in the circuit.

According to this model, if Wernicke's area is damaged, the person would have difficulty comprehending both spoken and written language. He should be unable to speak, repeat and write correctly. The fact that in such cases speech is fluent and well articulated suggests that Broca's area is intact but receiving inadequate information. If the damage were in Broca's area, the effect of the lesion would be to disrupt articulation. Speech would be slow and labored but comprehension should remain intact.

This model may appear to be rather simple, but it has shown itself to be remarkably fruitful. It is possible to use it to predict the sites of brain lesions on the basis of the type of language disorder. Moreover, it gave rise to some definite predictions that lesions in certain sites should produce types of aphasia not previously described. For example, if a lesion disconnected Wernicke's area from Broca's area while leaving the two areas intact, a special type of aphasia should be the result. Since Broca's area is preserved, speech should be fluent but abnormal. On the other hand, comprehension should be intact because Wernicke's area is still functioning. Rep-

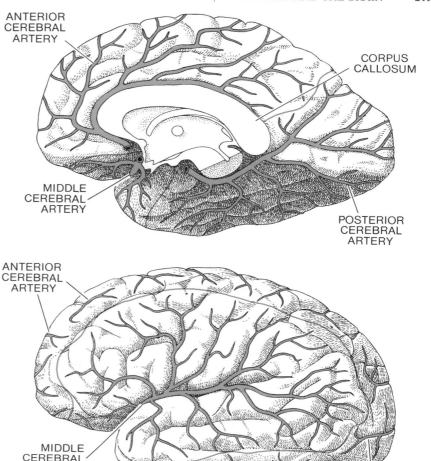

CEREBRAL AREAS are nourished by several arteries, each supplying blood to a specific region. The speech and auditory region is nourished by the middle cerebral artery. The visual areas at the rear are supplied by the posterior cerebral artery. In patients who suffer from inadequate oxygen supply to the brain the damage is often not within the area of a single blood vessel but rather in the "border zones" (*colored lines*). These are the regions between the areas served by the major arteries where the blood supply is marginal.

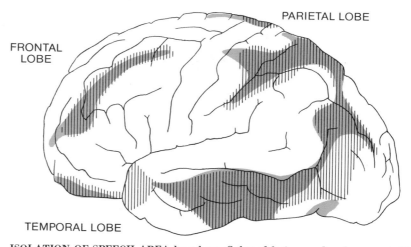

ISOLATION OF SPEECH AREA by a large *C*-shaped lesion produced a remarkable syndrome in a woman who suffered from severe carbon monoxide poisoning. She could repeat words and learn new songs but could not comprehend the meaning of words. Postmortem examination of her brain revealed that in the regions surrounding the speech areas of the left hemisphere, either the cortex (*colored areas*) or the underlying white matter (*hatched areas*) was destroyed but that the cortical structures related to the production of language (Broca's area and Wernicke's area) and the connections between them were left intact.

CLASSIC CASE of a man who lost the ability to read even though he had normal visual acuity and could copy written words was described in 1892 by Joseph Jules Dejerine. Post-mortem analysis of the man's brain showed that the left visual cortex and the splenium (*dark colored areas*) were destroyed as a result of an occlusion of the left posterior cerebral artery. The splenium is the section of the corpus callosum that transfers visual information between the two hemispheres. The man's left visual cortex was inoperative, making him blind in his right visual field. Words in his left visual field were properly received by the right visual cortex, but could not cross over to the language areas in the left hemisphere because of the damaged splenium. Thus words seen by the man remained as meaningless patterns.

etition of spoken language, however, should be grossly impaired. This syndrome has in fact been found. It is termed conduction aphasia.

The basic pattern of speech localization in the brain has been supported by the work of many investigators. A. R. Luria of the U.S.S.R. studied a large number of patients who suffered brain wounds during World War II [see the article "The Functional Organization of the Brain," by A. R. Luria, beginning on page 230]. When the wound site lay over Wernicke's or Broca's area, Luria found that the result was almost always severe and permanent aphasia. When the wounds were in other areas, aphasia was less frequent and less severe.

A remarkable case of aphasia has provided striking confirmation of Wernicke's model. The case, described by Fred Quadfasel, Jose Segarra and myself, involved a woman who had suffered from accidental carbon monoxide poisoning. During the nine years we studied her she was totally helpless and required complete nursing care. She never uttered speech spontaneously and showed no evidence of comprehending words. She could, however, repeat perfectly sentences that had just been said to her. In addition she would complete certain phrases. For example, if she heard "Roses are red," she would say "Roses are red, violets are blue, sugar is sweet and so are you." Even more surprising was her ability to learn songs. A song that had been written after her illness would be played to her and after a few repetitions she would begin to sing along with it. Eventually she would begin to sing as soon as the song started. If the song was stopped after a few bars, she would continue singing the song through to the end, making no errors in either words or melody.

On the basis of Wernicke's model we predicted that the lesions caused by the carbon monoxide poisoning lay outside the speech and auditory regions, and that both Broca's area and Wernicke's area were intact. Postmortem examination revealed a remarkable lesion that isolated the speech area from the rest of the cortex. The lesion fitted the prediction. Broca's area, Wernicke's area and the connection between them were intact. Also intact were the auditory pathways and the motor pathways to the speech organs. Around the speech area, however, either the cortex or the underlying white matter was destroyed [see *bottom illustration on preceding page*]. The woman could not comprehend speech because the words did not arouse associations in other portions of the cortex. She could repeat speech correctly because the internal connections of the speech region were intact. Presumably well-learned word sequences stored in Broca's area could be triggered by the beginning phrases. This syndrome is called isolation of the speech area.

Two important extensions of the Wernicke model were advanced by a French neurologist, Joseph Jules Dejerine. In 1891 he described a disorder called alexia with agraphia: the loss of the ability to read and write. The patient could, however, speak and understand spoken language. Postmortem examination showed that there was a lesion in the angular gyrus of the left hemisphere, the area of the brain that acts as a way station between the visual and the auditory region. A lesion here would separate the visual and auditory language areas. Although words and letters would be seen correctly, they would be meaningless visual patterns, since the visual pattern must first be converted to the auditory form before the word can be comprehended. Conversely, the auditory pattern for a word must be transformed into the visual pattern before the word can be spelled. Patients suffering from alexia with agraphia cannot recognize words spelled aloud to them nor can they themselves spell aloud a spoken word.

Dejerine's second contribution was showing the importance of information transfer between the hemispheres. His patient was an intelligent businessman who had awakened one morning to discover that he could no longer read. It was found that the man was blind in the right half of the visual field. Since the right half of the field is projected to the left cerebral hemisphere, it was obvious that the man suffered damage to the visual pathways on the left side of the brain [see illustration on opposite page]. He could speak and comprehend spoken language and could write, but he could not read even though he had normal visual acuity. In fact, although he could not comprehend written words, he could copy them correctly. Postmortem examination of the man's brain by Dejerine revealed two lesions that were the result of the occlusion of the left posterior cerebral artery. The visual cortex of the left hemisphere was totally destroyed. Also destroyed was a portion of the corpus callosum: the mass of nerve fibers that interconnect the two cerebral hemispheres. That portion was the splenium, which carries the visual information between the hemispheres. The destruction of the splenium prevented stimuli from the visual cortex of the right hemisphere

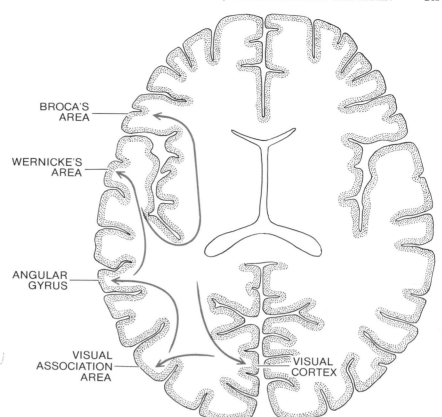

SAYING THE NAME of a seen object, according to Wernicke's model, involves the transfer of the visual pattern to the angular gyrus, which contains the "rules" for arousing the auditory form of the pattern in Wernicke's area. From here the auditory form is transmitted by way of the arcuate fasciculus to Broca's area. There the articulatory form is aroused, is passed on to the face area of the motor cortex and the word then is spoken.

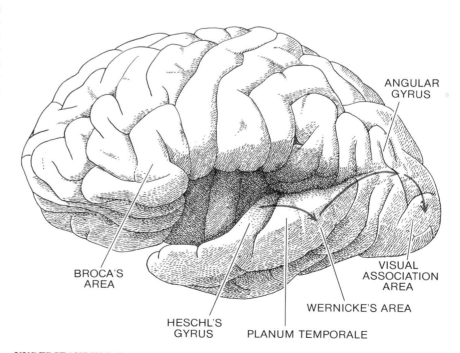

UNDERSTANDING the spoken name of an object involves the transfer of the auditory stimuli from Heschl's gyrus (the primary auditory cortex) to Wernicke's area and then to the angular gyrus, which arouses the comparable visual pattern in the visual association cortex. Here the Sylvian fissure has been spread apart to show the pathway more clearly.

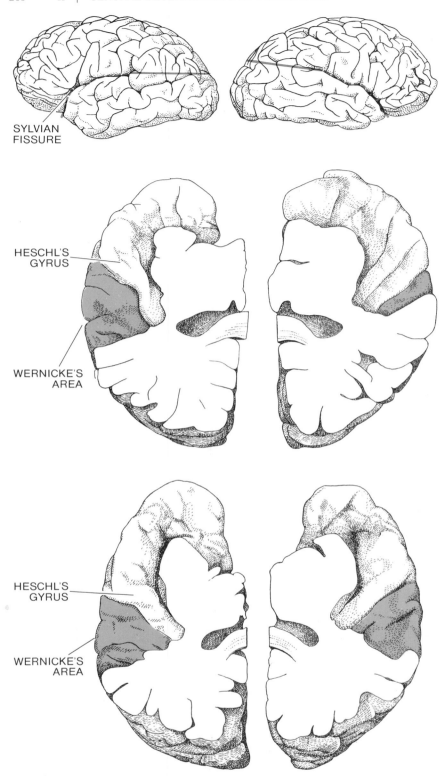

SYLVIAN
FISSURE

HESCHL'S
GYRUS

WERNICKE'S
AREA

HESCHL'S
GYRUS

WERNICKE'S
AREA

ANATOMICAL DIFFERENCES between the two hemispheres of the human brain are found on the upper surface of the temporal lobe, which cannot be seen in an intact brain because it lies within the Sylvian fissure. Typically the Sylvian fissure in the left hemisphere appears to be pushed down compared with the Sylvian fissure on the right side (*top illustration*). In order to expose the surface of the temporal lobe a knife is moved along the fissure (*broken line*) and then through the brain, cutting away the top portion (*solid line*). The region studied was the planum temporale (*colored areas*), an extension of Wernicke's area. The middle illustration shows a brain with a larger left planum; the bottom illustration shows left and right planums of about the same size. In a study of 100 normal human brains planum temporale was larger on the left side in 65 percent of the cases, equal on both sides in 24 percent of the cases and larger on the right side in 11 percent.

from reaching the angular gyrus of the left hemisphere. According to Wernicke's model, it is the left angular gyrus that converts the visual pattern of a word into the auditory pattern; without such conversion a seen word cannot be comprehended. Other workers have since shown that when a person is blind in the right half of the visual field but is still capable of reading, the portion of the corpus callosum that transfers visual information between the hemispheres is not damaged.

In 1937 the first case in which surgical section of the corpus callosum stopped the transfer of information between the hemispheres was reported by John Trescher and Frank Ford. The patient had the rear portion of his corpus callosum severed during an operation to remove a brain tumor. According to Wernicke's model, this should have resulted in the loss of reading ability in the left half of the visual field. Trescher and Ford found that the patient could read normally when words appeared in his right visual field but could not read at all in his left visual field.

Hugo Liepmann, who was one of Wernicke's assistants in Breslau, made an extensive study of syndromes of the corpus callosum, and descriptions of these disorders were a standard part of German neurology before World War I. Much of this work was neglected, and only recently has its full importance been appreciated. Liepmann's analysis of corpus callosum syndromes was based on Wernicke's model. In cases such as those described by Liepmann the front four-fifths of the corpus callosum is destroyed by occlusion of the cerebral artery that nourishes it. Since the splenium is preserved the patient can read in either visual field. Such a lesion, however, gives rise to three characteristic disorders. The patient writes correctly with his right hand but incorrectly with the left. He carries out commands with his right arm but not with the left; although the left hemisphere can understand the command, it cannot transmit the message to the right hemisphere. Finally, the patient cannot name objects held in his left hand because the somesthetic sensations cannot reach the verbal centers in the left hemisphere.

The problem of cerebral dominance in humans has intrigued investigators since Broca first discovered it. Many early neurologists claimed that there were anatomical differences between the hemispheres, but in the past few decades there has been a tendency to assume that the left and right hemispheres are

MEANING	BROCA'S APHASIA				WERNICKE'S APHASIA
	KANA		KANJI		
	PATIENT'S	CORRECT	PATIENT'S	CORRECT	
INK	キンヌ (KINSU)	インキ (INKI)	墨 (SUMI)	墨	参 答 微 社 久 兵 美 (LONG TIME) (SOLDIER)
UNIVERSITY	タイ (TAI)	ダイガク (DAIGAKU)	大学	大學 (GREAT LEARNING)	
TOKYO	トウ (TOU)	トウキヨウ (TOKYO)	東京	東京 (EAST CAPITAL)	

JAPANESE APHASICS display some characteristics rarely found in Western patients because of the unique writing system used in Japan. There are two separate forms of such writing. One is Kana, which is syllabic. The other is Kanji, which is ideographic. Kana words are articulated syllable by syllable and are not easily identified at a glance, whereas each Kanji character simultaneously represents both a sound and a meaning. A patient with Broca's aphasia, studied by Tsuneo Imura and his colleagues at the Nihon University College of Medicine, was able to write a dictated word correctly in Kanji but not in Kana (*top left*). When the patient was asked to write the word "ink," even though there is no Kanji character for the word, his first effort was the Kanji character "sumi," which means india ink. When required to write in Kana, the symbols he produced were correct but the word was wrong. Another patient who had Wernicke's aphasia wrote Kanji quickly and without hesitation. He was completely unaware that he was producing meaningless ideograms, as are patients who exhibit paraphasias in speech. Only two of characters had meaning (*top right*).

symmetrical. It has been thought that cerebral dominance is based on undetected subtle physiological differences not reflected in gross structure. Walter Levitsky and I decided to look again into the possibility that the human brain is anatomically asymmetrical. We studied 100 normal human brains, and we were surprised to find that striking asymmetries were readily visible. The area we studied was the upper surface of the temporal lobe, which is not seen in the intact brain because it lies within the depths of the Sylvian fissure. The asymmetrical area we found and measured was the planum temporale, an extension of Wernicke's area [*see illustration on opposite page*]. This region was larger on the left side of the brain in 65 percent of the cases, equal in 24 percent and larger on the right side in 11 percent. In absolute terms the left planum was nine millimeters longer on the average than the right planum. In relative terms the left planum was one-third longer than the right. Statistically all the differences were highly significant. Juhn A. Wada of the University of British Columbia subsequently reported a study that confirmed our results. In addition Wada studied a series of brains from infants who had died soon after birth and found that the planum asymmetry was present. It seems likely that the asymmetries of the brain are genetically determined.

It is sometimes asserted that the anatomical approach neglects the plasticity of the nervous system and makes the likelihood of therapy for language disorders rather hopeless. This is not the case. Even the earliest investigators of aphasia were aware that some patients developed symptoms that were much milder than expected. Other patients recovered completely from a lesion that normally would have produced permanent aphasia. There is recovery or partial recovery of language functions in some cases, as Luria's large-scale study of the war wounded has shown. Of all the patients with wounds in the primary speech area of the left hemisphere, 97.2 percent were aphasic when Luria first examined them. A follow-up examination found that 93.3 percent were still aphasic, although in most cases they were aphasic to a lesser degree.

How does one account for the apparent recovery of language function in some cases? Some partial answers are available. Children have been known to make a much better recovery than adults with the same type of lesion. This suggests that at least in childhood the right hemisphere has some capacity to take over speech functions. Some cases of adult recovery are patients who had suffered brain damage in childhood. A number of patients who have undergone surgical removal of portions of the speech area for the control of epileptic seizures often show milder language disorders than had been expected. This probably is owing to the fact that the patients had suffered from left temporal epilepsy involving the left side of the brain from childhood and had been using the right hemisphere for language functions to a considerable degree.

Left-handed people also show on the average milder disorders than expected when the speech regions are damaged, even though for most left-handers the left hemisphere is dominant for speech just as it is for right-handers. It is an interesting fact that right-handers with a strong family history of left-handedness show better speech recovery than people without left-handed inheritance.

Effective and safe methods for studying cerebral dominance and localization of language function in the intact, normal human brain have begun to appear. Doreen Kimura of the University of Western Ontario has adapted the technique of dichotic listening to investigate the auditory asymmetries of the brain. More recently several investigators have found increased electrical activity over the speech areas of the left hemisphere during the production or perception of speech. Refinement of these techniques could lead to a better understanding of how the normal human brain is organized for language. A deeper understanding of the neural mechanisms of speech should lead in turn to more precise methods of dealing with disorders of man's most characteristic attribute, language.

The Asymmetry of the Human Brain

by Doreen Kimura
March 1973

*The cerebral hemispheres, though physically alike,
have different functions: the right is specialized
for analyzing information about the environment
and the left for skilled motor acts, including speech*

In most animals the structure of the nervous system is essentially symmetrical. In mammals the symmetry is made more striking by the prominence of the uppermost part of the brain: the cerebral hemispheres. In man, however, the two cerebral hemispheres differ greatly in their functions. It is well known that the left hemisphere plays a dominant role in speech [see the article "Language and the Brain," by Norman Geschwind, beginning on page 238]. The right hemisphere also has specialized functions, but until recently we have had less information about them because of the emphasis on studying language disorders. It turns out that the right hemisphere plays a dominant role in man's perception of his environment.

For more than a century the principal source of knowledge about the division of labor between the two cerebral hemispheres of man has been malfunctions of the brain caused by accident, surgery or disease. Although studies of intellectual impairments in patients with various kinds of brain lesion have provided much valuable information, such studies have the disadvantage that the damage may have affected not only the specific functional systems but also their interaction. In the past few years I have been involved in developing methods for studying the asymmetry of hemispheric functions in normal people.

I first became aware of the possibility that some aspects of brain function could be readily studied in normal people while I was doing research with patients at the Montreal Neurological Institute. One of the tests administered to the patients was a modification of a dichotic listening technique devised by Donald E. Broadbent of the British Medical Research Council's Applied Psychology Research Unit. His technique involves simultaneously presenting a spoken digit to one ear and a different spoken digit to the other ear. Three such pairs are usually delivered in sequence during one trial, and the subject is asked to report all the numbers he has heard. Patients with damage to the left temporal region of the brain reported fewer digits correctly than patients with damage to the right temporal region. A quite unexpected and intriguing finding was that most patients, no matter what part of the brain had been damaged, reported the words they had heard with their right ear more accurately than those they had heard with their left. The same turned out to be true for a group of normal people. There is evidence from numerous studies of pure-tone thresholds that the left and right ears do not differ in their basic capacity for detecting sounds, and so we concluded that the perceptual superiority of the right ear for words was somehow related to that ear's connections with the brain.

A peculiarity of the human nervous system is that each cerebral hemisphere receives information primarily from the opposite half of the body. Man's visual system is so arranged that vision to the right of a fixation point is mediated by the left half of the brain and vice versa. The auditory system is somewhat less crossed in that each half of the brain receives input from both ears, but the crossed connections are nevertheless stronger than the uncrossed ones. The tactual and motor systems of the brain are almost completely crossed: sensations from the left half of the body and movement of the left half of the body are served primarily by the right cerebral hemisphere and vice versa. The two hemispheres are themselves interconnected by nerve pathways. These pathways, the largest of which is the corpus callosum, play an important role in coordinating the activities of the hemispheres.

Since the auditory system is a predominantly crossed system, the neural input from the right ear to the left cerebral hemisphere should be stronger than that from the right ear to the right hemisphere. And since the left hemisphere usually contains the neural system for perception of speech, it is reasonable to suppose speech sounds presented to the right ear would have readier access to the speech-perception system. This supposition can be directly tested by observing people whose speech functions are not in the left hemisphere but in the right. Which side serves speech can be determined by the sodium amytal test, devised by Juhn A. Wada. The test involves injecting sodium amytal (a sedative) into the carotid artery of one side of the neck or the other. The drug disturbs the functioning of the cerebral hemisphere on that side for a few minutes, and if the subject's speech is disturbed as well one infers that speech is represented in that hemisphere.

Thirteen patients whom I tested at the Montreal Neurological Institute were found to have speech represented in the right hemisphere rather than in the left. The scores of these patients on the dichotic listening task were higher for the left ear. The results supported the hypothesis that the superiority of the right ear in normal subjects is due to better connections between that ear and the left (speech) hemisphere than between that ear and the right hemisphere.

We found further evidence that the superior performance of one ear on dichotic listening tasks did in fact reflect a hemispheric specialization of function. Brenda Milner of the Montreal Neurological Institute found that whereas damage to the left temporal lobe of the brain impaired comprehension of spoken material, damage to the right temporal lobe impaired the perception of certain other kinds of auditory material, particularly the discrimination of tonal quality and tonal pattern. I developed a dichotic listening task in which a headset was used to simultaneously play one melodic pattern to one ear and a different melodic pattern to the other ear. The subject was then asked to pick out the two melodies he (or she) had just heard from four melodies, each of which was played one at a time to both ears. Since melodies are processed predominantly by the right temporal lobe, normal subjects were able to pick out the melody presented to the left ear better than the one presented to the right ear.

The results were particularly exciting because they opened the way for exploration of the characteristics of verbal and nonverbal processes in the brain with relatively simple techniques. Although it has been known for more than a century that the left hemisphere is involved in speech functions, we still do not have a very clear idea of what the

characteristics of those functions are. The traditional way of distinguishing them is to use a term such as "symbolic," which implies that the defining characteristics have to do with the capacity to let an event stand for something else. When we applied the dichotic listening technique, we got a rather different answer. The right ear was found to be superior for nonsense syllables and nonsensical sounds (such as recorded speech played backward or a foreign language unknown to the subject). Donald Shankweiler and Michael Studdert-Kennedy of the Haskins Laboratories in New Haven, Conn., have also applied the dichotic method to the problems of defining the characteristics of speech. They found that there was no right-ear superiority for the perception of isolated vowels but that there was such an effect for consonant-vowel syllables. It is difficult to reconcile all these findings with the notion that the left-hemisphere speech system primarily processes symbolic material. Why should vowels, which can have symbolic value, be

processed equally well by both hemispheres whereas nonsense sounds such as speech played backward, which do not have a symbolic value, are apparently processed primarily by the left hemisphere?

One is forced to conclude that in auditory perception the left hemisphere is specialized for the perception of certain kinds of sound generated by the human vocal cords and vocal tract. By cutting a tape recording of natural speech into small segments Laurain King and I found that the briefest duration that yielded a right-ear superiority was about 200 milliseconds, or about the duration of an average spoken syllable: a consonant and a vowel. That size of unit seems to be necessary, although not always sufficient, for asymmetrical processing, and it supports the notion that the syllable is a basic unit in speech.

We further studied the dichotic perception of different vocal nonspeech sounds, such as coughing, laughing and crying. Instead of finding a right-ear superiority with these sounds, we ob-

DICHOTIC LISTENING TASK consists in simultaneously playing one melody to one ear and a different melody to the other ear. The subject is then asked to select these melodies from a series of four melodies that are played subsequently one at a time to both ears. The melodies are played through earphones connected to a dual-channel tape recorder. Other dichotic listening tasks involved listening to pairs of digits, words, nonsense syllables, vowels, backward speech and vocal sounds such as laughing and crying.

tained a left-ear superiority. This result suggests that these sounds are processed primarily by the right hemisphere, just as melodic patterns are. Melodies hummed by another person were also identified better when heard by the left ear. Therefore if the left hemisphere distinguishes sounds by their articulatory features, these features must be rather specific.

With some justification speech is generally regarded as being primarily an auditory-vocal system. Insofar as comprehension of a written word is a consequence of prior experience with the spoken equivalent, one might expect the speech system to take part in the processing of printed and written material. In actuality when reading abilities are thoroughly tested, disturbances of speech are nearly always accompanied by at least a mild disorder in reading. We set out to find whether or not there were visual perceptual asymmetries analogous to the right- and left-ear effects we had found in the auditory modality. Some earlier studies had in fact shown that words and letters are more accurately reported from the right half of the field of vision than from the

left half, but the effects were explained as being caused by reading habits. In order to relate such effects specifically to the asymmetry of cerebral function, we needed to find tasks that tapped right-hemisphere visual functions as well.

Although the visual system is crossed, its connections are different from those of the auditory system. The connections are not from each eye to the opposite half of the brain but from each half of the visual field to the visual cortex on the opposite side [*see illustration on opposite page*]. Vision to the left of the point of fixation is received by the right half of each retina and the neural pathways from the right side of both retinas go to the visual cortex of the right hemisphere. Obviously the fibers from the right half of the retina of the left eye must cross the midline of the brain to get to the right hemisphere but the fibers from the right half of the retina of the right eye do not cross.

An important difference between vision and audition is that when the head is motionless, the ears are stationary but the eyes are not. Since the eyes are con-

stantly moving, under normal viewing conditions one cannot present an image in only one visual field. In order to overcome this difficulty stimuli must be presented very rapidly during some period when the point of fixation is known. This can be done with the instrument known as the tachistoscope [*see illustration on page 250*]. The subject looks into the instrument and is asked to fixate on a designated point. While he is fixating, a visual stimulus is presented very rapidly either to the left of the point or to the right. Before the subject can make a new fixation to look at the stimulus, the stimulus has disappeared. As a result only one side of each of the retinas and only one cerebral hemisphere are directly stimulated.

In most of our tachistoscope experiments we did not use competition between two stimuli, as we had in the dichotic listening tests. In fact, our findings have been less ambiguous when only one visual field is stimulated. In normal people, then, words and letters are reported more accurately from the right visual field than from the left, a finding compatible with the right-ear superiority for the recognition of spoken sounds. That is, the recognition of visual verbal material is also more accurate when such material initially stimulates the left hemisphere.

Much of our work with visual perception has dealt with uncovering some of the specialized functions of the right hemisphere. It has been known for some time that injury to the right posterior part of the brain (the parieto-occipital region) results in the impairment of complex abilities such as drawing, finding one's way from place to place and building models from a plan or picture. In our studies with normal subjects we found evidence that the right hemisphere is also primary for some very fundamental visual processes. We find, for example, that in the simplest kind of spatial task—the location of a single point in a two-dimensional area—the right hemisphere is dominant. We tested for this ability by presenting dots one at a time either in the left visual field or in the right for a hundredth of a second. The dot was presented at various locations within a circle drawn on a plain white card. The subject then identified the location of the dot on a similar card outside the tachistoscope. The scores for correctly locating dots were higher for dots presented in the left field than for dots presented in the right field. Moreover, ascertaining the number of dots and of geometric forms was more accurate for the left field.

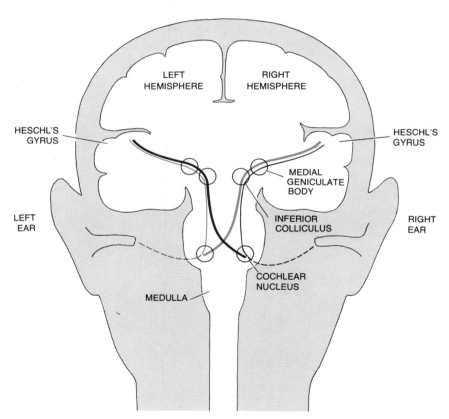

AUDITORY PATHWAYS from the ears to the cerebral auditory receiving areas in the right and left hemispheres are partially crossed. Although each hemisphere can receive input from both ears, the neural connections from one ear to the hemisphere on the opposite side are stronger than the connections to the hemisphere on the same side. When ipsilateral (same side) and contralateral (opposite side) inputs compete in the auditory neural system, it is thought that the stronger contralateral input inhibits or occludes the ipsilateral signals.

This ability is not due merely to some kind of heightened attention to stimuli on the left, since the simple detection of dots is no more accurate in one field than in the other. Detection was tested either by having the subject report whether or not a dot was present on any one trial with a fixed exposure time, or by determining the exposure time required for detection of a dot. In neither case is there a difference between the detection accuracy of the left field and of the right. It appears instead that the right hemisphere incorporates important components of a system of spatial coordinates that facilitates the location of a point in space. Of course, stimuli arriving at both visual cortexes must ordinarily have access to this system, but when input is deliberately limited to one visual field, it is possible to determine if one hemisphere has a functional advantage.

We then asked if the right hemisphere might also be important for depth perception. Locating objects in three dimensions can be mediated by one or more of several cues. Most of these cues are monocular, that is, they can be distinguished by one eye. The cues include the relative sizes of retinal images, the obscuring of one object by another or the relative speed with which two objects move across the field of vision. Another important cue to depth, binocular disparity, requires both eyes. Binocular disparity refers to the fact that because the two eyes are separated each eye receives a slightly different retinal image. The disparity between the two images can provide information about the depth of an object because nearer objects have a larger binocular disparity than farther ones.

Margaret Durnford and I initiated some studies in depth perception by attaching a classical depth-perception box to the back of the tachistoscope. The box contains a fixed vertical central rod in line with the fixation point. On each side of the central rod is a track on which another vertical rod can be moved. The movable rod is seen with both eyes for only a fraction of a second, and the subject was asked whether it was nearer than the central rod or farther. When the variable rod was in the left visual field, that is, when the information went to the right hemisphere, the reports were more accurate. Thus spatial information in the third dimension also is processed more accurately by the right hemisphere than by the left.

When the movable rod was viewed with only one eye, there was no difference in accuracy between the left field

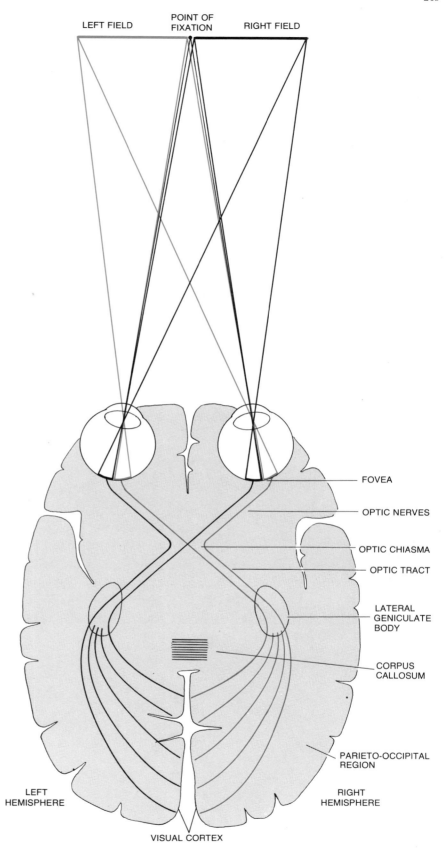

VISUAL PATHWAYS are completely crossed, so that when the eyes are fixated on a point, all of the field to the left of the fixation point excites the visual cortex in the right hemisphere and stimuli from the right visual field excite the left visual cortex. The visual cortexes can communicate via the corpus callosum, which connects the two hemispheres.

and the right. This result suggested that binocular information was processed primarily by the right hemisphere and that monocular information was processed by each hemisphere. As a further test of the specificity of hemispheric asymmetry we presented visual stimuli in which the only cue to depth was binocular disparity. When two slightly different views of a two-dimensional picture are seen separately by the two eyes by means of a stereoscope, the natural binocular disparity can be simulated. The subject reports seeing the two as being fused and as possessing the characteristics of depth that neither image alone yields.

Random-dot stereograms developed by Bela Julesz of the Bell Telephone Laboratories are ideal for this purpose, since each monocular image appears as a random array of dots. When the two images are viewed stereoscopically, a form such as a square or a triangle appears either in front of the rest of the array or behind it. A series of such stereograms with different forms was tachistoscopically presented to either the left or the right visual field, and the subject was asked to identify the form that stood out. For example, on a left-field trial one random-dot image would be presented to the left field of the left eye and its stereogram partner to the left field of the right eye. The two patterns thus presented are initially processed in the right cerebral hemisphere. A presentation to the right field, on the other hand, leads to stereoscopic processing in the left hemisphere.

We had anticipated some difficulty in getting binocular fusion because of the brief exposure (100 milliseconds) we had to use, but somewhat to our surprise most people we tested could do the task. The identification of stereoscopic stimuli was clearly better when stimuli were presented to the left visual field, that is, when the disparate images went to the right hemisphere. It may be, then, that the right-hemisphere processing of depth information is rather specifically connected to the utilization of such binocular cues.

Clearly the right hemisphere works better than the left hemisphere in analyzing information about where objects are located in space. The probability that we were tapping functions fundamental to orientation in space encouraged us to study hemispheric specialization for still another basic visual process: the perception of the slant of a line. Very short lines were presented one at a time in either the left visual field or the right. The lines varied in slope from 15 degrees to 165 degrees in 15-degree steps. After the subject had seen the line he was asked to pick it out of a multiple-choice array of slanted lines on a sheet of paper. There was a small but consistent superiority for slope identification in the left visual field, again suggesting that this information is asymmetrically processed in the brain. David H. Hubel and Torsten N. Wiesel of the Harvard Medical School have suggested that the initial processing of the orientation of a line is done in the visual cortex. The fact that we found a hemispheric asymmetry for such perceptual tasks opens the possibility that there may be some functional asymmetry between the hemispheres in primary processes as well as in the more complex associative processes.

We do not know precisely what neural systems in the brain we are sampling with our perceptual techniques. The evidence we have suggests that with the

TWO-FIELD TACHISTOSCOPE is used for study of visual perception. When the fixation field is lighted, an observer sees a reflection of the field in the partially silvered mirror. He is asked to fixate on a point in the center of the field. Then the fixation-field light is turned off and the exposure-field light is simultaneously turned on for a few milliseconds. The image on the exposure field passes through the partially silvered mirror and is briefly seen by the observer. At the end of the exposure the fixation-field light comes on and the exposure-field light goes off. By placing the exposure image in the left or right visual field as desired the experimenter can selectively stimulate either the right or the left visual cortex.

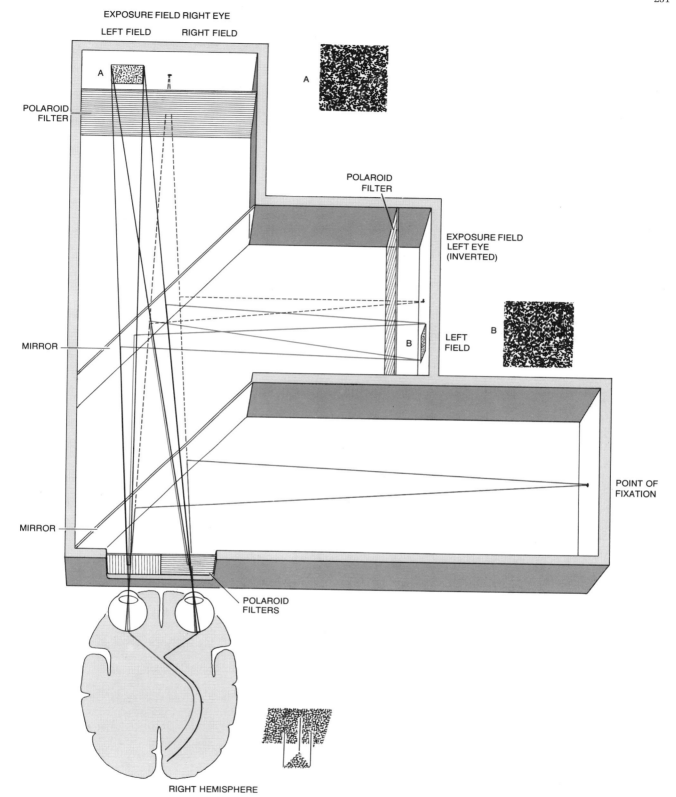

EXPOSURE FIELD RIGHT EYE

LEFT FIELD   RIGHT FIELD

A

POLAROID
FILTER

POLAROID
FILTER

EXPOSURE FIELD
LEFT EYE
(INVERTED)

LEFT
FIELD

B

MIRROR

MIRROR

POINT OF
FIXATION

POLAROID
FILTERS

RIGHT HEMISPHERE

A

B

THREE-FIELD TACHISTOSCOPE is used in studies of depth perception. The subject initially fixates on a point, which he sees as a reflection from a partially silvered mirror. The two exposure fields become visible when the light on the fixation field is turned off and the lights near the exposure fields are flashed on. The Polaroid filters are arranged so that each eye receives a different image. Using a technique developed by Bela Julesz of the Bell Telephone Laboratories, the author presented one random-dot pattern to the right hemiretina of the right eye and a slightly different random-dot pattern to the right hemiretina of the left eye. In other trials the pattern was presented to the left hemiretinas. When each pattern is viewed alone, no shapes or depth can be seen, but when the two patterns are fused somewhere in the visual system, the subject in this case sees a triangle floating in front of the background dot pattern. Most people are better at identifying the stereoscopic figure when the images are flashed onto the left visual field than when they are flashed onto the right visual field, indicating that the right hemisphere may be better at processing depth information.

tachistoscopic tests we are tapping the function of regions near the striate cortex, the major visual pathway to the hemispheres, rather than more remote regions such as the temporal lobes, which also have visual functions. With the auditory dichotic tests, on the other hand, we are probably tapping the functions of the temporal lobe area.

A related point of interest is that we have not found any left-visual-field superiority for the perception of form, although we have tried in several tests. We know that damage to the right temporal lobe impairs the perception of nonsense designs, suggesting that some portions of the right hemisphere may indeed be critical for form perception. The tachistoscopic methods we used, however, do not sample the function of the systems for perception of form. Apparently the neural systems involved in spatial processing are relatively independent of those involved in form perception, a suggestion that was made many years ago by the British neurologist Gordon Holmes and that is supported by recent studies of visual perception in hamsters conducted by Gerald Schneider of the Massachusetts Institute of Technology.

Although we have concentrated on visual and auditory perception, it appears that there is an analogous asym-

metry in tactual perception. Beata Hermelin and Neil O'Connor of the Medical Research Council's Developmental Psychology Unit have reported that the tactual perception of Braille dot patterns by blind people is more rapid with the left hand than with the right. Diana Ingram in our laboratory has found that when one arm is used to locate a point out of sight under a table on which the location of the point is indicated, the left arm performs more accurately than the right.

From these observations and others one can conclude that the posterior part of the right hemisphere is involved in the direct analysis of information about the external environment. The parieto-occipital area is particularly critical for the kinds of behavior that are dependent on spatial relations, whereas the temporal region takes part in processing nonspatial stimuli such as melodic patterns and nonsense designs. An important secondary process in the analysis of perceptual input is the attaching of a verbal label. We know that verbal transformation of information involves the left hemisphere, but we still have much to learn about the transfer from right-to-left-hemisphere processing and from left-to-right-hemisphere processing. For example, we can demonstrate left-visual-

field superiority in spatial perception in spite of the fact that the subject ultimately gives us a verbal response that is controlled from his left hemisphere. We explain this result by saying that the primary analysis is accomplished by the right hemisphere, and the verbal response is secondary. In other situations, however, the mode of response (manual or vocal) can influence which field dominates. Hence we do not yet have a completely satisfactory explanation.

We have seen that the left hemisphere is critical for the production and perception of certain sounds made by the human speech system. Recently my colleagues and I have obtained evidence from patients with cerebral strokes that the left hemisphere may also be essential for some types of movements of the hand. We found that patients with left-sided cerebral damage have difficulty copying a series of hand movements, whether the movements are meaningful or not. Moreover, there are reports in the clinical literature of deaf mutes who used hand movements as a means of communication and who, after suffering damage to the left hemisphere, displayed disturbances of these movements that were analogous to disturbances of speech. That the left hemisphere has a special control over some aspects of manual behavior is further suggested by the fact that most people use their right hand for many skilled acts. Although the relation between speech lateralization and hand preference is not perfect, the high incidence of both left-hemisphere control of speech and right-hand preference is probably not coincidental.

We have found further support for a relation between speech and certain manual activities by observing the hand movements of normal people while they are speaking. As everyone knows, speech is often accompanied by gestures, in which the hands are moved around freely in space without touching anything. Such movements are hardly ever seen during a nonspeech vocal activity such as humming. In both humming and speaking, however, there may be other kinds of manual activity, such as touching the body, rubbing the nose or scratching. Equally interesting is the fact that the free movements during speech are made primarily by the hand opposite the hemisphere that controls speech (as determined by means of the dichotic verbal method). If speech is controlled by the left hemisphere, as it is in most people, the right hand makes more of the free movements, whereas if speech is controlled by the right hemisphere, the left

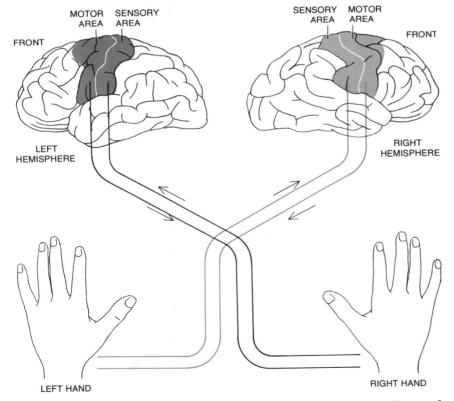

MOTOR AND SENSORY PATHWAYS from the hands are almost completely crossed, so that each hand is served primarily by the cerebral hemisphere on the opposite side.

GESTURES DURING SPEECH are made primarily by the hand that is opposite the cerebral hemisphere controlling speech. In most people speech is controlled by the left hemisphere, and the right hand of such people makes more free movements than the left hand during speech, as is shown in these pictures from a video tape recording made by the author during an experiment. The asymmetrical use of the hands during speech has been found only when the hands move freely in space without touching the body.

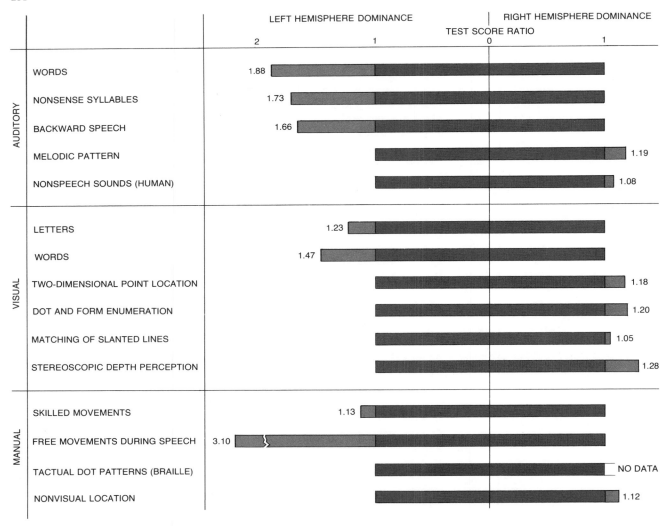

LEFT HEMISPHERE DOMINANCE | RIGHT HEMISPHERE DOMINANCE

TEST SCORE RATIO

2   1   0   1

AUDITORY
- WORDS — 1.88
- NONSENSE SYLLABLES — 1.73
- BACKWARD SPEECH — 1.66
- MELODIC PATTERN — 1.19
- NONSPEECH SOUNDS (HUMAN) — 1.08

VISUAL
- LETTERS — 1.23
- WORDS — 1.47
- TWO-DIMENSIONAL POINT LOCATION — 1.18
- DOT AND FORM ENUMERATION — 1.20
- MATCHING OF SLANTED LINES — 1.05
- STEREOSCOPIC DEPTH PERCEPTION — 1.28

MANUAL
- SKILLED MOVEMENTS — 1.13
- FREE MOVEMENTS DURING SPEECH — 3.10
- TACTUAL DOT PATTERNS (BRAILLE) — NO DATA
- NONVISUAL LOCATION — 1.12

FUNCTIONAL ASYMMETRIES of the cerebral hemispheres in normal, right-handed people are found in the auditory, visual and manual modalities. Test scores for the left and right sides were converted to ratios for comparison. The ratio for left-hemisphere dominance for perception of spoken words is 1.88 : 1, whereas the ratio for right-hemisphere dominance for melodies is 1.19 : 1. These ratios are not fixed values since they vary with the type of stimulus, the kind of response required and the difficulty of the task.

hand makes more of the free movements. Curiously, this asymmetry is restricted to free movements; it does not appear in self-touching movements. These findings and the clinical findings I have mentioned suggest that there is indeed some overlap between the speaking system in a hemisphere and the system controlling certain kinds of manual activity. It may be that the left hemisphere is particularly well adapted not for the symbolic function in itself but for the execution of some categories of motor activity that happen to lend themselves readily to communication.

In our work on cerebral asymmetry in normal people we have occasionally encountered sex differences. In right-hemisphere tasks males tend to have a greater left-visual-field superiority for dot location and dot enumeration than females. We also know that males are superior to females in certain visual-spatial tasks. It may be that right-hemisphere specialization is more pronounced in males than in females, and that such specialization may sometimes be advantageous. Recently Jeannette McGlone and Wilda Davidson in my laboratory at the University of Western Ontario found some evidence in favor of this idea. They administered a standard test of spatial perception in which the subject must identify a design after it has been rotated. They found, as is usual in this task, that males usually performed better than females. The females who did particularly poorly on the test were those who showed some left-hemispheric specialization for spatial functions (as inferred from the tachistoscopic dot-enumeration test). Usually such functions are controlled by the right hemisphere.

In contrast, females tend to have greater verbal fluency than males. There is no evidence, however, that adult females are more asymmetrical in speech lateralization than males. Dichotic studies nonetheless suggest that speech lateralization may develop earlier in girls than in boys. It appears that for some intellectual functions the brains of males and females may be differently organized. Most of human evolution must have taken place under conditions where for the male hunting members of society accurate information about both the immediate and the distant environment was of paramount importance. For the females, who presumably stayed closer to home with other nonhunting members of the group, similar selection processes may not have operated. It will be interesting to discover whether or not the sex differences in verbal and nonverbal asymmetries we have uncovered with our relatively simple techniques hold true for other cultures.

BIBLIOGRAPHIES

I PERIPHERAL MECHANISMS OF PERCEPTION AND CONTROL

1. Contour and Contrast

MACH BANDS: QUANTITATIVE STUDIES ON NEURAL NETWORKS IN THE RETINA. Floyd Ratliff. Holden-Day, Inc., 1965.

LINEAR SYSTEMS ANALYSIS OF THE *LIMULUS* RETINA. Frederick A. Dodge, Robert M. Shapley and Bruce W. Knight in *Behavioral Science,* Vol. 15, No. 1, pages 24–36; January, 1970.

CONTOUR AND CONTRAST. Floyd Ratliff in *Proceedings of the American Philosophical Society,* Vol. 115, No. 2, pages 150–163; April, 1971.

INHIBITORY INTERACTION IN THE RETINA OF *LIMULUS.* H. K. Hartline and F. Ratliff in *Handbook of Sensory Physiology: Vol. VII/Part IB.* Springer-Verlag, in print.

2. The Control of Sensitivity in the Retina

ORGANIZATION OF THE RETINA OF THE MUDPUPPY, NECTURUS MACULOSUS, I: SYNAPTIC STRUCTURE. John E. Dowling and Frank S. Werblin in *Journal of Neurophysiology,* Vol. 32, No. 3, pages 315–338; May, 1969.

ORGANIZATION OF THE RETINA OF THE MUDPUPPY, NECTURUS MACULOSUS, II: INTRACELLULAR RECORDING. Frank S. Werblin and John E. Dowling in *Journal of Neurophysiology,* Vol. 32, No. 3, pages 339–355; May, 1969.

ADAPTATION IN A VERTEBRATE RETINA: INTRACELLULAR RECORDING IN NECTURUS. Frank S. Werblin in *Journal of Neurophysiology,* Vol. 34, No. 2, pages 228–241; March, 1971.

LATERAL INTERACTIONS AT INNER PLEXIFORM LAYER OF VERTEBRATE RETINA: ANTAGONISTIC RESPONSES TO CHANGE. Frank S. Werblin in *Science,* Vol. 175, No. 4025, pages 1008–1010; March 3, 1972.

FUNCTIONAL ORGANIZATION OF A VERTEBRATE RETINA: SHARPENING UP IN SPACE AND INTENSITY. Frank S. Werblin in *Annals ,of the New York Academy of Sciences: Patterns of Integration from Biochemical to Behavioral Processes,* edited by George Hadu, Vol. 193; August, 1972.

3. Contrast and Spatial Frequency

ELECTROPHYSIOLOGICAL EVIDENCE FOR THE EXISTENCE OF ORIENTATION AND SIZE DETECTORS IN THE HUMAN VISUAL SYSTEM. F. W. Campbell and L. Maffei in *The Journal of Physiology,* Vol. 207, No. 3, pages 635–652; May, 1970.

THE CONTRAST SENSITIVITY OF THE CAT. F. W. Campbell, L. Maffei and M. Piccolino in *The Journal of Physiology,* Vol. 229, No. 3, pages 719–731; March, 1973.

BEHAVIOURAL CONTRAST SENSITIVITY OF THE CAT IN VARIOUS VISUAL MERIDIANS. S. Bisti and L. Maffei in *The Journal of Physiology,* Vol. 241, No. 1, pages 201–210; August, 1974.

4. Experiments in the Visual Perception of Texture

VISUAL PATTERN DISCRIMINATION. Bela Julesz in *IRE Transactions on Information Theory,* Vol. IT-8, pages 84–92; 1962.

High-Order Statistics and Short-Term Auditory Memory. Bela Julesz and Newman Guttman in *Proceedings of the 5th International Congress on Acoustics, Liège,* Vol. 1a, Report B15; 1965.

Foundations of Cyclopean Perception. Bela Julesz. University of Chicago Press, 1971.

Inability of Humans to Discriminate Between Visual Textures That Agree in Second-Order Statistics—Revisited. B. Julesz, H. L. Frisch, E. N. Gilbert and L. A. Shepp in *Perception,* Vol. 2, pages 391–405; 1973.

5. The Perception of Transparency

Gesetze des Sehens. Wolfgang Metzger. Verlag von Waldemar Kramer Frankfurt am Main, 1953.

Margini Quasi-Percettivi in Campi con Stimolazione Omogenea. Gaetano Kanizsa in *Rivista di Psicologia,* Vol. 49, No. 1, pages 7–30; January–March, 1955.

Zur Analyse der phanomenalen Durchsichtig Keitserscheinungen. F. Metelli in *Gestalt und Wirklichkeit.* Duncker und Humboldt, Berlin, 1967.

An Algebraic Development of the Theory of Perceptual Transparency. F. Metelli in *Ergonomics,* Vol. 13, 1970.

6. The Neurophysiology of Binocular Vision

The Neural Mechanism of Binocular Depth Discrimination. H. B. Barlow, C. Blakemore and J. D. Pettigrew in *Journal of Physiology,* Vol. 193, pages 327–342; 1967.

Binocular Interaction on Single Units in Cat Striate Cortex: Simultaneous Stimulation by Single Moving Slit with Receptive Fields in Correspondence. J. D. Pettigrew, T. Nikara and P. O. Bishop in *Experimental Brain Research,* Vol. 6, pages 391–410; 1968.

Eye Dominance in the Visual Cortex. Colin Blakemore and John D. Pettigrew in *Nature,* Vol. 225, No. 5231, pages 426–429; January 31, 1970.

Foundations of Cyclopean Perception. Bela Julesz. University of Chicago Press, 1971.

7. Visual Motion Perception

Perception of Motion and Changing Form. Gunnar Johansson in *The Scandinavian Journal of Psychology,* Vol. 5, No. 3, pages 181–208; 1964.

What Gives Rise to the Perception of Motion? James J. Gibson in *Psychological Review,* Vol. 75, No. 4, pages 335–346; July, 1968.

Visual Perception of Bending Motion. G. Jansson and G. Johansson in *Perception,* Vol. 2, pages 321–326; 1973.

Visual Perception of Motion in Depth: Application of a Vector Model to Three-Dot Motion Patterns. Erik Börjesson and Claes von Hofsten in *Perception & Psychophysics,* Vol. 13, No. 2, pages 169–179; April, 1973.

Visual Perception of Biological Motion and a Model for Its Analysis. Gunnar Johansson in *Perception & Psychophysics,* Vol. 14, No. 2, pages 201–211; October, 1973.

8. Auditory Beats in the Brain

Masking of Tonal Signals. Lloyd A. Jeffress, Hugh C. Blodgett, Thomas T. Sandel and Charles L. Wood III in *The Journal of the Acoustical Society of America,* Vol. 28, No. 3, pages 416–426; May, 1956.

Binaural Interaction in the Superior Olivary Complex of the Cat: An Analysis of Field Potentials Evoked by Binaural-Beat Stimuli. Joel S. Wernick and Arnold Starr in *Journal of Neurophysiology,* Vol. 31, No. 3, pages 428–441; May, 1968.

Limits for the Detection of Binaural Beats. David R. Perrott and Michael A. Nelson in *The Journal of the Acoustical Society of America,* Vol. 46, No. 6, Part 2, pages 1477–1481; December, 1969.

9. The Superior Colliculus of the Brain

The Role of the Superior Colliculus in Visually Guided Behavior. James M. Sprague and Thomas H. Meikle, Jr., in *Experimental Neurology,* Vol. 11, pages 115–146; 1965.

Visual Receptive Fields in the Superior Colliculus of the Cat. Peter Sterling and Barbara G. Wickelgren in *Journal of Neurophysiology,* Vol. 32, No. 1, pages 1–15; January, 1969.

Superior Colliculus: Some Receptive Field Responsive Cells. Barbara G. Wickelgren in *Science,* Vol. 173, No. 3991, pages 69–72; July 2, 1971.

The Primate Superior Colliculus and the Shift of Visual Attention. Robert H. Wurtz and Michael E. Goldberg in *Investigative Ophthalmology,* Vol. 11, No. 6, pages 441–450; June, 1972.

The Role of the Monkey Superior Colliculus in Eye Movement and Vision. Peter H. Schiller in *Investigative Ophthalmology,* Vol. 11, No. 6, pages 451–460; June, 1972.

10. The Neural Basis of Visually Guided Behavior

What the Frog's Eye Tells the Frog's Brain. J. Y. Lettvin, H. R. Maturana, W. S. McCulloch and W. H. Pitts in *Proceedings of the Institute of Radio Engineers,* Vol. 47, No. 11, pages 1940–1951; November, 1959.

A Quantitative Analysis of Movement Detecting Neurons in the Frog's Retina. O.-J. Grüsser, U. Grüsser-Cornehls, D. Finkelstein, V. Henn, M. Patutschnik and E. Butenandt in *Pflüger's Archiv für die gesamte Physiologie des Menschen und der Tiere*, Vol. 293, pages 100–106; 1967.

Neurophysiologie des Bewegungssehens. O.-J. Grüsser and U. Grüsser-Cornehls in *Ergebnisse der Physiologie*, Vol. 61, pages 178–265; 1969.

Neural Mechanisms of Prey-catching and Avoidance Behavior in the Toad (Bufo bufo L.). J.-P. Ewert in *Subcortical Visual Systems*, edited by D. Ingle. S. Karger, 1970.

Lokalisation und Identifikation im visuellen System der Wirbeltiere. J.-P. Ewert in *Fortschritte der Zoologie*, Vol. 21, pages 307–333; 1973.

11. Control Mechanisms of the Eye

Control Theory and Biological Systems. Fred S. Grodins. Columbia University Press, 1963.

The Eye, Vol. III: Muscular Mechanisms. Edited by Hugh Davson. Academic Press, 1962.

Stabilized Images on the Retina. Roy M. Pritchard in *Scientific American*, Vol. 204, No. 6, pages 72–78; June, 1961.

Variable Feedback Experiments Testing a Sampled Data Model for Eye Tracking Movements. L. R. Young and L. Stark in *IEEE Transactions on Human Factors in Electronics*, Vol. HFE-4, No. 1, pages 38–51; September, 1963.

12. The Coordination of Eye-Head Movement

Central Control of Movement—Neurosciences Research Progress Bulletin: Vol. 9. Edited by E. V. Evarts, E. Bizzi, R. Burke, M. DeLong and W. T. Thach, 1971.

Eye-Head Coordination in Monkeys: Evidence for Centrally Patterned Organization. Emilio Bizzi, Ronald E. Kalil and Vincenzo Tagliasco in *Science*, Vol. 173, No. 3995, pages 452–454; July 30, 1971.

Adjustment of Saccade Characteristics during Head Movements. P. Morasso, E. Bizzi and J. Dichgans in *Experimental Brain Research*, Vol. 16, pages 492–500; 1973.

Mechanisms Underlying Recovery of Eye-Head Coordination following Bilateral Labyrinthectomy in Monkeys. J. Dichgans, E. Bizzi, P. Morasso and V. Tagliasco in *Experimental Brain Research*, Vol. 18, pages 548–562; 1973.

13. The Cortex of the Cerebellum

Histologie du Systeme Nerveux de l'Homme & des Vertebres: Vol. II. Santiago Ramón y Cajal. A. Maloine, 1911.

The Cerebellum as a Neuronal Machine. John C. Eccles, Masao Itó and János Szentágothai. Springer-Verlag, 1967.

Neurobiology of Cerebellar Evolution and Development: Proceedings of the First International Symposium of the Institute for Biomedical Research. Edited by R. Llinás. The American Medical Association, 1969.

Cerebellar Cortex: Cytology and Organization. Sanford L. Palay and Victoria Chan-Palay. Springer-Verlag, 1974.

Eighteenth Bowditch Lecture: Motor Aspects of Cerebellar Control. Rodolfo Llinás in *The Physiologist*, Vol. 17, No. 1, pages 19–46; February, 1974.

II CENTRAL DETERMINANTS OF PERCEPTION

14. Multistability in Perception

The Analysis of Sensations and the Relation of the Physical to the Psychical. Ernst Mach. Dover Publications, Inc., 1959.

Ambiguity of Form: Old and New. Gerald H. Fisher in *Perception and Psychophysics*, Vol. 4, No. 3, pages 189–192; September, 1968.

Triangles as Ambiguous Figures. Fred Attneave in *The American Journal of Psychology*, Vol. 81, No. 3, pages 447–453; September, 1968.

15. Sources of Ambiguity in the Prints of Maurits C. Escher

Some Factors Determining Figure-Ground Articulation. M. R. Harrower in *British Journal of Psychology*, Vol. 26, No. 4, pages 407–424; 1936.

Perception. Hans-Lukas Teuber in *Handbook of Physiology: Section 1—Neurophysiology*, Vol. 3. Edited by H. W. Magoun. Williams & Wilkins, 1961.

The Graphic Work of M. C. Escher. M. C. Escher. Ballantine Books, Inc., 1971.

The World of M. C. Escher, edited by J. L. Locher. Harry N. Abrams, Inc., 1971.

New Aspects of Paul Klee's Bauhaus Style. M. L. Teuber in *Paul Klee, Paintings and Watercolors from the Bauhaus Years, 1921–1931*. Des Moines Art Center, 1973.

16. Auditory Illusions and Confusions

Verbal Transformation Effect and Auditory Perceptual Mechanisms. Richard M. Warren in

Psychological Bulletin, Vol. 70, No. 4, pages 261–270; October, 1968.

AUDITORY SEQUENCE: CONFUSION OF PATTERNS OTHER THAN SPEECH OR MUSIC. Richard M. Warren, Charles J. Obusek, Richard M. Farmer and Roslyn P. Warren in *Science,* Vol. 164, No. 3879, pages 586–587; May 2, 1969.

PERCEPTUAL RESTORATION OF MISSING SPEECH SOUNDS. Richard M. Warren in *Science,* Vol. 167, No. 3912, pages 392–393; January 23, 1970.

17. The Perception of Disoriented Figures

RECOGNITION UNDER OBJECTIVE REVERSAL. George V. N. Dearborn in *The Psychological Review,* Vol. 6, No. 4, pages 395–406; July, 1899.

THE ANALYSIS OF SENSATIONS AND THE RELATION OF THE PHYSICAL TO THE PSYCHICAL. Ernst Mach, translated from the German by C. M. Williams. Dover Publications, Inc., 1959.

ORIENTATION AND SHAPE I AND II in *Human Spatial Orientation.* I. P. Howard and W. B. Templeton. John Wiley & Sons, Inc., 1966.

SIMILARITY IN VISUALLY PERCEIVED FORMS. Erich Goldmeier in *Psychological Issues,* Vol. 8, No. 1, Monograph 29; 1972.

ORIENTATION AND FORM. Irvin Rock. Academic Press, 1974.

18. The Recognition of Faces

SOME ASPECTS OF RECOGNITION OF HUMAN FACES. L. D. Harmon in *Pattern Recognition in Biological and Technical Systems: Proceedings of the Fourth Congress of the Deutsche Gesellschaft für Kybernetik,* edited by Otto-Joachim Grüsser and Rainer Klinke. Springer-Verlag, 1971.

IDENTIFICATION OF HUMAN FACES. A. Jay Goldstein, Leon D. Harmon and Ann B. Lesk in *Proceedings of the IEEE,* Vol. 59, No. 5, pages 748–760; May, 1971.

MAN-MACHINE INTERACTION IN HUMAN-FACE IDENTIFICATION. A. J. Goldstein, L. D. Harmon and A. B. Lesk in *The Bell System Technical Journal,* Vol. 51, No. 2, pages 399–427; February, 1972.

MASKING IN VISUAL RECOGNITION: EFFECTS OF TWO-DIMENSIONAL FILTERED NOISE. Leon D. Harmon and Bela Julesz in *Science,* Vol. 180, No. 4091, pages 1194–1197; June 15, 1973.

19. Experiments in Reading

THE PSYCHOLOGY AND PEDAGOGY OF READING. Edmund Burke Huey. The M.I.T. Press, 1968.

CLUES TO A LETTER'S RECOGNITION: IMPLICATIONS FOR THE DESIGN OF CHARACTERS. Paul A. Kolers in *The Journal of Typographic Research* (now *Visible Language*), Vol. 3, No. 2, pages 145–168; April, 1969.

BASIC STUDIES ON READING. Edited by Harry Levin and Joanna P. Williams. Basic Books, Inc., 1970.

20. Eyewitness Testimony

ON THE WITNESS STAND: ESSAYS ON PSYCHOLOGY AND CRIME. Hugo Münsterberg. Doubleday, Page and Company, 1915.

EYEWITNESS IDENTIFICATION IN CRIMINAL CASES. Patrick M. Wall. Charles C. Thomas, Publisher, 1965.

EXPERIMENTOR EFFECTS IN BEHAVIORAL RESEARCH. Robert Rosenthal. Appleton-Century-Crofts, 1966.

THROUGH A BAG, DARKLY, Robert Buckhout in *American Psychologist,* Vol. 23, No. 11, pages 832–833; November, 1968.

21. Pictorial Perception and Culture

GEOGRAPHY AND ATLAS OF PROTESTANT MISSIONS. Harlan P. Beach. New York Volunteer Movement for Foreign Missions, 1901.

THE STUDY OF THE PROBLEM OF PICTORIAL PERCEPTION AMONG UNACCULTURATED GROUPS. William Hudson in *International Journal of Psychology,* Vol. 2, No. 2, pages 89–107; 1967.

DIFFICULTIES IN PICTORIAL DEPTH PERCEPTION IN AFRICA. Jan B. Deregowski in *The British Journal of Psychology,* Vol. 59, Part 3, pages 195–204; August, 1968.

PERCEPTION OF THE TWO-PRONGED TRIDENT BY TWO AND THREE-DIMENSIONAL PERCEIVERS. J. B. Deregowski in *Journal of Experimental Psychology,* Vol. 82, No. 1, Part 1, pages 9–13; October, 1969.

RESPONSES MEDIATING PICTORIAL RECOGNITION. Jan B. Deregowski in *The Journal of Social Psychology,* Vol. 84, First Half, pages 27–33; June, 1971.

22. The Object in the World of the Infant

THE CONSTRUCTION OF REALITY IN THE CHILD. Jean Piaget. Basic Books, Inc., 1954.

THE CHILD AND MODERN PHYSICS. Jean Piaget in *Scientific American,* Vol. 196, No. 3, pages 46–51; March, 1957.

CAUSALITÉ, PERMANENCE ET RÉALITÉ PHÉNOMÉNALES: ETUDES DE PSYCHOLOGIE EXPÉRIMENTALE. A. Michotte. Louvain, Belgium: Publications Universitaires, 1962.

THE NATURE OF PERCEPTUAL ADAPTATION. Irvin Rock. Basic Books, Inc., 1966.

THE VISUAL WORLD OF INFANTS. T. G. R. Bower in *Scientific American,* Vol. 215, No. 6, pages 80–92; December, 1966.

SPACE PERCEPTION IN EARLY INFANCY: PERCEPTION

WITHIN A COMMON AUDITORY-VISUAL SPACE. Eric Aronson and Shelley Rosenbloom in *Science,* Vol. 172, No. 3988, pages 1161–1163; June 11, 1971.

23. The Functional Organization of the Brain

HIGHER CORTICAL FUNCTIONS IN MAN. A. R. Luria. Basic Books, Inc., 1966.

HUMAN BRAIN AND PSYCHOLOGICAL PROCESSES. A. R. Luria. Harper & Row, Publishers, 1966.

THE CO-ORDINATION AND REGULATION OF MOVEMENTS. N. Bernstein. Pergamon Press, 1967.

TRAUMATIC APHASIA. A. R. Luria. Mouton Publishers, 1969.

24. Language and the Brain

CEREBRAL DOMINANCE AND ITS RELATION TO PSYCHOLOGICAL FUNCTION. O. L. Zangwill. Oliver and Boyd, 1960.

DISCONNEXION SYNDROMES IN ANIMALS AND MAN: PART I. Norman Geschwind in *Brain,* Vol. 88, Part 2, pages 237–294; June, 1965.

DISCONNEXION SYNDROMES IN ANIMALS AND MAN: PART II. Norman Geschwind in *Brain,* Vol. 88, Part 3, pages 585–644; September, 1965.

HUMAN BRAIN: LEFT-RIGHT ASYMMETRIES IN TEMPORAL SPEECH REGION. Norman Geschwind and Walter Levitsky in *Science,* Vol. 161, No. 3837, pages 186–187; July 12, 1968.

TRAUMATIC APHASIA: ITS SYNDROMES, PSYCHOLOGY AND TREATMENT. A. R. Luria. Mouton & Co., 1970.

25. The Asymmetry of the Human Brain

FUNCTIONAL ASYMMETRY OF THE BRAIN IN DICHOTIC LISTENING. Doreen Kimura in *Cortex,* Vol. 3, No. 2, pages 163–178; June, 1967.

SPATIAL LOCALIZATION IN LEFT AND RIGHT VISUAL FIELDS. Doreen Kimura in *Canadian Journal of Psychology,* Vol. 23, No. 6, pages 445–458; December, 1969.

HEMISPHERIC SPECIALIZATION FOR SPEECH PERCEPTION. Michael Studdert-Kennedy and Donald Shankweiler in *The Journal of the Accoustical Society of America.* Vol. 48, No. 2, Part 2, pages 579–594; August, 1970.

RIGHT HEMISPHERE SPECIALIZATION FOR DEPTH PERCEPTION REFLECTED IN VISUAL FIELD DIFFERENCES. Margaret Durnford and Doreen Kimura in *Nature,* Vol. 231, No. 4302, pages 394–395; June 11, 1971.

INDEX